Clashing Views on

Social Issues

FIFTEENTH EDITION, EXPANDED

TAKING SIDES

Clashing Views on

Social Issues

FIFTEENTH EDITION, EXPANDED

Selected, Edited, and with Introductions by

Kurt Finsterbusch
University of Maryland

 **Higher Education**

Boston   Burr Ridge, IL   Dubuque, IA   New York   San Francisco   St. Louis
Bangkok   Bogotá   Caracas   Kuala Lumpur   Lisbon   London   Madrid   Mexico City
Milan   Montreal   New Delhi   Santiago   Seoul   Singapore   Sydney   Taipei   Toronto

HN
59
.2
.T35
2010

Higher Education

TAKING SIDES: CLASHING VIEWS ON SOCIAL ISSUES, FIFTEENTH EDITION, EXPANDED

1 2 3 4 5 6 7 8 9 0 DOC/DOC 0 9

MHID: 0-07-812750-5
ISBN: 978-0-07-812750-2
ISSN: 95-83865

Managing Editor: *Larry Loeppke*
Senior Managing Editor: *Faye Schilling*
Editorial Coordinator: *Mary Foust*
Developmental Editor: *Jade Benedict*
Editorial Assistant: *Nancy Meissner*
Production Service Assistant: *Rita Hingtgen*
Permissions Coordinator: *Shirley Lanners*
Senior Marketing Manager: *Julie Keck*
Marketing Communications Specialist: *Mary Klein*
Marketing Coordinator: *Alice Link*
Senior Project Manager: *Jane Mohr*
Design Specialist: *Tara McDermott*

Compositor: Macmillan Publishing Solutions
Cover Image: Digital Vision/PunchStock

Library of Congress Cataloging-in-Publication Data
Main entry under title:
Taking Sides: Clashing Views on Social Issues/Selected, Edited, and with Introductions
by Kurt Finsterbusch—15th edition, expanded

Includes bibliographical references.
1. Social behavior. 2. Social problems. I. Finsterbusch, Kurt, *comp.*

302

www.mhhe.com

Clashing Views on

Social Issues

FIFTEENTH EDITION, EXPANDED

Kurt Finsterbusch
University of Maryland

Advisory Board

Preface

The English word *fanatic* is derived from the Latin *fanum,* meaning temple. It refers to the kind of madmen often seen in the precincts of temples in ancient times, the kind presumed to be possessed by deities or demons. The term first came into English usage during the seventeenth century, when it was used to describe religious zealots. Soon after, its meaning was broadened to include a political and social context. We have come to associate the term *fanatic* with a person who acts as if his or her views were inspired, a person utterly incapable of appreciating opposing points of view. The nineteenth-century English novelist George Eliot put it precisely: "I call a man fanatical when . . . he . . . becomes unjust and unsympathetic to men who are out of his own track." A fanatic may hear but is unable to listen. Confronted with those who disagree, a fanatic immediately vilifies opponents.

Most of us would avoid the company of fanatics, but who among us is not tempted to caricature opponents instead of listening to them? Who does not put certain topics off-limits for discussion? Who does not grasp at euphemisms to avoid facing inconvenient facts? Who has not, in George Eliot's language, sometimes been "unjust and unsympathetic" to those on a different track? Who is not, at least in certain very sensitive areas, a *little* fanatical? The counterweight to fanaticism is open discussion. The difficult issues that trouble us as a society have at least two sides, and we lose as a society if we hear only one side. At the individual level, the answer to fanaticism is listening. And that is the underlying purpose of this book: to encourage its readers to listen to opposing points of view.

This book contains 44 selections presented in a pro and con format. A total of 22 different controversial social issues are debated. The sociologists, political scientists, economists, and social critics whose views are debated here make their cases vigorously. In order to effectively read each selection, analyze the points raised, and debate the basic assumptions and values of each position, or, in other words, in order to think critically about what you are reading, you will first have to give each side a sympathetic hearing. John Stuart Mill, the nineteenth-century British philosopher, noted that the majority is not doing the minority a favor by listening to its views; it is doing *itself* a favor. By listening to contrasting points of view, we strengthen our own. In some cases, we change our viewpoints completely. But in most cases, we either incorporate some elements of the opposing view—thus making our own richer—or else learn how to answer the objections to our viewpoints. Either way, we gain from the experience.

Organization of the Book   Each issue has an issue *Introduction*, which sets the stage for the debate as it is argued in the YES and NO selections. Each issue concludes with a *Postscript* that makes some final observations and points the way to other questions related to the issue. In reading the issue and forming your own opinions, you should not feel confined to adopt one or the other of the positions presented. There are positions in between the given views or totally outside them, and the *Suggestions for Further Reading* that appear in each issue Postscript should help you find resources to continue your study of the subject. At the back of the book is a listing of all the *Contributors to This Volume*, which will give you information on the social scientists whose views are debated here. Also, on the *Internet References* page that accompanies each unit opener, you will find Internet site addresses (URLs) that are relevant to the issues in that unit.

Changes to This Edition This new edition has been updated with 14 newer articles and two slightly revised issues: the marriage issue became the divorce issue (4), and the drug issue became the marijuana issue (16). Today, the world is changing rapidly in many ways so that new issues arise, old ones fade, and some old issues become recast by events. Hence, we think that we must constantly revise this work.

A Word to the Instructor An *Instructor's Resource Guide with Test Questions* (multiple-choice and essay) is available through the publisher for the instructor using *Taking Sides* in the classroom. A general guidebook, *Using Taking Sides in the Classroom*, which discusses methods and techniques for integrating the pro-con approach into any classroom setting, is also available. An online version of *Using Taking Sides in the Classroom* and a correspondence service for *Taking Sides* adopters can be found at http://www.mhcls.com/usingts/.

Taking Sides: Clashing Views on Social Issues is only one title in the *Taking Sides* series. If you are interested in seeing the table of contents for any of the other titles, please visit the Taking Sides Web site at http://www.mhcls.com/takingsides/.

Acknowledgments I wish to acknowledge the encouragement and support given to this project by my editor, Susan Brusch.

I want to thank my wife, Meredith Ramsay, for her patience and support as I birthed this new edition. I also want to thank George McKenna for many years as a close colleague and co-editor through many early editions of this book.

Kurt Finsterbusch
University of Maryland

Contents In Brief

Contents

Robert H. Bork, famous for being nominated for the Supreme Court but not confirmed by the Senate, argues that modern liberalism is responsible for the decline in morals. Journalist Kay S. Hymowitz argues that the permissive culture of the sixties, which led to less respect for authority, crime, sexual promiscuity, and other indicators of moral decline, is waning. The cultural pendulum is swinging back to a more traditional culture of commitment, moderation, and family values.

Fred Barnes, Executive Editor of *The Weekly Standard*, argues from first-hand experience that the mainstream media has a pronounced liberal bias that is reflected in their hiring and news stories. Robert F. Kennedy, Jr., environmental and political activist, believes that the media have a conservative bias. Most people get much of their news and false information from conservative media.

Political analyst Patrick Buchanan asserts that the large influx of legal and illegal immigrants, especially from Mexico, threatens to undermine the cultural foundations of American unity. Linda Chavez, Chairman of the Center for Equal Opportunity, argues that immigrants do not lower wages and take jobs from citizens, as evidenced by the strong economy and low unemployment rate. Immigrants are also very hard workers with considerable drive and strong family values.

Elizabeth Marquardt, Director of the Center for Marriage and Families, draws on the literature to argue that divorce has devastating impacts on children and attacks Constance Ahrons' counter-thesis. Constance Ahron, co-chair of the Council on Contemporary Families, found the opposite true in her research on the children of divorced parents. These children do quite well in later life and most think that they were not harmed by the divorce.

Journalist Claudia Wallis reports that more and more mothers are choosing to quit work and stay home to care for their children. The work demands on professional women have increased to the point that very few can do both work and family. Forced to choose, growing numbers choose family. Neil Gilbert, Chernin Professor of Social Welfare at the University of California at Berkeley, challenges Wallis's thesis as resting on "thin" data. The real opt-out story is the growing number of professional women who are opting out of having children and, of those who do have children, most are using day-care services.

America's largest lesbian and gay organization, The Human Rights Campaign, presents many arguments for why same-sex couples should be able to marry. The main argument is fairness. Marriage confers many benefits that same-sex couples are deprived of. Researcher Peter Sprigg presents many arguments for why same-sex couples should not be able to marry. The main argument is that the state has the right and duty to specify who a person, whether straight or gay, can marry so no rights are violated.

UNIT 3   STRATIFICATION AND INEQUALITY   105

James Kurth, Claude Smith Professor of Political Science at Swarthmore College, warns of very negative consequences for America of the growing income inequality. Consequences range from the potential of under-consumption and overproduction that can cause a recession, to biased political policies and increasing terrorist threats. Gary S. Becker and Kevin M. Murphy, both economists teaching at the University of Chicago and Senior Fellows at the Hoover Institute, point out the positive consequences of the growing income inequality. The main reason for the increasing inequality is the increasing returns to education, which in turn inspire greater efforts by young people to increase their social capital.

History professor Barbara Epstein argues that the feminist movement has been highly successful in changing the consciousness of Americans to "an awareness of the inequality of women and a determination to resist it." She explains how feminists succeeded at the consciousness level but have declined as a movement for social change. Journalist Kate O'Beirne argues that feminism is unpopular with women and is pushing an agenda that most women do not support. She claims that most women have concluded "that the feminist movement is both socially destructive and personally disappointing."

Curtis Crawford, editor of the Web site http://www.DebatingRacial Preference.org, explores all possible options for bettering the situation of disadvantaged minorities in a truly just manner. He argues that the right of everyone, including white males, to nondiscrimination is clearly superior to the right of minorities to affirmative action. Sociologist Lawrence D. Bobo demonstrates that racial prejudice still exists even though it has become a more subtle type of racism, which he calls laissez-faire racism. Though it is harder to identify, it has significant effects, as Bobo illustrates. In fact, it plays a big role in current politics.

UNIT 4   POLITICAL ECONOMY AND INSTITUTIONS   181

Clint Bolick, vice president of the Institute for Justice, presents the argument for school choice that competition leads to improvements and makes the case that minorities especially need school choice to improve their educational performance. Educator and businessman Ron Wolk argues that school choice and most other educational reforms can only be marginally effective because they do not get at the heart of the educational problem, which is the way students learn. Too much attention is directed to the way teachers teach when the attention should be placed on how to stimulate students to learn more. Wolk advocates giving students more responsibility for their education.

Ronald Bailey, science editor for *Reason* magazine, discusses and advocates all the beneficial things that biotechnology can do for humans. Political science professor Michael J. Sandel cautions against many uses of biotechnology to alter and enhance humans. He praises many other uses of biotechnology, but he condemns using biotechnology to alter and enhance humans. In these activities, humans play God and attempt to inappropriately remake nature.

UNIT 5   CRIME AND SOCIAL CONTROL   255

David A. Anderson estimates the total annual cost of crime including law enforcement and security services. The costs exceed one trillion dollars, with fraud (mostly white collar crime) causing about one-fifth of the total. His calculations of the full costs of the loss of life and injury comes to about half of the total costs. It is right, therefore, to view personal and violent crime as the big crime problem. Professor of philosophy Jeffrey Reiman argues that the dangers posed by negligent corporations and white-collar criminals are a greater menace to society than are the activities of typical street criminals.

Ethan A. Nadelmann, director of the Lindesmith Center, a drug policy research institute, argues that marijuana should be legalized but treated like alcohol (i.e., illegal for children and regulated for adults). It is not nearly as harmful as a number of legal substances, so why is so much energy and money wasted in enforcing this unpopular law? John P. Walters, director of the Office of National Drug Control Policy, argues that marijuana has many harmful effects. Its legalization would greatly increase addiction to it.

Robert H. Bork, senior fellow at the American Enterprise Institute, recognizes that the values of security and civil rights must be balanced while we war against terrorism, but he is concerned that some commentators would hamstring security forces in order to protect nonessential civil rights. For example, to not use ethnic profiling of Muslim or Arab persons would reduce the effectiveness of security forces, while holding suspected terrorists without filing charges or allowing them council would increase their effectiveness. Larry Cox, Executive Director of Amnesty International USA, sees the U.S. as converting from a strong civil rights advocate to a civil rights violator. The record of U.S. rights abuses includes torture and degrading treatment, suspension of habeas corpus, denial of legal representation, and secret detention.

Lester R. Brown, founder of the Worldwatch Institute and now president of the Earth Policy Institute, argues the population growth and economic development are placing increasing harmful demands on the environment for resources and to grow food for improving diets. Bjorn Lomborg, a statistician at the University of Aarhus, Denmark, presents evidence that population growth is slowing down, natural resources are not running out, species are disappearing very slowly, the environment is improving in some ways, and assertions about environmental decline are exaggerated.

Author Johan Norberg argues that globalization is overwhelmingly good. Consumers throughout the world get better-quality goods at lower prices as the competition forces producers to be more creative, efficient, and responsive to consumers' demands. Even most poor people benefit greatly. Martin Hart-Landsberg, Professor of Economics at Lewis and Clark College, argues that globalization has served the capitalists well but has hurt the workers and the environment and may lead to economic instability.

Political sociologist G. William Domhoff argues that the "owners and top-level managers in large income-producing properties are far and away the dominant power figures in the United States" and that they have inordinate influence in the federal government. Political scientist Sheldon Kamieniecki's research finds that business interests do not participate at a high rate in policy issues that affect them, "and when they do, they have mixed success in influencing policy outcomes." In fact, environmental and other groups often have considerable influence vis-à-vis business interests.

Alice Eagly and Linda Carli argue that women seldom reach the highest levels of corporate America because they face obstacles at every stage of their career that decrease the woman/man ratio at each step upward. Kingsley Browne argues that biological differences between men and women account for many differences in their behaviors and choices that make women and men better suited for different types of jobs and differences in the way that they handle the same jobs.

Julia Galeota interprets the flooding of the rest of the world with American products and images as cultural imperialism. She argues that multinational corporations' strategy is to impose American values and ideals on the world community and to advance American culture at the expense of other cultures. Philippe Legrain examines the idea of American cultural imperialism and concludes that it is a myth. Furthermore, the advance of globalization and whatever cultural attachments that go with it are positive, not negative, developments.

Correlation Guide

The *Taking Sides* series presents current issues in a debate-style format designed to stimulate student interest and develop critical thinking skills. Each issue is thoughtfully framed with an issue summary, an issue introduction, and a postscript. The pro and con essays—selected for their liveliness and substance—represent the arguments of leading scholars and commentators in their fields.

Taking Sides: Clashing Views on Social Issues, 15/e Expanded is an easy-to-use reader that presents issues on important topics such as *social interaction, stratification, inequality* and *deviance*. For more information on *Taking Sides* and other *McGraw-Hill Contemporary Learning Series* titles, visit www.mhcls.com.

This convenient guide matches the issues in **Taking Sides: Social Issues, 15/e Expanded** with the corresponding chapters in three of our best-selling McGraw-Hill Sociology textbooks by Schaefer, Witt, and Hughes.

Taking Sides: Social Issues, 15/e Expanded by Finsterbusch	SOC, 1/e by Witt	Sociology: The Core, 9/e by Hughes	Sociology Matters, 4/e by Schaefer
Issue 1: Is America in Moral Decline?	**Chapter 3:** Culture	**Chapter 2:** Culture and Social Structure	**Chapter 1:** The Sociological View
Issue 2: Does the Media Have a Liberal Bias?	**Chapter 5:** Social Structure and Interaction	**Chapter 2:** Culture and Social Structure **Chapter 4:** Social Groups and Formal Organizations	**Chapter 2:** Culture and Socialization **Chapter 11:** Social Movements, Social Change, and Technology
Issue 3: Is Third World Immigration a Threat to America's Way of Life?	**Chapter 10:** Social Class **Chapter 11:** Global Inequality **Chapter 13:** Race and Ethnicity	**Chapter 7:** Inequalities of Race and Ethnicity	**Chapter 6:** Inequality by Race and Ethnicity **Chapter 9:** Social Institutions: Education, Government, and the Economy **Chapter 10:** Population, Community, Health, and the Environment
Issue 4: Does Divorce Have Long-Term Damaging Effects on Children?	**Chapter 7:** Families	**Chapter 10:** The Family	**Chapter 2:** Culture and Socialization **Chapter 8:** Social Institutions: Family and Religion
Issue 5: Should Mothers Stay Home with Their Children?	**Chapter 4:** Socialization **Chapter 7:** Families **Chapter 10:** Social Class	**Chapter 3:** Socialization **Chapter 10:** The Family	**Chapter 2:** Culture and Socialization **Chapter 7:** Inequality by Gender
Issue 6: Should Same-Sex Marriages Be Legally Recognized?	**Chapter 4:** Socialization **Chapter 7:** Families	**Chapter 10:** The Family	**Chapter 8:** Social Institutions: Family and Religion
Issue 7: Is Increasing Economic Inequality a Serious Problem?	**Chapter 11:** Global Inequality	**Chapter 6:** Social Stratification	**Chapter 5:** Stratification in the United States and Global Inequality

continued

Taking Sides: Social Issues, 15/e Expanded by Finsterbusch	SOC, 1/e by Witt	Sociology: The Core, 9/e by Hughes	Sociology Matters, 4/e by Schaefer
Issue 8: Has Feminism Benefited American Society?	**Chapter 12:** Gender and Age	**Chapter 8:** Gender Inequality	**Chapter 7:** Inequality by Gender
Issue 9: Has Affirmative Action Outlived Its Usefulness?	**Chapter 13:** Race and Ethnicity	**Chapter 7:** Inequalities of Race and Ethnicity	**Chapter 5:** Stratification in the United States and Global Inequality **Chapter 11:** Social Movements, Social Change, and Technology
Issue 10: Are Boys and Men Disadvantaged Relative to Girls and Women?	**Chapter 12:** Gender and Age	**Chapter 8:** Gender Inequality	**Chapter 7:** Inequality by Gender
Issue 11: Should Government Intervene in a Capitalist Economy?	**Chapter 9:** Government and Economy	**Chapter 9:** Political and Economic Power	**Chapter 9:** Social Institutions: Education, Government, and the Economy
Issue 12: Has Welfare Reform Benefited the Poor?	**Chapter 10:** Social Class	**Chapter 9:** Political and Economic Power	**Chapter 9:** Social Institutions: Education, Government, and the Economy **Chapter 11:** Social Movements, Social Change, and Technology
Issue 13: Is Competition the Reform That Will Fix Education?	**Chapter 8:** Education and Religion	**Chapter 11:** Religion, Education, and Medicine	**Chapter 9:** Social Institutions: Education, Government, and the Economy
Issue 14: Should Biotechnology Be Used to Alter and Enhance Humans?	**Chapter 14:** Health, Medicine and Environment	**Chapter 11:** Religion, Education, and Medicine	**Chapter 10:** Population, Community, Health, and the Environment
Issue 15: Is Street Crime More Harmful Than White-Collar Crime?	**Chapter 6:** Deviance	**Chapter 5:** Deviance and Crime	**Chapter 4:** Deviance and Social Control
Issue 16: Should Marijuana Be Legalized?	**Chapter 6:** Deviance	**Chapter 5:** Deviance and Crime	**Chapter 4:** Deviance and Social Control **Chapter 11:** Social Movements, Social Change, and Technology
Issue 17: Does the Threat of Terrorism Warrant the Curtailment of Civil Liberties?	**Chapter 9:** Government and Economy	**Chapter 9:** Political and Economic Power	**Chapter 9:** Social Institutions: Education, Government, and the Economy
Issue 18: Is Humankind Dangerously Harming the Environment?	**Chapter 14:** Health, Medicine and Environment	**Chapter 12:** Population and the Environment	**Chapter 10:** Population, Community, Health, and the Environment
Issue 19: Is Globalization Good for Humankind?	**Chapter 11:** Global Inequality	**Chapter 6:** Social Stratification	**Chapter 11:** Social Movements, Social Change, and Technology
Issue 20: Is America Dominated by Big Business?	**Chapter 9:** Government and Economy	**Chapter 9:** Political and Economic Power	**Chapter 5:** Stratification in the United States and Global Inequality
Issue 21: Are Barriers to Women's Success as Leaders Due to Societal Obstacles?	**Chapter 12:** Gender and Age	**Chapter 8:** Gender Inequality	**Chapter 7:** Inequality by Gender
Issue 22: Is the World a Victim of American Cultural Imperialism?	**Chapter 3:** Culture	**Chapter 9:** Political and Economic Power	**Chapter 2:** Culture and Socialization **Chapter 11:** Social Movements, Social Change, and Technology

Introduction

Debating Social Issues

Kurt Finsterbusch

What Is Sociology?

"I have become a problem to myself," St. Augustine said. Put into a social and secular framework, St. Augustine's concern marks the starting point of sociology. We have become a problem to ourselves, and it is sociology that seeks to understand the problem and, perhaps, to find some solutions. The subject matter of sociology, then, is ourselves—people interacting with one another in groups and organizations.

Although the subject matter of sociology is very familiar, it is often useful to look at it in an unfamiliar light, one that involves a variety of theories and perceptual frameworks. In fact, to properly understand social phenomena, it *should* be looked at from several different points of view. In practice, however, this may lead to more friction than light, especially when each view proponent says, "I am right and you are wrong," rather than, "My view adds considerably to what your view has shown."

Sociology, as a science of society, was developed in the nineteenth century. Auguste Comte (1798–1857), the French mathematician and philosopher who is considered to be the father of sociology, had a vision of a well-run society based on social science knowledge. Sociologists (Comte coined the term) would discover the laws of social life and then determine how society should be structured and run. Society would not become perfect, because some problems are intractable, but he believed that a society guided by scientists and other experts was the best possible society.

Unfortunately, Comte's vision was extremely naive. For most matters of state there is no one best way of structuring or doing things that sociologists can discover and recommend. Instead, sociologists debate more social issues than they resolve.

The purpose of sociology is to throw light on social issues and their relationship to the complex, confusing, and dynamic social world around us. It seeks to describe how society is organized and how individuals fit into it. But neither the organization of society nor the fit of individuals is perfect. Social disorganization is a fact of life—at least in modern, complex societies such as the one we live in. Here, perfect harmony continues to elude us, and "social problems" are endemic. The very institutions, laws, and policies that produce benefits also produce what sociologists call "unintended effects"—unintended and undesirable. The changes that please one sector of the society may displease another, or the changes that seem so indisputably healthy at first turn out to have a dark underside to them. The examples are endless. Modern urban life gives people privacy and freedom from snooping neighbors that the small town never afforded; yet that very privacy seems to breed an uneasy sense of anonymity and loneliness. Take another example: Hierarchy is necessary for organizations to function efficiently, but hierarchy leads to the creation of a ruling elite. Flatten out the hierarchy and you may achieve social equality—but at the price of confusion, incompetence, and low productivity.

This is not to say that all efforts to effect social change are ultimately futile and that the only sound view is the tragic one that concludes "nothing works." We can be realistic without falling into despair. In many respects, the human condition has improved over the centuries and has improved as a result of conscious social policies. But improvements are purchased at a price—not only a monetary price but one involving human discomfort and discontent. The job of policymakers is to balance the anticipated benefits against the probable costs.

It can never hurt policymakers to know more about the society in which they work or the social issues they confront. That, broadly speaking, is the purpose of sociology. It is what this book is about. This volume examines issues that are central to the study of sociology.

Culture and Values

A common value system is the major mechanism for integrating a society, but modern societies contain so many different groups with differing ideas and values that integration must be built as much on tolerance of differences as on common values. Furthermore, technology and social conditions change, so values must adjust to new situations, often weakening old values. Some people (often called *conservatives*) will defend the old values. Others (often called *liberals*) will make concessions to allow for change. For example, the protection of human life is a sacred value to most people, but some would compromise that value when the life involved is a 90-year-old comatose man on life-support machines who had signed a document indicating that he did not want to be kept alive under those conditions. The conservative would counter that once we make the value of human life relative, we become dangerously open to greater evils—that perhaps society will come to think it acceptable to terminate all sick, elderly people undergoing expensive treatments. This is only one example of how values are hotly debated today.

Three debates on values are presented in Unit 1. In Issue 1, Kay S. Hymowitz challenges the common perception that morals have declined in America, while Robert H. Bork argues for the declining morality thesis. Issue 2 examines a major institution that can be seen as responsible for instilling values and culture in people—the media. This issue focuses in particular on whether the news reporters and anchorpersons report and comment on the news with professional objectivity and relatively bias free. Fred Barnes argues that the major news outlets are liberal and hire liberal journalists. The selection and reporting of news, therefore, has a liberal bias. In contrast, Robert F. Kennedy, Jr., counters that most people get their news from conservative sources and believe many conservative myths as a result.

The final culture/values debate, Issue 3, concerns the cultural impact of immigration. Patrick Buchanan argues that current levels of immigration are too high and that immigrant cultures are too different from American culture to be assimilated. Thus, immigration is threatening America's cultural unity. Linda Chavez counters that most immigrants have good values. They are ambitious, work hard, and have strong family values. They also are not taking jobs away from citizens nor lowering wages. The strong economy and low unemployment prove that. . . .

Sex Roles, Gender, and the Family

An area that has experienced tremendous value change in the last several decades is sex roles and the family. Women in large numbers have rejected major aspects of their traditional gender roles and family roles while remaining strongly committed to much of the mother role and to many feminine characteristics. Men have changed much less but their situation has changed considerably. Issue 4 examines the consequences of divorce on children because it has become so common. Elizabeth Marquardt presents evidence that divorce damages children, but Constance Ahrons counters that her research with children of divorced parents shows otherwise. Issue 5 considers one of the current strains on mothers—the conflict between career and childrearing. Claudia Wallis presents the case for mothers staying home and Neil Gilbert argues this is true for some but overall the trend is for increasing proportion of mothers to be in the labor force. Issue 6 debates whether same-sex marriages should be legal. The Human Rights Campaign presents all the arguments in its favor and Peter Sprigg presents all the arguments against it.

Stratification and Inequality

Issue 7 centers around a sociological debate about whether or not increasing economic inequality is a serious problem. James Kurth asserts that it is, while Gary S. Becker and Kevin M. Murphy argue that the increasing inequality is largely the result of the education premium, which, in turn, encourages young people to get more education and better themselves. Issue 8 covers a major transformation in American stratification, which has been the dramatic change in women's position in society. The feminist movement was a major force in changing women's roles. Not all women, however, believe that the feminist movement has benefited society. In this vein, Kate O'Beirne blasts the feminist movement while Barbara Epstein praises feminists for the great things that they accomplished.

Today one of the most controversial issues regarding inequalities is affirmative action. Is justice promoted or undermined by such policies? Curtis Crawford and Lawrence D. Bobo take opposing sides on this question in Issue 9.

Issue 10 deals with male-female advantages and disadvantages. Michelle Conlin explains that the way schools operate and the behaviors that they reward or sanction favor females over males. As a result, females are graduating from high school, colleges, and most grad schools at higher rates than males. Joel Wendland points out the substantial advantages that males have over females in employment and wages and argues that the gender gap still favors males.

Political Economy and Institutions

The United States is a capitalist welfare state, and the role of the state in capitalism (more precisely, the market) and in welfare is examined in the next two issues. Issue 11 considers whether or not the government should step in and attempt to correct for the failures of the market through regulations, policies, and programs. Eliot Spitzer and Andrew F. Celli, Jr., argue that government intervention is necessary to make markets work well and to prevent various harms to society. John Stossel argues that even well-intended state interventions in the market usually only make matters worse and that governments cannot serve the public good as effectively as competitive markets can. One way in which the government intervenes in the economy is by providing welfare to people who cannot provide for their own needs in the labor market. Issue 12 debates the wisdom of the Work Opportunity Reconciliation Act of 1996, which ended Aid to Families of Dependent Children (which was what most people equated with welfare). David Coates presents the argument that the welfare reform was a great success because it greatly reduced welfare rolls and dramatically increased the employment of welfare mothers. David Coates also presents the counter argument. The real answer to poverty is higher wages for entry-level workers, which would draw them off of the welfare rolls instead of pushing them off into working poverty.

Education is one of the biggest jobs of the government as well as the key to individual prosperity and the success of the economy. For decades the American system of education has been severely criticized. Such an important institution is destined to be closely scrutinized, and many reforms have been attempted. The main debate on how to improve public schools concerns school choice as presented in Issue 13. Clint Bolick argues that competition improves performance in sports and business so it should do the same in education, and the data support this theory. Also, parents should be allowed to send their children to the school of their choice. Ron Wolk presents a more radical view of school reform. Many reform proposals today, including school choice, will do little to improve schools. He proposes shifting more responsibility for education from teachers to students.

The final issue in this section deals with a set of concerns about the use of present and soon-to-emerge biotechnologies. The value of biotechnologies for healing people is accepted by all. Issue 14, however, debates their use to alter and enhance humans. Ronald Bailey advocates the full use of biotechnologies to improve the genes of babies and to enhance everyone. The arguments against such practices are present by Michael Sandel.

Crime and Social Control

Crime is interesting to sociologists because crimes are those activities that society makes illegal and will use force to stop. Why are some acts made illegal and others (even those that may be more harmful) not made illegal? Surveys indicate that concern about crime is extremely high in America. Is the fear of crime, however, rightly placed? Americans fear mainly street crime, but Jeffrey Reiman argues in Issue 15 that corporate crime—also known as "white-collar crime"—causes far more death, harm, and financial loss to Americans than does street crime. In contrast, David A. Anderson calculates the full costs of crime, both direct and indirect, and concludes that the costs of murder and theft far exceed the cost of white-collar crime. These contradictory findings result from differing definitions of white-collar crime. A prominent aspect of the crime picture is the illegal drug trade. It has such bad consequences that some people are seriously talking about legalizing drugs in order to kill the illegal drug business. The case seems especially strong for marijuana. Ethan A. Nadelmann argues this view in Issue 16, while John P. Walters argues that legalization of marijuana would lead to more addiction and problems. Finally, Issue 17 deals with terrorism, perhaps the major problem in America today. We must defend against and prevent it. To do so effectively requires the expansion of police powers, so we passed the Patriot Act. But did the Patriot Act go too far and trample America's liberties? Larry Cox argues that America must stop denying civil rights and return to being a leader in advocating civil rights. On the other hand, Robert H. Bork believes that the complaints of people like Cox have tied the hands of the law in the past and that the grave danger we face today requires the strengthening, not weakening, of the Act.

The Future: Population/Environment/Society

Many social commentators speculate on "the fate of the earth." The environmentalists have their own vision of apocalypse. They see the possibility that the human race could degrade the environment to the point that population growth and increasing economic production could overshoot the carrying capacity of the globe. The resulting collapse could lead to the extinction of much of the human race and the end of free societies. Other analysts believe that these fears are groundless. In Issue 18, Lester R. Brown shows how human actions are degrading the environment in ways that adversely affect humans. In contrast, Bjorn Lomborg argues that the environment is improving in many ways and that environmental problems are manageable or will have mild adverse effects.

Issues 20–22 assess the benefits and costs of globalization. Johan Norberg argues that economic globalization has been a demonstration of the basic economic theory that global markets and relatively free trade economically benefit all nations that participate. Martin Hart-Landsberg counters that globalization, which increases corporate profits, hurts both workers and the environment.

The Social Construction of Reality

An important idea in sociology is that people construct social reality in the course of interaction by attaching social meanings to the reality they are experiencing and then responding to those meanings. Two people can walk down a city street and derive very different meanings from what they see around them. Both, for example, may see homeless people—but they may see them in different contexts. One fits them into a picture of once-vibrant cities dragged into decay and ruin because of permissive policies that have encouraged pathological types to harass citizens; the other observer fits them into a picture of an America that can no longer hide the wretchedness of its poor. Both feel that they are seeing something deplorable, but their views of what makes it deplorable are radically opposed. Their differing views of what they have seen will lead to very different prescriptions for what should be done about the problem.

The social construction of reality is an important idea for this book because each author is socially constructing reality and working hard to persuade you to see his or her point of view; that is, to see the definition of the situation and the set of meanings he or she has assigned to the situation. In doing this, each author presents a carefully selected set of facts, arguments, and values. The arguments contain assumptions or theories, some of which are spelled out and some of which are unspoken. The critical reader has to judge the evidence for the facts, the logic and soundness of the arguments, the importance of the values, and whether or not omitted facts, theories, and values invalidate the thesis. This book facilitates this critical thinking process by placing authors in opposition. This puts the reader in the position of critically evaluating two constructions of reality for each issue instead of one.

Conclusion

Writing in the 1950s, a period that was in some ways like our own, the sociologist C. Wright Mills said that Americans know a lot about their "troubles" but they cannot make the connections between seemingly personal concerns and the concerns of others in the world. If they could only learn to make those connections, they could turn their concerns into *issues*. An issue transcends the realm of the personal. According to Mills, "An issue is a public matter: some value cherished by publics is felt to be threatened. Often there is a debate about what the value really is and what it is that really threatens it."

It is not primarily personal troubles but social issues that I have tried to present in this book. The variety of topics in it can be taken as an invitation to discover what Mills called "the sociological imagination." This imagination, said Mills, "is the capacity to shift from one perspective to another—from the political to the psychological; from examination of a single family to comparative assessment of the national budgets of the world. . . . It is the capacity to range from the most impersonal and remote transformations to the most intimate features of the human self—and to see the relations between the two." This book, with a range of issues well suited to the sociological imagination, is intended to enlarge that capacity.

Internet References . . .

Internet Philosophical Resources on Moral Relativism

This Web site for *Ethics Updates* offers discussion questions, a bibliographical guide, and a list of Internet resources concerning moral relativism.

http://ethics.sandiego.edu/relativism.html

The National Institute on Media and the Family

The National Institute on Media and the Family Web site is a national resource for teachers, parents, community leaders, and others who are interested in the influence of electronic media on early childhood education, child development, academic performance, culture, and violence.

http://www.mediaandthefamily.com

The International Center for Migration, Ethnicity, and Citizenship

The International Center for Migration, Ethnicity, and Citizenship is engaged in scholarly research and public policy analysis bearing on international migration, refugees, and the incorporation of newcomers in host countries.

http://www.newschool.edu/icmec/

National Immigrant Forum

The National Immigrant Forum is a pro-immigrant organization that examines the effects of immigration on U.S. society. Click on the links for discussion of underground economies, immigrant economies, race and ethnic relations, and other topics.

http://www.immigrationforum.org

The National Network for Immigrant and Refugee Rights (NNIRR)

The National Network for Immigrant and Refugee Rights (NNIRR) serves as a forum to share information and analysis, to educate communities and the general public, and to develop and coordinate plans of action on important immigrant and refugee issues.

http://www.nnirr.org

Culture and Values

*S*ociologists *recognize that a fairly strong consensus on the basic values of a society contributes greatly to the smooth functioning of that society. The functioning of modern, complex urban societies, however, often depends on the tolerance of cultural differences and equal rights and protections for all cultural groups. In fact, such societies can be enriched by the contributions of different cultures. But at some point the cultural differences may result in a pulling apart that exceeds the pulling together. One cultural problem is the perceived moral decline, which may involve a conflict between old and new values. Another cultural problem in America is whether the media has a bias that is significantly removed from the epicenter of American culture. The final problem is whether current immigrants to the United States bring appropriate values and skills.*

- Is American in Moral Decline?

- Does the News Media Have a Liberal Bias?

- Is Third World Immigration a Threat to America's Way of Life?

ISSUE 1

Is America in Moral Decline?

YES: Robert H. Bork, from *Slouching Towards Gomorrah: Modern Liberalism and American Decline* (Regan Books, 1996)

NO: Kay S. Hymowitz, from "Our Changing Culture: Abandoning the Sixties," *Current* (June 2004)

ISSUE SUMMARY

YES: Robert H. Bork, famous for being nominated for the Supreme Court but not confirmed by the Senate, argues that modern liberalism is responsible for the decline in morals.

NO: Journalist Kay S. Hymowitz argues that the permissive culture of the sixties, which led to less respect for authority, crime, sexual promiscuity, and other indicators of moral decline, is waning. The cultural pendulum is swinging back to a more traditional culture of commitment, moderation, and family values.

Morality is the glue that holds society together. It enables people to deal with each other in relative tranquility and generally to their mutual benefit. Morality influences us both from the outside and from the inside. The morality of others affects us from outside as social pressure. Our conscience is morality affecting us from inside, even though others, especially parents, influence the formation of our conscience. Because parents, churches, schools, and peers teach us their beliefs and values (their morals) and the rules of society, most of us grow up wanting to do what is right. We also want to do things that are pleasurable. In a well-functioning society the right and the pleasurable are not too far apart, and most people lead morally respectable lives. On the other hand, no one lives up to moral standards perfectly. In fact, deviance from some moral standards is common, and when it becomes very common the standard changes. Some people interpret this as moral decline, while others interpret it as simply a change in moral standards or even as progress. Take, for example, the new morality that wives should be equal to rather than subservient to their husbands.

The degree of commitment to various moral precepts varies from person to person. Some people even act as moral guardians and take responsibility for encouraging others to live up to the moral standards. One of their major tactics is to cry out against the decline of morals. There are a number of such voices speaking out in public today. In fact, many politicians seem to try to outdo each other in speaking out against crime, teenage pregnancy, divorce, violence in the media, latchkey children, irresponsible parenting, etc.

Cries of moral decline have been ringing out for centuries. In earlier times the cries were against sin, debauchery, and godlessness. Today the cries are often against various aspects of individualism. Parents are condemned for sacrificing their children for their own needs, including their careers. Divorced people are condemned for discarding spouses instead of working hard to save their marriages. Children of elderly parents are condemned for putting their parents into nursing homes to avoid the inconvenience of caring for them. The general public is condemned for investing so little time in others and their communities while pursuing their own interests. These criticisms against individualism may have some validity. On the other hand, individualism has some more positive aspects, including enterprise and inventiveness, which contribute to economic growth; individual responsibility; advocacy of human rights; reduced clannishness and reduced prejudice toward other groups; and an emphasis on self-development, which includes successful relations with others.

The morality debate is important because moral decline not only increases human suffering but also weakens society and hinders the performance of its institutions. The following selections require some deep reflection on the moral underpinnings of American society as well as other societies, and they invite the reader to strengthen those underpinnings.

Many have decried the high levels of crime, violence, divorce, and opportunism, but few argue the thesis of the moral decline of America as thoroughly and as passionately as Robert H. Bork, the author of the following selection. But is he reading the facts correctly? Kay S. Hymowitz presents the counter thesis of moral improvement. The main indicators of morals are reversing, which she explains by the cultural shift from the permissive values of the sixties to more traditional values of today's youth including more respect for parents and traditional values.

Modern Liberalism and American Decline

This is an [article] about American decline. Since American culture is a variant of the cultures of all Western industrialized democracies, it may even, inadvertently, be . . . about Western decline. In the United States, at least, that decline and the mounting resistance to it have produced what we now call a culture war. It is impossible to say what the outcome will be, but for the moment our trajectory continues downward. This is not to deny that much in our culture remains healthy, that many families are intact and continue to raise children with strong moral values. American culture is complex and resilient. But it is also not to be denied that there are aspects of almost every branch of our culture that are worse than ever before and that the rot is spreading.

"Culture," as used here, refers to all human behavior and institutions, including popular entertainment, art, religion, education, scholarship, economic activity, science, technology, law, and morality. Of that list, only science, technology, and the economy may be said to be healthy today, and it is problematical how long that will last. Improbable as it may seem, science and technology themselves are increasingly under attack, and it seems highly unlikely that a vigorous economy can be sustained in an enfeebled, hedonistic culture, particularly when that culture distorts incentives by increasingly rejecting personal achievement as the criterion for the distribution of rewards.

With each new evidence of deterioration, we lament for a moment, and then become accustomed to it. We hear one day of the latest rap song calling for killing policemen or the sexual mutilation of women; the next, of coercive left-wing political indoctrination at a prestigious university; then of the latest homicide figures for New York City, Los Angeles, or the District of Columbia; of the collapse of the criminal justice system, which displays an inability to punish adequately and, often enough, an inability even to convict the clearly guilty; of the rising rate of illegitimate births; the uninhibited display of sexuality and the popularization of violence in our entertainment; worsening racial tensions; the angry activists of feminism, homosexuality, environmentalism, animal rights—the list could be extended almost indefinitely.

So unrelenting is the assault on our sensibilities that many of us grow numb, finding resignation to be the rational, adaptive response to an environment that is increasingly polluted and apparently beyond our control.

That is what Senator Daniel Patrick Moynihan calls "defining deviancy down." Moynihan cites the "Durkheim constant." Emile Durkheim, a founder of sociology, posited that there is a limit to the amount of deviant behavior any community can "afford to recognize." As behavior worsens, the community adjusts its standards so that conduct once thought reprehensible is no longer deemed so. As behavior improves, the deviancy boundary moves up to encompass conduct previously thought normal. Thus, a community of saints and a community of felons would display very different behavior but about the same amount of recognized deviancy.

But the Durkheim constant is now behaving in a very odd way. While defining deviancy down with respect to crime, illegitimacy, drug use, and the like, our cultural elites are growing intensely moralistic and disapproving about what had always been thought normal behavior, thus accomplishing what columnist Charles Krauthammer terms "defining deviancy up." It is at least an apparent paradox that we are accomplishing both forms of redefining, both down and up, simultaneously. One would suppose that as once normal behavior became viewed as deviant, that would mean that there was less really bad conduct in the society. But that is hardly our case. Instead, we have redefined what we mean by such things as child abuse, rape, and racial or sexual discrimination so that behavior until recently thought quite normal, unremarkable, even benign, is now identified as blameworthy or even criminal. Middle-class life is portrayed as oppressive and shot through with pathologies. "As part of the vast social project of moral leveling," Krauthammer wrote, "it is not enough for the deviant to be normalized. The normal must be found to be deviant." This situation is thoroughly perverse. Underclass values become increasingly acceptable to the middle class, especially their young, and middle-class values become increasingly contemptible to the cultural elites.

That is why there is currently a widespread sense that the distinctive virtues of American life, indeed the distinctive features of Western civilization, are in peril in ways not previously seen. . . . This time we face, and seem to be succumbing to, an attack mounted by a force not only within Western civilization but one that is perhaps its legitimate child.

The enemy within is modern liberalism, a corrosive agent carrying a very different mood and agenda than that of classical or traditional liberalism. . . . Modernity, the child of the Enlightenment, failed when it became apparent that the good society cannot be achieved by unaided reason. The response of liberalism was not to turn to religion, which modernity had seemingly made irrelevant, but to abandon reason. Hence, there have appeared philosophies claiming that words can carry no definite meaning or that there is no reality other than one that is "socially constructed." A reality so constructed, it is thought, can be decisively altered by social or cultural edict, which is a prescription for coercion. . . .

The defining characteristics of modern liberalism are radical egalitarianism (the equality of outcomes rather than of opportunities) and radical individualism (the drastic reduction of limits to personal gratification). . . .

Men were kept from rootless hedonism, which is the end stage of unconfined individualism, by religion, morality, and law. These are commonly cited.

To them I would add the necessity for hard work, usually physical work, and the fear of want. These constraints were progressively undermined by rising affluence. . . .

The mistake the Enlightenment founders of liberalism made about human nature has brought us to this—an increasing number of alienated, restless individuals, individuals without strong ties to others, except in the pursuit of ever more degraded distractions and sensations. And liberalism has no corrective within itself; all it can do is endorse more liberty and demand more rights. Persons capable of high achievement in one field or another may find meaning in work, may find community among colleagues, and may not particularly mind social and moral separation otherwise. Such people are unlikely to need the more sordid distractions that popular culture now offers. But very large segments of the population do not fall into that category. For them, the drives of liberalism are catastrophic.

The consequences of liberalism, liberty, and the pursuit of happiness pushed too far are now apparent. Irving Kristol writes of the clear signs of rot and decadence germinating within American society—a rot and decadence that was no longer the consequence of liberalism but was the actual agenda of contemporary liberalism. . . . [S]ector after sector of American life has been ruthlessly corrupted by the liberal ethos. It is an ethos that aims simultaneously at political and social collectivism on the one hand, and moral anarchy on the other." I would add only that current liberalism's rot and decadence is merely what liberalism has been moving towards for better than two centuries.

We can now see the tendency of the Enlightenment, the Declaration of Independence, and *On Liberty.* Each insisted on the expanding liberty of the individual and each assumed that order was not a serious problem and could be left, pretty much, to take care of itself. And, for a time, order did seem to take care of itself. But that was because the institutions—family, church, school, neighborhood, inherited morality—remained strong. The constant underestimation of their value and the continual pressure for more individual autonomy necessarily weakened the restraints on individuals. The ideal slowly became the autonomous individual who stood in an adversarial relationship to any institution or group that attempted to set limits to acceptable thought and behavior.

That process continues today, and hence we have an increasingly disorderly society. The street predator of the underclass may be the natural outcome of the mistake the founders of liberalism made. They would have done better had they remembered original sin. Or had they taken Edmund Burke seriously. Mill wrote: "Liberty consists in doing what one desires." That might have been said by a man who was both a libertine and an anarchist; Mill was neither, but his rhetoric encouraged those who would be either or both. Burke had it right earlier: "The only liberty I mean is a liberty connected with order; that not only exists along with order and virtue, but which cannot exist at all without them." "The effect of liberty to individuals is, that they may do what they please: We ought to see what it will please them to do, before we risque congratulations, which may soon be turned into complaints." Burke, unlike the Mill of *On Liberty,* had a true understanding of the nature of men, and balanced liberty with restraint and order, which are, in truth, essential to the preservation of liberty.

The classical liberalism of the nineteenth century is widely and correctly admired, but we can now see that it was inevitably a transitional phase. The tendencies inherent in individualism were kept within bounds by the health of institutions other than the state, a common moral culture, and the strength of religion. Liberalism drained the power from the institutions. We no longer have a common moral culture and our religion, while pervasive, seems increasingly unable to affect actual behavior.

Modern liberalism is one branch of the rupture that occurred in liberalism in the last century. The other branch is today called conservatism. American conservatism, neo or otherwise, in fact represents the older classical liberal tradition. Conservatism of the American variety is simply liberalism that accepts the constraints that a clear view of reality, including a recognition of the nature of human beings, places upon the main thrusts of liberalism—liberty and equality. The difference, it has been said, is that between a hard-headed and a sentimental liberalism. Sentimental liberalism, with its sweet view of human nature, naturally evolves into the disaster of modern liberalism.

"During the past 30 years," William Bennett writes, "we have witnessed a profound shift in public attitudes." He cites polls showing that "we Americans now place less value on what we owe others as a matter of moral obligation; less value on sacrifice as a moral good, on social conformity, respectability, and observing the rules; less value on correctness and restraint in matters of physical pleasure and sexuality—and correlatively greater value on things like self-expression, individualism, self-realization, and personal choice." Though I think the shift in public attitudes merely accelerated in the past thirty years, having been silently eroding our culture for much longer, it is clear that our current set of values is inhospitable to the self-discipline required for such institutions as marriage and education and hospitable to no-fault divorce and self-esteem training.

Our modern, virtually unqualified, enthusiasm for liberty forgets that liberty can only be "the space between the walls," the walls of morality and law based upon morality. It is sensible to argue about how far apart the walls should be set, but it is cultural suicide to demand all space and no walls. . . .

The Collapse of Popular Culture

The distance and direction popular culture has travelled in less than one lifetime is shown by the contrast between best-selling records. A performer of the 1930s hit "The Way You Look Tonight" sang these words to romantic music:

> *Oh, but you're lovely, /With your smile so warm, /And your cheek so soft, /There is nothing for me but to love you, /Just the way you look tonight.*

In our time, Snoop Doggy Dogg's song "Horny" proclaims to "music" without melody:

> *I called you up for some sexual healing. /I'm callin' again so let me come get it. /Bring the lotion so I can rub you. /Assume the position so I can f . . . you.*

Then there is Nine Inch Nails' song, "Big Man with a Gun." Even the expurgated version published by the *Washington Post* gives some idea of how rapidly popular culture is sinking into barbarism:

> *I am a big man (yes I am). And I have a big gun. Got me a big old [expletive] and I, I like to have fun. Held against your forehead, I'll make you suck it. Maybe I'll put a hole in your head. . . . I can reduce it if you want. I can devour. I'm hard as [expletive] steel and I've got the power. . . . Shoot, shoot, shoot, shoot, shoot. I'm going to come all over you. . . . me and my [expletive] gun, me and my [expletive] gun.*

The obscenity of thought and word is staggering, but also notable is the deliberate rejection of any attempt to achieve artistic distinction or even mediocrity. The music is generally little more than noise with a beat, the singing is an unmelodic chant, the lyrics often range from the perverse to the mercifully unintelligible. It is difficult to convey just how debased rap is. . . .

What America increasingly produces and distributes is now propaganda for every perversion and obscenity imaginable. If many of us accept the assumptions on which that is based, and apparently many do, then we are well on our way to an obscene culture. The upshot is that American popular culture is in a free fall, with the bottom not yet in sight. This is what the liberal view of human nature has brought us to. The idea that men are naturally rational, moral creatures without the need for strong external restraints has been exploded by experience. There is an eager and growing market for depravity, and profitable industries devoted to supplying it. Much of such resistance as there is comes from people living on the moral capital accumulated by prior generations. That capital may be expected to dwindle further—cultures do not unravel everywhere all at once. Unless there is vigorous counterattack, which must, I think, resort to legal as well as moral sanctions, the prospects are for a chaotic and unhappy society, followed, perhaps, by an authoritarian and unhappy society. . . .

The Rise of Crime, Illegitimacy, and Welfare

The United States has surely never before experienced the social chaos and the accompanying personal tragedies that have become routine today: high rates of crime and low rates of punishment, high rates of illegitimate births subsidized by welfare, and high rates of family dissolution through no-fault divorce. These pathologies are recent, and it is now widely accepted that they are related to one another.

The proximate cause of these pathologies is the infatuation of modern liberalism with the individual's right to self-gratification along with the kind of egalitarianism, largely based on guilt, that inhibits judgment and reform. These pathologies were easy to fall into and will be very difficult to climb out of. There is, in fact, no agreement about how to cure them. It may be, in fact, that a democratic nation will be unable to take the measures necessary, once we know what those measures are.

If radical individualism and egalitarianism are the causes, we should expect to see their various effects produced at about the same time as one another. And that is what we do see. During the same years that popular culture was becoming ever more sordid, the pathologies of divorce, illegitimacy, and crime exploded. The story is well documented and may be quickly summarized. The more difficult question, particularly about illegitimacy and welfare, is how to escape what we have done.

Rates of illegitimate births and the commission of serious crimes began rising together and did so at the same time in both the United States and England. National illegitimacy statistics were first gathered in the United States in 1920. Illegitimate births then constituted 3 percent of all births. The proportion slowly went up to just over 5 percent in 1960, and then shot up to 11 percent in 1970, above 18 percent in 1980, and 30 percent by 1991. These are figures for the entire population. Black illegitimacy started from a higher base than white and skyrocketed sooner, reaching 68 percent in 1991. White illegitimacy had reached a little over 2 percent by 1960 and then shot up to 6 percent in 1970, 11 percent in 1980, and just under 22 percent in 1991. Combined black and white illegitimacy in 1992 was 32 percent. These are national averages; illegitimacy is much higher in lower-income communities and neighborhoods.

Crime displays the same pattern. National records about violent crime in the United States were first kept in 1960. The number of violent crimes in that year was just under 1,900 per 100,000 people; the number doubled within ten years, and more than tripled to almost 6,000 by 1980. After a brief decline, the crime rate began rising again and had reached almost 5,700 by 1992. It is thus apparent that crime and illegitimacy trends began rising at almost the same time and then rose together. . . .

Rising crime, illegitimacy, and student rebellion had a common cause. While the middle-class student radicals turned to dreams of revolution and the destruction of institutions, some of the lower classes turned to crime and sexual license, and probably for the same reasons. That fact bodes ill because it suggests a long-developing weakening of cultural constraints, constraints it will be very hard to put back in place. . . .

Crime rates in a number of areas have stopped rising and in some places have begun to decline. It is possible that the rate of violent crimes has gone down in the nation as a whole. This appears to be partially due to better policing, slightly higher rates of incarceration, and a decline in the number of young males, who are almost entirely responsible for violent crime though more and more women are taking up the practice. But, as the Council on Crime report puts it: "Recent drops in serious crime are but the lull before the coming crime storm." That is because the population of young males in the age groups that commit violent crime is about to increase rapidly, producing more violence than we know at present. It is also likely that the coming young felons will commit more serious crimes than today's juvenile offenders do. According to the report, the literature indicates that "each generation of crime-prone boys is several times more dangerous than the one before it, and that over 80 percent of the most serious and frequent offenders escape detection and arrest." . . .

When physical safety becomes a major problem even for the middle classes, we must of necessity become a heavily policed, authoritarian society, a society in which the middle classes live in gated and walled communities and make their places of work hardened targets. After the Oklahoma City bombing, there were serious proposals in Washington to use the Army to provide security. The mayor of Washington, D.C., proposed using the National Guard to supplement the police in that drug-ridden and murder-racked city. Whites tend to dismiss the violence of the inner cities as a black problem. As the killing and the drugs spread to white neighborhoods and suburbs, as they are doing, the response will be far more repressive. Both the fear of crime and the escalating harshness of the response to it will sharply reduce Americans' freedom of movement and peace of mind. Ours will become a most unpleasant society in which to live. Murray poses our alternatives: "Either we reverse the current trends in illegitimacy—especially white illegitimacy—or America must, willy-nilly, become an unrecognizably authoritarian, socially segregated, centralized state." . . .

Kay S. Hymowitz

→ **NO**

Our Changing Culture: Abandoning the Sixties

Sex doesn't sell: Miss Prim is in. No, editors at the *New York Times* "Sunday Styles" section were not off their meds when they came up with that headline recently. Just think about some of the Oscar nominees this year: there was *Seabiscuit,* a classic inspirational story of steadfast outsiders beating huge odds to win the race; *Return of the King: Lord of the Rings,* a mythic battle of good defeating evil, featuring female characters as pure as driven snow; *Master and Commander,* a nineteenth-century naval epic celebrating courage, discipline, and patriarchal authority. And then there was *Lost in Translation,* in which a man in the throes of a midlife crisis spends hours in a hotel room with a luscious young woman, and . . . they talk a lot.

If you listen carefully, you can hear something shifting deep beneath the manic surface of American culture. Rap stars have taken to wearing designer suits. Miranda Hobbs, *Sex and the City*'s redhead, has abandoned hooking up and a Manhattan co-op for a husband and a Brooklyn fixer-upper, where she helps tend her baby and ailing mother-in-law; even nympho Samantha has found a "meaningful relationship." Madonna is writing children's books. Gloria Steinem is an old married lady.

Family Values

Yessiree, family values are hot! Capitalism is cool! Seven-grain bread is so yesterday, and red meat is back!

Wave away the colored smoke of the Jackson family circus, Paris Hilton, and the antics of San Francisco, and you can see how Americans have been self-correcting from a decades-long experiment with "alternative values." Slowly, almost imperceptibly during the 1990s, the culture began a lumbering, Titanic turn away from the iceberg, a movement reinforced by the 1990s economic boom and the shock of the 9/11 terrorist attacks. During the last ten years, most of the miserable trends in crime, divorce, illegitimacy, drug use, and the like that we saw in the decades after 1965 either turned around or stalled. Today Americans are consciously, deliberately embracing ideas about sex, marriage, children, and the American dream that are coalescing into a viable—though admittedly much altered—sort of bourgeois normality. What is emerging is a vital, optimistic, family-centered, entrepreneurial, and yes, morally thoughtful, citizenry.

Not the 1950s

To check a culture's pulse, first look at the kids, as good a crystal ball as we have. Yes, there's reason to worry: guns in the schools, drugs, binge drinking, cheating, Ritalin, gangs, bullies, depression, oral sex, Internet porn, you name it. Kids dress like streetwalkers and thugs, they're too fat, they don't read, they watch too much television, they never play outside, they can't pay attention, they curse like *South Park's* Eric Cartman. The 1950s, this ain't.

Yet marketers who plumb people's attitudes to predict trends are noticing something interesting about "Millennials," the term that generation researchers Neil Howe and William Strauss invented for the cohort of kids born between 1981 and 1999: they're looking more like Jimmy Stewart than James Dean. They adore their parents, they want to succeed, they're optimistic, trusting, cooperative, dutiful, and civic-minded. "They're going to 'rebel' by being, not worse, but better," write Howe and Strauss.

However counterintuitive, there's plenty of hard evidence to support this view. Consider the most basic indicator of social health: crime. The juvenile murder rate plummeted 70 percent between 1993 and 2001. By 2001, the arrest rate for all violent crime among juveniles was down 44 percent from its 1994 peak, reaching its lowest level since 1983. Juvenile arrests for burglary were also down 56 percent in that time period. Vandalism is at its lowest level in two decades. Despite all the headlines to the contrary, schools are a lot safer: school-based crimes dropped by close to half in the late 1990s. According to the Youth Risk Behavior Survey, the percentage of ninth- through 12th-graders who reported being in a fight anywhere in the previous 12 months dropped from 42 percent in 1991 to 33 percent in 2001, while those who had been in a fight on school property fell from 16 percent to 13 percent.

Drinking

Something similar looks like it may be happening with adolescent drinking and drug use, on the rise throughout much of the nineties. But suddenly, around the turn of the millennium, the nation's teens started to climb back on the wagon. Monitoring the Future, an annual University of Michigan survey of the attitudes and behavior of high school students, reports that by 2002 the percentage of kids who reported binge drinking in the last 30 days was close to its lowest level in the 12 years that the survey has been following eighth- and tenth-graders and in the 30 years that it has been following high school seniors. Though during the 1990s marijuana use rose sharply among eighth-graders and less dramatically among tenth- and 12th-graders, by late in the decade the numbers began to fall. More broadly, the Department of Health and Human Services reports that all illicit teen drug use dropped 11 percent between 2001 and 2003. Ecstasy use, which soared between 1998 and 2001, fell by more than half among high schoolers. A 2003 National Center on

Addiction and Substance Abuse study found that 56 percent of teenagers have no friends who drink regularly, up from 52 percent in 2002, and 68 percent say they have no friends using marijuana, up from 62 percent—even though 40 percent of them say they would have no trouble finding the stuff if they wanted it. They're just not interested.

And what about teen sex? Only yesterday, you'd have thought there was no way to wrangle that horse back into the barn. No more. According to the Alan Guttmacher Institute, out-of-wedlock teen pregnancy rates have come down 28 percent from their high in 1990, from a peak of 117 per thousand girls ages 15 to 19 to 83.6 per thousand in 2000. The teen abortion rate also fell—by a third—during the same period. True, American kids still get pregnant at higher rates than those in other major Western nations, but the U.S. is the only country that saw a dramatic drop in teen pregnancy during the last decade.

While American kids are more often saying yes to birth control, even more of them, remarkably, are just saying no to sex, just as they are passing up marijuana and beer. According to the 1991 Youth Risk Behavior Survey, 54 percent of teens reported having had sex; a decade later, the number was 46 percent. The number of high schoolers who reported four or more partners also fell from 18.7 percent to 14.2 percent.

Making the decline in sexual activity more striking is that it began just around the same time that Depo-Provera, a four-shots-a-year birth control technology specifically aimed at teens, came on the market. It's often been said that the birth control pill, which became available to the public in the early 1960s, propelled the sexual revolution. The lesson of Depo-Provera, which was accompanied by a decrease in sexual activity, is that it isn't technology that changes sexual behavior. It's the culture.

If you need more proof, check the surveys not just on kids' sexual behavior but on their attitudes toward sex. Millennial are notably more strait-laced than many of their let's-spend-the-night-together parents. American Freshman, an annual survey of over a quarter of a million first-year kids at 413 four-year colleges, has found that young people have become less accepting of casual sex in the last 15 years. Between 1987 and 2001, those who agree with the statement "If two people really like each other, it's all right for them to have sex if they've known each other for a very short time" fell from 52 percent to 42 percent. Similarly, a recent National Campaign to Prevent Teen Pregnancy survey found that 92 percent of teenagers believe it is important for them "to get strong messages from society that they should not have sex until they are at least out of high school." Twenty-eight percent say they have become more opposed to teens having sex over the past several years, compared to 11 percent who say they are less opposed. It seems that it is adults who are skittish about abstinence, not kids: almost half of the parents interviewed believe it is embarrassing for teens to admit they are virgins, yet only a quarter of teenagers think so.

Keep in mind that these beliefs do not exist in an isolated room of the teen brain marked "sex" or "pregnancy." They are part of a welter of attitudes and values that reinforce each other. . . .

Fed up with the fall-out from the reign of "if it feels good, do it"—not only as it played out in the inner city but in troubled middle-class families across the land—Americans are looking more favorably on old-fashioned virtues like caution, self-restraint, commitment, and personal responsibility. They are in the midst of a fundamental shift in the cultural Zeitgeist that is driving so many seemingly independent trends in crime, sex, drugs, and alcohol in the same positive direction.

Look, for instance, at what's happening to teen alienation. If Millennials have a problem with authority, it's that they wish they had *more* of it. Poll after poll depicts a generation that thinks their parents are just grand. A 2003 *American Demographics* survey shows 67 percent of teens "give Mom an A." They tell interviewers for the National Campaign to Prevent Teen Pregnancy that they want *more* advice about sex from their parents. Summarizing opinion polls, researcher Neil Howe says that this generation is at least as attached to their parents and their values as any generation before. "When it comes to 'Do you get along with your family?' it's never been as high. Same thing for 'Do you believe in the values of your parents?' When they're asked 'Do you trust your parents to help you with important life decisions?' they don't see parents as meddling or interfering," Howe concludes. "They're grateful."

Hallmark Card

In fact, when it comes to families, this generation is as mushy as a Hallmark card. A Harris Interactive survey of college seniors found that 81 percent planned to marry (12 percent already had) at a mean age of 28. Ninety-one percent hope to have children—and get this: on average, they'd like to have three. The 2001 Monitoring the Future survey found 88 percent of male high school seniors and 93 percent of females believing that it is extremely or quite important to have a good marriage and family life. In a survey of college women conducted by the Institute for American Values, 83 percent said, "Being married is a very important goal for me." Over half of the women surveyed said they would like to meet their husbands in college. . . . Americans at or approaching marriageable age—are marriage nuts.

In real life, the number of married-couple families, after declining in the seventies and eighties, rose 5.7 percent in the nineties, according to demographer William H. Frey.

Marrying Later

And in fact, the incredible shrinking married-couple-with-children statistic cited by Kipnis is a statistical mirage, an artifact of two demographic trends, unconnected with American attitudes toward knot tying. First, young people are marrying later; the average age is 25 for women, 27 for men, up from 20 and 23 three decades ago. That means there are a lot more young singles out there than there were in 1970. Further swelling the ranks of these un-Ozzies and Harriets is the vastly increased number of empty nesters, retirees, and widows, beneficiaries of major health-care improvements over the past decades.

There are 34 million Americans over 65, and it's a safe bet that only those few living with their adult kids would be counted as part of a married-couple household with children. What it comes down to is that a smaller proportion of married couples with children is no more evidence of the decline of the family than more cars on the road is evidence of a decline in trucks.

Even on the fraught issue of out-of-wedlock births and divorce, there are grounds for hope. In the population at large, the decades-long trend toward family fragmentation has finally halted and, according to some numbers, is even reversing itself. Overall, the proportion of children in married-parent families rose from 68 percent in 1998 to 69 percent in 2002—a tiny boost, to be sure, but the first upward tick in decades. More encouragingly, after plummeting between 1965 and 1992, the number of black children living with married parents rose from 34 percent in 1995 to 39 percent in 2000. Moreover, the longitudinal Fragile Families and Child Wellbeing Study has found that half of the poor, largely black, new mothers it surveys are living with the father at the time of their baby's birth. Two-thirds of them agree "it is better for children if their parents are married," and 77 percent say that chances of marrying their child's father are 50 percent or higher. If history is any guide, most won't; but the fact that so many want to marry and understand that it is better to do so is an unexpected bit of social capital to build on.

Americans are even beginning to look at divorce with a more jaded eye. The divorce rate—statistically hard to pin down—is certainly stabilizing, and possibly even declining from its record high of 50 percent. Not so long ago, orthodox opinion would natter on about marital breakup as an opportunity for adults' "personal growth" or about "resilient children" who were "better off when their parents were happy." For the children of divorce who are now in their childbearing years, such sunny talk grates. They saw their mothers forced to move to one-bedroom apartments while their fathers went off with new girlfriends; they found out what it was like when your father moved from being the love object who read to you every night, to a guy who lives across the country whom you see once a year. When it comes to marriage and children, a lot of these damaged young adults are determined to do better. Nic Carothers, the 18-year-old son of divorced parents interviewed by the *Indianapolis Star,* explained his determination to avoid sex until he marries for life: "My father wasn't a very responsible man. I want to be a better father when the time is right." "I can't tell you how many 30-somethings are still in therapy because of their parents' divorce," Catherine Stellin, of Youth Intelligence, told me. "Now we're hearing that maybe it's a good thing to stay together for the sake of the kids."

Dr. Laura

This change of view is not limited to the heartland. Writing in the mainstream *Atlantic Monthly,* Caitlin Flanagan recently offered mild praise for *The Proper Care & Feeding of Husbands,* by much reviled talk-show host Dr. Laura: "There are many of us who understand that once you have children, certain doors ought to be closed to you forever. That to do right by a child means more than buying the latest bicycle helmet and getting him on the best soccer team. . . . It means investing oneself completely in the marriage that wrought him." Flanagan went on to chastise feminist male-bashing. "Our culture is quick to point out the responsibilities husbands have to wives—they should help out with the housework, be better listeners, understand that a woman wants to be more than somebody's mother and somebody's wife—but very reluctant to suggest that a wife has a responsibility to a husband." Such views didn't sink Flanagan's career; she will now be publishing her marriage-happy essays in *bienpensant New Yorker.*

In fact, applause for the nuclear family is now coming even from the American academy and from left-leaning advocacy groups. For decades, elites jeered at the assumption that changes in family structure would harm children; remember the guffaws that greeted Vice President Dan Quayle's pro-marriage *Murphy Brown* speech in 1992? But by the 1990s, study after study began showing, as Barbara Dafoe Whitehead put it in a landmark 1993 *Atlantic Monthly* article, that "Dan Quayle Was Right"—that, on average, children in married, two-parent families do better than other kids by every measure of success. Once-skeptical experts began acknowledging that the traditionalists had it right all along, and advocates announced, in the words of ChildTrends, that "[m]arriage is one of the most beneficial resources for adults and children." Just a decade ago it seemed impossible to imagine a leftish organization like the Center for Law and Social Policy going on record that "society should try to help more children grow up with their two biological, married parents in a reasonably healthy, stable relationship," but that's what has happened.

Home Alone

Still not convinced that there's anything to cheer about? Think about how much more child-centered Americans have become compared with 15 or 20 years ago—the era of the latchkey kid, when the Nickelodeon children's network touted itself as a "parent-free zone," and *Home Alone* was the signature kids' movie. But by the nineties, soccer moms had the keys to the house and the minivan, which was mounting up thousands of miles on trips to soccer matches, violin lessons, and swim meets. Studies showed a big drop in children's unstructured time. Even older kids came under their parents' hothouse scrutiny: "helicopter parents," in Neil Howe and William Strauss's term, hover over their children even after they leave for college, talking on the phone every day, visiting frequently, and helping them with their papers via e-mail.

The 30-somethings who are today's young parents show every sign of keeping the hearth fires burning bright. According to *American Demographics,* Gen-X parents are "nostalgic for the childhood that boomers supposedly had. It's informed their model of the perfect, traditional marriage." Gen-X women are abandoning Ms. for Mrs.: according to a recent Harvard study, the past decade has seen a "substantial decrease" in the percentage of college-educated brides keeping their maiden names. If they can afford to, these Missuses are also choosing the nursery over the cubicle; by 2000, the number of women in the workforce with infants under one dropped from 59 percent to 55 percent, the first decline in decades. The *New York Times Magazine* has run high-profile stories of six-figure MBAs and lawyers leaving their jobs to be at home with their babies. *Time* published a recent cover story on the trend toward professional-class stay-at-homes, and *Cosmopolitan,* of all places, has found a new group of "housewife wannabes" who would like nothing more than to do a Donna Reed. And these young mothers want big families: *USA Today* reports that "the rate of women having more than two children rose steadily in the late 1990s."

Their traditionalism also embraces old-fashioned discipline. A 1999 Yankelovich survey found that 89 percent of Gen Xers think modern parents let kids get away with too much; 65 percent want to return to a more traditional sense of parental duty. "Character education" is hot in school districts across the country—as are the Girl Scouts, because, as official Courtney Shore told the *Washington Times,* "parents and communities are returning to values-based activities." Today's parenting magazines do a brisk trade in articles with titles like ARE YOU A PARENT OR A PUSHOVER? GET A DISCIPLINE MAKEOVER and TEACHING YOUR CHILD RIGHT FROM WRONG.

Hard Workers

. . . [R]esearchers Howe and Strauss say that Millennials "are the first generation in living memory to be actually less violent, vulgar, and sexually charged than the popular culture adults are producing for them." How can that be?

Generational backlash counts for a lot: what we're seeing now is a rewrite of the boomer years. The truth is, Gen Xers and Millennials have some real gripes about the world their boomer parents constructed. When a 1999 Peter D. Hart Research Associates poll asked Americans between the ages of 18 to 30 what experience had shaped their generation, the most common answer was "divorce and single-parent families." Growing up in the aftermath of America's great marriage meltdown, no wonder that young people put so much stock in marriage and family, their bedrock in the mobile twenty-first century.

The Silent Generation

In fact, in some respects young Gen-X adults resemble their Silent Generation grandparents more than their boomer parents, especially in their longing for suburban nesting as a dreamlike aspiration. . . .

Immigration

Also changing the Zeitgeist is immigration. Marketers often characterize today's young generation by its "diversity"; a better way to put it is to say that it teems with immigrants and the sons and daughters of immigrants. Only 64 percent of Gen Xers and 62 percent of Millennial are non-Hispanic whites, compared with three-quarters of baby boomers. Twenty percent of today's teens have at least one immigrant parent. These kids often have a fervent work ethic—which can raise the bar for slacker American kids, as any high schooler with more than three Asian students in his algebra class will attest. Their parents tend toward traditionalism when it comes to marriage and family, with minuscule divorce and illegitimacy rates among Asians (though not among Hispanics, where families headed by a single mother have expanded rapidly). Immigrant kids are more likely to listen to their parents, and they tend not to be alienated ingrates who take their country's prosperity and opportunities for granted. As a Vietnamese high schooler wrote on PopPolitics.com: "When your parents have traveled thousands of miles to live here, when they spend three hours a day driving you and your siblings to various activities, when they paid hundreds of thousands of dollars for a cramped house they could have bought half-price elsewhere, you feel a debt."

And that drive and seriousness take us to reason number four: the information economy. According to the American Freshman survey, 73.8 percent of college kids say succeeding financially is an important life goal—a huge rise from the 40 percent who thought so in the late 1960s. These kids know they have to be hardworking, forward-looking, and pragmatic. But they know opportunity is out there, having just witnessed one of the most remarkable booms in American history, a time when black family poverty fell from 44 percent in 1992 to 23 percent in 1999, and when an astonishing 23 percent of households began earning over $75,000. Though plenty of Gen Xers lost their shirts when the dot-com bubble burst in 2000, there's little sign that they are souring on the free market. J. Walker Smith, president of the Yankelovich consultancy group, told Adweek that Gen Xers "feel more comfortable than boomers in reinventing themselves—they're more self-reliant and more self-directed. They're at home in an uncertain market and are going to look for a way to reengineer opportunities for themselves right here."

Some argue that we are witnessing the rise of a shallow, money-grubbing generation. After all, the number of kids who say "developing a meaningful philosophy of life" is an important goal has plummeted during the same period in which the number of those valuing financial success has soared. But remember: living in an age of "ecstatic capitalism," middle-class young people, who often have had opportunities to hone their talents in everything from computer science to theater to debate, expect work to be gratifying as well as remunerative. They see work itself as a source of meaning—as well as an engine of self-discipline.

Comfort with the advanced market economy also helps explain how it is that a vulgar popular culture has not had the corrupting influence on behavior that we might have feared. Growing up steeped in entertainment media, the young learn early on to be skeptical toward its blandishments. They don't believe they take their ideas about how to live a decent life from *Dawson's Creek*, or 50 Cent. In a recent survey from the National Campaign to Prevent Teen Pregnancy, for instance, teens were asked who influences their values about sex: only 4 percent answered "the media," while 45 percent answered "my parents." Of course, kids don't necessarily know where they're getting their ideas. And of course popular culture has some influence on their behavior. Presumably, suburban middle-school boys who grab and fondle girls in the halls, while the girls hint at their availability for oral sex, did not learn any of this at the dinner table.

"Bobos"

Even after all these changes, of course, we still live in a post-sexual revolution culture. Nobody pretends we're going back to the 1950s. Americans may have abandoned the credo of "if it feels good, do it," but they still embrace sexual pleasure as a great human good and take pride in advertising their own potential for success in that area. David Brooks coined the term "bobo" to refer to bourgeois bohemians, but the newest generation of bobos might be better described as bourgeois booty-shakers. Young mothers go to "strip aerobics" classes, where they do their workout by pole dancing, before they go off to pick up little Tiffany at kindergarten. Madonna does some provocative tongue wrestling with Britney Spears on national television, but everyone knows that in reality she glories in being a Hollywood soccer mom (and Mrs. Guy Ritchie, as she would have it). An edgy exterior no longer necessarily connotes a radical life-style: not long ago, I watched a heavily pierced couple, as the bride-to-be, with her stringy, dyed red hair, torn jeans, and bright green sneakers, squealed over the pear-shaped diamond engagement ring she was trying on. Go figure.

Gilmore Girls

The popular media has been trying to make sense of these crosscurrents. Some writers seem to grasp that they can bombard their viewers with breast and fart jokes, but in the end people are still interested in how to live meaningful lives. Consider the WB network's popular series *Gilmore Girls*. The main character, Lorelai Gilmore, is a single 30-something who had a baby when she was 16. A motor-mouthed girl-woman, she picks fights with her now-teenage daughter over the size of their "boobs," makes pop-culture allusions as obsessively as any teeny-bopper, and mugs and pouts during her weekly adolescent-style riffs with her own parents. The daughter, Rory, on the other hand, is the proto-Millennial: sober, hardworking, respectful, and chaste. Her hell-raiser mother's jaw drops when she hears that her daughter hasn't really thought about having sex with her boyfriend. Meanwhile, this season Rory is a freshman at Yale, where she writes for the school paper and reads, you know, literature. *(The Sun Also Rises?* On the network that gave us *Dawson 's Creek?)* Yes, this is a piece of pop-culture effluvium, but its point, made weekly, is that Rory has the promising future, while her mother reflects the childish past. . . .

With their genius for problem solving and compromise, pragmatic Americans have seen the damage that their decades-long fling with the sexual revolution and the transvaluation of traditional values wrought. And now, without giving up the real gains, they are earnestly knitting up their unraveled culture. It is a moment of tremendous promise.

POSTSCRIPT

Is America in Moral Decline?

Handwringing over weakening morals has long been a favorite pastime. Yet are Americans less moral today than they were a century ago? Consider that slavery has been abolished, civil rights for minorities have been won and generally accepted, tolerant attitudes have greatly increased, and genocide toward Native Americans ceased a long time ago. How could Americans have made so much progress if they have been getting much worse for hundreds of years? Such reflections cast suspicion over the moral decline thesis. On the other hand, this thesis is supported by many trends, such as the increases in crime and divorce (which have recently declined or leveled off). The issue is important because morality is a distinctive trait of the human species and essential to cooperative interactions. If morality declines, coercive restraint must increase to hold harmful behaviors in check, but self-restraint is much less costly than police restraint.

The issue of the trends in morality requires an examination of the blessings and curses of individualism and capitalism. One tenet of individualism is that the rights of the individual generally have priority over the rights of government or of the community. This may provide the freedom for wonderful human achievements but might also protect hateful and even dangerous speech and weaken society in the long run. Capitalism would be another demoralizing factor because it encourages self-interest and the passion for personal gain. Higher education may be another culprit because it relativizes values. In general, the forces behind the demoralization of society as described by Bork are not likely to be reversed in the medium-term future.

Most of the relevant literature is on aspects of the moral decline. Few works challenge the decline thesis. Examples include Nicholas Lemann's "It's Not as Bad as You Think It Is," *The Washington Monthly* (March 1997), David Whitman, *The Optimism Gap: The I'm OK—They're not Syndrome and the Myth of American Decline* (Walker & Company, 1998), and Gregg Easterbrook's "America the O.K.," *The New Republic* (January 4 & 11, 1999). For an exposition of the moral decline thesis, see Charles Derber's *The Wilding of America: How Greed and Violence Are Eroding Our Nation's Character* (St. Martin's Press, 1996); and Richard Sennett's *The Corrosion of Character* (W. W. Norton, 1998). Richard Stivers attributes the moral decline to a culture of cynicism in *The Culture of Cynicism: American Morality in Decline* (Basil Blackwell, 1994), while Neal Wood attributes it to capitalism in *Tyranny in America: Capitalism and National Decay* (Verso, 2004). Perhaps the solution to whatever decline may exist is moral education, but according to Tianlong Yu in *In the Name of Morality: Character Education and Political Control* (P. Lang, 2004) this may create the potential for some degree of public mind control by the state.

ISSUE 2

Does the News Media Have a Liberal Bias?

YES: Fred Barnes, from "Is Mainstream Media Fair and Balanced?" *Imprimis* (August 2006)

NO: Robert F. Kennedy Jr., from *Crimes Against Nature* (Harper-Collins, 2005)

ISSUE SUMMARY

YES: Fred Barnes, journalist, executive editor of *The Weekly Standard*, and TV commentator, argues that the mainstream media has a pronounced liberal bias. They do not hire conservatives and an analysis of specific news stories shows their bias.

NO: Robert F. Kennedy Jr., environmentalist and political activist, agrees with Barnes that the media is biased, but believes that it has a conservative bias. Surveys show that most Americans have many false beliefs that are fed them by conservative talk radio shows and other conservative media outlets. Many media owners are very conservative and stifle investigative reporting.

"**A** small group of men, numbering perhaps no more than a dozen 'anchormen,' commentators and executive producers . . . decide what forty to fifty million Americans will learn of the day's events in the nation and the world." The speaker was Spiro Agnew, vice president of the United States during the Nixon administration. The thesis of Agnew's speech, delivered to an audience of midwestern Republicans in 1969, was that the television news media are controlled by a small group of liberals who foist their liberal opinions on viewers under the guise of "news." The upshot of this control, said Agnew, "is that a narrow and distorted picture of America often emerges from the televised news." Many Americans, even many of those who were later shocked by revelations that Agnew took bribes while serving in public office, agreed with Agnew's critique of the "liberal media."

Politicians' complaints about unfair news coverage go back much further than Agnew and the Nixon administration. The third president of the United States, Thomas Jefferson, was an eloquent champion of the press, but after six years as president, he could hardly contain his bitterness. "The man who never looks into a newspaper," he wrote, "is better informed than he who reads them, inasmuch as he who knows nothing is nearer to truth than he whose mind is filled with falsehoods and errors."

The press today is much different than it was in Jefferson's day. Newspapers then were pressed in hand-operated frames in many little printing shops around the country; everything was local and decentralized, and each paper averaged a few hundred subscribers. Today, newspaper chains have taken over most of the once independent local newspapers. Other newspapers, like the *New York Times* and the *Washington Post,* enjoy nationwide prestige and help set the nation's news agenda. Geographical centralization is even more obvious in the case of television. About 70 percent of the national news on television comes from three networks whose programming originates in New York City.

A second important difference between the media of the eighteenth century and the media today has to do with the ideal of "objectivity." In past eras, newspapers were frankly partisan sheets, full of nasty barbs at the politicians and parties the editors did not like; they made no distinction between "news" and "editorials." The ideal of objective journalism is a relatively recent development. It traces back to the early years of the twentieth century. Disgusted with the sensationalist "yellow journalism" of the time, intellectual leaders urged that newspapers cultivate a core of professionals who would concentrate on accurate reporting and who would leave their opinions to the editorial page. Journalism schools cropped up around the country, helping to promote the ideal of objectivity. Although some journalists now openly scoff at it, the ideal still commands the respect—in theory, if not always in practice—of working reporters.

These two historical developments, news centralization and news professionalism, play off against one another in the current debate over news "bias." The question of bias was irrelevant when the press was a scatter of little independent newspapers. Bias started to become an important question when newspapers became dominated by chains and airwaves by networks, and when a few national press leaders like the *New York Times* and the *Washington Post* began to emerge. Although these "mainstream" news outlets have been challenged in recent years by opinions expressed in a variety of alternative media—such as cable television, talk radio, newsletters, and computer mail—they still remain powerful conveyers of news.

Is media news reporting biased? The media constitutes a major socializing institution, so this is an important question. Defenders of the media usually hold that although journalists, like all human beings, have biases, their professionalism compels them to report news with considerable objectivity. Media critics insist that journalists constantly interject their biases into their news reports. The critics, however, often disagree about whether such bias is liberal or conservative, as is the case with this issue. In the following selections, Fred Barnes argues that the news media tilt to the left, while Robert F. Kennedy Jr. contends that the slant of the news media to which most people are exposed supports a conservative status quo.

YES ↵

Fred Barnes

Is the Mainstream Media Fair and Balanced?

Let me begin by defining three terms that are thrown around in debates about the media today. The first is objectivity, which means reporting the news with none of your own political views or instincts slanting the story one way or another. Perfect objectivity is pretty hard for anyone to attain, but it can be approximated. Then there's fairness. Fairness concedes that there may be some slant in a news story, but requires that a reporter will be honest and not misleading with regard to those with whom he disagrees. And finally there's balance, which means that both sides on an issue or on politics in general—or more than two sides, when there are more than two—get a hearing.

My topic today is how the mainstream media—meaning nationally influential newspapers like the *Washington Post*, the *New York Times*, the *Wall Street Journal* and *USA Today*; influential regional papers like the *Miami Herald*, the *Chicago Tribune* and the *Los Angeles Times*; the broadcast networks and cable news stations like CNN; and the wire services, which now are pretty much reduced to the Associated Press—stacks up in terms of the latter two journalistic standards, fairness and balance. In my opinion, they don't stack up very well.

Twenty years ago I wrote a piece in *The New Republic* entitled "Media Realignment," and the thrust of it was that the mainstream media was shedding some of its liberal slant and moving more to the center. This was in the Reagan years, and I pointed to things like *USA Today*, which was then about five years old and was a champion of the Reagan economic recovery. CNN was younger then, too, and quite different from the way it is now; Ted Turner owned it, but he wasn't manipulating it the way he did later, which turned it into something quite different. Financial news was suddenly very big in the midst of the 401 (k) revolution, and the stock market boom was getting a lot of coverage. *The New Republic*, where I worked, had been pro-Stalin in the 1930s, but by the 1980s had become very pro-Reagan and anti-communist on foreign policy. I also cited a rise of new conservative columnists like George Will. But looking back on that piece now, I see that I couldn't have been more wrong. The idea that the mainstream media was moving to the center was a mirage. In fact, I would say that compared to what I was writing about back in the 1980s, the mainstream media today is more liberal, more elitist, more secular, more biased, more hostile to conservatives and Republicans, and more self-righteous.

Liberal and Impenetrable

Liberalism is endemic in the mainstream media today. Evan Thomas—the deputy editor of *Newsweek* and one of the honest liberals in the media—noted this very thing with regard to coverage of the 2004 presidential race, which I'll discuss later. It was obvious, he said, that the large majority in the media wanted John Kerry to win and that this bias slanted their coverage. And indeed, every poll of the media—and there have been a lot of them—shows that they're liberal, secular and so on. Polls of the Washington press corps, for instance, about who they voted for in 2004 always show that nine-to-one or ten-to-one of them voted Democratic. Peter Brown, a columnist who just recently left the *Orlando Sentinel*, conducted a poll a few years ago of newspaper staffs all around the country—not just at the big papers, but midsize papers and even some small papers—and found that this disparity existed everywhere.

Nor is this likely to change. Hugh Hewitt, the California lawyer and blogger and talk radio host, spent a few days recently at the Columbia Journalism School, supposedly the premiere journalism school in America. He spoke to a couple of classes there and polled them on who they had voted for. He found only one Bush voter in all the classes he spoke to. Steve Hayes, a fine young writer and reporter at *The Weekly Standard*, went to Columbia Journalism School and says that during his time there he was one of only two or three conservative students out of hundreds.

This is not to say that there aren't many fine young conservative journalists. But they aren't likely to be hired in the mainstream media. When I was at *The New Republic* for ten years—and *The New Republic* was quite liberal, despite its hawkish foreign policy—any young person who joined the staff and wrote stories that were interesting and demonstrated that he or she could write well was grabbed immediately by the *New York Times* or other big newspapers, *Newsweek*, *Time* or the networks. But that doesn't happen at *The Weekly Standard*, where I work now. Some of our young writers are the most talented I have ever met in my 30-plus years in journalism. But they don't get those phone calls. Why? Because they're with a conservative magazine. Of course there has been one famous exception—David Brooks, who is now the conservative columnist with the *New York Times*. But he was probably the least conservative person at *The Weekly Standard*. Conservatives are tokens on most editorial pages, just as they are on the broadcast networks and on cable news stations like CNN and MSNBC. Of course, I have a vested interest, since I work for FOX News; but if you compare the number of liberal commentators on FOX—and there are a lot of them—with the number of conservatives on those other stations, you'll see what I mean.

The fact is that the mainstream media doesn't want conservatives. It doesn't matter whether they're good reporters or writers. They go out of their way not to hire them. This was true 20 years ago, and it's true today. This impenetrability is why conservatives have had to erect the alternative media—talk radio, the blogs, conservative magazines and FOX News. Together, these form a real infrastructure that's an alternative to the mainstream media. But it's still a lot smaller, it's not as influential and it's largely reactive. It's not the equal of the mainstream media, that's for sure.

Powerful and Unfair

One way to see the unequaled power of the mainstream media is in how it is able to shape and create the stories that we're stuck talking about in America. A good example is Cindy Sheehan last summer. The Sheehan story was a total creation of the mainstream media. And in creating the story, the media shamelessly mischaracterized Sheehan. It portrayed her as simply a poor woman who wanted to see President Bush because her son had been killed in Iraq. Well, in the first place, she had already seen President Bush once. Also, though you would never know it from the dominant coverage, she was in favor of the Iraqi insurgency—the beheaders, the killers of innocent women and children. She was on their side, and she said so. She was also filled with a deep hatred of Israel. Yet the media treated her in a completely sympathetic manner, failing to report the beliefs that she made little attempt to hide. In any case, the Cindy Sheehan story came to dominate the news for the latter part of the summer; only the mainstream media still has the power to *make* stories big.

To see how distorted the mainstream media's view of the world can be, one need only compare its coverage of the Valerie Plame "leak" story with its coverage of the NSA surveillance leak story. Plame is the CIA agent whose name was written about by reporter Robert Novak in a column, following which the media portrayed her as having been outed as an undercover CIA agent. The simple facts from the beginning were that she was not an undercover agent any more; she was not even overseas. The story had no national security repercussions at all—none. But that didn't stop the media, which built the story up to great heights—apparently in the groundless hope that it would lead to an indictment of Karl Rove—and kept it front page news, at least intermittently, for what seemed like forever. The NSA surveillance story, on the other hand, also created by the media—this time pursuant to a real leak, and one that was clearly in violation of the law—had tremendous national security implications. After all, it revealed a secret and crucial program that was being used to uncover plots to bomb and massacre Americans and probably rendered that program no longer effective. Not only was this important story treated on an equal basis with the non-story of Valerie Plame, but the media was not interested, for the most part, in its national security repercussions. Instead the media mischaracterized the story as a "domestic spying scandal," suggesting constitutional overreach by the Bush administration. Well, a domestic spying story is exactly what the story was *not*. Those being spied on were Al-Qaeda members overseas who were using the telephone. If some of those calls were with people in the U.S., they were monitored for that reason only. But the media's stubborn mischaracterization of the story continued to frame the debate.

This brings me to the use of unfair and unbalanced labeling by the media. How often, if ever, have you heard or read the term "ultraliberal"? I don't think I've ever heard or read it. You'll hear and see the term "ultraconservative" a lot, but not "ultraliberal"—even though there are plenty of ultraliberals. Another widely used labeling term is "activist." If people are working to block a shopping center from being built or campaigning against Wal-Mart, they are called "activists." Of course, what the term "activist" means is *liberal*. But while conservatives are called conservatives by the media, liberals are "activists." For years we've seen something similar with regard to debates over judicial nominees. The Federalist Society, with which many conservative judicial nominees tend to be associated, is always referred to as the *conservative* Federalist Society, as if that's part of its name. But the groups opposing conservative nominees are rarely if ever labeled as liberal—giving the impression that they, unlike the Federalist Society, are somehow objective.

Related to this, I would mention that conservatives are often labeled in a way to suggest they are mean and hateful. Liberals criticize, but conservatives hate. Have you noticed that the media never characterizes individuals or groups as Bush haters? There are Bush critics, but there are no Bush haters— whereas in the Clinton years, critics of the president were often referred to as Clinton haters. I'm not saying that there weren't Clinton haters on the fringes in the 1990s. But far-left groups have been treated as acceptable . . . within the mainstream of American politics today by the media, while in truth they are as clearly animated by hatred as the most rabid anti-Clinton voices ever were.

Secular and Partisan Bias

With regard to religion, Christianity in particular—but also religious faith in general—is reflexively treated as something dangerous and pernicious by the mainstream media. Back in the early 1990s when I was still at *The New Republic*, I was invited to a dinner in Washington with Mario Cuomo. He was then governor of New York, and had invited several reporters to dinner because he was thinking about running for president. At one point that night he mentioned that he sent his children to Catholic schools in New York because he wanted them to be taught about a God-centered universe. This was in the context of expressing his whole-hearted support for public schools. But from the reaction, you would have thought he had said that one day a week he would bring out the snakes in his office and make policy decisions based on where they bit him. He was subsequently pummeled with stories about how improper it was for him, one, to send his kids to religious schools, and two, to talk about it. It was amazing. The most rigid form of secularism passes as the standard in mainstream journalism these days.

President Bush is similarly treated as someone who is obsessive about his religion. And what does he do? Well, he reads a devotional every day; he tries to get through the Bible, I think, once a year; and he prays. Now, I know many, many people who do this. Tens of millions of people do it. And yet the media treats Bush as some religious nut and pursues this story inaccurately. Again, it is clear that partisan bias is involved, too, because in fact, Bush talks publicly about his faith much less than other presidents have. There is a good book about Bush's religion by Paul Kengor, who went back to every word President Clinton spoke and found out that Clinton quoted scripture and mentioned God and Jesus Christ more than President Bush has. You would never get that from the mainstream media.

The partisan bias of the mainstream media has been at no time more evident than during the last presidential election. Presidential candidates used to be savaged equally by the media. No matter who—Republican or Democrat— they both used to take their hits. But that's not true any more. Robert Lichter, at the Center for Media and Public Affairs in Washington, measures the broadcast news for all sorts of things, including how they treat candidates. He's been doing it now for nearly 20 years. And would anyone care to guess what presidential candidate in all those years has gotten the most favorable treatment from the broadcast media? The answer is John Kerry, who got 77 percent favorable coverage in the stories regarding him on the three broadcast news shows. For Bush, it was 34 percent. This was true despite the fact that Kerry made his Vietnam service the motif of the Democratic National Convention, followed weeks later by 64 Swift Boat vets who served with Kerry in Vietnam claiming that he didn't do the things he said he did. It was a huge story, but the mainstream media didn't want to cover it and didn't cover it, for week after week after week.

There was an amazingly well documented book written by a man named John O'Neill—himself a Swift Boat vet—who went into great detail about why John Kerry didn't deserve his three Purple Hearts, etc. It might have been a right-wing screed, but if you actually read it, it wasn't a screed. It backed up its claims with evidence. Normally in journalism, when somebody makes some serious charges against a well-known person, reporters look into the charges to see if they're true or not. If they aren't, reporters look into the motives behind the false charges—for instance, to find out if someone paid the person making the false charges, and so on. But that's not what the media did in this case. The *New York Times* responded immediately by investigating the financing of the Swift Boat vets, rather than by trying to determine whether what they were saying was true. Ultimately, grudgingly—after bloggers and FOX News had covered the story sufficiently long that it couldn't be ignored—the mainstream media had to pick up on the story. But its whole effort was aimed at knocking down what the Swift Boat vets were saying.

Compare this with September 8, 2004, when Dan Rather reported on documents that he said showed not only that President Bush used preferential treatment to get into the Texas National Guard, but that he hadn't even done all his service. The very next morning, the whole story—because CBS put one of the documents on its Web site—was knocked down. It was knocked down because a blogger on a Web site called Little Green Footballs made a copy on his computer of the document that was supposedly made on a typewriter 30 years earlier and demonstrated that it was a fraud made on a modern computer. Then, only a few weeks after that embarrassment, CBS came up with a story, subsequently picked up by the *New York Times*, that an arms cache of

400 tons of ammunition in Iraq had been left unguarded by the American military and that the insurgents had gotten hold of it. Well, it turned out that they didn't know whether the insurgents had gotten that ammunition or not, or whether indeed the American military had possession of it. It was about a week before the election that these major news organizations broke this unsubstantiated story, something that would have been unimaginable in past campaigns. Why would they do that? Why would Dan Rather insist on releasing fraudulent documents when even his own experts recommended against it? Why would CBS and the *New York Times* come back with an explosive but unsubstantiated arms cache story only weeks later? They did it for one reason: They wanted to defeat President Bush for re-election. There is no other motive that would explain disregarding all the precautions you're taught you should have in journalism.

❧❀❧

I'll wind up on a positive note, however. Forty years ago, John Kenneth Galbraith—the great liberal Harvard economist—said that he knew conservatism was dead because it was bookless. Conservatives didn't publish books. And to some extent, it was true at the time. But it's no longer true. Conservatives have become such prolific writers and consumers of books that Random House and other publishing companies have started separate conservative imprints. Nowadays it is common to see two or three or four conservative books—some of them kind of trashy, but some of them very good—on the bestseller list. Insofar as books are an indication of how well conservatives are doing—at least in the publishing part of the media world—I would say they're doing quite well. They're not winning, but they're much better off than they were before—something that can't be said about how they are faring in the unfair and unbalanced mainstream media.

Robert F. Kennedy Jr.　　　　　　　　　　　　**NO**

The Disinformation Society

Many Democratic voters marveled at the election results. George W. Bush, they argued, has transformed a projected $5.6 trillion, 10-year Bill Clinton surplus into a projected $1.4 trillion deficit—a $7 trillion shift in wealth from our national treasury into the pockets of the wealthiest Americans, particularly the president's corporate paymasters. Any discerning observer, they argued, must acknowledge that the White House has repeatedly lied to the American people about critical policy issues—Medicare, education, the environment, the budget implications of its tax breaks, and the war in Iraq—with catastrophic results.

President Bush has opened our national lands and sacred places to the lowest bidder and launched a jihad against the American environment and public health to enrich his corporate sponsors. He has mired us in a costly, humiliating war that has killed more than 1,520 American soldiers and maimed 11,300. He has made America the target of Islamic hatred, caused thousands of new terrorists to be recruited to al-Qaeda, isolated us in the world, and drained our treasury of the funds necessary to rebuild Afghanistan and to finance our own vital homeland-security needs. He has shattered our traditional alliances and failed to protect vulnerable terrorist targets at home—chemical plants, nuclear facilities, air-cargo carriers, and ports. He has disgraced our nation and empowered tyrants with the unpunished excesses at Guantánamo and Abu Ghraib. These baffled Democrats were hard-pressed to believe that their fellow Americans would give a man like this a second term.

To explain the president's victory, political pundits posited a vast "values gap" between red states and blue states. They attributed the president's success in the polls, despite his tragic job failures, to the rise of religious fundamentalism. Heartland Americans, they suggested, are the soldiers in a new American Taliban, willing to vote against their own economic interests to promote "morality" issues that they see as the critical high ground in a life-or-death culture war.

I believe, however, that the Democrats lost the presidential contest not because of a philosophical chasm between red and blue states but due to an information deficit caused by a breakdown in our national media. Traditional broadcast networks have abandoned their former obligation to advance democracy and promote the public interest by informing the public about both sides of issues relevant to those goals. To attract viewers and advertising revenues, they entertain rather than inform. This threat to the flow of information, vital to democracy's survival, has been compounded in recent years by the growing power of right-wing media that twist the news and deliberately deceive the public to advance their radical agenda.

According to an October 2004 survey by the Program on International Policy Attitudes (PIPA), a joint program of the Center on Policy Attitudes, in Washington, D.C., and the Center for International and Security Studies at the University of Maryland:

- Seventy-two percent of Bush supporters believed Iraq had weapons of mass destruction (or a major program for developing them), versus 26 percent of Kerry voters. A seven-month search by 1,500 investigators led by David Kay, working for the C.I.A., found no such weapons.
- Seventy-five percent of Bush supporters believed that Iraq was providing substantial support to al-Qaeda, a view held by 30 percent of Kerry supporters. *The 9/11 Commission Report* concluded that there was no terrorist alliance between Iraq and al-Qaeda.
- Eighty-two percent of Bush supporters erroneously believed either that the rest of the world felt better about the U.S. thanks to its invasion of Iraq or that views were evenly divided. Eighty-six percent of Kerry supporters accurately understood that a majority of the world felt worse about our country.
- Most Bush supporters believed the Iraq war had strong support in the Islamic world. Kerry's supporters accurately estimated the low level of support in Islamic countries. Even Turkey, the most Westernized Islamic country, was 87 percent against the invasion.
- Most significant, the majority of Bush voters agreed with Kerry supporters that if Iraq did not have W.M.D. and was not providing assistance to al-Qaeda the U.S. should not have gone to war. Furthermore, most Bush supporters, according to PIPA, favored the Kyoto Protocol to fight global warming, the Mine Ban Treaty to ban land mines, and strong labor and environmental standards in trade agreements, and wrongly believed that their candidate favored these things. In other words, the values and principles were the same. Bush voters made their choice based on bad information.

It's no mystery where the false beliefs are coming from. Both Bush and Kerry supporters overwhelmingly believe that the Bush administration at the time of the 2004 U.S. election was telling the American people that Iraq had W.M.D. and that Saddam Hussein had strong links to al-Qaeda. The White House's false message was carried by right-wing media in bed with the administration. Prior to the election, FOX News reporters, for example, regularly made unsubstantiated claims about Iraq's W.M.D. FOX anchor Brit Hume, on his newscast in July 2004, announced that W.M.D. had actually been found. Sean Hannity repeatedly suggested without factual support that the phantom weapons had been moved to Syria and would soon be found. An October 2003 survey by PIPA showed that people who watch FOX News are disproportionately afflicted with the same misinformation evidenced by the 2004 PIPA report. The earlier study probed for the source of public misinformation about the Iraq war that might account for the common misperceptions that Saddam Hussein had been involved in the 9/11 attacks, that he supported al-Qaeda, that W.M.D. had been found, and that world opinion favored the U.S. invasion. The study discovered that "the extent of Americans' misperceptions vary significantly depending on their source of news. Those who receive most of their news from FOX News are more likely than average to have misperceptions."

Unfortunately for John Kerry, many Americans now do get their information from FOX—according to Nielsen Media Research, in February, FOX was the cable news leader, with an average of 1.57 million prime-time viewers, nearly 2.5 times CNN's average viewership in the same time slot—and from FOX's similarly biased cable colleagues, CNBC and MSNBC. Millions more tune to the Sinclair Broadcast Group—one of the nation's largest TV franchises. After 9/11, Sinclair forced its stations to broadcast spots pledging support for President Bush, and actively censored unfavorable coverage of the Iraq war—blacking out Ted Koppel's *Nightline* when it ran the names of the U.S. war dead. It retreated from its pre-election proposal to strong-arm its 62 TV stations into pre-empting their prime-time programming to air an erroneous and blatantly biased documentary about John Kerry's war record only when its stock dropped 17 percent due to Wall Street fears of sponsor boycotts and investor worries that Sinclair was putting its right-wing ideology ahead of shareholder profits.

Americans are also getting huge amounts of misinformation from talk radio, which is thoroughly dominated by the extreme right. A Gallup Poll conducted in December 2002 discovered that 22 percent of Americans receive their daily news from talkradio programs. An estimated 15 million people listen to Rush Limbaugh alone, and on the top 45 AM radio stations in the country, listeners encounter 310 hours of conservative talk for every 5 hours of liberal talk. According to the nonprofit Democracy Radio, Inc., 90 percent of all political talk-radio programming is conservative, while only 10 percent is progressive. All the leading talk-show hosts are right-wing radicals—Rush Limbaugh, Sean Hannity, Michael Savage, Oliver North, G. Gordon Liddy, Bill O'Reilly, and Michael Reagan—and the same applies to local talk radio.

Alas, while the right-wing media are deliberately misleading the American people, the traditional corporately owned media—CBS, NBC, ABC, and CNN—are doing little to remedy those wrong impressions. They are, instead, focusing on expanding viewership by hawking irrelevant stories that appeal to our prurient interest in sex and celebrity gossip. None of the three major networks gave gavel-to-gavel coverage of the party conventions or more than an hour in prime time, opting instead to entertain the public with semi-pornographic reality shows. "We're about to elect a president of the United States at a time when we have young people dying in our name overseas, we just had a report from the 9/11 commission which says we are not safe as a nation, and one of these two groups of people is going to run our country," commented PBS newsman Jim Lehrer, in disgust at the lack of convention coverage. CBS anchor Dan Rather said that "I argued the conventions were part of the dance of democracy. I found myself increasingly like the Mohicans, forced farther and farther back into the wilderness and eventually eliminated."

The broadcast reporters participating in the presidential debates were apparently so uninterested in real issues that they neglected to ask the candidates a single question about the president's environmental record. CBS anchor Bob Schieffer, who M.C.'d the final debate, asked no questions about the environment, focusing instead on abortion, gay marriage, and the personal faith of the candidates, an agenda that could have been dictated by Karl Rove.

Where is that dreaded but impossible-to-find "liberal bias" that supposedly infects the American press? The erroneous impression that the American media have a liberal bias is itself a mark of the triumph of the right-wing propaganda machine.

⌖

The Republican Noise Machine: Right-Wing Media and How It Corrupts Democracy, by David Brock—the president and C.E.O. of Media Matters for America, a watchdog group that documents misinformation in the right-wing media—traces the history of the "liberal bias" notion back to the Barry Goldwater presidential campaign, in 1964, in which aggrieved conservatives railed against Walter Cronkite and the "Eastern Liberal Press" at the Republican National Convention. In response to Spiro Agnew's 1969 attack on the networks as insufficiently supportive of Nixon's policies in Vietnam, conservatives formed an organization called Accuracy in Media, whose purpose was to discredit the media by tagging it as "liberal," and to market that idea with clever catchphrases. Polluter-funded foundations, including the Adolph Coors Foundation and the so-called four sisters—the Lynde and Harry Bradley Foundation, the John M. Olin Foundation, Richard Mellon Scaife's foundations, and the Smith Richardson Foundation—all of which funded the anti-environmental movement, spent hundreds of millions of dollars to perpetuate the big lie of liberal bias, to convince the conservative base that it should not believe the mainstream, to create a market for right-wing media, and to intimidate and discipline the mainstream press into being more accommodating to conservatism.

According to Brock, right-wing groups such as the Heritage Foundation and Scaife's Landmark Legal Foundation helped persuade Ronald Reagan and his Federal Communications Commission, in 1987, to eliminate the Fairness Doctrine—the F.C.C.'s 1949 rule which dictated that broadcasters provide equal time to both sides of controversial public questions. It was a "godsend for conservatives," according to religious-right pioneer and Moral Majority co-founder Richard Viguerie, opening up talk radio to one-sided, right-wing broadcasters. (Rush Limbaugh nationally launched his talk show the following year.) Radical ideologues, faced with Niagara-size flows of money from the Adolph Coors Foundation, the four sisters, and others, set up magazines and newspapers and cultivated a generation of young pundits, writers, and propagandists, giving them lucrative sinecures inside right-wing think tanks, now numbering more than 500, from which they bombard the media with carefully honed messages justifying corporate profit taking.

Brock himself was one of the young stars recruited to this movement, working in turn for the Heritage Foundation, the Reverend Sun Myung Moon's

Washington Times, and Scaife's *American Spectator.* "If you look at this history," Brock told me recently, "you will find that the conservative movement has in many ways purchased the debate. You have conservative media outlets day after day that are intentionally misinforming the public." Brock, who admits to participating in the deliberate deception while he was a so-called journalist on the right-wing payroll, worries that the right-wing media are systematically feeding the public "false and wrong information. It's a really significant problem for democracy.

"We're in a situation," continues Brock, "where you have 'red facts' and 'blue facts.' And I think the conservatives intentionally have done that to try to confuse and neutralize accurate information that may not serve the conservative agenda."

The consolidation of media ownership and its conservative drift are growing ever more severe. Following the election, Clear Channel, the biggest owner of radio stations in the country, announced that FOX News will now supply its news feed to many of the company's 1,240 stations, further amplifying the distorted drumbeat of right-wing propaganda that most Americans now take for news. . . .

Furthermore, Fox's rating success has exerted irresistible gravities that have pulled its competitors' programming to starboard. In the days leading up to the Iraq war, MSNBC fired one of television's last liberal voices, Phil Donahue, who hosted its highest-rated show; an internal memo revealed that Donahue presented "a difficult public face for NBC in a time of war." CBS's post-election decision to retire Dan Rather, a lightning rod for rightwing wrath, coincided with Tom Brokaw's retirement from NBC. He was replaced by Brian Williams, who has said, "I think Rush [Limbaugh] has actually yet to get the credit he is due." According to NBC president Jeff Zucker, "No one understands this NASCAR nation more than Brian."

Conservative noise on cable and talk radio also has an echo effect on the rest of the media. One of the conservative talking points in the last election was that terrorists supported the candidacy of John Kerry. According to Media Matters, this pearl originated on Limbaugh's radio show in March 2004 and repeatedly surfaced in mainstream news. In May, CNN's Kelli Arena reported "speculation that al-Qaeda believes it has a better chance of winning in Iraq if John Kerry is in the White House"; in June it migrated to Dick Morris's *New York Post* column. Chris Matthews mentioned it in a July edition of *Hardball.* In September, Bill Schneider, CNN's senior political analyst, declared that al-Qaeda "would very much like to defeat President Bush," signaling that Limbaugh's contrivance was now embedded firmly in the national consciousness.

That "echo effect" is not random. Brock shows in his book how the cues by which mainstream news directors decide what is important to cover are no longer being suggested by *The New York Times* and other responsible media outlets, but rather by the "shadowy" participants of a Washington, D.C., meeting convened by Grover Norquist's Americans for Tax Reform, an anti-government organization that seeks to prevent federal regulation of business.

Every Wednesday morning the leaders of 80 conservative organizations meet in Washington in Norquist's boardroom. This radical cabal formulates policy with the Republican National Committee and the White House, developing talking points that go out to the conservative media via a sophisticated fax tree. Soon, millions of Americans are hearing the same message from cable news commentators and thousands of talk jocks across America. Their precisely crafted message and language then percolate through the mainstream media to form the underlying assumptions of our national debate. . . .

A typical meeting might focus on a new tax proposal released by President Bush. Following conference calls throughout the week, the decision will be made to call the plan "bold." Over the next 10 days, radio and cable will reiterate that it's "bold, bold, bold." The result, according to Brock, is that "people come to think that there must be something 'bold' about this plan."

This highly integrated network has given the right frightening power to disseminate its propaganda and has dramatically changed the way Americans get their information and formulate policy. In *The Republican Noise Machine*, Brock alleges routine fraud and systematically dishonest practices by his former employer the Reverend Sun Myung Moon's *Washington Times,* which is the primary propaganda organ for Moon's agenda to establish America as a Fascist theocracy. The paper doesn't reach more than a hundred thousand subscribers, but its articles are read on the air by Rush Limbaugh, reaching 15 million people, and are posted on Matt Drudge's Web site, to reach another 7 million people, and its writers regularly appear on *The O'Reilly Factor,* before another 2 million. Network TV talk-show producers and bookers use those appearances as a tip sheet for picking the subject matter and guests for their own shows. And so the capacity of the conservative movement to disseminate propaganda has increased exponentially.

This right-wing propaganda machine can quickly and indelibly brand Democratic candidates unfavorably—John Kerry as a flip-flopper, AL Gore as a liar. The machine is so powerful that it was able to orchestrate Clinton's impeachment despite the private and trivial nature of his "crime"—a lie about an extramarital tryst—when compared with President Bush's calamitous lies about Iraq, the budget, Medicare, education, and the environment. During the 2000 campaign, AL Gore was smeared as a liar—a charge that was completely false—by rightwing pundits such as gambling addict Bill Bennett and prescription-painkiller abuser Rush Limbaugh, both of whom the right wing has sold as moral paradigms. Meanwhile, George Bush's chronic problems with the truth during the three presidential debates that year were barely mentioned in the media, as Brock has noted. Americans accepted this negative characterization of Gore, and when they emerged from the voting booths in 2000, they told pollsters that Bush won their vote on "trust."

In the 2004 campaign, the so-called Swift Boat Veterans for Truth launched dishonest attacks which, amplified and repeated by the right-wing media, helped torpedo John Kerry's presidential ambitions. No matter who the Democratic nominee was, this machinery had the capacity to discredit and destroy him. . . .

Furthermore, America's newspapers, like most other media outlets, are owned predominantly by Republican conservatives. Newspapers endorsed Bush by two to one in the 2000 election. According to a recent survey, the op-ed columnists who appear in the most newspapers are conservatives Cal Thomas and George Will. Republican-owned newspapers often reprint misinformation from the right. And red-state journalists, whatever their personal political sympathies, are unlikely to offend their editors by spending inordinate energy exposing right-wing lies.

Print journalism is a victim of the same consolidation by a few large, profit-driven corporations that has affected the broadcasters. Today, a shrinking pool of owners—guided by big business rather than journalistic values—forces news executives to cut costs and seek the largest audience. The consolidation has led to demands on news organizations to return profits at rates never before expected of them. Last summer, just a few months after winning five Pulitzer Prizes, the *Los Angeles Times* was asked by its parent company to drop 60 newsroom positions.

The pressure for bottomline news leaves little incentive for investment in investigative reporting. Costcutting has liquidated news staffs, leaving reporters little time to research stories. According to an Ohio University study, the number of investigative reporters was cut almost in half between 1980 and 1995. . . .

When veteran television journalist and former CBS news analyst Bill Moyers resigned as host of PBS's *Now* in December, he observed, "I think my peers in commercial television are talented and devoted journalists, but they've chosen to work in a corporate mainstream that trims their talent to fit the corporate nature of American life. And you do not get rewarded for telling the hard truths about America in a profit-seeking environment." Moyers called the decline in American journalism "the biggest story of our time." He added, "We have an ideological press that's interested in the election of Republicans, and a mainstream press that's interested in the bottom line. Therefore, we don't have a vigilant, independent press whose interest is the American people." . . .

POSTSCRIPT

Does the News Media Have a Liberal Bias?

As the opposing arguments in this issue indicate, we can find critics on both the Left and the Right who agree that the media are biased. What divides such critics is the question of whether the bias is left-wing or right-wing. Defenders of the news media may seize upon this disagreement to bolster their own claim that "bias is in the eye of the beholder." But the case may be that the news media are unfair to both sides. If that were true, however, it would seem to take some of the force out of the argument that the news media have a distinct ideological tilt at all.

A study by S. Robert Lichter et al., *The Media Elite* (Adler & Adler, 1986), tends to support Barnes's contention that the media slant leftward, as does Ann Coulter in *Slander: Liberal Lies about the American Right* (Crown Publishers, 2002); and Bernard Goldberg in *BIAS: A CBS Insider Exposes How the Media Distort the News* (Regency Publishing, 2002); and *Arrogance: Rescuing America form the Media Elite* (Warner Books 2003). On the other hand, those who think the media are biased rightward include Ben Bagdikian, *The Media Monopoly,* 6th edition (Beacon Press, 2000); Mark Hertsgaard, *On Bended Knee: The Press and the Reagan Presidency* (Schocken, 1989); Eric Alterman, *What Liberal Media? The Truth about Bias and the News* (Basic Books, 2003); David Edwards and David Cromwell, *Guardians of Power: The Myth of the Liberal Media* (Pluto Press, 2006); Jeffery Klaehn, ed., *Bound by Power: Intended Consequences* (Black Rose Books, 2006); and Robert Waterman McChesney, *The Problem of the Media: U.S. Communication Politics in the Twenty-First Century* (Monthly Review Press, 2004). In *South Park Conservatives: The Revolt Against Liberal Media Bias* (Regnery Publications, 2005), Brian C. Anderson observes that the media were very liberal but America revolted and now conservative voices are being heard.

S. Robert Lichter, Linda Lichter, and Stanley Rothman's *Watching America* (Prentice Hall, 1991) surveys the political and social messages contained in television "entertainment" programs. Several recent memoirs of journalists are very useful for the debate on media bias. See Tom Wicker's *On the Record* (Bedford/St. Martin's, 2002); Ted Koppel's *Off Camera* (Alfred A. Knopf, 2000); and Bill O'Reilly's *The No-Spin Zone* (Broadway Books, 2001). David Halberstam's *The Powers That Be* (Alfred A. Knopf, 1979), a historical study of CBS, the *Washington Post, Time* magazine, and the *Los Angeles Times,* describes some of the political and ideological struggles that have taken place within major media organizations.

ISSUE 3

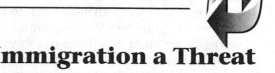

Is Third World Immigration a Threat to America's Way of Life?

YES: Patrick Buchanan, from "Shields Up!" *The American Enterprise* (March 2002)

NO: Linda Chavez, from "The Realities of Immigration," *Commentary* (July/August 2006)

ISSUE SUMMARY

YES: Political analyst Patrick Buchanan asserts that the large influx of legal and illegal immigrants, especially those from Mexico, threatens to undermine the cultural foundations of American unity.

NO: Linda Chavez, chairman of the Center for Equal Opportunity and a high-ranking official in several Republican administrations, challenges the thesis that immigrants lower wages and take jobs from citizens. The strong economy and low unemployment refute this thesis. Immigrants are also cultural assets. They are very hard workers with considerable drive and strong family values.

Before September 11, 2001, many Americans favored the reduction of immigration. After the terrorist attacks on the World Trade Center and the Pentagon by immigrants, some felt even stronger about limiting immigration. But is immigration bad for America, as this sentiment assumes, or does it strengthen America?

Today the number of legal immigrants to America is close to 1 million per year, and illegal ("undocumented") immigrants probably number well over that figure. In terms of numbers, immigration is now comparable to the level it reached during the early years of the twentieth century, when millions of immigrants arrived from southern and eastern Europe. A majority of the new immigrants, however, do not come from Europe but from what has been called the "Third World"—the underdeveloped nations. The largest percentages come from Mexico, the Philippines, Korea, and the islands of the Caribbean, while European immigration has shrunk to about 10 percent. Much of the reason for this shift has to do with changes made in U.S. immigration laws during the 1960s. Decades earlier, in the 1920s, America had narrowed its gate to people from certain regions of the world by imposing quotas designed to preserve the balance of races in America. But, in 1965, a series of amendments to the Immigration Act put all the world's people on an equal footing in terms of immigration. The result, wrote journalist Theodore H. White, was "a stampede, almost an invasion" of Third World immigrants. Indeed, the 1965 amendments made it even easier for Third World immigrants to enter the country because the new law gave preference to those with a family member already living in the United States. Because most of the European immigrants who settled in the early part of the century had died off, and few Europeans had immigrated in more recent years, a greater percentage of family-reuniting immigration came from the Third World.

Immigrants move to the United States for various reasons: to flee tyranny and terrorism, to escape war, or to join relatives who have already settled. Above all, they immigrate because in their eyes America is an island of affluence in a global sea of poverty; here they will earn many times what they could only hope to earn in their native countries. One hotly debated question is: What will these new immigrants do to the United States—or for it?

Part of the debate has to do with bread-and-butter issues: Will new immigrants take jobs away from American workers? Or will they fill jobs that American workers do not want anyway, which will help stimulate the economy? Behind these economic issues is a more profound cultural question: Will these new immigrants add healthy new strains to America's cultural inheritance, broadening and revitalizing it? Or will they cause the country to break up into separate cultural units, destroying America's unity? Of all the questions relating to immigration, this one seems to be the most sensitive.

In 1992, conservative columnist Patrick Buchanan set off a firestorm of controversy when he raised this question: "If we had to take a million immigrants next year, say Zulus or Englishmen, and put them in Virginia, which group would be easier to assimilate and cause less problems for the people of Virginia?" Although Buchanan later explained that his intention was not to denigrate Zulus or any other racial group but to simply talk about assimilation into Anglo-American culture, his remarks were widely characterized as racist and xenophobic (related to a fear of foreigners). Whether or not that characterization is justified, Buchanan's question goes to the heart of the cultural debate over immigration—the tension between unity and diversity. In the selections that follow, Buchanan contends that immigrants are harming the United States both economically and culturally. He argues that the sheer number of immigrants from other cultures threatens to overwhelm traditional safeguards against cultural disintegration and that this foreign influx is changing America from a nation into a collection of separate nationalities. Linda Chavez counters that the accusations against immigrants are false and that immigrants contribute greatly to America.

YES ↵

Patrick Buchanan

Shields Up!

In 1821, a newly independent Mexico invited Americans to settle in its northern province of Texas—on two conditions: Americans must embrace Roman Catholicism, and they must swear allegiance to Mexico. Thousands took up the offer. But, in 1835, after the tyrannical General Santa Anna seized power, the Texans, fed up with loyalty oaths and fake conversions, and outnumbering Mexicans in Texas ten to one, rebelled and kicked the tiny Mexican garrison back across the Rio Grande.

Santa Anna led an army north to recapture his lost province. At a mission called the Alamo, he massacred the first rebels who resisted. Then he executed the 400 Texans who surrendered at Goliad. But at San Jacinto, Santa Anna blundered straight into an ambush. His army was butchered, he was captured. The Texans demanded his execution for the Alamo massacre, but Texas army commander Sam Houston had another idea. He made the dictator an offer: his life for Texas. Santa Anna signed. And on his last day in office, Andrew Jackson recognized the independence of the Lone Star Republic.

Eight years later, the U.S. annexed the Texas republic. An enraged Mexico disputed the American claim to all land north of the Rio Grande, so President James Polk sent troops to the north bank of the river. When Mexican soldiers crossed and fired on a U.S. patrol, Congress declared war. By 1848, soldiers with names like Grant, Lee, and McClellan were in the city of Montezuma. A humiliated Mexico was forced to cede all of Texas, the Southwest, and California. The U.S. gave Mexico $15 million to ease the anguish of amputation.

Mexicans seethed with hatred and resentment, and in 1910 the troubles began anew. After a revolution that was anti-church and anti-American, U.S. sailors were roughed up and arrested in Tampico. In 1914, President Woodrow Wilson ordered the occupation of Vera Cruz by U.S. Marines. As Wilson explained to the British ambassador, "I am going to teach the South Americans to elect good men." When the bandit Pancho Villa led a murderous raid into New Mexico in 1916, Wilson sent General Pershing and 10,000 troops to do the tutoring.

Despite FDR's Good Neighbor Policy, President Cárdenas nationalized U.S. oil companies in 1938—an event honored in Mexico to this day. Pemex was born, a state cartel that would collude with OPEC in 1999 to hike up oil prices to $35 a barrel. American consumers, whose tax dollars had supported a $50 billion bailout of a bankrupt Mexico in 1994, got gouged.

From *The Death of the West* by Patrick J. Buchanan (Thomas Dunne Books, 2002). Copyright © 2002 by Patrick J. Buchanan. Reprinted by permission of St. Martin's Press.

39

ϫϴ

The point of this history? Mexico has an historic grievance against the United States that is felt deeply by her people. This is one factor producing deep differences in attitudes toward America between today's immigrants from places like Mexico and the old immigrants from Ireland, Italy, and Eastern Europe. With fully one-fifth of all people of Mexican ancestry now residing in the United States, and up to 1 million more crossing the border every year, we need to understand these differences.

1. The number of people pouring in from Mexico is larger than any wave from any country ever before. In the 1990s alone, the number of people of Mexican heritage living in the U.S. grew by 50 percent to at least 21 million. The Founding Fathers wanted immigrants to spread out among the population to ensure assimilation, but Mexican Americans are highly concentrated in the Southwest.
2. Mexicans are not only from another culture, but of another race. History has taught that different races are far more difficult to assimilate than different cultures. The 60 million Americans who claim German ancestry are fully assimilated, while millions from Africa and Asia are still not full participants in American society.
3. Millions of Mexicans broke the law to get into the United States, and they break the law every day they remain here. Each year, 1.6 million illegal aliens are apprehended, almost all of them at our bleeding southern border.
4. Unlike the immigrants of old, who bade farewell to their native lands forever, millions of Mexicans have no desire to learn English or become U.S. citizens. America is not their home; they are here to earn money. They remain proud Mexicans. Rather than assimilate, they create their own radio and TV stations, newspapers, films, and magazines. They are becoming a nation within a nation.
5. These waves of Mexican immigrants are also arriving in a different America than did the old immigrants. A belief in racial rights and ethnic entitlements has taken root among America's minorities and liberal elites. Today, ethnic enclaves are encouraged and ethnic chauvinism is rife in the barrios. Anyone quoting Calvin Coolidge's declaration that "America must remain American" today would be charged with a hate crime.

Harvard professor Samuel P. Huntington, author of *The Clash of Civilizations*, calls migration "the central issue of our time." He has warned in the pages of this magazine:

> If 1 million Mexican soldiers crossed the border, Americans would treat it as a major threat to their national security. . . . The invasion of over 1 million Mexican civilians . . . would be a comparable threat to American societal security, and Americans should react against it with vigor.

Mexican immigration is a challenge to our cultural integrity, our national identity, and potentially to our future as a country. Yet, American leaders are far from reacting "with vigor," even though a Zogby poll found that 72 percent of Americans want less immigration, and a Rasmussen poll in July 2000 found that 89 percent support English as America's official language. The people want action. The elites disagree—and do nothing. Despite our braggadocio about being "the world's only remaining superpower," the U.S. lacks the fortitude to defend its borders and to demand, without apology, that immigrants assimilate to its society.

Perhaps our mutual love of the dollar can bridge the cultural chasm, and we shall all live happily in what Ben Wattenberg calls the First Universal Nation. But Uncle Sam is taking a hellish risk in importing a huge diaspora of tens of millions of people from a nation vastly different from our own. It is not a decision we can ever undo. Our children will live with the consequences. "If assimilation fails," Huntington recognizes, "the United States will become a cleft country with all the potentials for internal strife and disunion that entails." Is that a risk worth taking?

A North American Union of Canada, Mexico, and the United States has been proposed by Mexican President Fox, with a complete opening of borders to the goods and peoples of the three countries. *The Wall Street Journal* is enraptured. But Mexico's per capita GDP of $5,000 is only a fraction of America's—the largest income gap on earth between two adjoining countries. Half of all Mexicans live in poverty, and 18 million people exist on less than $2 a day, while the U.S. minimum wage is headed for $50 a day. Throw open the border, and millions could flood into the United States within months. Is America nothing more than an economic system?

❦

Our old image is of Mexicans as amiable Catholics with traditional values. There are millions of hard-working, family-oriented Americans of Mexican heritage, who have been quick to answer the call to arms in several of America's wars. And, yes, history has shown that any man or woman, from any country on the planet, can be a good American.

But today's demographic sea change, especially in California, where a fourth of the residents are foreign-born and almost a third are Latino, has spawned a new ethnic chauvinism. When the U.S. soccer team played Mexico in Los Angeles a few years ago, the "Star-Spangled Banner" was jeered, an American flag was torn down, and the U.S. team and its few fans were showered with beer bottles and garbage.

In the New Mexico legislature in 2001, a resolution was introduced to rename the state "Nuevo Mexico," the name it carried before it became a part of the American Union. When the bill was defeated, sponsor Representative Miguel Garcia suggested to reporters that "covert racism" may have been the cause.

A spirit of separatism, nationalism, and irredentism has come alive in the barrio. Charles Truxillo, a professor of Chicano Studies at the University of New Mexico, says a new "Aztlan," with Los Angeles as its capital, is inevitable. José Angel Gutierrez, a political science professor at the University of Texas at

Arlington and director of the UTA Mexican-American Study Center, told a university crowd: "We have an aging white America. They are not making bables. They are dying. The explosion is in our population. They are shitting in their pants in fear! I love it."

More authoritative voices are sounding the same notes. The Mexican consul general José Pescador Osuna remarked in 1998, "Even though I am saying this part serious, part joking, I think we are practicing La Reconquista in California." California legislator Art Torres called Proposition 187, to cut off welfare to illegal aliens, "the last gasp of white America."

"California is going to be a Mexican State. We are going to control all the institutions. If people don't like it, they should leave," exults Mario Obledo, president of the League of United Latin American Citizens, and recipient of the Medal of Freedom from President Clinton. Former Mexican president Ernesto Zedillo told Mexican-Americans in Dallas: "You are Mexicans, Mexicans who live north of the border."

❧

Why should nationalistic and patriotic Mexicans not dream of a *reconquista*? The Latino student organization known by its Spanish acronym MEChA states, "We declare the independence of our *mestizo* nation. We are a bronze people with a bronze culture. Before the world, before all of North America . . . we are a nation." MEChA demands U.S. "restitution" for "past economic slavery, political exploitation, ethnic and cultural psychological destruction and denial of civil and human rights."

MEChA, which claims 400 campus chapters across the country, is unabashedly racist and anti-American. Its slogan—Por la Raza todo. Fuera de La Raza nada.—translates as "For our race, everything. For those outside our race, nothing." Yet it now exerts real power in many places. The former chair of its UCLA chapter, Antonio Villaraigosa, came within a whisker of being elected mayor of Los Angeles in 2001.

That Villaraigosa could go through an entire campaign for control of America's second-largest city without having to explain his association with a Chicano version of the white-supremacist Aryan Nation proves that America's major media are morally intimidated by any minority that boasts past victimhood credentials, real or imagined.

❧

Meanwhile, the invasion rolls on. America's once-sleepy 2,000-mile border with Mexico is now the scene of daily confrontations. Even the Mexican army shows its contempt for U.S. law. The State Department reported 55 military incursions in the five years before an incident in 2000 when truckloads of Mexican soldiers barreled through a barbed-wire fence, fired shots, and pursued two mounted officers and a U.S. Border Patrol vehicle. U.S. Border Patrol agents believe that some Mexican army units collaborate with their country's drug cartels.

America has become a spillway for an exploding population that Mexico is unable to employ. Mexico's population is growing by 10 million every decade. Mexican senator Adolfo Zinser conceded that Mexico's "economic policy is dependent on unlimited emigration to the United States." The *Yanqui*-baiting academic and "onetime Communist supporter" Jorge Casteñada warned in *The Atlantic Monthly* six years ago that any American effort to cut back immigration "will make social peace in . . . Mexico untenable. . . . Some Americans dislike immigration, but there is very little they can do about it." With Señor Casteñada now President Fox's foreign minister and Senator Zinser his national security adviser, these opinions carry weight.

The Mexican government openly supports illegal entry of its citizens into the United States. An Office for Mexicans Abroad helps Mexicans evade U.S. border guards in the deserts of Arizona and California by providing them with "survival kits" of water, dry meat, granola, Tylenol, anti-diarrhea pills, bandages, and condoms. The kits are distributed in Mexico's poorest towns, along with information on where illegal aliens can get free social services in California. Mexico is aiding and abetting an invasion of the United States, and the U.S. responds with intimidated silence and moral paralysis.

With California the preferred destination for this immigration flood, sociologist William Frey has documented an out-migration of African Americans and Anglo Americans from the Golden State in search of cities and towns like the ones in which they grew up. Other Californians are moving into gated communities. A country that cannot control its borders isn't really a country, Ronald Reagan warned some two decades ago.

Concerns about a radical change in America's ethnic composition have been called un-American. But they are as American as Benjamin Franklin, who once asked, "Why should Pennsylvania, founded by the English, become a Colony of Aliens, who will shortly be so numerous as to Germanize us instead of our Anglifying them?" Franklin would never find out if his fears were justified, because German immigration was halted during the Revolutionary War.

Theodore Roosevelt likewise warned that "The one absolutely certain way of bringing this nation to ruin, of preventing all possibility of its continuing to be a nation at all, would be to permit it to become a tangle of squabbling nationalities."

Immigration is a subject worthy of national debate, yet it has been deemed taboo by the forces of political correctness. Like the Mississippi, with its endless flow of life-giving water, immigration has enriched America throughout history. But when the Mississippi floods its banks, the devastation can be enormous. What will become of our country if the levees do not hold?

◦⟨◎⟩◦

Harvard economist George Borjas has found no net economic benefit from mass migration from the Third World. In his study, the added costs of schooling, health care, welfare, prisons, plus the added pressure on land, water, and power resources, exceeded the taxes that immigrants pay. The National Bureau of

Economic Research put the cost of immigration at $80 billion in 1995. What are the benefits, then, that justify the risk of the balkanization of America?

Today there are 28.4 million foreign-born persons living in the United States. Half are from Latin America and the Caribbean, one fourth from Asia. The rest are from Africa, the Middle East, and Europe. One in every five New Yorkers and Floridians is foreign-born, as is one of every four Californians. As the United States allots most of its immigrant visas to relatives of new arrivals, it is difficult for Europeans to be admitted to the U.S., while entire villages from El Salvador have settled here easily.

- A third of the legal immigrants who come to the United States have not finished high school. Some 22 percent do not even have a ninth-grade education, compared to less than 5 percent of our native-born.
- Of the immigrants who have arrived since 1980, 60 percent still do not earn $20,000 a year.
- Immigrant use of food stamps, Supplemental Security Income, and school lunch programs runs from 50 percent to 100 percent higher than use by the native born.
- By 1991, foreign nationals accounted for 24 percent of all arrests in Los Angeles and 36 percent of all arrests in Miami.
- In 1980, federal and state prisons housed 9,000 criminal aliens. By 1995, this number had soared to 59,000, a figure that does not include aliens who became citizens, or the criminals sent over from Cuba by Fidel Castro in the Mariel boat lift.

Mass emigration from poor Third World countries is good for business, especially businesses that employ large numbers of workers at low wages. But what is good for corporate America is not necessarily good for Middle America. When it comes to open borders, the corporate interest and the national interest do not coincide; they collide. Mass immigration raises more critical issues than jobs or wages—immigration is ultimately about America herself. Is the U.S. government, by deporting scarcely 1 percent of illegal aliens a year, failing in its Constitutional duty to protect the rights of American citizens?

⁓◦⟨◉⟩◦⁓

Most of the people who leave their homelands to come to America, whether from Mexico or Mauritania, are good, decent people. They seek the same freedom and opportunities our ancestors sought.

But today's record number of immigrants arriving from cultures that have little in common with our own raises a question: What is a nation? Some define a nation as one people of common ancestry, language, literature, history, heritage, heroes, traditions, customs, mores, and faith who have lived together over time in the same land under the same rulers. Among those who pressed this definition were Secretary of State John Quincy Adams, who laid down these conditions on immigrants: "They must cast off the European skin, never to resume it. They must look forward to their posterity rather than backward to their ancestors." Woodrow Wilson, speaking to newly naturalized

Americans in 1915 in Philadelphia, declared: "A man who thinks of himself as belonging to a particular national group in America has yet to become an American."

But Americans no longer agree on values, history, or heroes. What one half of America sees as a glorious past, the other views as shameful and wicked. Columbus, Washington, Jefferson, Jackson, Lincoln, and Lee—all of them heroes of the old America—are under attack. Equality and freedom, those most American of words, today hold different meanings for different Americans.

Nor is a shared belief in democracy sufficient to hold a people together. Half the nation did not even bother to vote in the Presidential election of 2000. Millions cannot name their congressman, senator, or the justices of the Supreme Court. They do not care. We live in the same country, we are governed by the same leaders. But are we one nation and one people?

It is hard to believe that over one million immigrants every year, from every country on earth, a third of them entering illegally, will reforge the bonds of our disuniting nation. John Stuart Mill cautioned that unified public opinion is "necessary to the working of representative government." We are about to find out if he was right.

Linda Chavez  **NO**

The Realities of Immigration

. . . CONTRARY TO popular myth, immigrants have never been particularly welcome in the United States. Americans have always tended to romanticize the immigrants of their grandparents' generation while casting a skeptical eye on contemporary newcomers. In the first decades of the 20th century, descendants of Northern European immigrants resisted the arrival of Southern and Eastern Europeans, and today the descendants of those once unwanted Italians, Greeks, and Poles are deeply distrustful of current immigrants from Latin America. Congressman Tom Tancredo, a Republican from Colorado and an outspoken advocate of tighter restrictions, is fond of invoking the memory of his Italian immigrant grandfather to argue that he is not anti-immigrant, just anti-illegal immigration. He fails to mention that at the time his grandfather arrived, immigrants simply had to show up on American shores (or walk across the border) to gain legal entry.

With the exception of the infamous Alien and Sedition Acts of 1798, there were few laws regulating immigration for the first hundred years of the nation's history. Though nativist sentiment increased throughout the later decades of the 19th century, giving rise to the 1882 Chinese Exclusion Act, it was not until 1917 that Congress began methodically to limit all immigration, denying admission to most Asians and Pacific Islanders and, in 1924, imposing quotas on those deemed undesirable: Jews, Italians, and others from Southern and Eastern Europe. These restrictions remained largely in effect until 1952, when Congress lifted many of them, including the bar on Asians.

The modern immigration era commenced in 1965 with the passage of the Immigration and Nationality Act, which abolished all national-origin quotas, gave preference to close relatives of American citizens, refugees, and individuals with certain skills, and allowed for immigrants from the Western hemisphere on a first-come, first-served basis. The act's passage drew a huge wave, much of it from Latin America and Asia. From 1970 to 2000, the United States admitted more than 20 million persons as permanent residents.

By 2000, some 3 million of these new residents were formerly illegal aliens who had gained amnesty as part of the 1986 Immigration Reform and Control Act (IRCA). This, Congress's first serious attempt to stem the flow of illegal immigration, forced employers to determine the status of their workers and imposed heavy penalties on those hiring illegal entrants. But from the beginning, the law was fraught with problems. It created huge bureaucratic burdens, even for private individuals wanting to hire someone to cut their lawn or care for their children, and spawned a vast new document-fraud industry for immigrants eager to get hold of the necessary paperwork. The law has been a monumental failure. Today, some 11.5 million illegal aliens reside in the U.S.—quadruple the population of two decades ago, when IRCA was enacted—and the number is growing by an estimated 500,000 a year. . . .

THE REAL question is not whether the U.S. has the means to stop illegal immigration—no doubt, with sufficient resources, we could mostly do so—but whether we would be better off as a nation without these workers. Restrictionists claim that large-scale immigration—legal and illegal—has depressed wages, burdened government resources, and acted as a net drain on the economy. The Federation for American Immigration Reform (FAIR), the most prominent of the pressure groups on the issue, argues that, because of this influx, hourly earnings among American males have not increased appreciably in 30 years. As the restrictionists see it, if the U.S. got serious about defending its borders, there would be plenty of Americans willing to do the jobs now performed by workers from abroad. . . .

As for the more conventional claims advanced by restrictionists, they, too, are hard to credit. Despite the presence in our workforce of millions of illegal immigrants, the U.S. is currently creating slightly more than two million jobs a year and boasts an unemployment rate of 4.7 percent, which is lower than the average in each of the past four decades. More to the point perhaps, when the National Research Council (NRC) of the National Academy of Sciences evaluated the economic impact of immigration in its landmark 1997 study The New Americans: Economic, Demographic, and Fiscal Effects of Immigration, it found only a small negative impact on the earnings of Americans, and even then, only for workers at lower skill and education levels.

Moreover, the participation of immigrants in the labor force has had obvious positive effects. The NRC estimated that roughly 5 percent of household expenditures in the U.S. went to goods and services produced by immigrant labor—labor whose relative cheapness translated into lower prices for everything from chicken to new homes. These price advantages, the study found, were "spread quite uniformly across most types of domestic consumers," with a slightly greater benefit for higher-income households.

Many restrictionists argue that if Americans would simply cut their own lawns, clean their own houses, and care for their own children, there would be no need for immigrant labor. But even if this were true, the overall economy would hardly benefit from having fewer workers. If American women were unable to rely on immigrants to perform some household duties, more of them would be forced to stay home. A smaller labor force would also have devastating consequences when it comes to dealing with the national debt and government-funded entitlements like Social Security and Medicare, a point repeatedly made by former Federal Reserve Board Chairman Alan Greenspan. As he told a Senate committee in 2003, "short of a major increase in immigration, economic growth cannot be safely counted upon to eliminate deficits and the difficult choices that will be required to restore fiscal discipline." The following year, Greenspan noted that offsetting the fiscal effects of our own declining birthrate would require a level of immigration "much larger than almost all current projections assume."

THE CONTRIBUTIONS that immigrants make to the economy must be weighed, of course, against the burdens they impose. FAIR and other restrictionist groups contend that immigrants are a huge drain on society because of the cost of providing public services to them—some $67 to $87 billion a year, according to one commonly cited study. Drawing on numbers from the NRC's 1997 report, FAIR argues that "the net fiscal drain on American taxpayers [from immigration] is between $166 and $226 a year per native household."

There is something to these assertions, though less than may at first appear. Much of the anxiety and resentment generated by immigrants is, indeed, a result of the very real costs they impose on state and local governments, especially in border states like California and Arizona. Providing education and health care to the children of immigrants is particularly expensive, and the federal government picks up only a fraction of the expense. But, again, there are countervailing factors. Illegal immigrants are hardly free-riders. An estimated three-quarters of them paid federal taxes in 2002, amounting to $7 billion in Social Security contributions and $1.5 billion in Medicare taxes, plus withholding for income taxes. They also pay state and local sales taxes and (as homeowners and renters) property taxes.

Moreover, FAIR and its ilk have a penchant for playing fast and loose with numbers. To support its assessment of immigration's overall fiscal burden, for instance, FAIR ignores the explicit cautions in a later NRC report about cross-sectional analyses that exclude the "concurrent descendants" of immigrants— that is, their adult children. These, overwhelmingly, are productive members of the workforce. As the NRC notes, when this more complete picture is taken into account, immigrants have "a positive federal impact of about $1,260 [per capita], exceeding their net cost [$680 per capita on average] at the state and local levels." Restrictionists also argue that fewer immigrants would mean more opportunities for low-skilled native workers. Of late, groups like the Minuteman Project have even taken to presenting themselves as champions of unemployed American blacks (a curious tactic, to say the least, considering the views on race and ethnicity of many in the anti-immigrant camp(B)).

But here, too, the factual evidence is mixed. Wages for Americans workers who have less than a high-school education have probably been adversely affected by large-scale immigration; the economist George Borjas estimates a reduction of 8 percent in hourly wages for native-born males in that category. But price competition is not the only reason that many employers favor immigrants over poorly educated natives. Human capital includes motivation, and there could hardly be two more disparately motivated groups than U.S.-born high-school drop-outs and their foreign-born rivals in the labor market. Young American men usually leave high school because they become involved with drugs or crime, have difficulty with authority, cannot maintain regular hours, or struggle with learning. Immigrants, on the other hand, have demonstrated enormous initiative, reflecting, in the words of President Reagan, "a special kind of courage that enabled them to leave their own land, leave their friends and their countrymen, and come to this new and strange land."

Just as important, they possess a strong desire to work. Legal immigrants have an 86-percent rate of participation in the labor force; illegal immigrant males have a 94-percent rate. By contrast, among white males with less than a high-school education, the participation rate is 46 percent, while among blacks it is 40 percent. If all immigrants, or even only illegal aliens, disappeared from the American workforce, can anyone truly believe that poorly skilled whites and blacks would fill the gap? To the contrary, productivity would likely decline, and employers in many sectors would simply move their operations to countries like Mexico, China, and the Philippines, where many of our immigrants come from in the first place. . . .

Evidence from the culture at large is also encouraging. On most measures of social and economic integration, Hispanic immigrants and their descendants have made steady strides up the ladder. English is the preferred language of virtually all U.S.-born Hispanics; indeed, according to a 2002 national survey by the Pew Hispanic Center and the Kaiser Family Foundation, 78 percent of third-generation Mexican-Americans cannot speak Spanish at all. In education, 86 percent of U.S.-born Hispanics complete high school, compared with 92 percent of non-Hispanic whites, and the drop-out rate among immigrant children who enroll in high school after they come here is no higher than for the native-born.

It remains true that attendance at four-year colleges is lower among Hispanics than for other groups, and Hispanics lag in attaining bachelor's degrees. But neither that nor their slightly lower rate of high-school attendance has kept Hispanic immigrants from pulling their economic weight. After controlling for education, English proficiency, age, and geographic location, Mexican-born males actually earn 2.4 percent more than comparable U.S.-born white males, according to a recent analysis of 2000 Census data by the National Research Council. Hispanic women, for their part, hold their own against U.S.-born white women with similar qualifications.

As for the effect of Hispanic immigrants on the country's social fabric, the NRC found that they are more likely than other Americans to live with their immediate relatives: 88.6 percent of Mexican immigrant households are made up of families, compared with 69.5 percent of non-Hispanic whites and 68.3 percent of blacks. These differences are partially attributable to the age structure of the Hispanic population, which is younger on average than the white or black population. But even after adjusting for age and immigrant generation, U.S. residents of Hispanic origin—and especially those from Mexico—are much more likely to live in family households. Despite increased out-of-wedlock births among Hispanics, about 67 percent of American children of Mexican origin live in two-parent families, as compared with 77 percent of white children but only 37 percent of black children.

Perhaps the strongest indicator of Hispanic integration into American life is the population's high rate of intermarriage. About a quarter of all Hispanics marry outside their ethnic group, almost exclusively to non-Hispanic white spouses, a rate that has remained virtually unchanged since 1980. And here a significant fact has been noted in a 2005 study by the Population Reference

Bureau—namely, that "the majority of inter-Hispanic children are reported as Hispanic." Such intermarriages themselves, the study goes on, "may have been a factor in the phenomenal growth of the U.S. Hispanic population in recent years."

It has been widely predicted that, by mid-century, Hispanics will represent fully a quarter of the U.S. population. Such predictions fail to take into account that increasing numbers of these "Hispanics" will have only one grandparent or great-grandparent of Hispanic heritage. By that point, Hispanic ethnicity may well mean neither more nor less than German, Italian, or Irish ethnicity means today.

HOW, THEN, to proceed? Congress is under growing pressure to strengthen border control, but unless it also reaches some agreement on more comprehensive reforms, stauncher enforcement is unlikely to have much of an effect. With a growing economy and more jobs than our own population can readily absorb, the U.S. will continue to need immigrants. Illegal immigration already responds reasonably well to market forces. It has increased during boom times like the late 1990's and decreased again when jobs disappear, as in the latest recession. Trying to determine an ideal number makes no more sense than trying to predict how much steel or how many textiles we ought to import; government quotas can never match the efficiency of simple supply and demand. As President Bush has argued—and as the Senate has now agreed—a guest-worker program is the way to go.

Does this mean the U.S. should just open its borders to anyone who wants to come? Hardly. We still need an orderly process, one that includes background checks to insure that terrorists and criminals are not being admitted. It also makes sense to require that immigrants have at least a basic knowledge of English and to give preference to those who have advanced skills or needed talents.

Moreover, immigrants themselves have to take more responsibility for their status. Illegal aliens from Mexico now pay significant sums of money to "coyotes" who sneak them across the border. If they could come legally as guest workers, that same money might be put up as a surety bond to guarantee their return at the end of their employment contract, or perhaps to pay for health insurance. Nor is it good policy to allow immigrants to become welfare recipients or to benefit from affirmative action: restrictions on both sorts of programs have to be written into law and stringently applied.

A market-driven guest-worker program might be arranged in any number of ways. A proposal devised by the Vernon K. Krieble Foundation, a policy group based in Colorado, suggests that government-licensed, private-sector employment agencies be put in charge of administering the effort, setting up offices in other countries to process applicants and perform background checks. Workers would be issued tamper-proof identity cards only after signing agreements that would allow for deportation if they violated the terms of their contract or committed crimes in the U.S. Although the Krieble plan would offer no path to citizenship, workers who wanted to change their status could still apply for permanent residency and, ultimately, citizenship through the normal, lengthy process. . . .

IN 1918, at the height of the last great wave of immigrants and the hysteria that it prompted in some circles, Madison Grant, a Yale-educated eugenicist and leader of the immigration-restriction movement, made a prediction:

The result of unlimited immigration is showing plainly in the rapid decline in the birth rate of native Americans because the poorer classes of colonial stock, where they still exist, will not bring children into the world to compete in the labor market with the Slovak, the Italian, the Syrian, and the Jew. . . . The man of the old stock is being crowded out of many country districts by these foreigners, just as he is today being literally driven off the streets of New York City by the swarms of Polish Jews. These immigrants adopt the language of the native American, they wear his clothes, they steal his name, and they are beginning to take his women, but they seldom adopt his religion or understand his ideals, and while he is being elbowed out of his own home, the American looks calmly abroad and urges on others the suicidal ethics which are exterminating his own race.

Today, such alarmism reads as little more than a historical curiosity. Southern and Eastern European immigrants and their children did, in fact, assimilate, and in certain cases—most prominently that of the Jews—they exceeded the educational and economic attainments of Grant's "colonial stock."

Present-day restrictionists point to all sorts of special circumstances that supposedly made such acculturation possible in the past but render it impossible today. Then as now, however, the restrictionists are wrong, not least in their failure to understand the basic dynamic of American nationhood. There is no denying the challenge posed by assimilating today's newcomers, especially so many of them in so short a span of time. Nor is there any denying the cultural forces, mainly stemming from the Left, that have attenuated the sense of national identity among native-born American elites themselves and led to such misguided policies as bilingual education. But, provided that we commit ourselves to the goal, past experience and progress to date suggest the task is anything but impossible.

As jarring as many found the recent pictures of a million illegal aliens marching in our cities, the fact remains that many of the immigrants were carrying the American flag, and waving it proudly. They and their leaders understand what most restrictionists do not and what some Americans have forgotten or choose to deny: that the price of admission to America is, and must be, the willingness to become an American. . . .

POSTSCRIPT

Is Third World Immigration a Threat to America's Way of Life?

Former representative Silvio Conte (R-Massachusetts) said at a citizenship ceremony, "You can go to France, but you will never be a Frenchman. You can go to Germany but you will never be a German. Today you are all Americans, and that is why this is the greatest country on the face of the earth." At one time, America's open door to immigrants was one of the prides of America. For some people, like Chavez, it still is. She thinks that immigration is making America stronger. Many people disagree because they fear the consequences of today's immigration. Buchanan worries that, although the new immigrants may want to assimilate, they have reached such a critical mass that the United States has lost the ability to absorb everyone into its own, slowly dissipating culture. The result is that immigrants are encouraged to maintain and promote the cultures that they arrive with, which further dilutes the original culture of America. The issue is based on what one thinks will happen as America becomes more diverse. Buchanan sees America as coming apart and Chavez sees America as becoming stronger.

Stanley Lieberson and Mary C. Waters, in *From Many Strands* (Russell Sage Foundation, 1988), argue that ethnic groups with European origins are assimilating, marrying outside their groups, and losing their ethnic identities. Richard D. Alba's study "Assimilation's Quiet Tide," *The Public Interest* (Spring 1995) confirms these findings. Latinos, however, are assimilating more slowly.

Several major works debate whether or not immigrants, on average, benefit America economically and whether they are assimilating. Sources that argue that immigrants largely benefit America include Julian L. Simon, *The Economic Consequences of Immigration,* 2d ed. (University of Michigan Press, 1999) and *Immigration: The Demographic and Economic Facts* (Cato Institute, 1995). Sources that argue that immigrants have more negative than positive impacts include George Borjas, *Heaven's Door: Immigration Policy and the American Economy* (Princeton University Press, 1999); Roy Beck, *The Case Against Immigration* (W. W. Norton, 1996); Patrick Buchanan, *The Death of the West: How Dying Populations and Immigrant Invasions Imperil Our Country and Civilization* (Thomas Dunne Books, 2002); and Otis L. Graham, Jr., *Unguarded Gates: A History of American's Immigration Crisis* (Rowman and Littlefield, 2004). For a more even-handed discussion, see Nancy Foner, ed., *Not Just Black and White: Historical and Contemporary Perspectives on Immigration, Race, and Ethnicity in the United States* (Russell Sage Foundation, 2004); Carol M. Swain ed., *Debating Immigration* (Cambridge University Press 2007); and

Frank D. Bean and Gilian Stevens, *America's Newcomers and the Dynamics of Diversity* (Russell Sage Foundation, 2003).

On the issue of Mexican immigration, see Douglas S. Massey, Jorge Durand, and Nolan J. Malone's *Beyond Smoke and Mirrors: Mexican Immigration in an Era of Economic Integration* (Russell Sage Foundation, 2003) and Victor Davis Hanson's *Mexifornia: A State of Becoming* (Encounter Books, 2003).

Internet References . . .

American Men's Studies Association

The American Men's Studies Association is a not-for-profit professional organization of scholars, therapists, and others interested in the exploration of masculinity in modern society.

http://mensstudies.org

Feminist Majority Foundation

The Feminist Majority Foundation Web site provides affirmative action links, resources from women's professional organizations, information for empowering women in business, sexual harassment information, and much more.

http://www.feminist.org

GLAAD: Gay and Lesbian Alliance Against Defamation

The Gay and Lesbian Alliance Against Defamation (GLAAD), formed in New York in 1985, seeks to improve the public's attitudes toward homosexuality and to put an end to discrimination against lesbians and gay men.

http://www.glaad.org

International Lesbian and Gay Association

The resources on the International Lesbian and Gay Association Web site are provided by a worldwide network of lesbian, gay, bisexual, and transgendered groups.

http://www.ilga.org

SocioSite: Feminism and Women's Issues

The Feminism and Women's Issues SocioSite provides insights into a number of issues that affect family relationships. It covers wide-ranging issues regarding women and men, family and children, and much more.

http://www.sociosite.net/index.php

Sex Roles, Gender, and the Family

*T*he modern feminist movement has advanced the causes of women to the point where there are now more women in the workforce in the United States than ever before. Professions and trades that were traditionally regarded as the provinces of men have opened up to women, and women now have easier access to the education and training necessary to excel in these new areas. But what is happening to sex roles, and what are the effects of changing sex roles? How have men and women been affected by the stress caused by current sex roles, the demand for the right to same-sex marriages, and the deterioration of the traditional family structure? The issues in this part address these sorts of questions.

- Does Divorce Have Long-Term Damaging Effects on Children?

- Should Mothers Stay Home with Their Children?

- Should Same-Sex Marriages Be Legally Recognized?

ISSUE 4

Does Divorce Have Long-Term Damaging Effects on Children?

YES: Elizabeth Marquardt, from "The Bad Divorce," *First Things* (February 2005)

NO: Constance Ahrons, from *We're Still Family: What Grown Children Have to Say about Their Parents' Divorce* (Harper Collins, 2004)

ISSUE SUMMARY

YES: Elizabeth Marquardt, Director of the Center for Marriage and Families, defends the common belief that divorce has devastating impacts on children and attacks Constance Ahrons's counter-thesis.

NO: Constance Ahron, co-chair of the Council on Contemporary Families, found in her research on the children of divorced parents that they do quite well in later life and most think that they were not harmed by the divorce.

T he state of the American family deeply concerns many Americans. About 40 percent of marriages end in divorce, and only 27 percent of children born in 1990 are expected to be living with both parents by the time they reach age 17. Most Americans, therefore, are affected personally or are close to people who are affected by structural changes in the family. Few people can avoid being exposed to the issue: violence in the family and celebrity divorces are standard fare for news programs, and magazine articles decrying the breakdown of the family appear frequently. Politicians today try to address the problems of the family. Academics have affirmed that the family crisis has numerous significant negative effects on children, spouses, and the rest of society.

But is the situation as bad as portrayed? Many of you reading this come from divorced homes and can evaluate how much you suffered and whether you have been scarred for life. All of you can look around you and judge for yourselves how your acquaintances have been affected by divorce. Obviously, divorce is much worse for children than a good marriage but is it worse than a bad marriage? Because the answer is not obvious, the debate heats up.

One reason divorce is a very important issue is the important role that the family plays in the functioning of society. For a society to survive, its population must reproduce (or take in many immigrants), and its young must be trained to perform adult roles and to have the values and attitudes that will motivate them to contribute to society. Procreation and socialization are two vital roles that families traditionally have performed. In addition, the family provides economic and emotional support for its members, which is vital to their effective functioning in society. Stable, well-functioning families best perform these roles and divorce jeopardizes them.

Although most experts agree that the American family is in crisis, there is little agreement about what, if anything, should be done about it. After all, most of these problems result from the choices that people make to try to increase their happiness. People end unhappy marriages. When they do, most of them also carefully consider the best interests of the children. These considerations obviously prevent or delay many divorces and probably should prevent many more. Obviously, however, many situations are improved by divorce, especially if the divorce and aftermath arrangements are conducted in a compassionate manner. So, which way is best is a judgment call, both by the potentially divorcing parents and by the academics who study the issue.

In the selections that follow, Constance Ahrons draws from her extensive work on the children of divorce to show that divorce has far fewer negative consequences on children than is commonly assumed. Elizabeth Marquardt's article is totally devoted to refuting Ahrons's thesis.

YES

Elizabeth Marquardt

The Bad Divorce

It is often said that those who are concerned about the social and personal effects of divorce are nostalgic for the 1950s, yearning for a mythical time when men worked, women happily stayed home baking cookies for the kids, and marriages never dissolved. Yet often the same people who make the charge of mythology are caught in a bit of nostalgia of their own, pining for the sexual liberationism of the 1970s, when many experts began to embrace unfettered divorce, confident that children, no less than adults, would thrive once "unhappy" marriages were brought to a speedy end.

Constance Ahrons, who coined the term "the good divorce" in the title of an influential 1992 book that examined ninety-eight divorcing couples, is very much a member of the latter camp. In her new book, *We're Still Family: What Grown Children Have to Say About Their Parents' Divorce,* Ahrons returns to those ninety-eight couples to survey their now-grown children. The result is a study based on telephone interviews with 173 young adults from eighty-nine families that tries to advance the idea it is not divorce itself that burdens children but rather the way in which parents divorce. As in her earlier book, Ahrons argues that the vocabulary we use to discuss divorce and remarriage is negative; she would prefer that we regard divorced families as "changed" or "rearranged" rather than broken, damaged, or destroyed. She claims that upbeat language will, above all, help children feel less stigmatized by divorce. Both of her books offer many new terms, such as "binuclear" and "tribe," to describe divorced families. The specific novelty of the new book is Ahrons' claim that her interviewees view their parents' divorces in a positive light.

It is with delight, then, that Ahrons shares surprising new findings from her on-going study. According to Ahrons, over three quarters of the young people from divorced families who she interviewed do not wish their parents were still together. A similar proportion feel their parents' decision to divorce was a good one, that their parents are better off today, and that they themselves are either better off or not affected by the divorce. To general readers who have been following the debates about children of divorce in recent years, such findings might sound like big news. But there are problems.

According to Ahrons, over three-quarters of the young people whom she interviewed do not wish that their parents were still together. A similar proportion feel that their parents' decision to divorce was a good one, that their parents are better off today, and that they themselves are either better off because of the divorce or have not been affected by it. Statistically, that sounds overwhelmingly convincing. But an answer to a survey question tells us very little unless we have a context for interpreting it and some grasp of the actual experiences that gave rise to it.

Like those whom Ahrons interviewed, I grew up in a divorced family, my parents having split when I was two years old. Like Ahrons, I am a researcher in the field, having led, with Norval Glenn, a study of young adults from both divorced and intact families that included a nationally representative telephone survey of some 1,500 people. As someone who studies children of divorce and who is herself a grown child of divorce, I have noticed that the kinds of questions that get asked in such studies and the way the answers are interpreted often depend on whether the questioner views divorce from the standpoint of the child or the parent.

Take, for example, Ahrons' finding that the majority of people raised in divorced families do not wish that their parents were together. Ahrons did not ask whether as children these young people had hoped their parents would reunite. Instead, she asked if they wish today their parents were still together. She presents their negative answers as gratifying evidence that divorce is affirmed by children. But is that really the right conclusion to draw?

Imagine the following scenario. One day when you are a child your parents come to you and tell you they are splitting up. Your life suddenly changes in lots of ways. Dad leaves, or maybe Mom does. You may move or change schools or lose friendships, or all of the above. Money is suddenly very tight and stays that way for a long time. You may not see one set of grandparents, aunts, uncles, and cousins nearly as much as you used to. Then, Mom starts dating, or maybe Dad does. A boyfriend or girlfriend moves in, perhaps bringing along his or her own kids. You may see one or both of your parents marry again; you may see one or both of them get divorced a second time. You deal with the losses. You adjust as best you can. You grow up and try to figure out this "relationship" thing for yourself. Then, some interviewer on the telephone asks if you wish your parents were still together today. A lifetime of pain and anger and adjustment flashes before your eyes. Any memory of your parents together as a couple—if you can remember them together at all—is buried deep under all those feelings. Your divorced parents have always seemed like polar opposites to you. No one could be more different from your mother than your father, and vice versa. "No," you reply to the interviewer, "I don't wish my parents were still together." Of course, one cannot automatically attribute such a train of thought to all of Ahrons' interview subjects. Still, it is plausible, and it might explain at least some of the responses. But Ahrons does not even consider it.

Ahrons tells us that the vast majority of young people in her study feel that they are either better off or not affected by their parents' divorce. For a child of divorce there could hardly be a more loaded question than this one. The generation that Ahrons is interviewing grew up in a time of massive changes in family life, with experts assuring parents that if they became happier after divorce, their children would as well. There wasn't a lot of patience for people who felt otherwise—especially when those people were children, with their aggravating preference for conventional married life over the adventures of divorce, and their tendency to look askance at their parents' new love interests.

However, a child soon learns the natural lesson that complaining about a parent's choices is a surefire way to be ignored or worse, and that what parents want above all is praise for those choices. Few things inspire as much admiration among divorced parents and their friends as the words of a child reassuring them that the divorce was no big deal—or even better, that it gave the child something beneficial, like early independence, or a new brother or sister. Parents are proud of a resilient child. They are embarrassed and frustrated by a child who claims to be a victim. And who among us wants to be a victim? Who would not rather be a hero, or at least a well-adjusted and agreeable person? When the interviewer calls on the telephone, what will the young adult be more likely to say? Something like "I'm damaged goods"? Or "Yes, it was tough at times but I survived it, and I'm stronger for it today." It is the second reply that children of divorce have all their lives been encouraged to give; and the fact that they are willing to give it yet again is hardly, as Ahrons would have it, news.

Thus, Ahrons' statistics on their own hardly constitute three cheers for divorce. Far more meaningful and revealing are the extended quotations from interview subjects with which the book is liberally studded. She writes, for instance, that Andy, now thirty-two, sees "value" in his parents' divorce. Why? Because:

> "I learned a lot. I grew up a lot more quickly than a lot of my friends. Not that that's a good thing or a bad thing. People were always thinking I was older than I was because of the way I carried myself."

Treating a sad, unfortunate experience (like being forced to grow up more quickly than one's peers) as something neutral or even positive is merely one example of what can happen when a person attempts to conform to a culture that insists that divorce is no big deal. To take such an ambivalent response as clear evidence that divorce does no damage, as Ahrons does is inexcusable.

Ahrons cheerfully reports other "good" results of divorce. Here for example is Brian, whose parents split when he was five:

> "In general, I think [the divorce] has had very positive effects. I see what happens in divorces, and I have promised myself that I would do anything to not get a divorce. I don't want my kids to go through what I went through."

Tracy, whose parents divorced when she was twelve, sees a similar upside to divorce:

> "I saw some of the things my parents did and know not to do that in my marriage and see the way they treated each other and know not to do that to my spouse and my children. I know [the divorce] has made me more committed to my husband and my children."

These are ringing endorsements of divorce as a positive life event? Like the testimony of a child who's learned a painful but useful lesson about the dangers of playing with fire, such accounts indicate that the primary benefit of divorce is to encourage young people to avoid it in their own lives if at all possible.

Then there are the significant problems with the structure of Ahrons' study itself. While the original families were recruited using a randomized method, the study lacks any control group. In other words, Ahrons interviewed plenty of young people from divorced families but spoke to no one of similar ages from intact families. So she really can't tell us anything at all about how these young people might differ from their peers.

Rather than acknowledging that her lack of a control group is a serious limitation, Ahrons sidesteps the issue. In several places she compares her subjects to generalized "social trends" or "their contemporaries" and decides, not surprisingly, that they are not all that different. Thus, Ahrons notes that many of the young people from divorced families told her they frequently struggled with issues of "commitment, trust, and dealing with conflict," but on this finding she comments, "These issues are precisely the ones that most adults in this stage of their development grapple with, whether they grow up in a nuclear family or not." Never mind that she has not interviewed any of those other young people, or cited any studies to back up her contention, or acknowledged the possibility that, while all young people do have to deal with these kinds of interpersonal issues, some have a much harder time doing it than others. Ahrons instead wholly dismisses the pain expressed by the children of divorce and assures us that they are simply passing through a normal development phase.

When it comes to her conclusions, Ahrons claims that "if you had a devitalized or high-conflict marriage, you can take heart that the decision to divorce may have been the very best thing you could have done for your children." While research does show that children, on average, do better after a high-conflict marriage ends (the same research, by Paul Amato and Alan Booth, also shows that only one-third of divorces end high-conflict marriages), no one—Ahrons included—has shown that children do better when an adult ends a marriage he or she perceives as "devitalized." Children don't much care whether their parents have a "vital" marriage. They care whether their mother and father live with them, take care of them, and don't fight a lot. . . .

Ahrons' also remains preoccupied with the concept of stigma. She writes, for instance, that we are seeing "progress" because a high divorce rate has the effect of reducing the stigma experienced by children of divorce. That's all well and good, but one wonders why Ahrons gives stigma so much attention while saying nothing about a far more damaging social problem for children of divorce—namely, silence. Consider my own experience. The type of family in which I grew up was radically different from the intact family model. Yet no one around me, not even therapists, ever once acknowledged that fact. Never mind that my beloved father lived hours away, or that the mother I adored was often stressed as she tried to earn a living while also acting as a single parent. I was left to assume, like many children of divorce, that whatever problems I struggled with were no one's fault but my own. The demand that children of divorce keep quiet and get with the program puts them in the position of protecting adults from guilt and further stress—effectively reversing the natural order of family life in which the adults are the protectors of children.

Ahrons is remarkably unsympathetic to the children on whom this burden is laid. What do children of divorce long for? According to Ahrons, they nurture unrealistic hopes for "tidy," "perfect" families. She uses these words so frequently—the first term appears at least six times in the book and the second at least four times—that she sometimes appears to be portraying children of divorce as weird obsessives. Speaking directly to children of divorce, Ahrons offers the following advice: "You may not have the idyllic family you dreamed of . . . [but] often the only thing within our control is how we perceive or interpret an event." "For example, you can choose to see your family as rearranged, or you can choose to see it as broken." Indeed, the curative powers of social constructivism are nothing short of miraculous. Encouraging readers to stop using the descriptive term "adult child of divorce," she asserts that "it's a stigmatizing label that presumes you are deficient or traumatized. . . . If you have fallen prey to using it to explain something about yourself, ask yourself if it is keeping you from making changes that might bring you more satisfaction in your life." Apparently, coming to grips with one's family history and the deepest sources of one's sadness and loneliness is the worst thing a child can do. . . .

Ahrons surely knows more about the tragedies of divorce than her thesis allows her to admit. She has studied divorced families for years. She has worked with them as a clinician. She has been through divorce herself. Yet she inevitably follows up heartbreaking observations of interviewees with the confident assertion that everyone involved would be so much happier if only they talked themselves out of—and even walked away from—their anguish. As she writes in one (unintentionally haunting) passage, "Over the years I have listened to many divorcing parents in my clinical practice talk about how much they look forward to the day when their children will be grown and they won't have to have anything more to do with their exes." Is it possible to image a sadder or more desperate desire than this one—the longing for one's children to grow up faster so that relations with one's ex-spouse can be more effectively severed? In such passages it becomes obvious that all of Ahrons' efforts to explain away the tragedy of divorce and its legacy are in vain. In the end, the theory collapses before reality.

Ahrons' poorly structured study and far too tendentious thesis are of no help to us in thinking through our approach to divorce and its consequences. Children of divorce are real, complex people who are deeply shaped by a new kind of fractured family life—one whose current prevalence is unprecedented in human history. These children are not nostalgic for "tidy," "perfect," "idyllic" families. They grieve the real losses that follow from their parents' divorce. They don't need new words to describe what they've been through. Ordinary words will serve quite well—provided that people are willing to listen to them.

Constance Ahrons

NO

No Easy Answers: Why the Popular View of Divorce Is Wrong

. . . Although it may appear strange, my exhusband's untimely death brought his second and first families closer together. I had mourned at his funeral and spent time with his family and friends for several days afterward. A different level of kinship formed, as we—his first and second families— shared our loss and sadness. Since then, we have chosen to join together at several family celebrations, which has added a deeper dimension to our feelings of family.

You may be thinking, "This is all so rational. There's no way my family could pull this off." Or perhaps, like the many people who have shared their stories with me over the years, you are nodding your head knowingly, remembering similar occasions in your own family. The truth is we are like many extended families rearranged by divorce. My ties to my exhusband's family are not close but we care about one another. We seldom have contact outside of family occasions, but we know we're family. We hear stories of each other's comings and goings, transmitted to us through our mutual ties to my daughters, and now, through grandchildren. But if many families, like my own, continue to have relationships years after divorce, why don't we hear more about them?

Quite simply, it's because this is not the way it's supposed to be. My family, and the many others like mine, don't fit the ideal images we have about families. They appear strange because they're not tidy. There are "extra" people and relationships that don't exist in nuclear families and are awkward to describe because we don't have familiar and socially defined kinship terms to do so. Although families rearranged and expanded by divorce are rapidly growing and increasingly common, our resistance to accepting them as normal makes them appear deviant.

Societal change is painfully slow, which results in the situation wherein the current realities of family life come into conflict with our valued images. Sociologists call this difference "cultural lag," the difference between what is real and what we hold as ideal. This lag occurs because of our powerful resistance to acknowledging changes that challenge our basic beliefs about what's good and what's bad in our society.

Why Good Divorces Are Invisible

Good divorces are those in which the divorce does not destroy meaningful family relationships. Parents maintain a sufficiently cooperative and support- ive relationship that allows them to focus on the needs of their children. In good divorces children continue to have ties to both their mothers and their fathers, and each of their extended families, including those acquired when either parent remarries.

Good divorces have been well-kept secrets because to acknowledge them in mainstream life threatens our nostalgic images of family. If the secret got out that indeed many families that don't fit our "mom and pop" household ideal are healthy, we would have to question the basic societal premise that marriage and family are synonymous. And that reality upsets a lot of people, who then respond with familiar outcries that divorce is eroding our basic values and destroying society.

Although we view ourselves as a society in which nuclear families and lifelong monogamous marriages predominate, the reality is that 43 percent of first marriages will end in divorce. Over half of new marriages are actually remarriages for at least one of the partners. Not only have either the bride or groom (or both) been divorced but increasingly one of them also has parents who are divorced.

Families are the way we organize to raise children. Although we hold the ideal image that marriage is a precursor to establishing a family, modern parents are increasingly challenging this traditional ideal. Families today arrange—and rearrange—themselves in many responsible ways that meet the needs of children for nurturance, guidance and economic support. Family historian Stephanie Coontz, in her book *The Way We Never Were,* shows how the "tremendous variety of workable childrearing patterns in history suggests that, with little effort, we should be able to forge new institutions and values."

One way we resist these needed societal changes is by denying that divorce is no longer deviant. We demean divorced families by clinging to the belief that families can't exist outside of marriage. It follows then that stories of healthy families that don't fit the tidy nuclear family package are rare and stories that show how divorce destroys families and harms children are common. In this way, bad divorces appear to represent the American way of divorce and good divorces become invisible.

Messages That Hinder Good Divorces

When the evils of divorce are all that families hear about, it makes coping with the normal transitions and changes that inevitably accompany divorce all the more difficult. Negative messages make children feel different and lesser, leading to feelings of shame and guilt. Parents who feel marginalized in this way are less likely to think about creative solutions to their problems. That all of this unnecessary anxiety is fueled by sensationalized reports of weak findings, half-truths and myths of devastation is deplorable. Only by sorting out the truths about divorce from the fiction can we be empowered to make better decisions, find healthy ways to maintain family relationships, and develop important family rituals after divorce. Let's take a close look at the most common misconceptions about divorce.

Misconception 1: Parents Should Stay Married for the Sake of the Kids

This is message that pervades our culture, and it rests on a false duality: Marriage is good for kids, divorce is bad. Underlying this premise is the belief that parents who divorce are immature and selfish because they put their personal needs ahead of the needs of their children, that because divorce is too easy to get, spouses give up on their marriages too easily and that if you're thinking about divorcing your spouse, you should "stick it out till the kids are grown." A popular joke takes this message to its extreme. A couple in their nineties, married for seventy years, appears before a judge in their petition for a divorce. The judge looks at them quizzically and asks, "Why now, why after all these years?" The couple responds: "We waited until the children were dead."

The research findings are now very clear that reality is nowhere near as simple and tidy. Unresolved, open interparental conflict between married spouses that pervades day-to-day family life has been shown again and again to have negative effects on children. Most experts agree that when this is the case it is better for the children if parents divorce rather than stay married. Ironically, prior to the initiation of no-fault legislation over twenty years ago, in most states this kind of open conflict in the home was considered "cruel and inhumane" treatment and it was one of the few grounds on which a divorce would be granted—if it could be proved.

But the majority of unsatisfying marriages are not such clearcut cases. When most parents ask themselves if they should stay married for the sake of their children, they have clearly reached the point where they are miserable in their marriages but wouldn't necessarily categorize them as "high-conflict." And here is where, in spite of the societal message, there is no agreement in the research findings or among clinical experts. That's because it's extremely complex and each individual situation is too different to allow for a "one-size-fits-all" answer.

A huge list of factors comes into play when assessing whether staying married would be better for your kids. For example,

- Is the unhappiness in your marriage making you so depressed or angry that your children's needs go unmet because you can't parent effectively?
- Do you and your spouse have a cold and distant relationship that makes the atmosphere at home unhealthy for your children?
- Do you and your spouse lack mutual respect, caring or interests, setting a poor model for your children?
- Would the financial hardships be so dire that your children will experience a severely reduced standard of living?

Add to this your child's temperament, resources and degree of resilience, and then the personal and family changes that take place in the years after the divorce, and you can see how the complexities mount.

It is a rare parent who divorces *too easily*. Most parents are responsible adults who spend years struggling with the extremely difficult and complex decision of whether to divorce or stay married "for the sake of the children." The bottom line is that divorce is an adult decision, usually made by one spouse, entered into in the face of many unknowns. Without a crystal ball, no one knows whether their decision will be better for their children. As you read further in this book, however, you may gain some perspective on what will be most helpful in your situation, with your children, by listening carefully to the reactions and feelings of various children of divorce *as they have changed over twenty years.*

Misconception 2: "Adult Children of Divorce" Are Doomed to Have Lifelong Problems

. . . The truth is that, for the great majority of children who experience a parental divorce, the divorce becomes part of their history but it is not a defining factor. Like the rest of us, most of them reach adulthood to lead reasonably happy, successful lives. Although children who grew up with divorced parents certainly share an important common experience, their ability to form healthy relationships, be good parents, build careers, and so on, are far more determined by their individual temperaments, their sibling relationships, the dynamics within their parents' *marriages* and the climate of their *postdivorce* family lives.

Misconception 3: Divorce Means You Are no Longer a Family

There's this myth that as long as you stay married your family is good but as soon as you announce you're separating, your family is thrown into the bad zone. Your family goes from being "intact" to being "dissolved," form two-parent to single parent, from functional to dysfunctional. Even though we all know that people don't jump from happy marriages right into divorce, there is an assumption that the decision to separate is the critical marker. It doesn't seem to matter whether your marital relationship was terrible, whether you were miserable and your children troubled. Just as long as you are married and living together in one household, the sign over the front door clearly states to the world, "We're a normal family."

The inaccurate and misleading message that divorce destroys families is harmful to both parents and children because it hides and denies all the positive ways that families can be rearranged after divorce. It sends the destructive message to children that divorce means they only get to keep one parent and they will no longer be part of a family. Although two-parent first-married households now represent less than 25 percent of all households, and an increasing number of children each year are raised by unmarried adults, many people cling to the belief that healthy families can only be two-parent married families and social change is always bad and threatening to our very foundations. . . .

⋅◖⦿◗⋅

The truth is that although some divorces result in family breakdown, the vast majority do not. While divorce changes the form of the family from one household to two, from a nuclear family to a binuclear one, it does not need to change the way children think and feel about the significant relationships within their families. This does not mean that divorce is not painful or difficult, but over the years, as postdivorce families change and even expand, most remain capable of meeting children's needs for family.

Misconception 4: Divorce Leaves Children without Fathers

This message is linked closely with the preceding one because when we say that divorce destroys families we really mean that fathers disappear from the family. The myths that accompany this message are that fathers are "deadbeat dads" who abandon their kids and leave their families impoverished. The message strongly implies that fathers don't care and are unwilling or unable to make continuing commitments to their children. While this reflects the reality for a minority of divorced fathers, the majority of fathers continue to have loving relationships with their children and contribute financially to their upbringing. . . .

Misconception 5: Exspouses Are Incapable of Getting Along

. . . Although we have come to realize that parents who divorce still need to have some relationship with one another, the belief that it's not really possible still lingers. In fact, when exspouses remain friends they are viewed as a little strange and their relationship is suspect. Yet, the truth is that many divorced parents *are* cooperative and effective coparents. Like good divorces and involved fathers, they are mostly invisible in the media. . . .

Misconception 6: Divorce Turns Everyone into Exfamily; In-Laws Become Outlaws

When it comes to the semantics of divorce-speak, all of the kinship ties that got established by marriage dissolve abruptly. On the day of the legal divorce, my husband and all of his relatives suddenly became exes. But even though the kinship is *legally* terminated, meaningful relationships often continue. My friend Jan, during her fifteen-year marriage, formed a very close relationship with her mother-in-law. Now, twenty years later, she still calls her eighty-two-year-old exmother-in-law "Mom," talks with her several times a week and has dinner with her weekly. Exmother-in-law is certainly not an adequate description of this ongoing relationship.

As a culture we continue to resist accepting divorce as a normal endpoint to marriage even though it is an option chosen by almost half of those who marry. It is this cultural lag, this denial of current realities that causes the inaccurate language, not only for the family ties that continue but also for the family we inherit when we, our former spouses, our parents or our children remarry. Kinship language is important because it provides a shorthand way for us to identify relationships without wading through tedious explanations. . . .

Misconception 7: Stepparents Aren't Real Parents

. . . Children and their new stepparents start off their relationships with two strikes against them. They have to fight an uphill battle to overcome negative expectations, and they have to do so without much help from society. Since almost 85 percent of the children with divorced parents will have a stepparent at some time in their lives, it is shocking that we know so little about how these relationships work. Clearly, societal resistance to recognizing the broad spectrum of postdivorce families has hindered the development of good role models for stepchildren and their stepparents.

Painting a False Picture

Taken together, these negative messages paint a false picture of divorce, one that assumes family ties are irretrievably broken so that postdivorce family relationships appear to be nonexistent. Despite these destructive messages, many divorced parents meet the needs of their children by creating strong families after divorce. Without a doubt, divorce is painful and creates stress for families, but it is important to remember that most recover, maintaining some of their kinship relationships and adding new ones over time.

By making good divorces invisible we have accepted bad divorces as the norm. In so doing, children and their divorced parents are being given inaccurate messages that conflict with the realities they live and make them feel deviant and stigmatized. It is time we challenge these outdated, ill-founded messages and replace them with new ones that acknowledge and accurately reflect current realities.

The Distortions of Oversimplifying

Just a little over a decade ago, in January 1989, the *New York Times* Magazine ran a cover story called "Children after Divorce," which created a wave of panic in divorced parents and their children. Judith Wallerstein and her coauthor, Sandra Blakeslee, a staff writer for the *New York Times,* noted their newest unexpected finding. Calling it the "sleeper effect," they concluded that only ten years after divorce did it become apparent that girls experience "serious effects of divorce at the time they are entering young adulthood."

When one of the most prestigious newspapers in the world highlights the findings of a study, most readers take it seriously. "That 66 percent of young women in our study between the ages of nineteen and twenty-three will suffer debilitating effects of their parents' divorce years later" immediately became generalized to the millions of female children with divorced parents. The message—just when you think everything may be okay, the doom of divorce will rear its ugly head—is based on a *mere eighteen out of the grand total of twenty-seven women* interviewed in this age group. This detail wasn't mentioned in the fine print of the article but is buried in the appendix of the book that was scheduled for publication a month after the *New York Times* story appeared. And it is on this slim data that the seeds of a myth are planted. We are still living with the fallout.

In sharp contrast to Wallerstein's view that parental divorce has a powerful devastating impact on children well into adulthood, another psychologist made headlines with a completely opposite thesis. In her book, *The Nurture Assumption: Why Children Turn Out the Way They Do,* Judith Rich Harris proposes that what parents do makes little difference in how their children's lives turn out. Half of the variation in children's behavior and personality is due to genes, claims Harris, and the other half to environmental factors, mainly their peer relationships. For this reason, Harris asserts parental divorce is not responsible for all the ills it is blamed for.

These extreme positions—of divorce as disaster and divorce as inconsequential—oversimplify the realities of our complex lives. Genes and contemporary relationships notwithstanding, we have strong evidence that parents still make a significant difference in their children's development. Genetic inheritance and peer relationships are part of the story but certainly not the whole story.

Sorting Out the Research Findings

Drawing conclusions across the large body of research on divorce is difficult. Studies with different paradigms ask different questions that lead to different answers. A classic wisdom story shows the problem. Three blind men bumped into an elephant as they walked through the woods. They didn't know what it was, but each prided himself on his skill at "seeing." So one blind man reached out and carefully explored the elephant's leg. He described in great detail the rough, scratchy surface that was huge and round. "Aha, this is an ancient mighty tree. We're in a new forest." "No, no," said the blind man who had taken hold of the elephant's trunk. "We're in great danger—this is a writhing snake, bigger than any in our hometown. Run!" The third man laughed at them both. He'd been touching the elephant's tusk, noticing the smooth hard surface, the gentle curve, the rounded end. "Nonsense! We have discovered an exquisitely carved horn for announcing the emperor's arrival."

The blind men described what they "saw" accurately. Their mistake was to claim that what they saw was the whole. Much like the three blind men, researchers see different parts of the divorce elephant, which then frames their investigations.

It should come, then, as no surprise that reports of the findings about divorce are often contradictory and confusing. It is impossible for any study to take account of all the complexities of real life, or of the individual differences that allow one family to thrive in a situation that would create enormous stress, and frayed relationships, in another. But it is in these variations that we can begin to make sense of how divorce impacts the lives of individuals and families.

Facing Reality

Hallmark Cards recently launched a line of greeting cards called "Ties That Bind" aimed at various nontraditional unions—from stepfamilies to adopted child households to unmarried partnerships. "Our cards reflect the times," says Marita Wesely-Clough, trend group manager at Hallmark. "Relationships today are so nebulous that they are hard to pin down, but in creating products, we have to be aware that they are there. Companies need to respect and be sensitive to how people are truly living their lives now, and not how they might wish or hope for them to live."

Advertising agencies and marketing services make it their business to assess social realities. To sell their products, they have to evaluate the needs and desires of their potential consumers. They do not share the popular cultural anxiety about the changes in families. Instead they study them and alter their products to suit. Policy makers would do well to take some lessons from them and alter their preconceived notions about families to reflect current realities.

While the political focus today is on saving marriages and preserving traditional family values, Americans in large numbers are dancing to their own drummers. They're cohabiting in increasingly large numbers, having more children "out of wedlock" and engaging in serial marriages. While the rates of divorce have come down from their 1981 highs, they have leveled off at a high rate that is predicted to remain stable. To meet the needs of children and parents, we need to burst the balloon about idealized families and support families as they really live their lives. And that means we have to face the true complexities of *our* families and not search for simple answers.

As you read this book, keep in mind that we can all look back on our childhoods and note something about our mothers or fathers or sisters or brothers that has had lasting effects on our personalities. If you are looking to answer the question of whether a parental divorce results in children having more or less problems than children who grew up in other living situations, you will be disappointed. Nor will you find answers to whether the stresses of divorce are worse for children than other stresses in life. However, you will find answers here to questions about how and why individual children respond in different ways to the variations in their divorced families.

Divorce is a stressful life event that requires increased focus on parenting. The effort and care that parents put into establishing their postdivorce families are crucial and will pay off over the years in their many benefits to the children. But remember, families are complex, and if you find easy answers, they are likely to be wrong.

POSTSCRIPT

Does Divorce Have Long-Term Damaging Effects on Children?

Because about 45 percent of first marriages and about 60 percent of second marriages end in divorce, it is a major problem for the individuals involved and, potentially, for the society as a whole. Most writings emphasize the negative effects of divorce, especially for the children. These include Maggie Gallagher, *The Abolition of Marriage: How We Destroy Lasting Love* (Regnery, 1996); Barbara Dafoe Whitehead, *The Divorce Culture: How Divorce Became an Entitlement and How It Is Blighting the Lives of Our Children* (Alfred A. Knopf, 1997); Richard T. Gill, *Posterity Lost: Progress, Ideology, and the Decline of the American Family* (Rowman & Littlefield, 1997); James Q. Wilson, *The Marriage Problem: How Our Culture Has Weakened Families* (HarperCollins, 2002); Judith Wallerstein, *The Unexpected Legacy of Divorce* (Hyperion, 2000); Elizabeth Marquardt, *Between Two Worlds: The Inner Lives of Children of Divorce* (Crown, 2006); and Linda Waite and Maggie Gallagher, *The Case for Staying Married* (Oxford University Press, 2005).

The writings that minimize the harmful effects of divorce include Constance Ahrons, *We're Still Family: What Grown Children Have to Say about Their Parents' Divorce*, (Harper Collins, 2004); E. L. Kain, *The Myth of Family Decline* (D. C. Heath, 1990); and Mavis Hetherington and John Kelly, *For Better or for Worse: Divorce Reconsidered* (W. W. Norton, 2002). David Popenoe and Jean Bethke Elshtain's book *Promises to Keep: Decline and Renewal of Marriage in America* (Rowman & Littlefield, 1996) discusses the negative impacts of divorce but also discusses signs of the renewal of marriage.

Works that analyze changes in marriage and the family along with divorce include Betty Farrell's *Family: The Making of an Idea, an Institution, and a Controversy in American Culture* (Westview Press, 1999); Karla B. Hackstaff's *Marriage in a Culture of Divorce* (Temple University Press, 1999); Jessica Weiss's *To Have and to Hold: Marriage, the Baby Boom, and Social Change* (University of Chicago Press, 2000); Barbara J. Risman's *Gender Vertigo: American Families in Transition* (Yale University Press, 1998); Ronald D. Taylor and Margaret C. Wang, eds., *Resilience Across Contexts: Family, Work, Culture, and Community* (Lawrence Erlbaum, 2000); Linda J. Waite and Maggie Gallagher, *The Case for Marriage: Why Married People Are Happier, Healthier, and Better Off Financially* (Doubleday, 2000); Daniel P. Moynihan, et al., eds., *Future of the Family* (Russell Sage Foundation, 2004); and Lynne M. Casper and Suzanne M. Bianchi, *Continuity and Change in the American Family* (Sage, 2002). For council on how to strengthen marriages, see David P. Gushee, *Getting Marriage Right: Realistic Counsel for Saving and*

Strengthening Relationships (Baker Books, 2004). For information on divorce among seniors, see Deirdre Bair, *Calling it Quits: Late-life Divorce and Starting Over,* 1st ed. (Random House, 2007). For advice on handling divorce issues, see Mark A. Fine and John H. Harvey (eds.), *Handbook of Divorce and Relationship Dissolution* (Lawrence Erlbaum, 2006). Finally, for information on the adjustment of children, see Robert E. Emery, *Marriage, Divorce, and Children's Adjustment,* 2nd ed. (Sage Publications, 1999).

ISSUE 5

Should Mothers Stay Home with Their Children?

YES: Claudia Wallis, from "The Case for Staying Home," *Time* (March 22, 2004)

NO: Neil Gilbert, from "What Do Women Really Want?" *The Public Interest* (Winter 2005)

ISSUE SUMMARY

YES: Journalist Claudia Wallis reports that more and more mothers are choosing to quit work and stay home to care for their children. The work demands on professional women have increased to the point that very few can do both work and family. Forced to choose, growing numbers choose family.

NO: Neil Gilbert, Chernin Professor of Social Welfare at the University of California at Berkeley, challenges the opt-out myth, which rests on "thin" data. The real opt-out story is the growing number of professional women who are not having children and, of those who do have children, the increasing number who use day-care services.

The fascinating aspect of social life is how many different trends and changes significantly affect our lives and choices. For example, consider married women and their work-family choices. Ever since the 1950s, married women have increasingly participated in the labor force. Why? The reasons are numerous. Women want the money for themselves. Women need the money for the family. Women want the challenge of a career. Women want the social life that work provides. Women want independence. The list of reasons goes on and on. These reasons change, however, as the context changes. For example, since 1965 the median price of the one-family home, compared to the average income of private nonagricultural workers, has doubled. Thus, the single earner family is having much more difficulty buying a house. This trend helps explain why married women increasingly enter or stay in the labor force. Attitudes have also changed. In 1968, a large survey asked young people what they expected to be doing at age 35. About 30 percent of the 20- to 21-year-olds said that they would be working. Seven years later, 65 percent of 20- to 21-year olds said they would be working. That is an astounding change.

Educational changes in the past half century have also been dramatic. As is pointed out in Issue 10, females have overtaken males in most aspects of education. Reversing 350 years of history, women are now outnumbering men in college and currently earn 57 percent of all bachelor degrees, 58 percent of all masters degrees, and are rapidly closing the M.D. and Ph.D. gaps. Women are also more focused on professional degrees while in college as demonstrated by their selection of majors. In 1966, 40 percent of college women graduates majored in education and 17 percent majored in English/literature, but only 2 percent majored in business. Women have stopped shying away from the business world. The percentage of female BA business degrees went from 9 percent in 1971 to 49 percent in 1997, while it went from 4 percent to 39 percent for MA business degrees and from 5 percent to 70 percent for law degrees.

Many other changes are associated with these and other changes in the labor force participation of women. The feminist movement, which surged in the 1960s and 1970s, encouraged women to fully develop their abilities and have challenging careers. It also spearheaded a social and political movement for equality for women. The Civil Rights Act of 1964 included gender in its equality protections, and years of discrimination lawsuits and voluntary changes by employers have greatly altered the workplace. Perhaps the most important factor was the invention of the birth control pill, because it gave women control over their fertility and changed the ramifications of engaging in sex. It contributed to the increasing age of individuals at marriage, which made educational preparation for careers more feasible. It also contributed to the substantial decline in fertility. Women are having fewer children on average and are increasingly choosing not to have any children.

Another trend affecting choices and behaviors is the increasing time scarcity. The percentage of males working more than 50 hours a week increased from 21.0 to 26.5 from 1970 to 2000 and, for females, from 5.2 to 11.3. Many women with professional careers are in this group and suffer from time scarcity. This brings us to the debate question: Should mothers stay home with their children? Most mothers want to both work and raise children at home, but most mothers find it very difficult to manage both. For decades, the trend for mothers was to increasingly enter or stay in the labor market. According to Claudia Wallis, a journalist for *Time*, this trend has stopped and started to decline slightly. She explains the opting-out trend as the preferred choice of women when their husband's income is sufficient. She even argues that this is the responsible thing to do. Neil Gilbert argues that Wallis's view is a fiction that melts away when the data are properly analyzed.

YES ↵

Claudia Wallis

The Case for Staying Home

It's 6:35 in the morning, and Cheryl Nevins, 34, dressed for work in a silky black maternity blouse and skirt, is busily tending to Ryan, 2½, and Brendan, 11 months, at their home in the leafy Edgebrook neighborhood of Chicago. Both boys are sobbing because Reilly, the beefy family dog, knocked Ryan over. In a blur of calm, purposeful activity, Nevins, who is 8 months pregnant, shoves the dog out into the backyard, changes Ryan's diaper on the family-room rug, heats farina in the microwave and feeds Brendan cereal and sliced bananas while crooning *Open, Shut Them* to encourage the baby to chew. Her husband Joe, 35, normally out the door by 5:30 a.m. for his job as a finance manager for Kraft Foods, makes a rare appearance in the morning muddle. "I do want to go outside with you," he tells Ryan, who is clinging to his leg, "but Daddy has to work every day except Saturdays and Sundays. That stinks."

At 7:40, Vera Orozco, the nanny, arrives to begin her 10½-hour shift at the Nevinses'. Cheryl, a labor lawyer for the Chicago board of education, hands over the baby and checks her e-mail from the kitchen table. "I almost feel apprehensive if I leave for work without logging on," she confesses. Between messages, she helps Ryan pull blue Play-Doh from a container, then briefs Orozco on the morning's events: "They woke up early. Ryan had his poop this morning, this guy has not." Throughout the day, Orozco will note every meal and activity on a tattered legal pad on the kitchen counter so Nevins can stay up to speed.

Suddenly it's 8:07, and the calm mom shifts from cruise control into hyperdrive. She must be out the door by 8:10 to make the 8:19 train. Once on the platform, she punches numbers into her cell phone, checks her voice mail and then leaves a message for a co-worker. On the train, she makes more calls and proofreads documents. "Right now, work is crazy," says Nevins, who has been responsible for negotiating and administering seven agreements between the board and labor unions.

Nevins is "truly passionate" about her job, but after seven years, she's about to leave it. When the baby arrives, she will take off at least a year, maybe two, maybe five. "It's hard. I'm giving up a great job that pays well, and I have a lot of respect and authority," she says. The decision to stay home was a tough one, but most of her working-mom friends have made the same choice. She concludes, "I know it's the right thing."

Then, 15 years ago, it all seemed so doable. Bring home the bacon, fry it up in a pan, split the second shift with some sensitive New Age man. But slowly the snappy, upbeat work-life rhythm has changed for women in high-powered posts like Nevins. The U.S. workweek still averages around 34 hours, thanks in part to a sluggish manufacturing sector. But for those in financial services, it's 55 hours; for top executives in big corporations, it's 60 to 70, says Catalyst, a research and consulting group that focuses on women in business. For dual-career couples with kids under 18, the combined work hours have grown from 81 a week in 1977 to 91 in 2002, according to the Families and Work Institute. E-mail, pagers and cell phones promised to allow execs to work from home. Who knew that would mean that home was no longer a sanctuary? Today BlackBerrys sprout on the sidelines of Little League games. Cell phones vibrate at the school play. And it's back to the e-mail after *Goodnight Moon*. "We are now the workaholism capital of the world, surpassing the Japanese," laments sociologist Arlie Hochschild, author of *The Time Bind: When Work Becomes Home and Home Becomes Work.*

Meanwhile, the pace has quickened on the home front, where a mother's job has expanded to include managing a packed schedule of child-enhancement activities. In their new book *The Mommy Myth*, Susan Douglas, a professor of communication studies at the University of Michigan, and Meredith Michaels, who teaches philosophy at Smith College, label the phenomenon the New Momism. Nowadays, they write, our culture insists that "to be a remotely decent mother, a woman has to devote her entire physical, psychological, emotional, and intellectual being, 24/7, to her children." It's a standard of success that's "impossible to meet," they argue. But that sure doesn't stop women from trying.

For most mothers—and fathers, for that matter—there is little choice but to persevere on both fronts to pay the bills. Indeed, 72% of mothers with children under 18 are in the work force—a figure that is up sharply from 47% in 1975 but has held steady since 1997. And thanks in part to a dodgy economy, there's growth in another category, working women whose husbands are unemployed, which has risen to 6.4% of all married couples.

But in the professional and managerial classes, where higher incomes permit more choices, a reluctant revolt is under way. Today's women execs are less willing to play the juggler's game, especially in its current high-speed mode, and more willing to sacrifice paychecks and prestige for time with their family. Like Cheryl Nevins, most of these women are choosing not so much to drop out as to stop out, often with every intention of returning. Their mantra: You can have it all, just not all at the same time. Their behavior, contrary to some popular reports, is not a June Cleaver-ish embrace of old-fashioned motherhood but a new, nonlinear approach to building a career and an insistence on restoring some kind of sanity. "What this group is staying home from is the 80-hour-a-week job," says Hochschild. "They are committed to work, but many watched their mothers and fathers be ground up by very long hours, and they would like to give their own children more than they got. They want a work-family balance."

Because these women represent a small and privileged sector, the dimensions of the exodus are hard to measure. What some experts are zeroing in on is the first-ever drop-off in workplace participation by married mothers with a child less than 1 year old. That figure fell from 59% in 1997 to 53% in 2000. The drop may sound modest, but, says Howard Hayghe, an economist at the Bureau of Labor Statistics, "that's huge," and the figure was roughly the same in 2002. Significantly, the drop was mostly among women who were white, over 30 and well educated.

Census data reveal an uptick in stay-at-home moms who hold graduate or professional degrees—the very women who seemed destined to blast through the glass ceiling. Now 22% of them are home with their kids. A study by Catalyst found that 1 in 3 women with M.B.A.s are not working full-time (it's 1 in 20 for their male peers). Economist and author Sylvia Ann Hewlett, who teaches at Columbia University, says she sees a brain drain throughout the top 10% of the female labor force (those earning more than $55,000). "What we have discovered in looking at this group over the last five years," she says, "is that many women who have any kind of choice are opting out."

Other experts say the drop-out rate isn't climbing but is merely more visible now that so many women are in high positions. In 1971 just 9% of medical degrees, 7% of law degrees and 4% of M.B.A.s were awarded to women; 30 years later, the respective figures were 43%, 47% and 41%.

The Generation Factor

For an older group of female professionals who came of age listening to Helen Reddy roar, the exodus of younger women can seem disturbingly regressive. Fay Clayton, 58, a partner in a small Chicago law firm, watched in dismay as her 15-person firm lost three younger women who left after having kids, though one has since returned part time. "I fear there is a generational split and possibly a step backwards for younger women," she says.

Others take a more optimistic view. "Younger women have greater expectations about the work-life balance," says Joanne Brundage, 51, founder and executive director of Mothers & More, a mothers' support organization with 7,500 members and 180 chapters in the U.S. While boomer moms have been reluctant to talk about their children at work for fear that "people won't think you're a professional," she observes, younger women "feel more entitled to ask for changes and advocate for themselves." That sense of confidence is reflected in the evolution of her organization's name. When Brundage founded it in Elmhurst, Ill., 17 years ago, it was sheepishly called FEMALE, for Formerly Employed Mothers at Loose Ends.

Brundage may be ignoring that young moms can afford to think flexibly about life and work while pioneering boomers first had to prove they could excel in high-powered jobs. But she's right about the generational difference. A 2001 survey by Catalyst of 1,263 men and women born from 1964 to 1975 found that Gen Xers "didn't want to have to make the kind of trade-offs the previous generation made. They're rejecting the stresses and sacrifices," says Catalyst's Paulette Gerkovich. "Both women and men rated personal and family goals higher than career goals."

A newer and larger survey, conducted late last year by the Boston-area marketing group Reach Advisors, provides more evidence of a shift in attitudes. Gen X (which it defined as those born from 1965 to 1979) moms and dads said they spent more time on child rearing and household tasks than did boomer parents (born from 1945 to 1964). Yet Gen Xers were much more likely than boomers to complain that they wanted more time. "At first we thought, Is this just a generation of whiners?" says Reach Advisors president James Chung. "But they really wish they had more time with their kids." In the highest household-income bracket ($120,000 and up), Reach Advisors found that 51% of Gen X moms were home full time, compared with 33% of boomer moms. But the younger stay-at-home moms were much more likely to say they intended to return to work: 46% of Gen Xers expressed that goal, compared with 34% of boomers.

Chung and others speculate that the attitude differences can be explained in part by forces that shaped each generation. While boomer women sought career opportunities that were unavailable to their mostly stay-at-home moms, Gen Xers were the latchkey kids and the children of divorce. Also, their careers have bumped along in a roller-coaster, boom-bust economy that may have shaken their faith in finding reliable satisfaction at work.

Pam Pala, 35, of Salt Lake City, Utah, is in some ways typical. She spent years building a career in the heavily male construction industry, rising to the position of construction project engineer with a big firm. But after her daughter was born 11 months ago, she decided to stay home to give her child the attention Pala had missed as a kid. "I grew up in a divorced family. My mom couldn't take care of us because she had to work," she says. "We went to babysitters or stayed home alone and were scared and hid under the bathroom counter whenever the doorbell rang." Pala wants to return to work when her daughter is in school, and she desperately hopes she won't be penalized for her years at home. "I have a feeling that I'll have to start lower on the totem pole than where I left," she says. "It seems unfair."

Maternal Desire and Doubts

Despite such misgivings, most women who step out of their careers find expected delights on the home front, not to mention the enormous relief of no longer worrying about shortchanging their kids. Annik Miller, 32, of Minneapolis, Minn., decided not to return to her job as a business-systems consultant at Wells Fargo Bank after she checked out day-care options for her son Alex, now 11 months. "I had one woman look at me honestly and say she could promise that my son would get undivided attention eight times each day—four bottles and four diaper changes," says Miller. "I appreciated her honesty, but I knew I couldn't leave him."

Others appreciate a slower pace and being there when a child asks a tough question. In McLean, Va., Oakie Russell's son Dylan, 8, recently inquired, out of the blue, "Mom, who is God's father?" Says Russell, 45, who gave up a dream job at PBS: "So, you're standing at the sink with your hands in the dishwater and you're thinking, 'Gee, that's really complicated. But I'm awfully glad I'm the one you're asking.'"

Psychologist Daphne de Marneffe speaks to these private joys in a new book, *Maternal Desire* (Little Brown). De Marneffe argues that feminists and American society at large have ignored the basic urge that most mothers feel to spend meaningful time with their children. She decries the rushed fragments of quality time doled out by working moms trying to do it all. She writes, "Anyone who has tried to 'fit everything in' can attest to how excruciating the five-minute wait at the supermarket checkout line becomes, let alone a child's slow-motion attempt to tie her own shoes when you're running late getting her to school." The book, which puts an idyllic gloss on staying home, could launch a thousand resignations.

What de Marneffe largely omits is the sense of pride and meaning that women often gain from their work. Women who step out of their careers can find the loss of identity even tougher than the loss of income. "I don't regret leaving, but a huge part of me is gone," says Bronwyn Towle, 41, who surrendered a demanding job as a Washington lobbyist to be with her two sons. Now when she joins her husband Raymond, who works at the U.S. Chamber of Commerce, at work-related dinners, she feels sidelined. "Everyone will be talking about what they're doing," says Towle, "and you say, 'I'm a stay-at-home mom.' It's conference-buzz kill."

Last year, after her youngest child went to kindergarten, Towle eased back into the world of work. She found a part-time job in a forward-thinking architectural firm but hopes to return to her field eventually. "I wish there was more part-time or job-sharing work," she says. It's a wish expressed by countless formerly working moms.

Building On-Ramps

Hunter College sociologist Pamela Stone has spent the past few years interviewing 50 stay-at-home mothers in seven U.S. cities for a book on professional women who have dropped out. "Work is much more of a culprit in this than the more rosy view that it's all about discovering how great your kids are," says Stone. "Not that these mothers don't want to spend time with their kids. But many of the women I talked to have tried to work part time or put forth job-sharing plans, and they're shot down. Despite all the family-friendly rhetoric, the workplace for professionals is extremely, extremely inflexible."

That's what Ruth Marlin, 40, of New York City found even at the family-friendly International Planned Parenthood Federation. After giving birth to her second child, 15 months ago, she was allowed to ease back in part time. But Marlin, an attorney and a senior development officer, was turned down when she asked to make the part-time arrangement permanent. "With the job market contracted so much, the opportunities just aren't there anymore," says Marlin, who hates to see her $100,000 law education go to waste. "Back in the dotcom days, people just wanted employees to stay. There was more flexibility. Who knows? Maybe the market will change."

There are signs that in some corners it is changing. In industries that depend on human assets, serious work is being done to create more part-time and flexible positions. At PricewaterhouseCoopers, 10% of the firm's female partners are on a part-time schedule, according to the accounting firm's chief diversity officer, Toni Riccardi. And, she insists, it's not career suicide: "A three-day week might slow your progress, but it won't prohibit you" from climbing the career ladder. The company has also begun to address the e-mail ball and chain. In December PWC shut down for 11 days over the holidays for the first time ever. "We realize people do need to rejuvenate," says Riccardi. "They don't, if their eye is on the BlackBerry and their hand is on a keyboard."

PWC is hardly alone. Last month economist Hewlett convened a task force of leaders from 14 companies and four law firms, including Goldman Sachs and Pfizer, to discuss what she calls the hidden brain drain of women and minority professionals. "We are talking about how to create off-ramps and on-ramps, slow lanes and acceleration ramps" so that workers can more easily leave, slow down or re-enter the work force, she explains.

"This is a war for talent," says Carolyn Buck Luce, a partner at the accounting firm Ernst & Young, who co-chairs the task force. Over the past 20 years, half of new hires at Ernst & Young have been women, she notes, and the firm is eager not only to keep them but to draw back those who have left to tend their children. This spring Deloitte Touche Tohmatsu will launch a Personal Pursuits program, allowing above-average performers to take up to five years of unpaid leave for personal reasons. Though most benefits will be suspended, the firm will continue to cover professional licensing fees for those on leave and will pay to send them for weeklong annual training sessions to keep their skills in shape. Such efforts have spawned their own goofy jargon. Professionals who return to their ex-employers are known as boomerangs, and the effort to reel them back in is called alumni relations.

One reason businesses are getting serious about the brain drain is demographics. With boomers nearing retirement, a shortfall of perhaps 10 million workers appears likely by 2010. "The labor shortage has a lot to do with it," says Melinda Wolfe, managing director and head of Goldman Sachs' global leadership and diversity.

Will these programs work? Will part-time jobs really be part time, as opposed to full-time jobs paid on a partial basis? Will serious professionals who shift into a slow lane be able to pick up velocity when their kids are grown? More important, will corporate culture evolve to a point where employees feel genuinely encouraged to use these options? Anyone who remembers all the talk about flex time in the 1980s will be tempted to dismiss the latest ideas for making the workplace family-friendly. But this time, perhaps, the numbers may be on the side of working moms—along with many working dads who are looking for options.

On-ramps, slow lanes, flexible options and respect for all such pathways can't come soon enough for mothers eager to set examples and offer choices for the next generation. Terri Laughlin, 38, a stay-at-home mom and former psychology professor at the University of Nebraska at Lincoln, was alarmed a few weeks ago when her daughters Erin, 8, and Molly, 6, announced their intentions to marry men "with enough money so we can stay at home." Says Laughlin: "I want to make sure they realize that although it's wonderful staying at home, that's only one of many options. What I hope to show them is that at some point I can re-create myself and go back to work."

Neil Gilbert

→ **NO**

What Do Women Really Want?

With journalists as well as social scientists continually on the lookout for new trends, the public is regularly treated to the discovery of social "revolutions." One of the latest concerns women and work. In October 2003, Lisa Belkin detected an "opt-out revolution" in her *New York Times Magazine* article about accomplished women leaving high-powered jobs to stay home with their kids. Six months later, reports on the revolution were still going strong. For example, the March 22, 2004 cover of *Time* showed a young child clinging to his mother's leg alongside the headline, "The Case for Staying Home: Why More Young Moms Are Opting Out of the Rat Race." But the evidence on this score is thin. Both the *New York Times* and *Time* stories are based mainly on evocative anecdotes. Princeton college graduates with law degrees from Harvard staying home to change diapers may be absorbing as a human-interest story. But as the saying goes, the plural of anecdote is not data.

The limited empirical evidence offered in support of the opt-out revolution draws upon facts such as these: 22 percent of mothers with graduate degrees are at home with their children, one in three women with an MBA does not work full time, and 26 percent of women approaching the most senior levels of management do not want to be promoted. However, with information of this sort one needs a ouija board to detect a social trend, let alone a revolution. The fact that 57 percent of mothers from the Stanford University class of 1981 stayed home with their young children for at least a year gives no indication of whether the percentage of Stanford graduates remaining at home with their children has increased, decreased, or remained the same over time.

But we know that some things have changed over time. The main difference between women in the 1970s and today is that a substantially higher percentage are currently receiving degrees in law or medicine, or obtaining graduate education in general. Between 1970 and 1997 the proportion of degrees awarded to women soared by almost 500 percent in medicine, 800 percent in law, and 1000 percent in business. Even if one-third of all the women currently receiving these degrees opt out of professional life, the remaining two-thirds amount to a significant increase in women's employment in these areas over the last three decades.

At the moment, women opting out of high-powered careers to stay home with their children are a minor element in a profound life-style trend that has

Reprinted with permission from *The Public Interest*, Winter 2005, pp. 21–27, 38.

extended over the last several decades—a development deftly portrayed, some might say celebrated, in the media. After a six-year run, the popular HBO series "Sex and the City" ended in 2004 with what was widely reported as a happy ending. Each of the four heroines, in their late thirties and early forties, found partners and commitment, while also pursuing gratifying careers. The series finale was a paean to love and individual fulfillment. But as for family life, these four vibrant, successful women approaching the terminus of their childbearing years ended up with only two marriages and one child between them. As a mirror of society, the media shift from kids bouncing off the walls in the "Brady Bunch" to the .25 fertility rate in "Sex and the City" several decades later clearly reflects the cultural and demographic trends over this period.

Today, a little over one in five women in their early forties are childless. That is close to double the proportion of childless women in 1976. Compared to a relatively few Ivy-League law graduates who have traded the bar for rocking the cradle, the abdication of motherhood poses an alternative and somewhat more compelling answer to the question: Who is opting out of what? Women are increasingly having fewer children and a growing proportion are choosing not to have any children at all. And those who have children are delegating their care to others. If there has been an "opt-out revolution," the dramatic increase in childlessness—from one in ten to almost one in five women—and the rise in out-of-home care for young kids would probably qualify more than the shift of a relatively small group of professional-class women from high-powered careers to childrearing activities.

The Choices Women Make

Talk of social revolutions conveys a sense of fundamental change in people's values—a new awakening that is compelling women to substitute one type of life for another. The "opt-out revolution" implies that whatever it is women really want, they all pretty much want the same thing when it comes to career and family. It may have looked that way in earlier times. Although the question of what women want has plagued men for ages, it became a serious issue for women only in modern times in the advanced industrialized countries. Before the contraceptive revolution of the mid 1960s, biology may not have been destiny, but it certainly contributed to the childbearing fate of women who engaged in sexual activity. Most women needed men for their economic survival before the equal-opportunity movement in the 1960s, which opened access to most all careers. Moreover, the expansion of white-collar jobs and jobs for secondary earners since the 1960s has presented women with a viable range of employment alternatives to traditional domestic life. Taken together, these advances in contraceptive technology and civil rights along with labor market changes have transformed women's opportunities to control and shape their personal lives. As Catherine Hakim, a senior research fellow at the London School of Economics, has pointed out, this historic shift allows modern women to exercise work and family choices that were heretofore unknown to all but a privileged few.

And what are these preferences? Taking family size as a powerful indicator of life-style choice, we can distinguish at least four general categories that form a continuum of work-family preferences among women in the United States. At one end of the continuum are women with three or more children. Most of these women derive most of their sense of personal identity and achievement from the traditional childrearing responsibilities and from practicing the domestic arts. While all mothers tend to love their children, these women also enjoy being around kids on a daily basis. In 1976, about 59 percent of women over 40 years of age had three or more children. But as women gained control over procreation and employment opportunities opened, fewer of them took this traditional route. Today, only 29 percent of the women over 40 years of age have three or more children.

At the other end of the continuum are women who are childless—often by choice. Here personal success tends to be measured by achievements in business, political, intellectual, and artistic life rather than in the traditional realms of motherhood and childrearing. This is a highly individualistic, work-centered group engaged in what might be called the "postmodern" life style. As already noted, since 1976 the proportion of childless women over the age of 40 has almost doubled, representing 18 percent of all the women in that age cohort today.

In the middle of the life-style continuum, about 52 percent of women currently over 40 have either one or two children. These women are interested in paid work, but not so vigorously committed to a career that they would forego motherhood. Although a bare majority, this group is often seen as representative of all women—and of the women "who want it all." In balancing the demands of employment and family, women with one child normally tip the scales in favor of their careers, while the group with two children leans more toward domestic life. Thus the women clustered around the center of the continuum can be divided into two basic categories—"neo-traditional" and "modern"—that vary in degrees from the traditional and the postmodern life styles.

The neo-traditional group contains families with two children whose working mothers are physically and emotionally invested more in their home life than their jobs, which are often part-time. Since 1976 the proportion of women over age 40 with two children has increased by 75 percent and currently amounts to about 35 percent of the women in that cohort. The modern family usually involves a working mother with one child; these women are more career-oriented and devote greater time and energy to their paid employment than neo-traditional women. The proportion of women over 40 with one child has climbed by almost 90 percent since 1976, and currently amounts to 17 percent of the women in that cohort.

As general types, the traditional, neo-traditional, modern, and postmodern categories help draw attention to both the diversity of work and family choices and to how the size of these groups has shifted over the last three decades. Needless to say, in each group there are women who do not fit the ideal-type—childless women who do not work and women employed full-time with three or more children at home. Also, there are women in each group who would have preferred to have more or fewer children than they ended up with. And certainly some women who would prefer not to work and to have additional children are compelled out of economic necessity to participate in the labor force and have fewer children. However, for most people in the advanced industrial countries what is often considered economic "necessity" amounts to a preferred level of material comfort—home ownership, automobiles, vacations, cell phones, DVDs, and the like. The trade-off between higher levels of material consumption and a more traditional domestic life is largely a matter of individual choice. Health has also not played much of a role in these changing family patterns. There is no strong indication that the physical status of the U.S. population has deteriorated over the last three decades in any way that would systematically account for the increasing proportion of women with only one or two children.

Many feminists like to portray women as a monolithic group whose shared interests are dominated by the common struggle to surmount biological determinism, patriarchal socialization, financial dependence on men, and work-place discrimination. And they would like public policies to reflect this supposed reality. However, in the course of exercising preferences about how to balance the demands of work and family, the heterogeneity of women's choices has become increasingly evident. This substantial variance has great importance for social policy. For it compels us to ask which groups of women—traditional, neo-traditional, modern, and postmodern—are really best served by today's so-called family-friendly policies.

Family Policy in the United States

The conventional package of "family-friendly" public policies involves benefits designed to reduce the tensions between work and family life, such as parental leave, family services, and day care. For the most part these policies address the needs of women in the neo-traditional and modern categories—those trying to balance work and family obligations. The costs of publicly subsidized day care are born by all taxpayers, but the programs offer no benefits to childless women who prefer the postmodern life style and are of little use to traditional stay-at-home mothers. Indeed, with few exceptions, childless women in full-time careers and those who remain at home to care for children are not the subjects of family-related policy deliberations.

Among the advanced industrial democracies the United States is considered a laggard in dispensing parental leave, day care, and other public subsidies to reduce the friction between raising a family and holding a job. The right to take 12 weeks of job-protected family leave was initiated in 1993. But the scope of coverage is limited to companies with 50 employees or more—and the leave is unpaid. Needless to say, unpaid leave is not a serious option for many low-income families. However, low-income families have benefited from the considerable rise in public spending for child care during the 1990s. Testifying before Congress in 2002, American Enterprise Institute scholar Douglas Besharov estimated that between 1994 and 1999 federal and state expenditures on child care programs climbed by almost 60 percent, from $8.9 billion to

$14.1 billion, most of which served low-income families. About $2 billion of additional support was delivered to mainly middle- and upper-income families through the child-care tax credit. Although $16 billion in publicly subsidized care is no trivial sum, it amounts to less than $900 for each child under five years of age.

The United States has moved slowly toward expanding conventional family-friendly arrangements in part because of ideological ambivalence in this area. Public sympathy for welfare programs that pay unmarried women to stay home and care for their children evaporated as the labor-force participation of married women with children younger than six years of age multiplied threefold, from under 20 percent in 1960 to over 60 percent in 2000. The increased public spending on day care is largely related to making it possible for welfare mothers to enter the labor force. Conservatives have long argued for strengthening work requirements in welfare programs. At the same time, many conservatives also support the idea of "putting less emphasis on policies that free up parents to be better workers, and more emphasis on policies that free up workers to be better parents"—a view expressed in the *Report to the Nation from the Commission on Children at Risk*. Liberals have traditionally resisted demands that welfare recipients should work for their benefits. But this position softens when feminists on the Left push for universal day care and other policies that encourage all mothers to enter the paid workplace. . . .

The case for rethinking what we mean by "family-friendly" policies is put forth not to advance one pattern of motherhood and employment over another, but to give equal consideration to the diverse values that influence how women respond to the conflicting demands of work and family life. As things now stand, public policies are far from neutral on the question of whether parents should look after their children or go to work and outsource the job of caring for the kids. As seen in the growth of public child-care spending, children have become an increasing source of paid employment. There will always be a few women leaving well-paid jobs to care for their children. But as an avant garde of the opt-out revolution, this group is unlikely to draw many recruits in the face of current policies, the full thrust of which reinforce the abdication of motherhood.

POSTSCRIPT

Should Mothers Stay Home with Their Children?

Choices are often difficult and working mothers have tough choices to make about how to balance career and family. I know that I would feel very deprived if I had to quit my professor's job to raise children even though children are a great joy. But I do not have to make this choice. This is what is obviously unfair about this issue. It is mostly a female problem. Men are not expected to quit their jobs and stay home and raise their children. Some, in fact, are doing just this because their wives are making far more money than they are, but this is rare. Perhaps this is what makes Douglas and Michael so angry (for they are angry in their book). Mothers are being told by the media that they should stay home for the good of the children. Why are fathers not also being told to stay home for the good of the children? Life is not fair, but we should make it as fair as possible.

According to Neil Gilbert, the evidence for the "new momism" is all around us. Look for it when you watch TV. Look at a couple of years of *Redbook, Good Housekeeping, People, E!, Us, InStyle, Family Life*, or *Parents*. For analyses of the new momism look at Pamela Stone, *Opting Out?: Why Women Really Quit Careers and Head Home* (University of California Press, 2007); Lisa A. Mainiero and Sherry E. Sullivan, *The Opt-Out Revolt* (Davies-Black, 2006); Phyllis Moen, *The Career Mystique* (Rowan & Littlefield, 2005); Ruth Feldstein, *Motherthehood in Black and White* (Cornell University Press, 2000); Ann Crittenden, *The Price of Motherhood* (Metropolitan Books, 2001); Susan Chira, *A Mother's Place: Choosing Work and Family Without Guilt or Shame* (Perennial, 1999); and Susan Maushart, *The Mask of Motherhood* (The New Press, 1999). Leslie Bennetts strongly advises women not to give up their careers in *The Feminine Mistake* (Voice/Hyperion, 2007) and Sylvia Ann Hewlett does the same in *Off-Ramps and On-Ramps: Keeping Talented Women on the Road to Success* (Harvard Business School Press, 2007).

For some recent discussions of the demands of work and family on women, see Suzanne M. Bianchi, John P. Robinson, and Melissa Milkie, *Changing Rhythms of Family Life* (American Sociological Association, 2006); Susan Thistle, *From Marriage to the Market* (University of California Press, 2006); Arlie Russell Hochschild, *The Second Shift* (Penguin Books, 2003); Daphne Spain and Suzanne M. Bianchi, *Balancing Act: Motherhood, Marriage, and Employment Among American Women* (Russell Sage Foundation, 1996); Nancy Kaltreider, ed., *Dilemmas of a Double Life: Women Balancing Careers and Relationships* (Jason, Aronson, 1997); and Anna Fels, *Necessary Dreams: Ambition in Women's Changing Lives* (Pantheon Books, 2004). Mary Eberstadt is the major critic of the working mothers who leave much of the childrearing to others. See her *Home-Alone America: The Hidden Toll of Daycare, Behavioral Drugs, and Other Parent Substitutes* (Penguin, 2004).

On the issue of time scarcity and time use, which factors into the debate on the tension between work and family, see *Fighting for Time: Shifting Boundaries of Work and Social Life* edited by Cynthia Fuchs-Epstein and Arne L. Kalleberg (Russell Sage Foundation, 2004); Phyllis Moen, *It's About Time: Couples and Careers* (Cornell University Press, 2003); Harriet B. Presser, *Working in a 24/7 Economy: Challenges for American Families* (Russell Sage Foundation, 2003); John Robinson and Geoffrey Godbey, *Time for Life: The Surprising Ways Americans Use Their Time*, 2nd edition (State University Press, 1999); Juliet Schor, *The Overworked American: The Unexpected Decline of Leisure* (Basic Books, 1991); Jerry A. Jacobs and Kathleen Gerson, *The Time Divide: Work, Family, and Gender Inequality* (Harvard University Press, 2004); and Cynthia Fuchs Epstein et al., *Paradox: Time Norms, Professional Life, Family, and Gender* (Routledge, 1999).

The issue of the tension between family and work is recently receiving much attention. See Jerry A. Jacobs, *The Time Divide: Work, Family, and Gender Inequality* (Harvard University Press, 2004); Harriet B. Presser, *Working in a 24/7 Economy: Challenges for American Families* (Russell Sage Foundation, 2003); Arlie Russell Hochschild, *The Commercialization of Intimate Life* (University of California Press, 2003); and Janet C. Gornick and Marcia K. Meyers, *Families that Work: Policies for Reconciling Parenthood and Employment* (Russell Sage Foundation, 2003). Brid Featherstone points out that government policies can reduce this stress in *Family Life and Family Support: A Feminist Analysis* (Palgrave Macmillan, 2004).

ISSUE 6

Should Same-Sex Marriages Be Legally Recognized?

YES: Human Rights Campaign, from "Answers to Questions about Marriage Equality" (HRC's FamilyNet Project, 2004)

NO: Peter Sprigg, from "Questions and Answers: What's Wrong with Letting Same-Sex Couples 'Marry'?" (Family Research Council, 2004)

ISSUE SUMMARY

YES: America's largest lesbian and gay organization, The Human Rights Campaign, presents many arguments for why same-sex couples should be able to marry. The main argument is fairness. Marriage confers many benefits that same-sex couples are deprived of.

NO: Researcher Peter Sprigg presents many arguments for why same-sex couples should not be able to marry. The main argument is that the state has the right and duty to specify who a person, whether straight or gay, can marry so no rights are violated.

In 1979 in Sioux Falls, South Dakota, Randy Rohl and Grady Quinn became the first acknowledged homosexual couple in America to receive permission from their high school principal to attend the senior prom together. The National Gay Task Force hailed the event as a milestone in the progress of human rights. It is unclear what the voters of Sioux Falls thought about it, since it was not put up to a vote. However, if their views were similar to those of voters in Dade County, Florida; Houston, Texas; Wichita, Kansas; and various localities in the state of Oregon, they probably were not pleased. In referenda held in these and other areas, voters have reversed decisions by legislators and local boards that banned discrimination by sexual preference.

Yet the attitude of Americans toward the rights of homosexuals is not easy to pin down. Voters have also defeated resolutions such as the one in California in 1978 that would have banned the hiring of homosexual school-teachers, or the one on the Oregon ballot in 1992 identifying homosexuality as "abnormal, wrong, unnatural and perverse." In some states, notably Colorado, voters have approved initiatives widely perceived as antihomosexual. But, almost invariably, these resolutions have been carefully worded so as to appear to oppose "special" rights for homosexuals. In general, polls show that a large majority of Americans believe that homosexuals should have equal rights with heterosexuals with regard to job opportunities. On the other hand, many view homosexuality as morally wrong.

Currently, same-sex marriages are not legally recognized by Congress. In the Defense of Marriage Act of 1996, Congress defined marriage as heterosexual. A state does not have to recognize another state's nonheterosexual marriage. The legal situation is constantly changing. Several states have legalized same-sex civil unions, and San Francisco and Massachusetts have legalized same-sex marriages. These developments have prompted President Bush to propose a Constitutional Amendment limiting marriage to the union of a man and a women.

The issue of same-sex marriage fascinates sociologists because it represents a basic change in a major social institution and is being played out on several fields: legal, cultural/moral, and behavioral. The legal debate will be decided by courts and legislatures; the cultural/moral debate is open to all of us; and the behavioral debate will be conducted by the activists on both sides. In the readings that follow, the Human Rights Campaign presents the major arguments for same-sex marriages, and Peter Sprigg argues that marriage must remain heterosexual.

YES ⤶

Answers to Questions About Marriage Equality

Why Same-Sex Couples Want to Marry

Many same-sex couples want the right to legally marry because they are in love—either they just met the love of their lives, or more likely, they have spent the last 10, 20 or 50 years with that person—and they want to honor their relationship in the greatest way our society has to offer, by making a public commitment to stand together in good times and bad, through all the joys and challenges family life brings.

Many parents want the right to marry because they know it offers children a vital safety net and guarantees protections that unmarried parents cannot provide.

And still other people—both gay and straight—are fighting for the right of same-sex couples to marry because they recognize that it is simply not fair to deny some families the protections all other families are eligible to enjoy.

Currently in the United States, same-sex couples in long-term, committed relationships pay higher taxes and are denied basic protections and rights granted to married heterosexual couples. Among them:

- **Hospital visitation.** Married couples have the automatic right to visit each other in the hospital and make medical decisions. Same-sex couples can be denied the right to visit a sick or injured loved one in the hospital.
- **Social Security benefits.** Married people receive Social Security payments upon the death of a spouse. Despite paying payroll taxes, gay and lesbian partners receive no Social Security survivor benefits—resulting in an average annual income loss of $5,528 upon the death of a partner.
- **Immigration.** Americans in binational relationships are not permitted to petition for their same-sex partners to immigrate. As a result, they are often forced to separate or move to another country.
- **Health insurance.** Many public and private employers provide medical coverage to the spouses of their employees, but most employers do not provide coverage to the life partners of gay and lesbian employees. Gay employees who do receive health coverage for their partners must pay federal income taxes on the value of the insurance.
- **Estate taxes.** A married person automatically inherits all the property of his or her deceased spouse without paying estate taxes. A gay or lesbian

taxpayer is forced to pay estate taxes on property inherited from a deceased partner.

- **Retirement savings.** While a married person can roll a deceased spouse's 401(k) funds into an IRA without paying taxes, a gay or lesbian American who inherits a 401(k) can end up paying up to 70 percent of it in taxes and penalties.
- **Family leave.** Married workers are legally entitled to unpaid leave from their jobs to care for an ill spouse. Gay and lesbian workers are not entitled to family leave to care for their partners.
- **Nursing homes.** Married couples have a legal right to live together in nursing homes. Because they are not legal spouses, elderly gay or lesbian couples do not have the right to spend their last days living together in nursing homes.
- **Home protection.** Laws protect married seniors from being forced to sell their homes to pay high nursing home bills; gay and lesbian seniors have no such protection.
- **Pensions.** After the death of a worker, most pension plans pay survivor benefits only to a legal spouse of the participant. Gay and lesbian partners are excluded from such pension benefits.

Why Civil Unions Aren't Enough

Comparing marriage to civil unions is a bit like comparing diamonds to rhinestones. One is, quite simply, the real deal; the other is not. Consider:

- Couples eligible to marry may have their marriage performed in any state and have it recognized in every other state in the nation and every country in the world.
- Couples who are joined in a civil union in Vermont (the only state that offers civil unions) have no guarantee that its protections will even travel with them to neighboring New York or New Hampshire—let alone California or any other state.

Moreover, even couples who have a civil union and remain in Vermont receive only second-class protections in comparison to their married friends and neighbors. While they receive state-level protections, they do not receive any of the *more than 1,100 federal benefits and protections of marriage.*

In short, civil unions are not separate but equal—they are separate *and* unequal. And our society has tried separate before. It just doesn't work. . . .

Answers to Questions People Are Asking

"I Believe God Meant Marriage for Men and Women. How Can I Support Marriage for Same-Sex Couples?"

Many people who believe in God—and fairness and justice for all—ask this question. They feel a tension between religious beliefs and democratic values that has been experienced in many different ways throughout our nation's history. That is why the farmers of our Constitution established the principle of separation of church and state. That principle applies no less to the marriage issue than it does to any other.

Indeed, the answer to the apparent dilemma between religious beliefs and support for equal protections for all families lies in recognizing that marriage has a significant religious meaning for many people, but that it is also a legal contract. And it is strictly the legal—not the religious—dimension of marriage that is being debated now.

Granting marriage rights to same-sex couples would *not* require Christianity, Judaism, Islam or any other religion to perform these marriages. It would not require religious institutions to permit these ceremonies to be held on their grounds. It would not even require that religious communities discuss the issue. People of faith would remain free to make their own judgments about what makes a marriage in the eyes of God—just as they are today.

Consider, for example, the difference in how the Catholic Church and the U.S. government view couples who have divorced and remarried. Because church tenets do not sanction divorce, the second marriage is not valid in the church's view. The government, however, recognizes the marriage by extending to the remarried couple the same rights and protections as those granted to every other married couple in America. In this situation—as would be the case in marriage for same-sex couples—the church remains free to establish its own teachings on the religious dimension of marriage while the government upholds equality under law.

It should also be noted that there are a growing number of religious communities that have decided to bless same-sex unions. Among them are Reform Judaism, the Unitarian Universalist Association and the Metropolitan Community Church. The Presbyterian Church (USA) also allows ceremonies to be performed, although they are not considered the same as marriage. The Episcopal Church and United Church of Christ allow individual churches to set their own policies on same-sex unions.

"This Is Different From Interracial Marriage. Sexual Orientation Is a Choice."

. . . Decades of research all point to the fact that sexual orientation is not a choice, and that a person's sexual orientation cannot be changed. Who one is drawn to is a fundamental aspect of who we are.

In this way, the struggle for marriage equality for same-sex couples is just as basic as the fight for interracial marriage was. It recognizes that Americans should not be coerced into false and unhappy marriages but should be free to marry the person they love—thereby building marriage on a true and stable foundation.

"Won't This Create a Free-For-All and Make the Whole Idea of Marriage Meaningless?"

Many people share this concern because opponents of gay and lesbian people have used this argument as a scare tactic. But it is not true. Granting same-sex couples the right to marry would in no way change the number of people who could enter into a marriage (or eliminate restrictions on the age or familial relationships of those who may marry). Marriage would continue to recognize the highest possible commitment that can be made between two adults, plain and simple. . . .

"I Strongly Believe Children Need a Mother and a Father."
Many of us grew up believing that everyone needs a mother and father, regardless of whether we ourselves happened to have two parents, or two *good* parents.

But as families have grown more diverse in recent decades, the researchers have studied how these different family relationships affect children, it has become clear that the *quality* of a family's relationship is more important than the particular *structure* of families that exist today. In other words, the qualities that help children grow into good and responsible adults—learning how to learn, to have compassion for others, to contribute to society and be respectful of others and their differences—do not depend on the sexual orientation of their parents but on their parents' ability to provide a loving, stable and happy home, something no class of Americans has an exclusive hold on.

That is why research studies have consistently shown that children raised by gay and lesbian parents do just as well on all conventional measure of child development, such as academic achievement, psychological well-being and social abilities, as children raised by heterosexual parents.

That is also why the nation's leading child welfare organizations, including the American Academy of Pediatrics, the American Academy of Family Physicians and others, have issued statements that dismiss assertions that only heterosexual couples can be good parents—and declare that the focus should now be on providing greater protections for the 1 million to 9 million children being raised by gay and lesbian parents in the United States today. . . .

"How Could Marriage for Same-Sex Couples Possibly Be Good for the American Family—or Our Country?"
. . . The prospect of a significant change in our laws and customs has often caused people to worry more about dire consequences that could result than about the potential positive outcomes. In fact, precisely the same anxiety arose when some people fought to overturn the laws prohibiting marriage between people of different races in the 1950s and 1960s. (One Virginia judge even declared that "God intended to separate the races.")

But in reality, opening marriage to couples who are so willing to fight for it could only strengthen the institution for all. It would open the doors to more supporters, not opponents. And it would help keep the age-old institution alive.

As history has repeatedly proven, institutions that fail to take account of the changing needs of the population are those that grow weak; those that recognize and accommodate changing needs grow strong. For example, the U.S. military, like American colleges and universities, grew stronger after permitting African Americans and women to join its ranks.

Similarly, granting same-sex couples the right to marry would strengthen the institution of marriage by allowing it to better meet the needs of the true diversity of family structures in America today. . . .

"Can't Same-Sex Couples Go to a Lawyer to Secure All the Rights They Need?"
Not by a long shot. When a gay or lesbian person gets seriously ill, there is no legal document that can make their partner eligible to take leave from work under the federal Family and Medical Leave Act to provide care—because that law applies only to married couples.

When gay or lesbian people grow old and in need of nursing home care, there is no legal document that can give them the right to Medicaid coverage without potentially causing their partner to be forced from their home—because the federal Medicaid law only permits married spouses to keep their home without becoming ineligible for benefits.

And when a gay or lesbian person dies, there is no legal document that can extend Social Security survivor benefits or the right to inherit a retirement plan without severe tax burdens that stem from being "unmarried" in the eyes of the law.

These are only a few examples of the critical protections that are granted through more than 1,100 federal laws that protect only married couples. In the absence of the right to marry, same-sex couples can only put in place a handful of the most basic arrangements, such as naming each other in a will or a power of attorney. And even these documents remain vulnerable to challenges in court by disgruntled family members.

"Won't This Cost Taxpayers Too Much Money?"
No, it wouldn't necessarily cost much at all. In fact, treating same-sex couples as families under law could even save taxpayers money because marriage would require them to assume legal responsibility for their joint living expenses and reduce their dependence on public assistance programs, such as Medicaid, Temporary Assistance to Needy Families, Supplemental Security Income disability payments and food stamps.

Put another way, the money it would cost to extend benefits to same-sex couples could be outweighed by the money that would be saved as these families rely more fully on each other instead of state or federal government assistance.

For example, two studies conducted in 2003 by professors at the University of Massachusetts, Amherst, and the University of California, Los Angeles, found that extending domestic partner benefits to same-sex couples in California and New Jersey would save taxpayers millions of dollars a year.

Specifically, the studies projected that the California state budget would save an estimated $8.1 million to $10.6 million each year by enacting the most comprehensive domestic partner law in the nation. In New Jersey, which passed a new domestic partner law in 2004, the savings were projected to be even higher—more than $61 million each year.

(Sources: "Equal Rights, Fiscal Responsibility: The Impact of A.B. 205 on California's Budget," by M. V. Lee Badgett, Ph.D., IGLSS, Department of Economics, University of Massachusetts, and R. Bradley Sears, J.D., Williams Project, UCLA School of Law, University of California, Los Angeles, May 2003, and "Supporting Families, Saving Funds: A Fiscal Analysis of New Jersey's

Domestic Partnership Act," by Badgett and Sears with Suzanne Goldberg, J.D., Rutgers School of Law-Newark, December 2003.)

"Where Can Same-Sex Couples Marry Today?"

In 2001, the Netherlands became the first country to extend marriage rights to same-sex couples. Belgium passed a similar law two years later. The laws in both of these countries, however, have strict citizenship or residency requirements that do not permit American couples to take advantage of the protections provided.

In June 2003, Ontario became the first Canadian province to grant marriage to same-sex couples, and in July 2003, British Columbia followed suit—becoming the first places that American same-sex couples could go to get married.

In November 2003, the Massachusetts Supreme Judicial Court recognized the right of same-sex couples to marry—giving the state six months to begin issuing marriage licenses to same-sex couples. It began issuing licenses May 17, 2004.

In February 2004, the city of San Francisco began issuing marriage licenses to same-sex couples after the mayor declared that the state constitution forbade him to discriminate. The issue is being addressed by California courts, and a number of other cities have either taken or are considering taking steps in the same direction.

Follow the latest developments in California, Oregon, New Jersey, New Mexico, New York and in other communities across the country. . . .

Other nations have also taken steps toward extending equal protections to all couples, though the protections they provide are more limited than marriage. Canada, Denmark, Finland, France, Germany, Iceland, Norway, Portugal and Sweden all have nationwide laws that grant same-sex partners a range of important rights, protections and obligations.

For example, in France, registered same-sex (and opposite-sex) couples can be joined in a civil "solidarity pact" that grants them the right to file joint tax returns, extend social security coverage to each other and receive the same health, employment and welfare benefits as legal spouses. It also commits the couple to assume joint responsibility for household debts.

Other countries, including Switzerland, Scotland and the Czech Republic, also have considered legislation that would legally recognize same-sex unions.

"What Protections Other Than Marriage Are Available to Same-Sex Couples?"

At the federal level, there are no protections at all available to same-sex couples. In fact, a federal law called the "Defense of Marriage Act" says that the federal government will discriminate against same-sex couples who marry by refusing to recognize their marriages or providing them with the federal protections of marriage. Some members of Congress are trying to go even further by attempting to pass a Federal Marriage Amendment that would write discrimination against same-sex couples into the U.S. Constitution.

At the state level, only Vermont offers civil unions, which provide important state benefits but no federal protections, such as Social Security survivor benefits. There is also no guarantee that civil unions will be recognized outside

10 FACTS

7. Same-sex couples live in 99.3 percent of all counties nationwide.
8. There are an estimated 3.1 million people living together in same-sex relationships in the United States.
9. Fifteen percent of these same-sex couples live in rural settings.
10. One out of three lesbian couples is raising children. One out of five gay male couples is raising children.
11. Between 1 million and 9 million children are being raised by gay, lesbian and bisexual parents in the United States today.
12. At least one same-sex couple is raising children in 96 percent of all counties nationwide.
13. The highest percentages of same-sex couples raising children live in the South.
14. Nearly one in four same-sex couples includes a partner 55 years old or older, and nearly one in five same-sex couples is composed of two people 55 or older.
15. More than one in 10 same-sex couples include a partner 65 years old or older, and nearly one in 10 same-sex couples is composed of two people 65 or older.
16. The states with the highest numbers of same-sex senior couples are also the most popular for heterosexual senior couples: California, New York and Florida.

These facts are based on analyses of the 2000 Census conducted by the Urban Institute and the Human Rights Campaign. The estimated number of people in same-sex relationships has been adjusted by 62 percent to compensate for the widely-reported undercount in the Census. (See "Gay and Lesbian Families in the United States: Same-Sex Unmarried Partner Households" on www.hrc.org.)

Vermont. Thirty-nine states also have "defense of marriage" laws explicitly prohibiting the recognition of marriages between same-sex partners.

Domestic partner laws have been enacted in California, Connecticut, New Jersey, Hawaii and the District of Columbia. The benefits conferred by these laws vary; some offer access to family health insurance, others confer co-parenting rights. These benefits are limited to residents of the state. A family that moves out of these states immediately loses the protections.

Peter Sprigg ⇒ **NO**

Questions and Answers: What's Wrong With Letting Same-Sex Couples "Marry"?

What's Wrong With Letting Same-Sex Couples Legally "Marry"?
There are two key reasons why the legal rights, benefits, and responsibilities of civil marriage should not be extended to same-sex couples.

The first is that homosexual relationships are not marriage. That is, they simply do not fit the minimum necessary condition for a marriage to exist—namely, the union of a man and a woman.

The second is that homosexual relationships are harmful. Not only do they not provide the same benefits to society as heterosexual marriages, but their consequences are far more negative than positive.

Either argument, standing alone, is sufficient to reject the claim that same-sex unions should be granted the legal status of marriage.

Let's Look at the First Argument. Isn't Marriage Whatever the Law Says It Is?
No. Marriage is not a creation of the law. Marriage is a fundamental human institution that predates the law and the Constitution. At its heart, it is an anthropological and sociological reality, not a legal one. Laws relating to marriage merely recognize and regulate an institution that already exists.

But Isn't Marriage Just a Way of Recognizing People Who Love Each Other and Want to Spend Their Lives Together?
If love and companionship were sufficient to define marriage, then there would be no reason to deny "marriage" to unions of a child and an adult, or an adult child and his or her aging parent, or to roommates who have no sexual relationship, or to groups rather than couples. Love and companionship are usually considered integral to marriage in our culture, but they are not sufficient to define it as an institution. . . .

Why Should Homosexuals Be Denied the Right to Marry Like Anyone Else?
The fundamental "right to marry" is a right that rests with *individuals*, not with *couples*. Homosexual *individuals* already have exactly the same "right" to marry as anyone else. Marriage license applications do not inquire as to a person's "sexual orientation." . . .

From *Family Research Council*, Issue No. 256, 2004, pp. 173–179. Copyright © 2004 by Family Research Council. Reprinted by permission.

However, while every individual person is free to get married, *no* person, whether heterosexual or homosexual, has ever had a legal right to marry simply any willing partner. Every person, whether heterosexual or homosexual, is subject to legal restrictions as to whom they may marry. To be specific, every person, regardless of sexual preference, is legally barred from marrying a child, a close blood relative, a person who is already married, or a person of the same sex. There is no discrimination here, nor does such a policy deny anyone the "equal protection of the laws" (as guaranteed by the Constitution), since these restrictions apply equally to every individual.

Some people may wish to do away with one or more of these longstanding restrictions upon one's choice of marital partner. However, the fact that a tiny but vocal minority of Americans desire to have someone of the same sex as a partner does not mean that they have a "right" to do so, any more than the desires of other tiny (but less vocal) minorities of Americans give them a "right" to choose a child, their own brother or sister, or a group of two or more as their marital partners.

Isn't Prohibiting Homosexual "Marriage" Just as Discriminatory as Prohibiting Interracial Marriage, Like Some States Used to Do?

This analogy is not valid at all. Bridging the divide of the sexes by uniting men and women is both a worthy goal and a part of the fundamental purpose of marriage, common to all human civilizations.

Laws against interracial marriage, on the other hand, served only the purpose of preserving a social system of racial segregation. This was both an unworthy goal and one utterly irrelevant to the fundamental nature of marriage.

Allowing a black woman to marry a white man does not change the definition of marriage, which requires one man and one woman. Allowing two men or two women to marry would change that fundamental definition. Banning the "marriage" of same-sex couples is therefore essential to preserve the nature and purpose of marriage itself. . . .

How Would Allowing Same-Sex Couples to Marry Change Society's Concept of Marriage?

As an example, marriage will open wide the door to homosexual adoption, which will simply lead to more children suffering the negative consequences of growing up without both a mother and a father.

Among homosexual men in particular, casual sex, rather than committed relationships, is the rule and not the exception. And even when they do enter into a more committed relationship, it is usually of relatively short duration. For example, a study of homosexual men in the Netherlands (the first country in the world to legalize "marriage" for same-sex couples), published in the journal *AIDS* in 2003, found that the average length of "steady partnerships" was not more than 2 < years (Maria Xiridou et al., in *AIDS* 2003, 17:1029–1038).

In addition, studies have shown that even homosexual men who are in "committed" relationships are not sexually faithful to each other. While infidelity among heterosexuals is much too common, it does not begin to compare to the rates among homosexual men. The 1994 National Health and Social Life Survey, which remains the most comprehensive study of Americans' sexual practices ever undertaken, found that 75 percent of married men and 90 percent of married women had been sexually faithful to their spouse. On the other hand, a major study of homosexual men in "committed" relationships found that only seven out of 156 had been sexually faithful, or 4.5 percent. The Dutch study cited above found that even homosexual men in "steady partnerships" had an average of eight "casual" sex partners per year.

So if same-sex relationships are legally recognized as "marriage," the idea of marriage as a sexually exclusive and faithful relationship will be dealt a serious blow. Adding monogamy and faithfulness to the other pillars of marriage that have already fallen will have overwhelmingly negative consequences for Americans' physical and mental health. . . .

Don't Homosexuals Need Marriage Rights So That They Will Be Able to Visit Their Partners in the Hospital?

The idea that homosexuals are routinely denied the right to visit their partners in the hospital is nonsense. When this issue was raised during debate over the Defense of Marriage Act in 1996, the Family Research Council did an informal survey of nine hospitals in four states and the District of Columbia. None of the administrators surveyed could recall a single case in which a visitor was barred because of their homosexuality, and they were incredulous that this would even be considered an issue.

Except when a doctor limits visitation for medical reasons, final authority over who may visit an adult patient rests with that patient. This is and should be the case regardless of the sexual orientation or marital status of the patient or the visitor.

The only situation in which there would be a possibility that the blood relatives of a patient might attempt to exclude the patient's homosexual partner is if the patient is unable to express his or her wishes due to unconsciousness or mental incapacity. Homosexual partners concerned about this (remote) possibility can effectively preclude it by granting to one another a health care proxy (the legal right to make medical decisions for the patient) and a power of attorney (the right to make all legal decisions for another person). Marriage is not necessary for this. It is inconceivable that a hospital would exclude someone who holds the health care proxy and power of attorney for a patient from visiting that patient, except for medical reasons.

The hypothetical "hospital visitation hardship" is nothing but an emotional smokescreen to distract people from the more serious implications of radically redefining marriage.

Don't Homosexuals Need the Right to Marry Each Other in Order to Ensure That They Will Be Able to Leave Their Estates to Their Partner When They Die?

As with the hospital visitation issue, the concern over inheritance rights is something that simply does not require marriage to resolve it. Nothing in current law prevents homosexual partners from being joint owners of property such as a home or a car, in which case the survivor would automatically become the owner if the partner dies.

An individual may leave the remainder of his estate to whomever he wishes—again, without regard to sexual orientation or marital status—simply by writing a will. As with the hospital visitation issue, blood relatives would only be able to overrule the surviving homosexual partner in the event that the deceased had failed to record his wishes in a common, inexpensive legal document. Changing the definition of a fundamental social institution like marriage is a rather extreme way of addressing this issue. Preparing a will is a much simpler solution.

Don't Homosexuals Need Marriage Rights So That They Can Get Social Security Survivor Benefits When a Partner Dies?

... Social Security survivor benefits were designed to recognize the non-monetary contribution made to a family by the homemaking and child-rearing activities of a wife and mother, and to ensure that a woman and her children would not become destitute if the husband and father were to die.

The Supreme Court ruled in the 1970s that such benefits must be gender-neutral. However, they still are largely based on the premise of a division of roles within a couple between a breadwinner who works to raise money and a homemaker who stays home to raise children.

Very few homosexual couples organize their lives along the lines of such a "traditional" division of labor and roles. They are far more likely to consist of two earners, each of whom can be supported in old age by their own personal Social Security pension.

Furthermore, far fewer homosexual couples than heterosexual ones are raising children at all, for the obvious reason that they are incapable of natural reproduction with each other. This, too, reduces the likelihood of a traditional division of labor among them.

Survivor benefits for the legal (biological or adopted) *children* of homosexual parents (as opposed to their partners) are already available under current law, so "marriage" rights for homosexual couples are unnecessary to protect the interests of these children themselves. ...

Even If "Marriage" Itself Is Uniquely Heterosexual, Doesn't Fairness Require That the Legal and Financial Benefits of Marriage Be Granted to Same-Sex Couples—Perhaps Through "Civil Unions" or "Domestic Partnerships?"

No. The legal and financial benefits of marriage are not an entitlement to be distributed equally to all (if they were, single people would have as much reason to consider them "discriminatory" as same-sex couples). Society grants benefits to marriage because marriage has benefits for society—including, but not limited to, the reproduction of the species in households with the optimal household structure (i.e., the presence of both a mother and a father).

Homosexual relationships, on the other hand, have no comparable benefit for society, and in fact impose substantial costs on society. The fact that AIDS is at least ten times more common among men who have sex with men than among the general population is but one example. . . .

What About the Argument That Homosexual Relations Are Harmful? What Do You Mean by That?

Homosexual men experience higher rates of many diseases, including:

- Human Papillomavirus (HPV), which causes most cases of cervical cancer in women and anal cancer in men
- Hepatitis A, B, and C
- Gonorrhea
- Syphilis
- "Gay Bowel Syndrome," a set of sexually transmitted gastrointestinal problems such as proctitis, proctocolitis, and enteritis
- HIV/AIDS (One Canadian study found that as a result of HIV alone, "life expectancy for gay and bisexual men is eight to twenty years less than for all men.")

Lesbian women, meanwhile, have a higher prevalence of:

- Bacterial vaginosis
- Hepatitis C
- HIV risk behaviors
- Cancer risk factors such as smoking, alcohol use, poor diet, and being overweight . . .

Do Homosexuals Have More Mental Health Problems as Well?

Yes. Various research studies have found that homosexuals have higher rates of:

- Alcohol abuse
- Drug abuse
- Nicotine dependence
- Depression
- Suicide

Isn't It Possible That These Problems Result From Society's "Discrimination" Against Homosexuals?

This is the argument usually put forward by pro-homosexual activists. However, there is a simple way to test this hypothesis. If "discrimination" were the cause of homosexuals' mental health problems, then one would expect those problems to be much less common in cities or countries, like San Francisco or the Netherlands, where homosexuality has achieved the highest levels of acceptance.

In fact, the opposite is the case. In places where homosexuality is widely accepted, the physical and mental health problems of homosexuals are greater, not less. This suggests that the real problem lies in the homosexual lifestyle itself, not in society's response to it. In fact, it suggests that increasing the level of social support *for* homosexual behavior (by, for instance, allowing same-sex couples to "marry") would only increase these problems, not reduce them. . . .

Haven't Studies Shown That Children Raised by Homosexual Parents Are No Different From Other Children?

No. This claim is often put forward, even by professional organizations. The truth is that most research on "homosexual parents" thus far has been marred by serious methodological problems. However, even pro-homosexual sociologists Judith Stacey and Timothy Biblarz report that the actual data from key studies show the "no differences" claim to be false.

Surveying the research (primarily regarding lesbians) in an *American Sociological Review* article in 2001, they found that:

- Children of lesbians are less likely to conform to traditional gender norms.
- Children of lesbians are more likely to engage in homosexual behavior.
- Daughters of lesbians are "more sexually adventurous and less chaste."
- Lesbian "co-parent relationships" are more likely to end than heterosexual ones.

A 1996 study by an Australian sociologist compared children raised by heterosexual married couples, heterosexual cohabiting couples, and homosexual cohabiting couples. It found that the children of heterosexual married couples did the best, and children of homosexual couples the worst, in nine of the thirteen academic and social categories measured. . . .

Do the American People Want to See "Marriages" Between Same-Sex Couples Recognized by Law?

No—and in the wake of the June 2003 court decisions to legalize such "marriages" in the Canadian province of Ontario and to legalize homosexual sodomy in the United States, the nation's opposition to such a radical social experiment has actually grown.

Five separate national opinion polls taken between June 24 and July 27, 2003 showed opponents of civil "marriage" for same-sex couples outnumbering supporters by not less than fifteen percentage points in every poll. The wording of poll questions can make a significant difference, and in this case, the poll with the most straightforward language (a Harris/CNN/Time poll asking "Do you think marriages between homosexual men or homosexual women should be recognized as legal by the law?") resulted in the strongest opposition, with 60 percent saying "No" and only 33 percent saying "Yes."

POSTSCRIPT

Should Same-Sex Marriages Be Legally Recognized?

The issue of the rights of homosexuals creates a social dilemma. Most people would agree that all members of society should have equal rights. However, the majority may disapprove of the lifestyles of a minority group and pass laws against some of their behaviors. The question is: When do these laws violate civil rights? Are laws against same-sex marriage such a violation?

There is a considerable literature on homosexuality and the social and legal status of homosexuals. Recent works on gay marriage include David Moats, *Civil Wars: A Battle for Gay Marriage* (Harcourt, 2004); Evan Gerstmann, *Same-Sex Marriage and the Constitution* (Cambridge University Press, 2004); *Marriage and Same-Sex Unions: A Debate* edited by Lynn D. Wardle, et al. (Praeger, 2003); Martin Dupuis, *Same-Sex Marriage, Legal Mobilization, and the Politics of Rights* (Peter Lang, 2002); and Kevin Bourassa, *Just Married: Gay Marriage and the Expansion of Human Rights* (University of Wisconsin Press, 2002). Recent works on the history of the gay rights movement include Dudley Clendinen and Adam Nagourney, *Out for Good: The Struggle to Build a Gay Rights Movement in America* (Simon & Schuster, 1999); Ronald J. Hunt, *Historical Dictionary of the Gay Liberation Movement* (Scarecrow Press, 1999); JoAnne Myers, *Historical Dictionary of the Lesbian Liberation Movement: Still the Rage* (Scarecrow Press, 2003); and John Loughery, *The Other Side of Silence: Men's Lives and Gay Identities: A Twentieth-Century History* (Henry Holt, 1998). For broad academic works on homosexuality see Kath Weston, *Long Slow Burn: Sexuality and Social Science* (Routledge, 1998); and Michael Ruse, *Homosexuality: A Philosophical Inquiry* (Blackwell, 1998). Recent works that focus on homosexual rights include David A. J. Richards, *Identity and the Case for Gay Rights* (University of Chicago Press, 1999); Daniel R. Pinello, *Gay Rights and American Law* (Cambridge University Press, 2003); Carlos A. Ball, *The Morality of Gay Rights: An Exploration in Political Philosophy* (Routledge, 2003); Brette McWhorter Sember, *Gay and Lesbian Rights: A Guide for GLBT Singles, Couples, and Families* (Sphinx Publishing, 2003); and Nan D. Hunter, *The Rights of Lesbians, Gay Men, Bisexuals, and Transgender People: The Authoritative ACLU Guide to a Lesbian, Gay, Bisexual, or Transgender Person's Rights,* 4th edition (Southern Illinois University Press, 2004).

Internet References . . .

Statistical Resources on the Web: Sociology

This Statistical Resources on the Web site provides links to data on poverty in the United States. Included is a link that contains both current and historical poverty data.

http://www.lib.umich.edu/govdocs/stats

Institute for Research on Poverty (IRP)

The Institute for Research on Poverty researches the causes and consequences of social inequality and poverty in the United States. This Web site includes frequently asked questions about poverty and links to other Internet resources on the subject.

http://www.ssc.wisc.edu/irp/

About.com: Affirmative Action

About com's Web site on affirmative action contains information about resources and organizations that focus on affirmative action policies and current events. This site also enables you to search other topics related to race relations.

http://www.racerelations.about.com/
cs/affirmativeaction

Stratification and Inequality

*W*hy is there so much poverty in a society as rich as ours? Why has there been such a noticeable increase in inequality over the past quarter century? Although the ideal of equal opportunity for all is strong in the United States, many charge that the American political and economic system is unfair. Does extensive poverty demonstrate that policymakers have failed to live up to United States egalitarian principles? Are American institutions deeply flawed in that they provide fabulous opportunities for the educated and rich and meager opportunities for the uneducated and poor? Is the American stratification system at fault or are the poor themselves at fault? And what about the racial gap? The civil rights movement and the Civil Rights Act have made America more fair than it was, so why does a sizeable racial gap remain? Various affirmative action programs have been implemented to remedy unequal opportunities, but some argue that this is discrimination in reverse. In fact, California passed a referendum banning affirmative action. Where should America go from here? Social scientists debate these questions in this part.

- Is Increasing Economic Inequality a Serious Problem?

- Has Feminism Benefited American Society?

- Has Affirmative Action Outlived Its Usefulness?

- Are Boys and Men Disadvantaged Relative to Girls and Women?

ISSUE 7

Is Increasing Economic Inequality a Serious Problem?

YES: James Kurth, from "The Rich Get Richer," *The American Conservative* (September 25, 2006)

NO: Gary S. Becker and Kevin M. Murphy, from "The Upside of Income Inequality," *The American* (May–June 2007)

ISSUE SUMMARY

YES: James Kurth, Claude Smith Professor of Political Science at Swarthmore College, warns of very negative consequences for America of the growing income inequality from a conservative perspective. He also mentions the liberal criticisms of inequality but downplays their importance because America has institutions that mitigate them.

NO: Gary S. Becker and Kevin M. Murphy, both economists teaching at the University of Chicago and Senior Fellows at the Hoover Institute, swim upstream on this issue by pointing out the positive consequences of the growing income inequality. The main reason for the increasing inequality is the increasing returns to education, which, in turn, inspire greater efforts by young people to increase their social capital.

The cover of the January 29, 1996, issue of *Time* magazine bears a picture of 1996 Republican presidential candidate Steve Forbes and large letters reading: "DOES A FLAT TAX MAKE SENSE?" During his campaign, Forbes expressed his willingness to spend $25 million of his own wealth in pursuit of the presidency, with the major focus of his presidential campaign being a flat tax, that would reduce taxes substantially for the rich. It seems reasonable to say that if the rich pay less in taxes, others would have to pay more. Is it acceptable for the tax burden to be shifted away from the rich in America? Forbes believed that the flat tax would benefit the poor as well as the rich. He theorized that the economy would surge ahead because investors would shift their money from relatively nonproductive, but tax-exempt, investments to productive investments. Although Forbes has disappeared from the political scene, his basic argument still thrives today. It is an example of the trickle-down theory, which states that helping the rich stimulates the economy, which helps the poor. In fact, the trickle-down theory is the major rationalization for the view that great economic inequality benefits all of society.

Inequality is not a simple subject. For example, America is commonly viewed as having more social equality than do the more hierarchical societies of Europe and Japan, but America has more income inequality than almost all other industrial societies. This apparent contradiction is explained when one recognizes that American equality is not in income, but in the opportunity to obtain higher incomes. The issue of economic inequality is further complicated by other categories of equality/inequality, which include political power, social status, and legal rights.

Americans believe that everyone should have an equal opportunity to compete for jobs and rewards. This belief is backed up by free public school education, which provides poor children with a ladder to success, and by laws that forbid discrimination. Americans, however, do not agree on many specific issues regarding opportunities or rights. For example, should society compensate for handicaps such as disadvantaged family backgrounds or the legacy of past discrimination?

This issue has divided the country. Americans do not agree on programs such as income-based scholarships, quotas, affirmative action, or the Head Start compensatory education program for poor preschoolers.

America's commitment to political equality is strong in principle, though less strong in practice. Everyone over 18 years old gets one vote, and all votes are counted equally. However, the political system tilts in the direction of special interest groups; those who do not belong to such groups are seldom heard. Furthermore, as in the case of Forbes, money plays an increasingly important role in political campaigns.

The final dimension of equality/inequality is status. Inequality of status involves differences in prestige, and it cannot be eliminated by legislation. Ideally, the people who contribute the most to society are the most highly esteemed. To what extent does this principle hold true in the United States? The Declaration of Independence proclaims that "all men are created equal," and the Founding Fathers who wrote the Declaration of Independence went on to base the laws of the land on the principle of equality. The equality they were referring to was equality of opportunity and legal and political rights for white, property-owning males. In the two centuries following the signing of the Declaration, nonwhites and women struggled for and won considerable equality of opportunity and rights. Meanwhile, income gaps in the United States have been widening.

In the readings that follow, James Kurth mentions the danger of ever greater concentration of market power, but thinks that antitrust laws and global competition will keep this problem in check. Other economic problems are also manageable. He is most concerned about the numerous political consequences of inequality, which include increased terrorist threats. Gary S. Becker and Kevin M. Murphy focus on the increased value of higher education that is at the root of the increasing inequality. The main consequence is the substantial increase in college attendance of all groups in society.

YES ⤶

James Kurth

The Rich Get Richer

In 1914, Henry Ford paid his factory workers $5 a day, twice the going rate, with the aim of creating a broad middle class able to buy the cars they were building. Today, that project isn't faring so well: *The Economist* reports that in the U.S. "the gap between rich and poor is bigger than in any other advanced country." And it's growing. According to the Congressional Budget Office, from 1979 to 2001, the after-tax income of the top 1 percent of U.S. households soared 139 percent, while the income of the middle fifth rose only 17 percent and the income of the poorest fifth climbed just 9 percent. Last year American CEOs earned 262 times the average wage of their workers—up tenfold from 1970.

This widening gap can be seen virtually everywhere we look—in America; within other countries, even those hitherto distinguished by a high degree of equality (in particular, Japan, South Korea, and China); and between rich and poor countries in the world at large. This pervasive reality has been explored ably and comprehensively in recent books by the popular and learned conservative writer Kevin Phillips. But it has also been recognized by professional analysts at the very heart of the capitalist system: a recent study by Citigroup Global Markets entitled "Plutonomy: Buying Luxury, Explaining Global Imbalances" suggested investment strategy on the basis of these trends.

Since most of the writing on inequality is done by economists, it is natural that they focus on the fiscal consequences. But in this essay, our focus will be on the ramifications for politics and culture, both within America and within the world more generally.

As Phillips documents, there have been several previous eras in American history that were characterized by growing economic inequality. They include not only the famous (and infamous) Gilded Age of the 1880s but also the 1830s and the 1920s. These previous eras and their eventual end may provide some prototypes for our own. But as we shall see, there are certain unique features of our era of growing inequality that make it something new under the sun.

It would be one thing, and bad enough, if great personal wealth were simply expended on more goods, in order to engage in conspicuous consumption. The consequences for society would include ever greater public displays of materialistic values. But this phenomenon seems to be as old as recorded history, and it is hard for a conservative to get really angry about something that has so much tradition behind it.

It would be another thing, and even worse, if great personal wealth were simply translated into more great wealth—if capital were invested in capital in order to get even more capital. The consequences for society would include ever greater concentration of market power. But in the United States, this phenomenon has been around for more than a century, and we have dealt with it by permitting more competition, not only by antitrust legislation but also by opening the American economy to similar goods imported from abroad and, even more effectively, to entirely new goods and services that have resulted from technological innovation. It is difficult to get anxious about a problem that has been so readily and so often solved in the past.

A more serious problem results because the rich also like to buy people—personal servants who work in their homes and grounds as maids, cooks, nannies, painters, and gardeners. Nowadays, this largely means Mexican and Central American immigrants—and illegal ones at that. Of course, U.S. agricultural and manufacturing businesses want to hire illegal immigrants, too. However, the really animated core of the political lobby that supports illegal immigration—its mass base, so to speak—is composed of rich homeowners, who desperately want someone to do their dirty work and to do it cheaply. Although they are the largest beneficiaries of the American way of life, including the rule of law, when it comes to the issue of illegal immigration, the rich do everything they can to undermine the American way for the vast majority of other Americans. There is nothing conservative about these actions by the rich; rather, the true conservatives are the less well-off who oppose illegal immigration and who are trying to preserve (and conserve) what was once an established and respected order.

But immigration policy is only one example of the most serious problem with increasing economic inequality: the holders of great wealth—especially if they are organized into a political lobby of similar holders of great wealth—can buy not only more goods, more capital, and more people. They can also buy (through the vehicle of campaign contributions) more important people: politicians and other public officials and therefore public policies.

Some of these bought policies may be for the purpose of making the rich even richer, most obviously the current regressive tax policies of the Bush administration. The wealth of the very rich is never the product of free enterprise and the free market alone but comes by operating within and exploiting a network of government supports, such as licenses, regulations, subsidies, and contracts. It is the product of a sort of giveaway. Consequently, to reduce the taxes on wealth (estate taxes) or on the income from wealth (capital-gains taxes), when that wealth has been acquired with one or another kind of government support, is in effect to give the wealth holder an additional giveaway. Again, there is nothing authentically conservative about this process.

Having even more wealth than they had before, the very rich can thus buy even more government supports and giveaways and acquire even more wealth, enabling them to buy even more government supports and giveaways. And so on. The result of great wealth buying public policies is a positive feedback loop, or perhaps a vicious cycle, which transfers ever greater wealth and power to the very rich and away from everyone else.

What is to prevent this cycle from going on forever? Historically, there have been two major constraining (or reversing) processes: one derives from macroeconomics, and the other derives from mass politics. Both constraints were once very powerful but neither are really operating today.

If the rich are getting richer, and the poor, if they are not getting poorer in real terms are not seeing their fortunes rise at comparable rates, this would seem to mean that the increasingly opulent consumption by the rich will have as its counterpart the increasingly austere consumption by the poor, and even by the now shrinking middle class. Eventually, the newly poor will not be able to earn enough to maintain their previous levels of consumption. Consequently, some goods produced will not be consumed, thus there will be fewer goods produced, there will be fewer producers or workers, there will be fewer goods consumed, and so on. We have yet another kind of cycle. It is exactly this process that has long been identified (by John Maynard Keynes, among others) as one of the classical explanations of how the growing inequality of the 1920s led to a crisis of underconsumption and overproduction and then to the Great Depression of the 1930s. A similar cycle had occurred earlier, when the growing inequality of the 1880s had issued in the depression of the 1890s (which, at that time, had also been called the Great Depression).

Given this simple model and given the recent pattern of growing economic inequality, one would have expected that the American economy would already be in a new Great Depression. What element has been added that has suspended, perhaps only temporarily, the execution of this macroeconomic iron law? The answer, of course, is consumer credit and record levels of consumer debt. Over one billion credit cards are in circulation in the U.S.—four for every man, woman, and child—and with 40 percent of families spending more than they earn, this keeps consumption rising, even as income may be declining.

In addition, some of the American consumption is also financed, albeit in an indirect and complex way, through the credit extended to the U.S. government and to U.S. lending institutions by the producers (or more precisely, by their governments) of many of the very goods that Americans are consuming—those of China, Japan, and South Korea. On the one hand, these foreign creditors have enabled the United States to avoid another Great Depression. On the other, this has come at the cost of a growing Great Dependence: the proportion of foreign-held debt is half what we owe as a nation and interest alone totals nearly $100 billion per year. That dependence is more immediate and obvious with respect to the U.S. government than it is for the American consumer. It does mean, however, that our government will have to tax American citizens more in order to finance its debt. With the tax policies of the Bush administration, this will in turn add to the growing inequality. It also means that the U.S. government may come to be more constrained in confronting the creditor governments on a variety of foreign-policy issues.

It strains credulity to believe that this cycle of increasing credit—be its sources domestic or foreign—can go on forever. When it ends, the old macroeconomic iron law will impose its penalties.

When we turn from economic responses to growing inequality to political ones, we quickly recall a dramatic parade of social—and socialist—movements marching across the historical landscape, from the beginning of the Industrial Revolution to the end of the Cold War. In America, these included the Jacksonian movement of the 1830s; the Populist movement of the 1880s–1890s; and the New Deal, along with a variety of Marxist movements, in the 1930s. Each of these represented a popular, even mass, reaction to growing economic inequality.

In Europe, of course, these social movements were more massive and more radical. They included the Labour Party in Britain in its early decades; Marxist parties in most nations on the Continent; anarchist movements in Southern Europe; and of course a successful Communist revolution in Russia. Each of these also represented a mass reaction to growing inequality. Communist movements and parties also spread to Asia, where they represented not only the class conflict between rich and poor within countries but also the international conflict between rich and poor countries within the world at large, with these Communist movements becoming anti-colonialist and nationalist ones as well (as in China and Indochina). Marxist movements also spread to Latin America, but there the reaction against growing inequality more often took the form of populist ones (the most familiar case being Peronism in Argentina).

Wherever their locale, most of these mass social movement were eventually able to impose some kind of constraint upon, or even reversal of, the growing inequality within their countries (but not, however, upon the inequality between countries). Sometimes the constraint was imposed by democratic elections and egalitarian legislation as with the American New Deal, the British Labour Party, and the Scandinavian social democratic parties. Sometimes an electoral triumph by socialist parties was followed by a repressive reaction imposed by parties of the Right as in much of Continental Europe during the 1920s–1930s. And on a few occasions, a Communist party succeeded in making a revolution and imposing a reversal of inequality that was ruthless and terrible indeed as in Russia, China, and Indochina.

But of course, this long historical parade of mass social movements effectively came to an end with the end of the Cold War and with the discrediting and collapse of Communism and of much of Marxism more generally. With the end of the Marxist version of mass social movements, it is not surprising that the past 15 years have been a period of growing economic inequality that is now almost completely unconstrained.

Given the extensive historical record of equalitarian social movements and the recent pattern of growing economic inequality, however, one might have expected that some such movement would have already arisen. If we look around the world, perhaps we will be able to see it before our very eyes. Indeed, when we eventually turn our attention to particular poor countries or regions, this will be the case.

In regard to contemporary America, however, there is no evidence of any social movement at all. Has a new element been added to American politics that has suspended, perhaps only temporarily, operation of the social-movement constraint in our own time? Actually, we can identify three such new elements.

First, there has been a change in the nature of the working population, which always constitutes a good part of the poor or increasingly poor within a society. The conditions of the working class, including the conditions conducive to political organization, are one thing in an industrial economy and a very different thing in a post-industrial, or information, economy such as our own. Sociologists have long observed and specified the many reasons it is much more difficult to politically organize workers who perform clerical, technical, or professional tasks in offices than workers who perform industrial or manufacturing tasks in factories. In any event, there are very few labor unions that are composed of clerical, technical, or professional employees. When we remember that unions of industrial workers were a fundamental and major pillar of the Democratic Party in America, the Labour Party in Britain, and the socialist and Marxist parties in continental Europe, we can see how, by itself, the shift to an information economy has removed the most powerful political constraint on growing economic inequality.

Second, there has also been a change in the economic self-identification of the general population. The way people define themselves is different in a consumer society, with a total focus upon individual self-gratification, than it is in a producer society, with an emphasis on the social consequences and connections of one's work. It is obviously much more difficult to politically organize masses of people if they all think of themselves as individual consumers or as expressive individualists, each freely choosing his own unique (even if vapid and banal) lifestyle, than to organize masses of people who think of themselves as members of working classes or local communities, who share in common most of the important conditions of their lives.

Third, and a variation on the consumer mentality, there has been a change in the non-working or leisure activities—the preoccupations and not just the occupations—of much of the population. For many Americans today, especially those in what was once the working class, there is indeed a kind of mass activity, but it is not mass political or social activism. Rather, it involves spectator entertainment, especially sports. For them, there is no participation in anything involving real interaction with other human beings, be it political parties, labor unions, community associations, fraternal societies, or, if they have become adults, even in participatory team sports themselves. It is the poorer classes, in contrast to the richer ones, that spend most of their free time with spectator entertainment. As more and more people become poor or poorer and lose any reasonable hope of improving their economic status, either by their own economic efforts or by anything like political activism, it is not surprising that they would seek to fill their bleak hours and vent their sullen frustrations with escapist (and violent) entertainment. What would have been seen as juvenile and abnormal preoccupations in the society of half a century or more ago have become normal ones in the society of our own time.

The same three shifts that have essentially demolished the social-movement constraint on growing inequality in America have also gone far toward doing so in other Western countries as well and even in Japan. All of these have now followed America far along the path of becoming information economies, consumer societies, and spectator cultures. . . .

What happens when we turn our attention from America and the West to the world at large? Of course, due to the promotion of globalization by successive U.S. governments and by American elites, the United States is now very much in that world—and in its face.

As it happens, globalization adds to the processes producing a widening gap between rich and poor. First, as is well known, in any country that is immersed and enmeshed in globalization, it has resulted in both winners (those who already have international connections, English-language proficiency, or information-age skills) and losers (those engaged in traditional agricultural, industrial, and cultural occupations). Those who are already rich tend to benefit from globalization, and many of those who are already poor tend to be hurt by it. It is no accident that the era of globalization— which has largely been the era since the end of the Cold War—has also been an era of a widening gap between rich and poor. Anyone who claims that globalization is a conservative process is either a liar or a fool.

What has been true within countries has been true between countries as well. Over the past 15 years or so, globalization has generally increased the GNP per capita of the countries that were already rich—the United States, Europe, and Japan— although of course even in these countries there are some sectors and groups that have been hurt by it. More momentously, globalization has also increased the GNP per capita of some countries that were once poor or near-poor, particularly many countries in Asia and including such immense ones as China and India. This is a very impressive result indeed, although again, even in these countries there are very large sectors and groups in the traditional economy that have been hurt by globalization.

However, there are three big regions where a very large majority of the people have lost out from globalization, or are at least convinced that they have: Africa, Latin America, and most consequentially, the Middle East and more generally the Muslim world. The increasing economic inequality within the countries of these regions combined with the increasing economic inequality between these regions and the rest of the world has generated vast reservoirs of resentment toward the globalization process, toward the West, and especially toward that arch-promoter of globalization, the United States. And starting in the early 2000s, that popular resentment has developed into actual resistance movements, which bear some resemblance to the egalitarian movements of earlier eras.

The resistance to globalization has developed least in Africa, which in any case is the least developed—the poorest and the most anarchic—region of the world. In Latin America, however, populist—and anti-globalization and anti-American—movements have surged in the past few years. Radical versions have been voted into power in Venezuela and Bolivia; more moderate versions have been successful in Argentina, Chile, and Uruguay; and populist candidates have come close to electoral victory in Mexico and Peru. In many ways, these contemporary populist movements and leaders are reminiscent of earlier ones in Latin America history. If the United States were not now bogged down in the quagmire of Iraq, the attention of the U.S. government and the American media would be fixated upon what they would perceive as a dangerous populist threat sweeping Latin America.

But the really serious resistance movement to globalization, the West, and the United States has arisen within the Muslim world. This is Islamism, which is also often called political Islam. When we in America consider Islamism, we do not think of it as an egalitarian social movement. However, the theology (more accurately, ideology) of political Islam is permeated with egalitarian norms and sentiments, and Islamists are often animated by egalitarian resentments and anger as well. Islamists speak frequently about the injustices and exploitation inflicted by the rich upon the poor, and by the rich West upon the poor Muslim world. "Social justice" is a central concept in most Islamist programs. They have their own way of claiming, as the Communists claimed in an earlier era, to speak for "the wretched of the earth." . . .

Perhaps the most interesting place where the Islamist ideology of social justice will resonate is that part of the Muslim world within the West itself: Western Europe's communities of Muslim Immigrants and their European-born children and descendents. By now several major European countries— Spain, Britain, France, and the Netherlands—have suffered either Islamist terrorist attacks or Muslim youth riots and violence, and there will doubtless be more of this in the future.

Indeed, many Western European countries are becoming two nations. The first is the original, ethnic-European nation; it is now largely secular or even pagan, rich, and aging. And because of its extraordinarily low birth rates, it is shrinking in numbers. The second is the immigrant, non-European nation, the Muslim nation or *umma;* it is substantially religious or even Islamist, poor, and young. And because of its high birth rate, it will continue to grow in numbers.

The two nations are coming to view each other with mutual contempt, but in the new Muslim nation there is a growing rage, and in the old, ethnic-European nation there is a growing fear. This will provide the perfect conditions for a widespread Islamist sense of social injustice, a deep Islamist hatred of what are perceived as rich Europeans, and as a natural consequence, an endemic threat of Islamist violence. . . .

And finally, of course, Islamist terrorists may soon acquire weapons of mass destruction, something that only states have possessed up to now. States, being established, hierarchical institutions, have not really wanted to put their WMD at the service of egalitarian projects. With Islamist transnational networks, however, there is no obvious reason why they would not be willing, even eager, to use WMD to bring the rich and the powerful, and rich and powerful states, crashing down. Although Islamist terrorist networks are not really very good examples of mass social movements, they will be very good at achieving mass social destruction. And, brimming over with egalitarian envy and self-righteous wrath, they will delight in doing so.

And so, what will be the eventual fate of the current drive toward greater economic inequality, in America and around the world? Within America and the other rich countries (or rather, the countries with a lot of rich), there do not now seem to be any internal forces that will arrest this drive. As for external forces, only Islamism is now beginning to mount a serious threat to the security of the rich, and that threat is also directed at all the other groups and peoples that the Islamists despise as well. Still, whoever might be the specific target of a particular Islamist attack with a weapon of truly mass destruction, it will take a lot of the rich along with it. Furthermore, by exploding established expectations about the future of economic and financial assets, and therefore by reducing the value of those assets, it will take a lot of their wealth too.

In the course of the 20th century, there were several years of growing economic inequality. On a few occasions, they came to an end in a relatively gentle way, with democratic elections and more egalitarian legislation. More often, however, they were ended by a catastrophe, such as the Great Depression, a violent social revolution, or a world war. When the rich went out, it seems, they normally did so with a bang, and not with a whimper. The way things are now going, it is likely to be so in the future.

Gary S. Becker and
Kevin M. Murphy

The Upside of Income Inequality

Income inequality in China substantially widened, particularly between households in the city and the countryside, after China began its rapid rate of economic development around 1980, The average urban resident now makes 3.2 times as much as the average rural resident, and among city dwellers alone, the top 10 percent makes 9.2 times as much as the bottom 10 percent. But at the same time that inequality rose, the number of Chinese who live in poverty fell—from 260 million in 1978 to 42 million in 1998. Despite the widening gap in incomes, rapid economic development dramatically improved the lives of China's poor.

Politicians and many others in the United States have recently grown concerned that earnings inequality has increased among Americans. But as the example of China—or India, for that matter—illustrates, the rise in inequality does not occur in a vacuum. In the case of China and India, the rise in inequality came along with an acceleration of economic growth that raised the standard of living for both the rich and the poor. In the United States, the rise in inequality accompanied a rise in the payoff to education and other skills. We believe that the rise in returns on investments in human capital is beneficial and desirable, and policies designed to deal with inequality must take account of its cause.

To show the importance to inequality of the increased return to human capital, consider Figure 1 . . . , which shows the link between earnings and education by displaying the wage premium received by college-educated workers compared with high school graduates. In 1980, an American with a college degree earned about 30 percent more than an American who stopped education at high school. But, in recent years, a person with a college education earned roughly 70 percent more. Meanwhile, the premium for having a graduate degree increased from roughly 50 percent in 1980 to well over 100 percent today. The labor market is placing a greater emphasis on education, dispensing rapidly rising rewards to those who stay in school the longest.

This trend has contributed significantly to the growth in overall earnings inequality in the United States. And just as in China and India, this growing inequality gap is associated with growing opportunity—in this case, the opportunity to advance through education. The upward trend in the returns to education is not limited to one segment of the population. Education premiums for women and African Americans have increased as much as, or more than, the premiums for all workers.

From *The American*, May–June 2007, pp. 20–23. Copyright © 2007 by American Enterprise Institute. Reprinted by permission.

Figure 1

Percentage by which the wage of workers with college and graduate school educations exceeds that of workers with high school only.

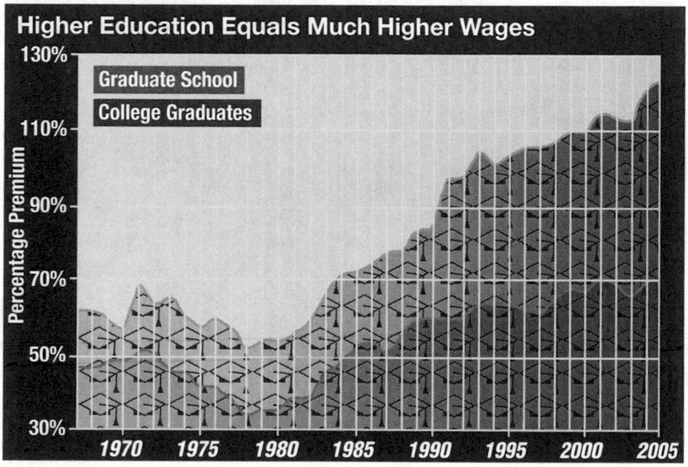

Higher Education Equals Much Higher Wages

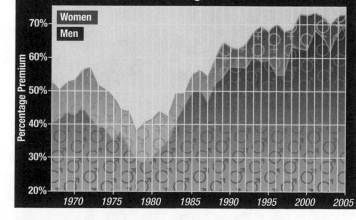

Source: Current Population Survey, U.S. Bureau of Labor Statistics.

Figure 2 shows that the growth in returns to education for women has paralleled that for men over the past 25 years, but has remained at a somewhat higher level. Figure 3 shows that returns for blacks have increased as much as those for whites. As these two figures show, the potential to improve one's

Figure 2

Percentage by which the wages of college-educated men and women exceed those of men and women with high school only.

Women Gain More From College...

Source: Current Population Survey, U.S. Bureau of Labor Statistics.

Figure 3

Percentage by which the wages of blacks and whites with college educations exceed those of both races with high school only.

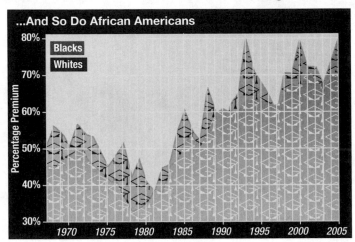

Source: Current Population Survey, U.S. Bureau of Labor Statistics.

labor-market prospects through higher education is greater now than at any time in the recent past, and this potential extends across gender and racial lines.

The growth in returns to college has generated a predictable response: as the education earnings gap increased, a larger fraction of high school graduates went on to college. As Figure 4 shows, the proportion of men and women

Figure 4

The proportion of Americans going to college roughly tracks the rising economic premium that college offers.

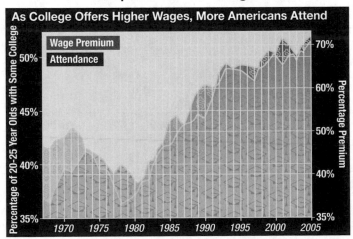

Source: Current Population Survey, U.S. Bureau of Labor Statistics.

ages 20 to 25 who attended college jumped by about half over the past 40 years, tracking the rise in the wage premium. When returns fell in the 1970s, the fraction going on to college declined. The rise in returns since 1980 has been accompanied by a significant rise in the fraction going on to college.

This increase in the proportion of persons going on to higher education is found among all racial and ethnic groups, but it is particularly important for women, who, in 2004, outnumbered men as students in degree-granting institutions of higher education by 33 percent.

Women have also shifted toward higher-earnings fields, such as business, law, and medicine: the number of women in graduate schools rose 66 percent between 1994 and 2004, while the number of men rose just 25 percent. And the greater education achievement of women compared to men is particularly prominent among blacks and Latinos: the proportion of black women who attend colleges and universities jumped from 24 percent to 43 percent between 1974 and 2003, while the proportion of white men rose only from 41 percent to 49 percent.

The potential generated by higher returns to education extends from individuals to the economy as a whole. Growth in the education level of the population has been a significant source of rising wages, productivity, and living standards over the past century. Higher returns to education will accelerate growth in living standards as existing investments have a higher return, and additional investments in education will be made in response to the higher returns. Gains from the higher returns will not be limited to GDP and other measures of economic activity; education provides a wide range of benefits not captured in GDP, and these will grow more rapidly as well due to the additional investments in schooling.

Why is the earnings gap widening? Because the demand for educated and other skilled persons is growing. That is hardly surprising, given developments in computers and the Internet, advances in biotechnology, and a general shift in economic activity to more education-intensive sectors, such as finance and professional services. Also, globalization has encouraged the importing of products using relatively low-skilled labor from abroad. At the same time, world demand has risen for the kinds of products and services that are provided by high-skilled employees.

When calculating the returns to education, we look at the *costs* of education as well. And even accounting for the rise in university tuition (it more than doubled, on average, in constant dollars between 1980 and 2005), overall returns to college and graduate study have increased substantially. Indeed, it appears that the increases in tuition were partly induced by the greater return to college education. Pablo Peña, in a Ph.D. dissertation in progress at the University of Chicago, argues convincingly that tuition rose in part because students want to invest more in the quality of their education, and increased spending per student by colleges is partly financed by higher tuition levels. More investment in the quality and quantity of schooling will benefit both individuals and society.

This brings us to our punch line. Should an increase in earnings inequality due primarily to higher rates of return on education and other skills be considered a favorable rather than an unfavorable development? We think so. Higher rates of return on capital are a sign of greater productivity in the economy, and that inference is fully applicable to human capital as well as to physical capital. The initial impact of higher returns to human capital is wider inequality in earnings (the same as the initial effect of higher returns on physical capital), but that impact becomes more muted and may be reversed over time as young men and women invest more in their human capital.

We conclude that the forces raising earnings inequality in the United States are beneficial to the extent that they reflect higher returns to investments in education and other human capital. Yet this conclusion should not produce complacency, for the response so far to these higher returns has been disturbingly limited. For example, why haven't more high school graduates gone on to a college education when the benefits are so apparent? Why don't more of those who go to college finish a four-year degree? (Only about half do so.) And why has the proportion of American youth who drop out of high school, especially African-American and Hispanic males, remained fairly constant?

The answers to these and related questions lie partly in the breakdown of the American family, and the resulting low skill levels acquired by many children in elementary and secondary school—particularly individuals from broken households. Cognitive skills tend to get developed at very early ages while, as our colleague James Heckman has shown, noncognitive skills—such as study habits, getting to appointments on time, and attitudes toward work—get fixed at later, although still relatively young, ages. Most high school dropouts certainly appear to be seriously deficient in the noncognitive skills that would enable them to take advantage of the higher rates of return to education and other human capital.

So instead of lamenting the increased earnings gap caused by education, policy makers and the public should focus attention on how to raise the fraction of American youth who complete high school and then go on for a college education. Solutions are not cheap or easy. But it will be a disaster if the focus remains so much on the earnings inequality itself that Congress tries to interfere directly with this inequality rather than trying to raise the education levels of those who are now being left behind.

For many, the solution to an increase in inequality is to make the tax structure more progressive—raise taxes on high-income households and reduce taxes on low-income households. While this may sound sensible, it is not. Would these same individuals advocate a tax on going to college and a subsidy for dropping out of high school in response to the increased importance of education? We think not. Yet shifting the tax structure has exactly this effect.

A more sensible policy is to try to take greater advantage of the opportunities afforded by the higher returns to human capital and encourage more human capital investment. Attempts to raise taxes and impose other penalties on the higher earnings that come from greater skills could greatly reduce the productivity of the world's leading economy by discouraging investments in its most productive and precious form of capital—human capital.

POSTSCRIPT

Is Increasing Economic Inequality a Serious Problem?

The list of negative consequences mentioned by James Kurth is quite long and varied. It includes conspicuous consumption, corporate concentration, biased immigration policies, regressive tax policies, many subsidies for the welloff, limitations on many policies benefitting lower groups, the coming of a crisis of overproduction and under-consumption and thus a bad recession, excessive debt, trade imbalances, and even greater danger from terrorism. Can anything good be said about the growing inequality?

According to Gary S. Becker and Kevin M. Murphy, it is making America much stronger. Inequality puts a high premium on higher education, which has driven up college enrollments and caused many Americans to better themselves.

Inequality, stratification, and social mobility are central concerns of sociology, and they are addressed by a large body of literature. Important discussions of income inequality include Robert H. Frank, *Falling Behind: How Rising Inequality Harms the Middle Class* (University of California Press, 2007); Allan C. Ornstein, *Class Counts: Education, Inequality, and the Shrinking Middle Class* (Rowman & Littlefield, 2007); Barry Bluestone and Bennett Harrison, *Growing Prosperity: The Battle for Growth With Equity in the Twenty-First Century* (Houghton Mifflin, 2000); D. G. Champernowne and F. A. Cowell, *Economic Inequality and Income Distribution* (Cambridge University Press, 1998); Sheldon Danziger and Peter Gottschalk, *America Unequal* (Harvard University Press, 1995); Richard B. Freeman, *When Earnings Diverge: Causes, Consequences, and Cures for the New Inequality in the U.S.* (National Policy Association, 1997); Andrew Hacker, *Money: Who Has How Much and Why* (Scribner's Reference, 1997); Chuck Collins and Felice Yeskel, *Economic Apartheid in America* (New Press, 2005); Paul Ryscavage, *Income Inequality in America: An Analysis of Trends* (M. E. Sharpe, 1999); Edward N. Wolff, *Top Heavy: The Increasing Inequality of Wealth in America and What Can Be Done about It* (New Press, 2002); *The Causes and Consequences of Increasing Inequality*, edited by Finis Welch (University of Chicago Press, 2001); James Tardner David Smith (eds.), *Inequality Matters: The Growing Ecomomic Divide in America and Its Poisonous Consequences* (New Press, 2005); and Samuel Bowles, et al. (eds.) *Unequal Chances* (Princeton University Press, 2005). A big part of the inequality picture is the conditions of the working poor, which is analyzed by Lawrence Mishel et al., *The State of Working America, 2002–2003* (Cornell University Press, 2003); *Low-Wage America: How Employers Are*

Reshaping Opportunity in the Workplace, edited by Eileen Appelbaum et al. (Russell Sage Foundation, 2003); and David K. Shipler, *The Working Poor: Invisible in America* (Knopf, 2004). For a poignant ethnographic study of the poor and their disadvantages, see Elliot Liebow, *Tell Them Who I Am: The Lives of Homeless Women* (Free Press, 1993).

ISSUE 8

Has Feminism Benefited
American Society?

YES: Barbara Epstein, from "The Successes and Failures of Feminism," *Journal of Women's History* (Summer 2002)

NO: Kate O'Beirne, from *Women Who Make the World Worse* (Sentinel, 2006)

ISSUE SUMMARY

YES: History Professor, Barbara Epstein argues that the feminist movement has been highly successful in changing the consciousness of Americans to "an awareness of the inequality of women and a determination to resist it." She explains how feminists succeeded at the consciousness level but have declined as a movement for social change.

NO: Journalist Kate O'Beirne argues that feminism is unpopular with women and is pushing an agenda that most women do not support. She claims that most women have concluded "that the feminist movement is both socially destructive and personally disappointing."

The publication of Betty Friedan's *The Feminine Mystique* (W. W. Norton, 1963) is generally thought of as the beginning of the modern women's movement, and since that time significant changes have occurred in American society. Data on advanced degrees and on income mark the profound changes. In 1960 only 35 percent of BAs were awarded to women but in 2003 that percentage had increased to 57 percent. The comparable figures for MAs were 32 percent in 1960 and 59 percent in 2003, for PhDs were 11 percent in 1960 and 48 percent in 2003, and for law degrees were 2.5 percent in 1960 and 48 percent in 2003. The number of women in Congress in 1960 was 20 percent and in 2002 was 73 percent. In 1963 the average full time adult women worker earned 58 percent of what the average adult male worker earned while in 2003 they earned 75 percent.

Many other changes marking women's progress are readily available. Occupations and professions, schools, clubs, associations, and governmental positions that were by tradition or law previously reserved for men only are now open to women. Women are found in increasing numbers among lawyers, judges, physicians, and elected officials. In 1981 President Ronald Reagan appointed the first woman, Sandra Day O'Connor, to the Supreme Court. In 1983 the first American woman astronaut, Sally Ride, was included in the crew of a space shuttle, and now women are on many of the space shuttle missions. The service academies have accepted women since 1976, and women in the military participated in the U.S. invasion of Panama in December 1989, the Persian Gulf War in 1990–1991, and the War to liberate Iraq in 2003. Elizabeth Watson became the first woman to head a big-city police department when the mayor of Houston appointed her chief of police in January 1990. New breakthroughs for women are now common and a woman president may not be far off.

These sorts of changes—quantifiable and highly publicized—signal a change in women's roles in the direction that feminists have championed. But more than three decades after Friedan's book there are still many inequalities that favor men including income and poverty indicators. Much change toward greater equality has also occurred in the cultural area, but full parity has not yet been achieved. Femininity and femaleness are not valued as highly as maleness and masculinity. Housework and child rearing are not shared equally in two career families though substantial progress has been made. Women are still adapting to a man's world.

Feminism—an ideology that, in its most basic form, directly opposes sexism by supporting gender equality and portraying women and men as essentially equals—has been a driving force in shaping the modern women's movement. The final legal victory of the women's movement was supposed to be the passage of the Equal Rights Amendment (ERA) to the Constitution, which would have made a person's sex an irrelevant distinction under the law. The ERA passed both houses of Congress by overwhelming margins in 1972, but it failed to win ratification from the required three-fourths of the state legislatures. The amendment was not ratified in part due to the efforts of a coalition of groups, composed overwhelmingly of women, who went to battle against it. Obviously, the women's movement did not represent the views of all women; many continued to believe in traditional gender roles. This pattern continues to today. Some of the prominent opponents against today's feminism are women.

In the readings that follow, a favorable view of feminism is presented by Barbara Epstein. The strongest arguments for feminism are the intolerable inequities that existed before the women's movement and the accomplishments of feminists since then as Epstein demonstrates. In contrast Kate O'Beirne argues that feminists falsely reconstruct gender realities to portray men as exploiters and women as victims and to blame women's unhappiness on being chained to child raising and homemaking. Her main criticism is that feminism attacks the family and seeks policies that run counter to natural differences between the sexes. She concludes that the feminist program of action will have largely adverse impacts such as undermining the family, encouraging divorce, and harming children.

YES ⤺

Barbara Epstein

The Successes and Failures
of Feminism

I have been trying to figure out for several years how feminism should go forward. This seems to me to be the perfect audience to present these ideas to, and get reactions from, so I am going to try out some of my thoughts on you. I want to talk about what the achievements of the women's movement have been and what remains undone—what the strengths were and what some of the weaknesses are.

Leaving aside the antiwar movement of the 1960s, which I think played an important role in bringing the war to an end, the women's movement was the most successful movement of the 1960s and 1970s. The idea that women should enjoy full equality with men was a startlingly radical idea then. That idea has been widely accepted. It seems clear that women in the United States think differently about themselves now than they did 30 years ago because of the women's movement. There have been advances in opportunities for women, especially in the professions, also to, I think, a lesser degree in working-class jobs. Such issues as child care, violence against women, and reproductive rights have been placed on the public agenda as legitimate issues—dramatically different from the political agenda of the 1950s and through the 1960s. There have also been some actual advances in other areas, around such issues as women's health and violence against women, though, given the rightward drift of politics in the United States generally over the last several decades, the record on these concerns has been somewhat mixed. But on a rhetorical level at least, women's equality has been accepted as a goal by mainstream society. The gap between rhetoric and reality remains, but the fact that women's equality has been accepted as a legitimate goal creates an opportunity for changing the reality. It seems to me that probably the most important contribution of the women's movement of the 1960s and 1970s was that it gave women a sense of their collective power. And I think it is useful to look at the difference between second-wave feminism and first-wave feminism in relation to this sort of issue. Women who participated in the women's movement of the late nineteenth and early twentieth centuries also learned this lesson, but the lesson had a narrower impact. First of all, that movement, particularly in the latter part of the nineteenth and early twentieth centuries, was largely confined to middle-class and upper-middle-class, overwhelmingly white women. Working-class women also participated, but they constituted quite a small element of the movement and the memory of that movement was quite effectively obliterated during the 1940s and 1950s, such that feminism in a sense had to be reinvented in the 1960s. The impact of the second wave of feminism has been broader and deeper and the obliteration of that lesson is not going to happen. So that's a very major accomplishment.

The second wave of feminism was successful not only because it led to changes in the lives of huge numbers of women, but also because the movement evolved over time. And I think in many ways, the movement evolved in positive directions. When the women's movement first emerged in the mid 1960s, it was largely confined to university students, other young people of more or less the same class and a slightly older group of women professionals. There were women of color and working-class women in these movements, but they tended to enter the movements through the same routes that everybody else did, namely the fact that they were in college or in the professions despite unusual origins. Their presence in the movement in the late 1960s did not mean that feminism was being adopted within working-class communities or within communities of color. In those years, there was a wide gap between the feminist claim to speak for all women and the reality, which had to do with the specific class and social origins of the women making up the movement. Most of them were from the middle class or the upper middle class, and I suspect actually that most of them were from the suburbs. In the 1970s and into the 1980s, women of color began to articulate their own versions of feminism, and working women, who had not been part of feminism's earlier university student cohort, began to organize around demands of equal treatment in the workplace and other issues working-class women faced. If one were to contrast the women's movement of the 1960s and beyond with the women's movement of the nineteenth and early twentieth centuries, I think one might say that while the first movement narrowed over time, in terms of its constituency and its class perspective, the latter movement—our movement—widened over time. Another way of putting this is to remember that the nineteenth-century women's movement emerged out of an alliance between white women and African Americans in the struggle for abolitionism. But after the Civil War, in the context of a white middle class shifting toward the political right in the late nineteenth century, the women's movement shifted away from earlier alliances. By the early twentieth century, the activists were arguing for women's suffrage on racist and anti-immigrant grounds. So there was a shift away from the alliance with black people specifically, and with a broader, progressive agenda, more generally. I do not think the women's movement of our era has ever been racist in that sense, but I also think it has improved over time. In the mid-1960s, the movement was largely composed of white women who were often blind to the fact that they could not actually speak for all women, but by the 1970s and certainly by the 1980s, there was a much greater awareness of the need to recognize difference within the women's movement, and a much greater awareness of the need to build alliances with other progressive constituencies, particularly groups of color.

Over the 1980s and 1990s, feminism as a perspective or as an identity spread widely and a kind of diffuse feminist consciousness has become a mass phenomenon. There are enormous numbers of women who identify as feminists or who think about women's issues in a different way as a result of feminism. There are also now countless projects, groups, and organizations that are, in one way or another, infused by a feminist perspective. But it is also the case that the main organizations of the women's movement, the most visible organizations such as the National Organization for Women and others, have narrowed in their perspective and are no longer mass-based. They are no longer connected to mass movements, and they have become organizations that are run by staffs rather than on the basis of membership engagement. These organizations have become more cautious in their approach than was the case with even the liberal wing of the women's movement in the late 1960s and 1970s, and they have become more identified with professional, middle-class women and their perspectives. This is not true of the whole women's movement, and actually this conference represents other strands within the movement. There are many organizations that rest on grassroots organizing among women, such as the National Congress of Neighborhood Women. There are many local groups focused on women of color and working women's concerns. There are many such groups in California, including the Mothers of East Los Angeles and the Women's Action for New Directions. While there are many grassroots-based women's organizations with broad social concerns, these do not make up the most visible wing of the women's movement. Despite a great deal of grassroots organizing, there is a way in which the women's movement has lost a sense of coherent direction and urgency. The wind has gone out of the sails. And I would like to address why.

The wind has gone out of the sails, not only of the women's movement but also of the progressive movement as a whole in the United States generally. There are hopeful signs. Among these is the struggle against globalization and corporate control that emerged in Seattle, and in which feminism has been a major component. Though it has not yet congealed into a movement, it holds out the possibility of something new and exciting. There are probably more people involved in grassroots organizing around progressive issues in the United States now than there were in the 1960s and 1970s. But despite these positive signs, the progressive movement as a whole has become institutionalized. It has become an arena in which many of us live and find consensus on many issues. But this progressive sector is not having much effect on the political direction of the country as a whole. Why is that? What has happened?

Part of the answer is that feminism has become more an idea than a movement. And even as a movement, it lacks some of the impetus that it once had. I think that in the case of the women's movement, the gap between the breadth of the original vision and the current state of activism comes from the gap between the feminism's broad and radical vision and the much narrower character of its actual tangible accomplishments—something Linda Gordon alluded to in her contribution to this conference when she said that the inspiration within the feminist movement came very largely from women's liberation in the 1960s and 1970s, but the liberal wing of feminism accomplished the concrete victories. I would go a little bit further and say that not only was it liberal feminists that were able to accomplish those victories, but that their victories were narrower than the intentions of the larger movement. There are many historical cases of popular movements that made broad and radical demands which then become winnowed down such that the final achievement was the least threatening element of the original set of demands. So it is not a big surprise that this should happen to the women's movement as it has happened to other movements, but it is worth looking at the fact that it did happen, and what the consequences have been.

Linda Gordon also mentioned that there were the two wings of the women's movement. People have categorized these differently. On the one hand, there was liberal feminism; on the other hand, there was women's liberation. People also sometimes talked about that wing as comprised of radical feminism and socialist feminism, with radical feminists regarding women's oppression as the root of all oppression, and socialist feminists placing women's oppression within the context of other forms of oppression, particularly race and class. But if one contrasts radical feminism with the liberal wing, you could say that the main goal of the liberal wing of the movement was to win equal access for women to the public sphere on equal terms with men, particularly to the sphere of work. While women's liberation or radical feminism supported that goal, it also aimed for two broader visions. One was that women's liberation insisted that the subordination of women in the public realm—both had to be addressed simultaneously. Radical feminists also insisted that it was not possible to win equality for women without winning equality in society across the board. In other words, women could not be equals in a society deeply stratified by race and class.

In the 1960s and 1970s, there was actually a lot of overlap between women's liberation or radical feminism, and liberal feminism. I think the influence tended to go from the radical sphere towards the liberal sphere; that liberal feminists were pushed by radical activists. Many liberals adopted radical ideas. Another element, particularly in the 1970s, was that people from women's liberation participated in an enormous amount of organizing around feminist issues among working-class women. Working-class women's caucuses demanded affirmative action to help themselves and others like them. So in a certain sense, it's not accurate to divide the women's movement up into different spheres because they overlapped, and because the goal of affirmative action—which is usually, and I think appropriately, associated with liberal feminism—also contained a very important working-class element.[1] However, despite the sort of ferment and intersection of liberal and radical demands that took place in the 1960s and 1970s, the fact of the matter is that demands and results are not always the same thing. Affirmative action campaigns in the end were more effective in the professions than elsewhere, and educated and overwhelmingly white women took the greatest advantage of these opportunities. I think that these gains in affirmative action, combined with the growing gap between the lower and higher rungs of the economy (which continued to increase divisions among women despite the gains of affirmative action), pushed the women's movement as a whole away from the radical demands of the 1960s and 1970s.

Meanwhile, radical feminism itself became stalled in the 1970s. It was torn apart by two things. The first was the kind of factionalism, ideological conflicts, and internal struggles that Linda Gordon addressed, which led to the decline of radical feminism and the emergence of a much less political version of feminism that we called cultural feminism by the end of the decade.[2] Such sectarianism is ordinarily associated with movements that are in decline, but feminism at the time was strong and growing. My analysis of why this happened is that the radical wing of the women's movement became a bit crazed in the late 1960s and early 1970s, for the same reason that radicalism in the United States as a whole was becoming a bit crazed (and I speak as someone who was part of this movement). Radicals not only adopted revolution as their aim, but also thought that revolution was within reach. Now there were many versions of revolution—feminist, Marxist/Leninist, Black, and so on. But everybody thought revolution was a good idea, and virtually everybody thought it was around the corner. In my view at least, there was nothing wrong with the commitment to revolution; I wish we had more of it now. But there was something unrealistic about the view that if we did just the right thing, it would happen.

At bottom, the war in Vietnam produced a major crisis in U.S. society. Protest against the war combined with protests against racism and sexism made it seem possible to create a new society. But the fact of the matter was that once the war was over, the major basis for protest evaporated. And those of us who thought that protest would go on to become a revolutionary movement in the United States turned out to be wrong. In fact, what happened was that when the war came to an end, the largest sector of the movement evaporated, and the radical core of the various movements began to find itself isolated. I think it took longer for this to happen in the case of radical feminism than it did in the case of other sectors of the radical movement simply because the mainstream feminist movement was strong and growing, and within the feminist movement, there were many people who were quite open to radical ideas. But nevertheless, the trajectory of American society as a whole was toward the right, and the idea that revolution would happen tomorrow if you did just the right thing was clearly not accurate. By the 1980s, radical feminism too had been pushed to the margins and it was no longer a central current within American politics.

So I am arguing that two things happened more or less simultaneously. First, affirmative action was more or less accomplished, but in a form that was relatively conservative. At the same time, the radical sector of the movement more or less evaporated—or more accurately, it moved into academia. While most radicals did not become academics, enough people did that there was a sort of a critical mass of radicals in academia. Because it was a safe space for radicals and because of access to publishing and whatnot, the university became one of the spaces where feminism was defined. At the same time, academic feminism was gradually losing its ties to activism outside the academy.

This did not happen to all academics, of course, and this conference is in a certain sense about the people who took a different path. I am very pleased that this conference and the collections have highlighted the work of

Frances Fox Piven, for example, who is a model in continuing to construct that bridge between activism and academia. Academic feminism, by and large, took a different path.

I suggested earlier that the politics and constituency of first-wave feminism narrowed and that was not the case with our feminist movement. But I think I was careful to say that there were also some problems. Even though I think our movement has not narrowed, particularly in relation to race, I think there is another respect in which the current women's movement has rather unconsciously narrowed its politics, which mirrors what happened in the nineteenth century. As the women's movement aged, so to speak, it became vulnerable to absorbing trends within its own class. And I think that is what has happened to the most visible and prominent aspects of our women's movement.

The women's movement of the 1960s and 1970s, especially the radical core of that movement, demanded not only equality for women, but also equality across the board. Feminists sought an egalitarian society governed by humane values. But since the early 1970s, economic inequalities have steadily widened in the United States. Most people now work longer hours at less secure jobs. Often these jobs are associated with increasing stress. Many people have spoken of work having become a religion in the United States. I think it might be more accurate to say that for many people, work has become the only meaningful source of identity. In a broader sense, the United States is becoming an increasingly individualistic, cold, and selfish society. It seems to me that we now live in a society in which people's concern for other people is becoming a kind of quaint, archaic value. People seem to assume that you should really be mostly concerned with yourself and maybe for other members of your nuclear family, if you happen to have one, but beyond that, it is a sort of silliness to be concerned with anybody else. Many progressives seem to have absorbed these ideas too. And I think the ways we have absorbed them has been by throwing ourselves into work and adopting or absorbing the view into the way we value ourselves. I know that this is true of me. I have the sense that it is also true of other people in our general community. I cannot really speak for the United States as a whole, but I am struck, even in visiting other countries, with the reigning individualism in the United States, which seems to be much further advanced than it is elsewhere in the world—even though I also think that individualism is a kind of global tendency.

Feminism is not marking a noticeable challenge to this cultural shift. In fact, I think that the version of feminism that was formed through the demand for women's equality in the workplace, and then, in practice, became focused around the success of the demand for affirmative action for professional women, has blindly absorbed many of the dominant cultural values of the middle class. In the 1970s, many feminists thought that if only we could get enough women into academic jobs, academia would change. It would become a less elitist, more humane place, concerned with social good. Well, a fair number of women are in the academy and I do not think that the academy has changed in those directions. Instead, I think the academy has gone in the opposite direction. This is not women's fault; it is because we are caught up in a wildly accelerating global version of capitalism that is drawing everything, including the universities, into its vortex and bringing market values to every area of life. Simply having more women in the academy does nothing to oppose this. As more people are in institutions that are adopting greater market values, the greater the pressures are for those people to adopt those values. We need a movement that explicitly and overtly criticizes this shift and the values associated with it.

I am suggesting here—and this is all completely impressionistic—that although the values of individualism, market values, and so forth, have taken on increased importance throughout the United States as a whole, there is a way in which the professional middle class has been the carrier of these values. We live in a society that is rapidly dividing between those who make it to the top and those who fall to the bottom, and generally speaking, people in the professional middle class would much rather rise than fall. There is a kind of scramble going on, and we are in the sector of society that is engaged in that scramble rather than critical of it. The media image of feminists as careerists was not entirely invented by a hostile press but feminists are no more careerists than other members of the same class. If this is true, then we are admitting that we have lost a grip on the social vision that feminism originally embraced. So I am calling for a return to a sort of revised version of radical feminism. It seems to me that we have to place feminism within the demand for an egalitarian society and a demand for a society that respects human connection and respects communities and promotes them rather than destroying them. And I do think we can look back to the legacy of women's liberation for at least some very good hints about how to do this.

Notes

1. I learned about this from Nancy Maclean, whose very important article on the use of affirmative action by working-class women appeared in a recent issue of *Feminist Studies*.

2. These developments are wonderfully described by Alice Echols in her book *Daring to Be Bad: Radical Feminism in America, 1967–1975*, and also by Ruth Rosen in her recent book *The World Split Open: How the Modern Women's Movement Changed America*. What is striking about both these books is that they are written from a perspective which is deeply feminist and deeply respectful of the women's movement, but also very clear-eyed about its problems.

Kate O'Beirne

 **NO**

Women Who Make the World Worse

How Radical Feminists Have Weakened the Family

The traditional family boosts the health, happiness, and wealth of husbands, wives, and children and raises the blood pressure of a certain kind of woman. Betty Friedan's 1963 *The Feminine Mystique* is typically included on lists of the one hundred most influential books of the last century. In a chapter entitled "The Comfortable Concentration Camp," she likened the passivity and hopelessness of American POWs in Korea to American women trapped at home with children in the suburbs. She later wrote, "For fear of being alone, I almost lost my own self-respect trying to hold on to a marriage that was based no longer on love but on dependent hate. It was easier for me to start the women's movement which was needed to change society than to change my own personal life."

Friedan got a divorce in 1969, but unfortunately not before she expounded on the merits of Marxist economics, persuaded far too many women that a selfless devotion to their families was a recipe for misery, helped to create the National Organization for Women (NOW), and destructively politicized relations between the sexes. Over the next decades, Friedan's fans moved beyond her criticisms of mothers at home and launched a hostile assault on marriage and family life.

The radical demand for androgyny and personal autonomy is irreconcilable with the need for different sex roles and mutual self-sacrifice between parents raising their offspring. Influential feminists see two major problems with the family that inhibit women's equality—husbands and fathers. Their advocacy and propaganda have eroded support for the family as an indispensable institution for both individuals and society.

Marriage Under Assault

In 1969, Marlene Dixon, a sociology professor at the University of Chicago, wrote, "The institution of marriage is the chief vehicle for the perpetuation of the oppression of women; it is through the role of wife that the subjugation of women is maintained. In a very real way the role of wife has been the genesis of women's rebellion throughout history."

That same year, Kate Millett's *Sexual Politics* was published. What began as a thesis for the Columbia University doctoral candidate became a celebrated call for the end of a patriarchal Institution that treated women like chattel. In 1970, Robin Morgan, a founder of Ms. magazine, was calling marriage "a slavery-like practice," and arguing, "We can't destroy the inequities between men and women until we destroy marriage." The following year, Australian feminist Germaine Greer's *The Female Eunuch* argued that married women had to save themselves by fleeing from their marriages in favor of "rambling organic structures."

By 1972, the angry screeds against marriage were being dressed up with academic adornments. In her influential book *The Future of Marriage*, Pennsylvania State University sociologist Jessie Bernard claimed that the "destructive nature" of marriage harmed women's mental and emotional health. In short, according to Bernard, "Being a housewife makes women sick." The fact that married women regularly reported that they were happier than unmarried women was dismissed as a symptom of this marital illness. "To be happy in a relationship which imposes so many impediments on her, as traditional marriage does, women must be slightly mentally ill." It was their oppression speaking when wives reported satisfaction with their lives. "Women accustomed to expressing themselves freely could not be happy in such a relationship."

Although the late Professor Bernard's pronouncements were those of a left-wing ideologue with a radical agenda, she was considered one of the top women sociologists in the world, and according to *The Boston Globe*, her twenty-three books established her as "the preeminent scholar of the women's movement." She held visiting professorships at Princeton and at the University of California. In *The Future of Motherhood* she argued that being a mother was also hazardous to women's health. She saw the desire for children as a sexist social construction and believed that many women preferred celibacy to "the degradation of most male-female sexual relationships." Professor Bernard sounded a warning about what truly liberated women could expect: "Men will resist and punish them; unliberated women, brainwashed not only to accept their slavery in marriage but also to love it, will resist them." The Center for Women's Policy Studies established a Jessie Bernard Wise Women award to recognize similar worthy insights.

Many establishment figures share Bernard's views. Laura Singer, who was president of the American Association for Marriage and Family Therapy in the 1970s, has explained, "I wouldn't say that marriage and self-actualization are *necessarily* mutually exclusive, but they are difficult to achieve together."

If these attacks on marriage strike you as extreme, you have some surprising company. Twenty years after she helped launch the modern women's movement, even Betty Friedan was criticizing her feminist sisters for their hostility to family life. In her 1981 book *The Second Stage*, she wrote: "The women's movement is being blamed, above all, for the destruction of the family." She cited the increase in divorces, in single-parent households, and in the number of women living alone and asked, "Can we keep on shrugging all this off as enemy propaganda— 'their problem, not ours'? I think we must at least admit and begin openly to discuss feminist denial of the importance of family, of women's own needs to give and get love and nurture, tender loving care."

This time Betty Friedan's appeals fell on deaf feminist ears. The scholarship and sentiment that sounded dire warnings about marriage's harmful effects on women's well-being and ambitions had found an enthusiastic audience in women's studies programs and was popularized by journalists like Barbara Ehrenreich, a former columnist for *Time* magazine.

Writing from that powerful perch, Ehrenreich repeatedly denigrated marriage and family life. She advocated that the government concentrate on promoting "good divorces" rather than attempt to strengthen marriages and argued that the only problem with single-parent households was the lack of sufficient government support. She used the Menendez brothers and O.J. Simpson cases as an opportunity to share her opinion about the malevolent forces afoot in American families. The murders should prompt us to think "that the family may not be the ideal and perfect living arrangement after all—that it can be a nest of pathology and a cradle of gruesome violence." She asserted that "millions flock to therapy groups" and "we are all, it is often said, 'in recovery.' And from what? Our families, in most cases." She cited the "long and honorable tradition of 'anti-family' thought" and quoted Edmund Leach, the renowned British anthropologist, stating that "far from being the basis of a good society, the family, with its narrow privacy and tawdry secrets, is the source of all discontents."

Marlo Thomas and her pals, including Lily Tomlin, Bea Arthur, and Whoopi Goldberg, literally sang the praises of never-formed or broken families. Thomas's earlier *Free to Be . . . You and Me* attempted to overcome nasty sex stereotypes and create a more welcoming world for boys who played with dolls. In her *Free to Be . . . a Family,* any arrangement at all was promoted as just fine for raising children. The book and album wanted to teach children that "if the people whom you live with are happy to see your face, that's a family." The stories, songs and poems were "really about the family as it exists today, not the family as a storybook idea."

During the 2004 campaign, Teresa Heinz Kerry reflected a casual contempt for the role of wife and mother when she proclaimed that Laura Bush hadn't worked at a "real job . . . since she's been grown up." Laura Bush worked as a teacher and librarian for ten years, before giving up her career in education to raise her twin daughters. Most people, who haven't inherited a condiments empire and the resources to allow them to keep busy handing out fat foundation grants, think being a wife and mother is a "real job" for a "grown-up".

Before long, the antipathy to marriage infected the academy and was reflected in social science textbooks. When a nonpartisan group studied twenty textbooks used in eight thousand college courses in the mid-nineties, they found, "These books repeatedly suggest that marriage is more a problem than a solution. The potential costs of marriage to adults, particularly women, often receive exaggerated treatment, while the benefits of marriage, both to individuals and society, are frequently downplayed or ignored."

In *Changing Families*, Judy Root Aulette, a sociology professor at the University of North Carolina at Charlotte, didn't mention a single beneficial effect of marriage in the three chapters she devoted to the subject (one of which was titled "Battering and Marital Rape"). She did find room to approvingly cite Friedrich Engels stating that marriage was "created for a particular purpose: to control women and children."

While Professor Aulette had a lot to learn about the institution of marriage, she was well schooled in the politics of phony grievances. She accused the report's author of trying "to get rid of my voice, and my right to be in a class-room and present a feminist point of view."

In her textbook, Marine Baca Zinn proved herself worthy of a Jessie Bernard Wise Women award when she wrote, "If marriage is so difficult for wives, why do the majority surveyed judge themselves as happy? . . . [The reason] is that happiness is interpreted by wives in terms of conformity. Since they are conforming to society's expectations, this must be happiness."

The study's author, Professor Norval Glenn of the University of Texas, explained that the textbooks studied represented "the distilled essence of the current conventional wisdom" and were used to train the next generation of counselors, social workers, therapists, and teachers. He illustrated the conventional wisdom by contrasting the number of pages in each book focusing on the benefits of marriage for adults—less than one—with the pages per book devoted to domestic violence—twelve."

Marriage Benefits Men and Women

Professor Linda Waite of the University of Chicago filled a well-researched book with the good news about marriage. In *The Case for Marriage: Why Married People Are Happier, Healthier, and Better Off Financially*, Waite, a self-described liberal Democrat, and her conservative co-author, Maggie Gallagher, detailed the research findings that thoroughly refute Jessie Bernard and her acolytes' case against marriage. Linda Waite saw the notion that marriage was a much better deal for men than women as "the most powerful and persuasive" of the modern myths about marriage. She thought it was important for young women to be well-informed before they make their choices. "If we pretend that women are not advantaged by being married, we are doing them a great disservice."

Among Waite and Gallagher's findings: Because wives influence husbands to take better care of themselves, men do get more health benefits from marriage than women, but both married men and women express "very high and very similar levels of satisfaction with their marriages" and are similarly committed to their spouses. Women gain more financially from marriage than men do, and while both sexes are winners in sexual satisfaction, women gain even more owing to the sense of commitment that improves their sex life. And, when a wide range of disorders is considered, both sexes enjoy a boost in mental health. In fact, married women are generally less depressed than *Sex and the City's* Carrie Bradshaw and her single sisters.

A well-respected study found that similar percentages of married women and men (41 percent and 38 percent) report they are "very happy," rates that are far higher than for those who have never married or are divorced. Social psychologist David G. Myers, author of *The Pursuit of Happiness*, strongly endorses Waite and Gallagher's conclusions. "The idea that women are happier if they are unmarried and men happier if they are married is blatantly untrue. The evidence is mountainous in the other direction."

Unlike other liberal women engaged in research on family issues, Dr. Waite had no preconceived notions or ideological axes to grind when she began to look at the data on marital status and mortality ten years ago. She was aware of other researchers looking at earnings data and health issues, but no one had put together the big picture. Waite recognized, "There's a general pattern here that nobody's noticed. All of the big things in life—good outcomes for children, health, long life—depend on marriage." This insight became the subject of a speech she delivered to the Population Association of America as its president in 1995.

Divorce Hurts

Professor Waite and her colleagues have more recently published a study on divorce that showed that unhappily married people were no happier after their marriages ended. They analyzed data from a national survey on families and households and found, "When the adults who said they were unhappily married in the late 1980s were interviewed again five years later, those who had divorced were on average still unhappy or even less happy, while those who stayed in their marriages on average had moved past the bad times and were at a happier stage."

Waite, who has been married for over thirty years, has a married daughter and a daughter with cerebral palsy who lives at home. She was married as an undergraduate and divorced from her first husband after four years with no children. She explains that her case against divorce is less applicable to the kind of short, early union she had. "It's very different. You're not leaving somebody who's financially dependent, you haven't built years of friendships, you don't have kids, you're not as much a working single unit as people who are married for a long time."

Waite explains that once children are present, the case against divorce becomes stronger. Professor Waite and Maggie Gallagher looked at the effect of divorce on children in their book and concluded that children were usually not better off when their parents split up. They pointed out that divorce might end marital conflict for parents, but it doesn't end "what really bothers kids: parental conflict." Their research indicates, "Children of divorce also have less money, live in poorer neighborhoods, go to poorer schools, and do worse in school than children of married parents—even if those marriages have a high degree of conflict."

In their book *Generation at Risk*, two liberal social scientists estimated that only about a third of divorces with children involved are so troubled that children are likely to benefit from the break-up. The remaining 70 percent of divorces involve low-conflict marriages where children are less harmed than they would be if their parents separated.

Fractured Families and Disposable Dads

In the past, the majority of Americans believed that unhappily married couples should stay together for the sake of their children. Now, only 15 percent agree that "when there are children in the family, parents should stay together even if they don't get along." When the traditional virtues of self-sacrifice and duty lose in a conflict with the feminist doctrine of self-fulfillment and personal autonomy, children pay a very steep price.

In an ominous sign that the well-being of children is unlikely to take precedence over the desires of adults any time soon, among young people there is little appreciation for the benefits of marriage and widespread support for "alternative lifestyles" as perfectly suitable for raising children. A national survey of high school seniors found that although a large majority of these teenagers expect to marry, less than a third of girls and only slightly more than a third of boys believe "that most people will have fuller and happier lives if they choose legal marriage rather than staying single or just living with someone." More than half of both boys and girls think out-of-wedlock child-bearing is a "worthwhile lifestyle."

In 1988, among never-married people between the ages of eighteen and thirty-four, 64 percent of males and 56 percent of females thought "those who want children should get married." In 2002, only 51 percent of males and 42 percent of females in this age group thought having children and being married shouldn't be separate pursuits.

While the pathetic plight of wives and mothers was being peddled by women like Bernard, Aulette, and Zinn, others were making the case that dads are dispensable.

Male lions roar to protect their young from threatening predators, penguin pops balance fragile eggs on their feet in frigid temperatures, while adult male elephants temper the delinquent behavior of the young bulls. When the National Fatherhood Initiative used these arresting thirty-second images from the animal kingdom to depict the importance of fathers in their "Nature of Fatherhood" ad campaign, they drove some feminists wild. NOW raised an alarm about the "dangerous policy" of paternal responsibility being promoted by the initiative, which hoped to encourage fathers to commit to marriage and parenting.

An article that argued "neither mothers nor fathers are unique or essential" was promoted to bolster the case that "NOW Knows Best." In "Deconstructing the Essential Father," published in the influential *American Psychologist* in 1999, the authors maintained that children are perfectly fine as long as they have "parenting figures" of either sex, who need not be biologically related. Predicatably, the authors favored policies that support the legitimacy of "diverse family structures" rather than "privileging the two-parent, heterosexual, married family." Fatherhood is a retrograde gender role and therefore verboten.

The academics did not just dismiss the unique contributions of fathers as unimportant. It was argued that a father's presence in the home extracts an overlooked cost because "some fathers' consumption of family resources in terms of gambling, purchasing alcohol, cigarettes, or other nonessential commodities, actually increases women's workload and stress level." So, message to moms: Throw the bums out.

Professor Louise B. Silverstein, a Yeshiva University psychology professor and family therapist, co-authored the study that sought "to create an ideology that defines the father-child bond as independent of the father-mother relationship." Professor Silverstein is a past president of the American Psychological Association's Division of Family Psychology and chairman (a title that could put her in therapy) of the Feminist Family Therapy Task Force within the APA Division of the Psychology of Women. Her 1999 article making the case for throwaway dads won the Association for Women in Psychology's Distinguished Publication Award.

From the indispensable Maggie Gallagher it won condemnation. Gallagher graduated from Yale University in 1982. Married with two sons, this Portland, Oregon, native lives in New York and is a syndicated columnist and president of the Institute for Marriage and Public Policy. The author of three books, she has been an editor of *National Review* and a senior editor of the Manhattan Institute's *City Journal*. George Gilder called her first book, *Enemies of Eros: How the Sexual Revolution Is Killing Family, Marriage, and Sex, and What We Can Do About It*, published in 1989, "the best book ever written on men, women and marriage."

Maggie Gallagher has mastered the social science research on marriage, the family, and child well-being to become a leading authority on the most personal public-policy questions we face. She devotes her formidable skills to debunking clichés and conventional wisdom about love, marriage, and children and has the fortitude to challenge a culture more interested in self-gratification to confront the consequences of our failure to keep our commitments.

After having some fun with Dr. Silverstein's conclusion that "both men and women have the same biological potential for nurturing" based on her examination of the behavior of marmoset fathers, Gallagher deconstructs Silverstein's deconstruction handiwork. "Our new desire to strengthen marriage is in their view just a scary attempt to reassert 'the cultural hegemony of traditional values, such as heterocentrism, Judeo-Christian marriage, and male power and privilege.' It leads to horrible, unrealistic policies—like giving job help to low-income married fathers (and not just welfare mothers), or a more marriage-friendly tax code. Instead, these hard- headed professors urge more practical solutions, like reconstructing traditional masculine ideology so men care for infants as much as women."

Maggie Gallagher incisively confronts the fundamental questions that Silverstein ignores. "Under what conditions are children likely to fare best? And, are adults obligated to provide, if they can, the best situation for their kids?" Answers: Living with their married biological parents, and Yes.

Louise Silverstein is the glorified guru of gender warriors, but Cornell University professor Urie Bronfenbrenner, who was widely regarded as one of the world's leading scholars in developmental psychology, child-rearing, and human ecology—the interdisciplinary field he created—strongly disagreed with her Dispensable Dad thesis. "Controlling for factors such as low income, children growing up in father-absent households are at a greater risk for experiencing a variety of behavioral and educational problems, including extremes of hyperactivity and withdrawal; lack of attentiveness in the classroom; difficulty in deferring gratification; impaired academic achievement; school misbehavior; absenteeism; dropping out; involvement in socially alienated peer groups; and the so-called 'teen-age syndrome' of behaviors that tend to hang together—smoking, drinking, early and frequent sexual experience, and in the more extreme cases, drugs, suicide, vandalism, violence and criminal acts."

In his defense of responsible fatherhood, Karl Zinsmeister counters Marlo Thomas's dismissal of the traditional family as a "storybook idea" by reminding us of its indispensability for men, women, and children. "It's when a culture stops upholding the paternal rituals, rules, and rewards that fathering withers. . . . Some people have actually convinced themselves families can do fine without fathers. They're wrong. Wherever men are not lured or corralled into concerning themselves with their children and mates, decent human society fades . . . the magic ingredients needed to tie men to their children are the ancient ones: Sexual restraint and enduring marriage." When men are committed to protecting and providing for their families, wives and children benefit and so too do husbands.

Studies show that men become more economically productive after they marry, with married men earning between 10 and 40 percent more than single men with similar education and job experience. Marriage also increases median family income, which more than doubled between 1947 and 1977. Over the past twenty years, the growth in median family income has slowed, increasing by just 9.6 percent, in large part because married couples, who do better economically, make up a decreasing proportion of all families.

In Britain, 49 percent of all births are illegitimate. In a sign that the British public has had its fill with the social and financial costs of unwed child-bearing, three unmarried sisters and their babies recently made front-page news. MUM AT 12, MUM AT 16, MUM AT 14, the headlines blared. The father of the sixteen-year-old's baby is a thirty-eight-year-old man in a "long-term relationship" with her; he lives with his parents. Their divorced mother had been married twice, but never to the fathers of her daughters. She became a grandmother three times in a year.

While most of the commentary criticized the intergenerational illegitimacy and complained that taxpayers had to pick up the considerable tab, Germaine Greer surfaced to celebrate the self-actualization of young girls doing their own thing. "Social historians will tell you that illegitimacy is highly hereditary. There have always been women like Yeats' Crazy Jane whose gardens grow 'nothing but babies and washing.' They live in an alternative society that is matrilineal, matrifocal, and matrilocal, a society that the patriarchy has always feared and hated." The "alternative society" Greer celebrates is on the brink of representing a majority of British births.

In 1960, only 9 percent of all children lived in single-parent, households. Presently in the United States, almost one third of children are born to single mothers. A large number of children will see their parents divorced before their eighteenth birthday. Two thirds of black children are born out of wedlock. Over half of American children will spend all or part of their childhood without their father in the home.

According to my former colleague, the Heritage Foundation's poverty guru Robert Rector, "The collapse of marriage is the principal cause of child poverty and a host of other social ills. A child raised by a never-married mother is seven times more likely to live in poverty than a child raised by his biological parents in an intact marriage." Nearly two thirds of poor children live in single-parent homes, and an additional 1.3 million children are born out of wedlock every year. We have never experienced so many children growing up without knowing what it means to live with the daily support and attention of their fathers.

Half of children living without their fathers have never been in their father's home, and one study found that only 27 percent of children over age four saw their father at least once a week, while 31 percent had no contact at all in the previous year.

In *The Abolition of Marriage*, Maggie Gallagher reminds us, "When we tell our girls that becoming a single mother—through divorce or failure to many—is a perfectly acceptable lifestyle choice, we forget that our boys are listening too. And this is what they hear: Men aren't necessary. Women can do it alone. Women and children are usually better off without men. Breadwinning oppresses women and children. Marriage and breadwinning can be hard. Why do it, if you are only oppressing the ones you love?"

Barbara Dafoe Whitehead is co-director of the National Marriage Project at Rutgers University. She famously concluded in *Atlantic Monthly* article that "Dan Quayle Was Right" following the feminist fits over the vice president's *Murphy Brown* comments. Dr. Whitehead recently reported, "According to some researchers, growing up with both married parents in a low-conflict marriage is so important to child well-being that it is replacing race, class, and neighborhood as the greatest source of difference in child outcomes."

According to the National Marriage Project, men today are increasingly staying single longer, fathering more illegitimate children, cohabiting rather than marrying, and divorcing in large numbers. In 1970, only 7 percent of men between the ages thirty-five and forty-four had never married, compared with 18 percent today.

The National Fatherhood Initiative that NOW's feminists rail against as a patriarchal plot offers some inescapable "Father Facts." The rate of child abuse in single-parent households is nearly twice the rate of child abuse in two-parent families. Even after controlling for factors like family background and neighborhood variables, boys who grew up outside of intact marriages were, on average, more than twice as likely to end up in jail as other boys, and twice as likely to use illegal drugs.

Intact families are a far more effective "program" than are most government schemes to reduce poverty, child abuse, crime, and drug abuse, or to boost educational outcomes.

Although costly to men, women, children, and taxpayers, opposition to the traditional family is growing. The influential American Law Institute (ALI) recently released a report arguing that family law should be reformed so that marriage and cohabitation are treated equally and that marriage should be redefined as a gender-neutral arrangement in order to accommodate same-sex couples. These lawyers want to wipe out biology as a basis for parenthood in order to ensure "family diversity."

Professor Katharine Bartlett, a feminist scholar and dean of Duke University's law school, is one of the principal authors of the ALI report.

She explains that her passion is "the value I place on family diversity and on the freedom of individuals to choose from a variety of family forms. This same value leads me to be generally opposed to efforts to standardize families into a certain type of nuclear family because a majority may believe this is the best kind of family or because it is the most deeply rooted ideologically in our traditions." Ignoring the overwhelming evidence about the benefits to family members and society from traditional marriage, Professor Bartlett attributes its support to either ignorant belief or blind ideology, befitting her status as a celebrated feminist scholar.

POSTSCRIPT

Has Feminism Benefited American Society?

The most convincing arguments of the anti-feminists are made against extremist positions, which "reasonable feminists" might not hold. For example, one can be a feminist and still love a husband, desire to mother children, and even leave the labor force in order to raise them. Nonetheless, there are legitimate issues in the debate about feminism. Does their demand for truly equal opportunity and affirmative action require the premise that men and women are essentially the same? Does feminist activism cultivate an antipathy to men as their oppressors? Has the feminist program adversely affected the family and gender relations? Do feminists deny that nondiscriminatory bases exist for many inequalities between men and women?

Over the past 40 years, there has been a deluge of books, articles, and periodicals devoted to expounding feminist positions. Among the earliest feminist publications was Betty Friedan's book *The Feminine Mystique* (W. W. Norton, 1963). Friedan later wrote *The Second Stage* (Summit Books, 1981), which was less antagonistic to men and more accepting of motherhood and traditional women's roles. In her latest book, *Life So Far* (Simon & Schuster, 2000) she presents her memoirs which largely cover the Women's movement that she helped start. Important statements by other past feminist leaders are Gloria Steinem, *Outrageous Acts and Everyday Rebellions*, 2nd ed. (Henry Holt, 1995) and "Revving Up for the Next 25 Years," *Ms* (September/October, 1997); Patricia Ireland, *What Women Want* (Penguin, 1996); and Susan Brownmiller, *In Our Time: Memoir of a Revolution* (Dial Press, 1999). For an attack on the attackers and misrepresentors of the women's movement see Susan Faludi's *Backlash: The Undeclared War on American Women* (Crown Publishers, 1991). For histories of the women's movement see Kathleen C. Berkeley, *The Women's Movement in America* (Greenwood Press, 1999); Dorothy Sue Cobble, *The Other Women's Movement: Workplace Justice and Social Rights in Modern America*, (Princeton University Press, 2004.); Barbara J. Love (ed.), *Feminists Who Changed America, 1963–1975*, (University of Illinois Press, 2006); and Judith M. Bennett, *History Matters: Patriarchy and the Challenge of Feminism*, (University of Pennsylvania Press, 2006). For discussions of the current state of feminism see Kristin Rowe-Finkbeiner, *The F-Word: Feminism in Jeopardy: Women, Politics, and the Future*, (Seal Press, 2004); Judith Lorber, *Breaking the Bowls: Degendering and Feminist Change*, (W.W. Norton, 2005); Maureen Dowd, *Are Men Necessary?*, (G.P. Putnam's Sons, 2005); Phyllis Chesler, *The Death of Feminism: What's Next in the Struggle for Women's Freedom*, (Palgrave Macmillan, 2005); Naomi Zack, *Inclusive Feminism: A Third Wave Theory of Women's*

Commonality, (Rowman & Littlefield, 2005); Stacy Gillis, Gillian Howie, and Rebbeca Munford (eds.), *Third Wave Feminism*, (Palgrave Macmillan, 2004). A superb analysis of the full range of gender issues is found in *Paradoxes of Gender* by Judith Lorber (Yale University Press, 1994). For radical feminist views, see Catharine A. MacKinnon's *Feminism Unmodified* (Harvard University Press, 1987); Marilyn French's *Beyond Power* (Summit Books, 1985); and Margaret Randall's *Gathering Rage: The Failure of Twentieth-Century Revolutions to Develop a Feminist Agenda* (Monthly Review Press, 1992). For a radical feminist analysis of the oppression of women, see Marilyn French, *The War Against Women* (Summit Books, 1992). For an insightful analysis of how ideology has been used by men to mute the rebellion of women against exploitative and subordinate relations, see Mary R. Jackman, *The Velvet Glove: Paternalism and Conflict in Gender, Class, and Race Relations* (University of California Press, 1994). A rich analysis of gender inequality and its social and psychological roots is provided by Sandra Lipsitz Bem in *The Lenses of Gender: Transforming the Debate on Sexual Inequality* (Yale University Press, 1994). For discussions of feminism around the world see Myra Marx Ferree and Aili Marl Tripp (eds.), *Global Feminism: Transnational Women's Activism, Organizing, and Human Rights*, (New York University Press, 2006); Mary E. Hawkesworth, *Globalization and Feminist Activism*, (Rowan & Littlefield, 2006); Valentine M. Moghadam, *Globalizing Women: Transnational Feminist Network*, Johns Hopkins University Press, 2005); Shamillah Wilson, Anasuya Sengupta, and Kristy Evans, (eds.), *Defending Our Dreams: Global Feminist Voices for a New Generation*, (Zed Books, 2005); Peggy Antrobus, *The Global Women's Movement*, (Zed, 2004); Trudie M. Eklund, *Sisters around the World: The Global Struggle for Female Equality*, (Hamilton Books, 2004). For a discussion of women's rights see Catharine A. MacKinnon, *Are Women Human?*, Belknap Press, 2006) and *Women's Lives, Men's Laws*, (Belknap Press); and Linda M.G. Zerilli, *Feminism and the Abyss of Freedom*, (University of Chicago Press, 2005).

Antifeminist works are rarer. One antifeminist, Nicholas Davidson, charges that it is "extremely difficult to find a publisher for a work critical of feminism." See Davidson's *The Failure of Feminism* (Prometheus Books, 1988). Other antifeminist arguments may be found in Elizabeth Powers', "A Farewell to Feminism," *Commentary* (January 1997); Ellen R. Klein, *Feminism Under Fire* (Prometheus, 1996) and *Undressing Feminism: A Philosophical Expose*, (Paragon House, 2002); Ariel Levy, *Female Chauvinist Pigs: Women and the Rise of Raunch Culture*, Free Press, 2005); Neil Boyd, *Big Sister: How Extreme Feminism Has Betrayed the Fight for Sexual Equality* (Greystone Press, 2004). Some like Christine Hoff Sommers advocate equity (liberal) feminism while criticizing feminist extremists and sloppy research in *Who Stole Feminism? How Women Have Betrayed Women* (Simon & Schuster, 1994).

For a defense of men against the accusations of feminists see Warren Farrell, *The Myth of Male Power* (Simon & Schuster, 1993) and David Thomas, *Not Guilty: The Case in Defense of Men* (William Morrow, 1993). For a pro feminist male viewpoint see Steven P. Schact and Doris W. Ewing, *Feminism with Men: Bridging the Gender Gap* (Rowan & Littlefield, 2004).

ISSUE 9

Has Affirmative Action Outlived Its Usefulness?

YES: Curtis Crawford, from "Racial Preference Versus Nondiscrimination," *Society* (March/April 2004)

NO: Lawrence D. Bobo, from "Inequalities that Endure?" in Maria Krysan and Amanda E. Lewis, eds., *The Changing Terrain of Race and Ethnicity* (Russell Sage Foundation, 2004)

ISSUE SUMMARY

YES: Curtis Crawford, editor of the Web site http://www. DebatingRacialPreference.org, explores all possible options for bettering the situation of disadvantaged minorities in a truly just manner. He argues that the right of everyone, including white males, to nondiscrimination is clearly superior to the right of minorities to affirmative action.

NO: Sociologist Lawrence D. Bobo demonstrates that racial prejudice still exists even though it has become a more subtle type of racism, which he calls laissez-faire racism. Though it is harder to identify, it has significant effects that Bobo illustrates. In fact, it plays a big role in current politics.

In America, equality is a principle as basic as liberty. "All men are created equal" is perhaps the most well known phrase in the Declaration of Independence. More than half a century after the signing of the Declaration, the French social philosopher Alexis de Tocqueville examined democracy in America and concluded that its most essential ingredient was the equality of condition. Today we know that the "equality of condition" that Tocqueville perceived did not exist for women, blacks, Native Americans, and other racial minorities, nor for other disadvantaged social classes. Nevertheless, the ideal persisted.

When slavery was abolished after the Civil War, the Constitution's newly ratified Fourteenth Amendment proclaimed, "No State shall . . . deny to any person within its jurisdiction the equal protection of the laws." Equality has been a long time coming. For nearly a century after the abolition of slavery,

American blacks were denied equal protection by law in some states and by social practice nearly everywhere. One-third of the states either permitted or forced schools to become racially segregated, and segregation was achieved elsewhere through housing policy and social behavior. In 1954 the Supreme Court reversed a 58-year-old standard that had found "separate but equal" schools compatible with equal protection of the law. A unanimous decision in *Brown v. Board of Education* held that separate is *not* equal for the members of the discriminated-against group when the segregation "generates a feeling of inferiority as to their status in the community that may affect their hearts and minds in a way unlikely ever to be undone." The 1954 ruling on public elementary education has been extended to other areas of both governmental and private conduct, including housing and employment.

Even if judicial decisions and congressional statutes could end all segregation and racial discrimination, would this achieve equality—or simply perpetuate-the status quo? Consider that the unemployment rate for blacks today is much higher than that of whites. Disproportionately higher numbers of blacks experience poverty, brutality, broken homes, physical and mental illness, and early deaths, while disproportionately lower numbers of them reach positions of affluence and prestige. It seems possible that much of this inequality has resulted from 300 years of slavery and segregation. Is termination of this ill treatment enough to end the injustices? No, say the proponents of affirmative action.

Affirmative action—the effort to improve the educational and employment opportunities for minorities—has had an uneven history in U.S. federal courts. In *Regents of the University of California v. Allan Bakke* (1978), which marked the first time the Supreme Court dealt directly with the merits of affirmative action, a 5-4 majority ruled that a white applicant to a medical school had been wrongly excluded in favor of a less qualified black applicant due to the school's affirmative action policy. Yet the majority also agreed that "race-conscious" policies may be used in admitting candidates—as long as they do not amount to fixed quotas. The ambivalence of *Bakke* has run through the Court's treatment of the issue since 1978. In 2003 the Supreme Court found the University of Michigan's admissions policy discriminatory but the University of Michigan Law School's admissions policy nondiscriminatory. As a result, race can still be used as one factor among many to create a diverse student body, but the weight of that factor must be far less than some universities had been using.

In the following selections, Curtis Crawford and Lawrence D. Bobo debate the merits of affirmative action. Crawford carefully lays out the options and arguments and balances the various rights and values involved. In the end, he argues, we must hold fast to the principle that the right to not be discriminated against supercedes all other values in this case and will produce the best results. Bobo counters that discrimination against minorities still exists, and affirmative actions—if not egregious—are still needed to bring about greater justice in society.

YES ⤸

Curtis Crawford

Racial Preference versus Nondiscrimination

After a 25-year silence on the subject, the Supreme Court has pronounced on the constitutionality of race-based affirmative action in university admissions. Those who had hoped that the issues would be wisely clarified and weighed must have been greatly disappointed. The two cases accepted for review, *Grutter v. Bollinger* and *Gratz v. Bollinger*, provided valuable information on how universities actually implement preferential admissions. . . .

The litigation of these two cases revealed large racial inequalities in the treatment of applicants with similar academic credentials. For example, at the trial in federal district court, the Michigan Law School admission grid for 1995 (the year Ms. Grutter was rejected) was offered in evidence. For all applicants, identified by race but not by name, the grid included data on their Undergraduate Grade Point Average (UGPA), Law School Aptitude Test score (LSAT), and admission or rejection. Each cell of the grid combined a small range of grades and scores. . . .

The size of the preference is indicated by the gap between the rates of admission for Favored Minorities and for Other Applicants. In the cell containing the median grade and score for all applicants (UGPA 3.25–3.49, LSAT 161–163), all Favored Minorities were admitted but only 5% of Other Applicants. . . . Down at the 30th percentile (applicants with grades and scores below 70% of their rivals), 83% of Favored Minorities but just 1% of Other Applicants gained admission. . . . In sum, Favored Minorities in the 10th percentile cell had a slightly better chance of admission than Other Applicants in the median cell, while Favored Minorities in the median cell had a slightly better chance than Other Applicants in the top cell. . . .

Racial affirmative action began almost forty years ago with efforts to make sure that people were not being treated unequally because of their race. It soon developed into programs conferring special treatment based on race, especially in higher education and employment. Decisions typically affected have been admission to college and graduate school; and hiring, promotion and training for private and government jobs. The groups now regularly designated for favorable treatment based on race or ethnicity are blacks, Latinos and Native Americans. Asians sometimes receive it; whites, almost never. The advantage is usually conferred by applying a double standard, whereby the requirements for selection are less exacting for members of the favored group.

From *Society*, March/April 2004, pp. 51–58. Copyright © 2004 by Springer Science and Business Media. Reprinted by permission.

These programs have been upheld as a remedy for past injustice, yet condemned as an instrument of present injustice. They have been praised for increasing minority access to business and professional careers, and blamed for debasing standards in the process. They are supposed by some to have raised and by others to have undermined the self-esteem of their recipients and the value placed on them by others. The controversy is fierce, partly because people on both sides believe that their position is what justice requires. But contrary views cannot both be right. We must dig deeper than usually occurs in public discussion to uncover and disentangle the relevant standards for moral judgment.

Unequal Treatment in General

At the outset, we need to distinguish between unequal treatment in general, and unequal treatment based on race. The latter may or may not be a special case, with special rules. Unequal treatment is simply treatment that favors one person over another. People are treated unequally for so many reasons, in so many contexts, that the existence of a general moral rule may seem impossible. But I suggest that we have such a rule. Ask yourself if and when you think that treating people unequally is the right thing to do. Is it all right when there is no reason for it? That would be arbitrary. Is it morally permissible if there is a good reason? For example, is it permissible to favor one applicant over another if they differ in ability, character, training, experience, and the like? Of course. Concerning something as important as the opportunity for education or employment, should people ever be treated unequally without good reason? No. But if there is a good reason, is it morally permissible to treat them unequally? It is not only permissible, it may be required.

What if the individual difference on which special treatment is based has nothing to do with an applicant's ability or need? Suppose that a public university gives an admissions preference to in-state residents, or a scholarship preference for veterans. Does the rule still hold, that unequal treatment is morally permissible when it is reasonable? The reasons commonly offered are, in the first case, that a state university is financed by, and owes a primary educational responsibility to, the residents of the state; in the second case, that such scholarships are both reward and incentive for service in the armed forces. The reasons seem good to me, and my sense of right and wrong does not bar the unequal treatment in either example. Others may think the reasons poor and the treatment wrong. In either view, whether unequal treatment is permissible depends on whether there is a good reason for it.

Preferential admission to a private university for the children of alumni is supposed to strengthen the school's relationship with its former students, thereby solidifying their continued interest and financial support, without which the quality and even the survival of the school might be jeopardized. Whether these are good reasons is disputed, but again the point is that, if one thinks the reasons good, one does not consider the preference immoral.

Supporters of racial preference think that the reasons for it are good: better, indeed, than for many kinds of preference that are generally accepted.

Hence they conclude that there is nothing morally wrong with the unequal treatment they advocate. This conclusion is valid, if the rule for unequal treatment based on race is the same as the rule for unequal treatment in general. But are the rules the same?

Does the rule, that unequal treatment is morally permissible when there is good reason, still hold when it is based on race? During the campaign to overthrow American discrimination against blacks and others, it was never suggested that if the discriminators had good reason, their actions would be morally acceptable. The legislatures, schools, professions, businesses and unions that practiced racial discrimination were not asked about their reasons; they were simply told to quit. Any claims that their policies were "reasonable means to legitimate ends" were rejected as rationalizations for racial injustice. The overriding conviction was that racial discrimination was morally out of bounds, no matter what reasons the discriminators might offer.

Based on this moral principle, laws were enacted between 1940 and 1970 at the local, state and national levels, barring unequal treatment in voting, housing, health care, public accommodations, public facilities, education and employment. These statutes established the right not to be discriminated against, and the corresponding duty not to discriminate, on account of "race, color or national origin." Rights are not absolute: they may be overridden by superior rights or by public necessity. But when unequal treatment on a particular basis is barred *as a matter of right*, people are not free to discriminate on that basis simply because they have good reasons. The right not to be racially discriminated against was not reserved for members of particular groups, but ascribed equally to every person in the United States.

Was the moral principle behind this legislation mistaken? For blacks it can be seen as a two-edged sword, banning adverse discrimination to be sure, but also prohibiting any discrimination in their favor. The antidiscrimination statutes left blacks with two important disadvantages. They were still held back by deficiencies in ability, training and motivation attributable at least in part to past discrimination; and they faced the prospect that discrimination against them in the future, though illegal, would often occur. No one doubts that the social and economic condition of American blacks would be better, absent their history of racial oppression. A plausible remedy would be racial preference, until both the effects of past, and the practice of current, anti-black discrimination had dissipated. But such a remedy would require important exceptions to the general ban on racial discrimination.

Any society that decides to end an era of discrimination faces the same moral dilemma. If everyone is granted the right not to be discriminated against on account of race, the possibility of helping the victims of past discrimination through racial preference is lost. If members of the previously excluded groups are favored on the basis of race, the right of others not to suffer racial discrimination is denied.

There is a way to slice through the dilemma, which would assist many disadvantaged individuals. Instead of racial preference, a program could assist those who had suffered specific, oppressive treatment, such as chronic and substantial racial discrimination. Any person, regardless of race, who could demonstrate such treatment in his own case would be eligible for the assistance. Such a program would satisfy the racial nondiscrimination rule, since the basis for assistance would be individual injury, not racial identity. But it would help only a fraction of those who currently benefit from race-based affirmative action.

Are there superior rights or public necessities that might override the right to racial nondiscrimination? The right to racial nondiscrimination, though momentous, is not the only care of the republic. Other (sometimes conflicting) rights and interests must also be protected. The moral dilemma of racial preference for some *versus* racial nondiscrimination for all might be avoided if, in certain circumstances, the right to racial nondiscrimination were superseded by a higher right or by public necessity.

Equity and Compensation

Some argue that there is a right to equal participation for racial groups, which overrides the individual right to nondiscrimination. According to this view, 'equal participation' means equal success in wealth, status, and achievement, not for every individual, but for the average person in each group, as compared with the average American. A belief in this right is often the moral basis for affirmative-action goals, adopted for the purpose of increasing the percentage of "underrepresented" minorities in the higher echelons of education and employment, to match their share of the general population. If such a right exists, it would conflict with the right to nondiscrimination, and might overrule it. . . .

If individuals who have been subjected to racial discrimination can be given compensatory help without running afoul of the nondiscrimination rule, why not an entire racial group? Could we thus escape from our moral dilemma? Is it possible that all we need is a finding by the national legislature that discrimination against certain racial groups has been and continues to be so pervasive that every member of the group is entitled to compensatory preference? Many proponents of affirmative action proceed as if such a finding had occurred, in their own minds if not in the legislative process. This helps them to think of racial preference as compensation, rather than discrimination.

A legislative finding of this sort, though based on evidence of injury to some, would be mere supposition concerning others. But the right of just compensation requires proof of specific injury to the person who invokes it. A legislative decision to compensate an entire racial group could not meet this criterion; it would be discrimination masquerading as compensation. Moreover, a legislature permitted to stereotype racial groups sympathetically would be free to do the contrary. Based on data that discrimination against Blacks is much more frequent than against whites, it would declare every black a victim. Based on statistics that crime by Blacks is much more frequent than by Whites, it could declare every Black a criminal. . . .

A Public Necessity to Achieve Diversity?

Some, giving a broader definition to public necessity, uphold two propositions, (a) that racial diversity in education and employment is a public necessity, and (b) that racial preference is essential to achieve such diversity. If by "diversity" they simply mean difference or variety, proposition (a) may be true, but proposition (b) is manifestly untrue. In a society composed of many different groups, all one needs in order to ensure racial and ethnic variety in colleges and workplaces is not to discriminate. But among supporters of race-based affirmative action, "diversity" often means having a larger number from "underrepresented groups" than would occur without racial preference. Using this definition, proposition (b) is true, but proposition (a) is false. There is no public necessity that racial groups be represented in education or employment in proportions higher than warranted by the fitness of their members, individually and impartially assessed.

A Need to Reduce Bias against Minorities?

Some argue that racial preference helps to prevent racial discrimination. They believe that unlawful discrimination against nonwhites in education and employment is common, since those in power are mostly white; they argue that when decision-makers have to meet goals for increasing minority participation, antiminority discrimination is effectively prevented. Racial goals and quotas are therefore imposed, by institutions over their officials or by courts over institutions, to ensure that people who might discriminate will not do so.

Paradoxically, this policy prevents violations of the right to racial non-discrimination by making certain that they occur. . . .

The Right to Racial Nondiscrimination

We have found that, if we recognize a general moral right to racial nondis-crimination, racial preference cannot be justified as serving a superior right or a public necessity. The supposed rights and necessities either do not exist, or do not conflict with the right to nondiscrimination. Is there another approach that might clear the way for racial preference?

The moral right to racial nondiscrimination could be expunged or lim-ited. One could (1) scrap the right altogether, (2) define the right more nar-rowly, (3) exempt education and employment from the nondiscrimination rule, (4) permit discrimination favorable to blacks, or (5) permit discrimina-tion favorable to all "underrepresented" minorities. Should the United States have chosen (or now choose) one of these options?

1. Scrap the Right Entirely?
This option would require us to repeal our antidiscrimination laws and to reject the moral principle on which they are based. No one advocates this. . . .

Wherever practiced, racial discrimination generates racial oppression, hostility and violence. Nondiscrimination is not easy, but it is the only stan-dard to which members of every racial and ethnic group might agree, since it is the only standard that places no one at a disadvantage because of his group membership. . . .

2. Redefine Wrongful Discrimination?

Instead of forbidding all unequal treatment based on race, we might bar such treatment only when it is motivated by racial prejudice or hostility. This would clear the way for "benign" discrimination in behalf of a previously excluded group, without sacrificing anyone's right to be free from "malign" discrimination.

A principal disadvantage to this approach is the extensive harm that it would legalize. A major reason for antidiscrimination laws is to protect people from being deprived of products, services, and opportunities by discriminatory acts. But this deprivation is just as great, whether the discrimination is motivated by prejudice or not. Discrimination is not benign to the person it injures. . . .

3. Exempt Education and Employment?

No one contends that racial discrimination should be outlawed in every kind of decision; to bar it in choosing a friend, a spouse, or a legislative representative would be invasive or unenforceable. Why not, then, withdraw the prohibition from the two areas in which preferential treatment might be most helpful for members of a previously excluded group, by bringing them more quickly into prestigious occupations and encouraging their fellows to aim higher and work harder?

A decision to exempt education and employment from the ban on discrimination would place both society and government in moral contradiction with themselves. The society, having decided that racial discrimination in general is wrong, would nevertheless be treating it in crucial areas as beneficial. The government, in its roles as educator and employer, would freely practice here that which elsewhere it must prosecute and punish. Such broad contradictions are fatal to the public consensus that racial discrimination is ordinarily unjust, a consensus that is necessary for general adherence to antidiscrimination laws. . . .

4. Favor Blacks Only?

This would respond forthrightly to the moral dilemma posed early in this essay, by making Blacks an exception to the nondiscrimination rule. The exception could apply to all areas of life that are covered by the rule, including housing, business, finance, voter registration, shopping, entertainment, criminal and civil justice, *etc.*, as well as education, employment, and government contracting. But an exception this large, which could easily sink the rule, has no champions. What is proposed instead is to limit the exception primarily to employment and higher education.

The exception faces two ways: Blacks would gain the privilege of favorable discrimination, by themselves or in their behalf; while all others would lose the right not to racially discriminated against when blacks are the beneficiaries.

A major argument against this option is the absence of a principled basis for making blacks the only beneficiaries of racial discrimination. If, when the nation decided to ban racial discrimination, blacks were the only group to have suffered it in the past, a basis for this exception would be clear. But Blacks were not alone. American Indians; Mexicans, Puerto Ricans, and other Latinos;

Japanese, Chinese, and other Asians; Poles, Italians, Slavs, Arabs, Jews, and other whites could all point to group wounds from past discrimination. . . .

5. Favor "Underrepresented" Minorities?

It may be argued that this, in effect, is the option we have chosen, not by amending the nondiscrimination statutes, but by creating affirmative-action programs. Under them, Blacks, Latinos, and Native Americans receive racial preference and are supposedly not discriminated against; whites do not receive preference and are often discriminated against; Asians are sometimes the beneficiaries, sometimes the victims. That many whites and Asians have lost their right to racial nondiscrimination in these areas is not made explicit. But it is surely implied, by the view that racial preference at their expense is morally permissible when serving a good purpose, and by the argument that they have no more reason to complain when disadvantaged by racial prefer-ence, than if the preference had been based on place of residence or family connections. . . .

Supporters of racial preference for black, Hispanic and Native Americans in education and employment typically invoke principles of racial justice, such as the right to compensation for past injury and/or a right to equal racial success. We have argued above that the latter right does not exist and the former right, properly applied, does not require special treatment based on race. We have argued also that the plea of public necessity is unfounded. . . .

Our inquiry began with a moral dilemma. If all have the right not to be subject to racial discrimination, no one may be assisted via racial preference; if racial preference is authorized for some, the right not to suffer racial dis-crimination is thereby denied to others. Two ways out of the dilemma were examined.

May the right to racial nondiscrimination, especially in education and employment, though belonging to everyone, be overridden by certain higher rights or public necessities? By a right to equal success for racial groups, or to just compensation for past discrimination? Or by a public necessity for racial preference as a means to racial peace, to racial diversity, or to the prevention of discrimination? These supposed rights and necessities were found to be either non-existent, or not in conflict with the right to racial nondiscrimina-tion, and therefore incapable of overriding it.

Should we rescind or limit the right to racial nondiscrimination, in order to make racial preference available? Five options were considered. The nondis-crimination rule could be scrapped altogether, redefined to cover only preju-diced or hostile acts, dropped from education and employment, or modified in these areas to allow preference for blacks only or for all "underrepresented" minorities. The arguments against these limits were in every case preponderant.

We cannot have the individual and social benefits of the nondiscrimina-tion rule if we decline to obey it. We cannot teach our children that racial discrimination is wrong if we persistently discriminate. We cannot preserve the right to nondiscrimination by systematically violating it. But, without breaking or bending the rule, we can respond to many people who need and deserve help. The racial nondiscrimination rule does not preclude compensation for specific injury. It does not bar special assistance, by the public or private sector, to persons who labor under social, cultural, or economic disadvantages, provided that the purpose of the help and the criteria for eligibility are colorblind.

Besides excluding racial preference, there are other important respects in which a desirable assistance program would not imitate current affirmative action. It would help people increase their ability to meet regular standards, instead of lowering standards to accommodate inferior ability. The role of government would be primarily determined by the legislative branch, not the bureaucracy or the judiciary. The participation of the private sector would be voluntary or contractual, not compulsory. The rules and operation of the program would be honestly described and freely accessible to public scrutiny. These guidelines are not mandates of the nondiscrimination rule, just counsels of good sense. They will be easier to meet in a racial policy that we really believe is right.

Lawrence D. Bobo

 **NO**

Inequities That Endure? Racial Ideology, American Politics, and the Peculiar Role of the Social Sciences

As part of research on the intersection of poverty, crime, and race, I conducted two focus groups in a major eastern city in early September 2001, just prior to the tragic events of September 11. The dynamics of the two groups, one with nine white participants and another with nine black participants, drove home for me very powerfully just how deep but also just how sophisticated, elusive, and enduring a race problem the United States still confronts. An example from each group begins to make the point that the very nature of this problem and our vocabularies for discussing it have grown very slippery, very difficult to grasp, and therefore extremely difficult to name and to fight.

First let's consider the white focus group. In response to the moderator's early question, "What's the biggest problem facing your community?" a young working-class white male eagerly and immediately chimed in, "Section 8 housing." "It's a terrible system," he said. The racial implications hung heavy in the room until a middle-aged white bartender tried to leaven things a bit by saying:

> All right. If you have people of a very low economic group who have a low standard of living who cannot properly feed and clothe their children, whose speech patterns are not as good as ours [and] are [therefore] looked down upon as a low class. Where I live most of those people happen to be black. So it's generally perceived that blacks are inferior to whites for that reason.

The bartender went on to explain: "It's not that way at all. It's a class issue, which in many ways is economically driven. From my perspective, it's not a racial issue at all. I'm a bartender. I'll serve anybody if they're a class [act]." At this, the group erupted in laughter, but the young working-class male was not finished. He asserted, a bit more vigorously:

> Why should somebody get to live in my neighborhood that hasn't earned that right? I'd like to live [in a more affluent area], but I can't afford to live

there so I don't. . . . So why should somebody get put in there by the government that didn't earn that right?

And then the underlying hostility and stereotyping came out more directly when he said: "And most of the people on that program are trashy, and they don't know how to behave in a working neighborhood. It's not fair. I call it unfair housing laws."

Toward the end of the session, when discussing why the jails are so disproportionately filled with blacks and Hispanics, this same young man said: "Blacks and Hispanics are more violent than white people. I think they are more likely to shoot somebody over a fender bender than a couple of white guys are. They have shorter fuses, and they are more emotional than white people."

In fairness, some members of the white group criticized antiblack prejudice. Some members of the group tried to point out misdeeds done by whites as well. But even the most liberal of the white participants never pushed the point, rarely moved beyond abstract observations or declarations against prejudice, and sometimes validated the racial stereotypes more overtly embraced by others. In an era when everyone supposedly knows what to say and what not to say and is artful about avoiding overt bigotry, this group discussion still quickly turned to racial topics and quickly elicited unabashed negative stereotyping and antiblack hostility.

When asked the same question about the "biggest problem facing your community," the black group almost in unison said, "Crime and drugs," and a few voices chimed in, "Racism." One middle-aged black woman reported: "I was thinking more so on the lines of myself because my house was burglarized three times. Twice while I was at work and one time when I returned from church, I caught the person in there."

The racial thread to her story became clearer when she later explained exactly what happened in terms of general police behavior in her community:

> The first two robberies that I had, the elderly couple that lived next door to me, they called the police. I was at work when the first two robberies occurred. They called the police two or three times. The police never even showed up. When I came in from work, I had to go . . . file a police report. My neighbors went with me, and they had called the police several times and they never came. Now, on that Sunday when I returned from church and caught him in my house, and the guy that I caught in my house lives around the corner, he has a case history, he has been in trouble since doomsday. When I told [the police] I had knocked him unconscious, oh yeah, they were there in a hurry. Guns drawn. And I didn't have a weapon except for the baseball bat, [and] I wound up face down on my living room floor, and they placed handcuffs on me.

The moderator, incredulous, asked: "Well, excuse me, but they locked you and him up?" "They locked me up and took him to the hospital."

Indeed, the situation was so dire, the woman explained, that had a black police officer who lived in the neighborhood not shown up to help after the patrol car arrived with sirens blaring, she felt certain the two white police officers who arrived, guns drawn, would probably have shot her. As it was, she was arrested for assault, spent two days in jail, and now has a lawsuit pending against the city. Somehow I doubt that a single, middle-aged, churchgoing white woman in an all-white neighborhood who had called the police to report that she apprehended a burglar in her home would end up handcuffed, arrested, and in jail alongside the burglar. At least, I am not uncomfortable assuming that the police would not have entered a home in a white community with the same degree of apprehension, fear, preparedness for violence, and ultimate disregard for a law-abiding citizen as they did in this case. But it can happen in black communities in America today.

To say that the problem of race endures, however, is not to say that it remains fundamentally the same and essentially unchanged. I share the view articulated by historians such as Barbara Fields and Thomas Holt that race is both socially constructed and historically contingent. As such, it is not enough to declare that race matters or that racism endures. *The much more demanding challenge is to account for how and why such a social construction comes to be reconstituted, refreshed, and enacted anew in very different times and places.* How is it that in 2001 we can find a working-class white man who is convinced that many blacks are "trashy people" controlled by emotions and clearly more susceptible to violence? How is it that a black woman defending herself and her home against a burglar ends up apprehended as if she were one of the "usual suspects"? Or cast more broadly, how do we have a milestone like the *Brown* decision and pass a Civil Rights Act, a Voting Rights Act, a Fair Housing Act, and numerous acts of enforcement and amendments to all of these, including the pursuit of affirmative action policies, and yet still continue to face a significant racial divide in America?

The answer I sketch here is but a partial one, focusing on three key observations. First, as I have argued elsewhere and elaborate in important ways here, I believe that we are witnessing the crystallization of a new racial ideology here in the United States. This ideology I refer to as laissez-faire racism. We once confronted a slave labor economy with its inchoate ideology of racism and then watched it evolve in response to war and other social, economic, and cultural trends into an explicit Jim Crow racism of the de jure segregation era. We have more recently seen the biological and openly segregationist thrust of twentieth-century Jim Crow racism change into the more cultural, free-market, and ostensibly color-blind thrust of laissez-faire racism in the new millennium. But make no mistake—the current social structure and attendant ideology reproduce, sustain, and rationalize enormous black-white inequality.

Second, race and racism remain powerful levers in American national politics. These levers can animate the electorate, constrain and shape political discourse and campaigns, and help direct the fate of major social policies. From the persistently contested efforts at affirmative action through a historic expansion of the penal system and the recent dismanding of "welfare as we know it," the racial divide has often decisively prefigured and channeled core features of our domestic politics.

Third, social science has played a peculiar role in the problem of race. And here I wish to identify an intellectual and scholarly failure to come to grips with the interrelated phenomena of white privilege and black agency. This failure may present itself differently depending on the ideological leanings of scholars. I critique one line of analysis on the left and one on the right. On the left, the problem typically presents as a failure of sociological imagination. It manifests itself in arguments that seek to reduce racialized social dynamics to some ontologically more fundamental nonracialized factor. On the right, the problem is typically the failure of explicit victim-blaming. It manifests itself in a rejection of social structural roots or causation of racialized social conditions. I want to suggest that both tactics—the left's search for some structural force more basic than race (such as class or skill levels or child-rearing practices) and the right's search for completely volitional factors (cultural or individual dispositions) as final causes of "race" differences—reflect a deep misunderstanding of the dynamics of race and racism. Race is not just a set of categories, and racism is not just a collection of individual-level anti-minority group attitudes. Race and racism are more fundamentally about sets of intertwined power relations, group interests and identities, and the ideas that justify and make sense out of (or challenge and delegitimate) the organized racial ordering of society. The latter analytic posture and theory of race in society is embodied in the theory of laissez-faire racism.

On Laissez-Faire Racism

There are those who doubt that we should be talking about racism at all. The journalist Jim Sleeper denounces continued talk of racism and racial bias as mainly so much polarizing "liberal racism." The political scientists Paul Sniderman and Edward Carmines write of the small and diminishing effects of racism in white public opinion and call for us to "reach beyond race." And the linguist John McWhorter writes of a terrible "culture of victimology" that afflicts the nation and ultimately works as a form of self-sabotage among black Americans. Even less overtly ideological writers talk of the growing victory of our Myrdalian "American Creed" over the legacy of racism. Some prominent black intellectuals, such as the legal scholar Randall Kennedy, while not as insensitive to the evidence of real and persistent inequality and discrimination, raise profound questions about race-based claims on the polity.

These analysts, I believe, are wrong. They advance a mistaken and counterproductive analysis of where we are today, how we got here, and the paths that we as a nation might best follow in the future. In many respects, these analysts are so patently wrong that it is easy to dismiss them.

Let's be clear first on what I mean by "racism." Attempts at definition abound in the scholarly literature. William Julius Wilson offers a particularly cogent specification when he argues that racism is an "an ideology of racial domination or exploitation that (1) incorporates belief in a particular race's cultural and/or inherent biological inferiority and (2) uses such beliefs to justify and prescribe inferior or unequal treatment for that group." I show here that there remains a profound tendency in the United States to blame racial inequality on the group culture and active choices of African Americans. This is abundantly clear in public opinion data, and it is exemplified by more than a few intellectual tracts, including McWhorter's *Losing the Race.* Closely attendant to this pattern is the profound tendency to downplay, ignore, or minimize the contemporary potency of racial discrimination. Again, this tendency is clear in public opinion and finds expression in the scholarly realm in the Thernstroms' book *America in Black and White.* These building blocks become part of the foundation for rejecting social policy that is race-targeted and aims to reduce or eliminate racial inequality. In effect, these attitudes facilitate and rationalize continued African American disadvantage and subordinated status. Our current circumstances, then, both as social structure and ideology, warrant description and analysis as a racist regime. Yet it is a different, less rigid, more delimited, and more permeable regime as well.

Laissez-faire racism involves persistent negative stereotyping of African Americans, a tendency to blame blacks themselves for the black-white gap in socioeconomic status, and resistance to meaningful policy efforts to ameliorate U.S. racist social conditions and institutions. It represents a critical new stage in American racism. As structures of racial oppression became less formal, as the power resources available to black communities grew and were effectively deployed, as other cultural trends paved the way for an assault on notions of biologically ranked "races," the stage was set for displacing Jim Crow racism and erecting something different in its place.

I have taken up a more complete development of the historical argument and the contemporary structural argument elsewhere. What is worth emphasizing here is, first, the explicit social groundedness and historical foundation of our theoretical logic—something that sets this theory of racial attitudes apart from notions like symbolic racism. Although not directly inspired by his work, our theoretical logic is a direct reflection of ideas articulated by the historian Thomas Holt. As he explains: "Racial phenomena and their meaning do change with time, with history, and with the conceptual and institutional spaces that history unfolds. More specifically they are responsive to major shifts in a political economy and to the cultural systems allied with that political economy."

The second point to emphasize here is that this is an argument about general patterns of group relations and ideology—not merely about variation in views among individuals from a single racial or ethnic category. As such, our primary concern is with the central tendency of attitudes and beliefs within and between racial groups and the social system as such, not within and between individuals. It is the collective dimensions of social experience that I most intend to convey with the notion of laissez-faire racism—not a singular attitude held to a greater or lesser degree by particular individuals. The intellectual case for such a perspective has been most forcefully articulated by the sociologist Mary R. Jackman. We should focus an analysis of attitudes and ideology on group-level comparisons, she writes, because doing so

> draws attention to the structural conditions that encase an intergroup
> relationship and it underscores the point that individual actors are not free

agents but caught in an aggregate relationship. Unless we assume that the individual is socially atomized, her personal experiences constitute only one source of information that is evaluated against the backdrop of her manifold observations of the aggregated experiences (both historical and contemporaneous) of the group as a whole.

The focus is thus more on the larger and enduring patterns and tendencies that distinguish groups than on the individual sources of variation.

With this in mind, I want to focus on three pieces of data, the first of which concerns the persistence of negative stereotypes of African Americans [in a survey he conducted]. . . . Several patterns stand out. It is easier for both blacks and whites to endorse the positive traits when expressing views about the characteristics of blacks than the negative traits. However, African Americans are always more favorable and less negative in their views than whites. Some of the differences are quite large. For instance, there is a thirty-percentage-point difference between white and black perceptions on the trait of intelligence and a thirty-three-percentage-point difference on the "hardworking" trait. . . .

Negative stereotypes of African Americans are common, though not uniform, and to a distressing degree they exist among both blacks and whites and presumably influence perceptions and behaviors for both groups. However, there is a sharp difference in central tendency within each group, in predictable directions. One cannot escape the conclusion that most whites have different and decidedly lesser views of the basic behavioral characteristics of blacks than do blacks themselves. And that generally these patterns indicate that African Americans remain a culturally dishonored and debased group in the American psyche. . . .

On American Politics

As a historic fact and experience as well as a contemporary political condition, racial prejudice has profoundly affected American politics. A wide body of evidence is accumulating to show that racial prejudice still affects politics. Black candidates for office typically encounter severe degree of difficulties securing white votes, partly owing to racial prejudice. There is some evidence, to be sure, that the potency of racial prejudice varies with the racial composition of electoral districts and the salience of race issues in the immediate political context.

Moreover, political candidates can use covert racial appeals to mobilize a segment of the white voting public under some circumstances. For example, the deployment of the infamous Willie Horton political ad during the 1988 presidential campaign heightened the voting public's concern over race issues. It also accentuated the impact of racial prejudice on electoral choices and did so in a way that did not increase concern with crime per se. That is, what appears to give a figure like Willie Horton such efficacy as a political symbol is not his violent criminal behavior per se, but rather his being a violent black man whose actions upset a racial order that should privilege and protect whites.

Major social policy decisions may also be driven by substantially racial considerations. The political psychologists David Sears and Jack Citrin make a strong case that antiblack prejudice proved to be a powerful source of voting in favor of California's historic property tax reduction initiative (Proposition 13), a change in law that fundamentally altered the resources available to government agencies.

On an even larger stage, the very design and early implementation of core features of the American welfare state were heavily shaped by racial considerations. Robert Lieberman has shown that the programs that became Social Security, Aid to Families with Dependent Children (AFDC), and unemployment insurance were initially designed to either exclude the great bulk of the black population or leave the judgment of qualification and delivery of benefits to local officials. The latter design feature of AFDC (originally ADC) had the effect in most southern states of drastically curtailing the share of social provision that went to African Americans. . . .

There are good reasons to believe that the push to "end welfare as we know it"—which began as a liberal reform effort but was hijacked by the political right and became, literally, the end of welfare as we had known it—was just as surely impelled by heavily racial considerations. The political sociologist Martin Gilens (1999) has carefully analyzed white opinion on the welfare state in the United States. Some features of the welfare state, he finds, lack an overtone of black dependency (such as Social Security) and enjoy high consensus support. Other programs (AFDC, food stamps, general relief) are heavily racialized, with much of the white voting public regarding these programs as helping lazy and undeserving blacks.

Indeed, the fundamental alignment of the U.S. national political panics has been centrally driven by a racial dynamic. Over the past thirty-five years we have witnessed a fundamental transformation in the Democratic and Republican party system, a transformation that political scientists call realignment. The more the Democratic Party was seen as advancing a civil rights agenda and black interests—in a manner that clearly set them apart from the Republican Party—the more race issues and race itself became central to party affiliations, political thinking, and voting in the mass white public. What was once a solid white Democrat-controlled South has thus shifted to a substantially white Republican-controlled South.

The end result of all of these patterns, simply put, is that African Americans do not enjoy a full range of voice, representation, and participation in politics. Black candidates, particularly if they are identified with the black community, are unlikely to be viable in majority white electoral districts. Even white candidates who come to be strongly associated with black interests run the risk of losing many white voters. As a consequence, party leaders on both sides have worked to organize the agenda and claims of African Americans out of national politics. In particular, the national Democratic Party, which should arguably reward its most loyal constituents in the black community, instead has often led the way in pushing black issues off the stage. As the political scientist Paul Frymer has explained, party leaders do so because they are at risk of losing coveted white "swing voters" in national elections if they come to be perceived as catering to black interests. Thus is the elite discourse around many domestic social policies, and their ultimate fate, bound up in racial considerations.

Against this backdrop it becomes difficult, if not counterproductive, to accept the widely shared view that American democracy is on an inexorable path toward ever-greater inclusivity and fuller realization of its democratic potential. In the context of such enduring and powerful racialization of American politics, such an assumption is naive at best.

There is an even more incisive point to be made. The presumption of ever-expanding American liberalism is mistaken. For example, the Pulitzer Prize winning–historian Joseph Ellis writes of the terrible "silence" on the subject of slavery and race that the "founding fathers" *deliberately* adopted. They waged a Revolutionary War for freedom, declared themselves the founders of a new nation, and in very nearly the same moment *knowingly* wedded democracy to slave-based racism. The philosopher Charles Mills extends the reach of this observation by showing the deep bias of Enlightenment thinkers toward a view of those on the European continent—whites—as the only real signatories to the "social contract." Others, particularly blacks, were never genuinely envisioned or embraced as fully human and thus were never intended to be covered by the reach of the social contract.

Considerations of this kind led the political theorist Rogers Smith to suggest that the United States has not one but rather multiple political traditions. One tradition is indeed more democratic, universalistic, egalitarian, and expansive. But this tradition competes with and sometimes decisively loses out to a sharply hierarchical, patriarchal, and racist civic tradition. The ultimate collapse of Reconstruction following the Civil War and the subsequent gradual development of de jure segregation and the Jim Crow racist regime provide one powerful case in point.

POSTSCRIPT

Has Affirmative Action Outlived Its Usefulness?

Crawford and Bobo approach the issue of affirmative action from different directions. Bobo starts with the end or goal of fairness to disadvantaged minorities and argues that affirmative action is a necessary means to that end. Crawford starts with the means and argues that affirmative action as morally unjustifiable. On the other hand, compensation for individuals who have been discriminated against is morally justifiable, but most of the people who benefit from affirmative action programs are not in this category. This argument would not persuade anyone who is passionate about justice for disadvantaged minorities, because our laws already allow discrimination victims to seek redress in the courts and that has not stopped or compensated for discrimination. Many believe that something more is needed, and affirmative action properly conducted is the best means.

The writings on this subject are diverse and numerous. For an in-depth discussion of the legal standing of affirmative action, see Girardeau A. Spann, *The Law of Affirmative Action: Twenty-Five Years of Supreme Court Decisions on Race and Remedies* (New York University Press, 2000). For a review of affirmative action programs, see M. Ali Raza et al., *The Ups and Downs of Affirmative Action Preferences* (Greenwood, 1999). William G. Bowen and Derek Bok review affirmative action in college admissions in *The Shape of the River: Long-Term Consequences of Considering Race in College and University Admissions* (Princeton University Press, 1998). Robert K. Fullinwider and Judith Lichtenberg provide a more recent assessment in *Leveling the Playing Field: Justice, Politics, and College Admissions* (Rowman & Littlefield, 2004) and Patricia Gurin et al. defend affirmative action at the University of Michigan in *Defending Diversity: Affirmative Action at the University of Michigan* (University of Michigan Press, 2004). For a history of affirmative action, see Philip F. Rubio, *A History of Affirmative Action* (University Press of Mississippi, 2001). The need for affirmative action or another effective means to address racial and gender inequality is provided in *Problem of the Century: Racial Stratification in the United States*, edited by Elijah Anderson and Douglas S. Massey (Russell Sage Foundation); Andrew Hacker, *Mismatch: The Growing Gulf between Women and Men* (Scribner, 2003); and David Neumark, *Sex Differences in Labor Markets* (Routledge, 2004). The debate on affirmative action is covered by Carl Cohen and James P. Sterba in *Affirmative Action and Racial Preference: A Debate* (Oxford University Press, 2003). Recently an anti-affirmative action movement has mobilized. Three works that try to counter this movement are Fred L. Pincus, *Reverse Discrimination: Dismantling the Myth* (Lynne Rienner, 2003); Faye J. Crosby,

Affirmative Action Is Dead: Long Live Affirmative Action (Yale University Press, 2004); and Lee Cokorinos, *The Assault on Diversity: An Organized Challenge to Racial and Gender Justice* (Rowman & Littlefield, 2003). Andrew Hacker argues that affirmative action has relatively minor adverse consequences for whites in *Two Nations: Black and White, Separate, Hostile, Unequal* (Charles Scribner's Sons, 1992). Dinesh D'Souza, in *The End of Racism* (Free Press, 1995), argues that white racism has pretty much disappeared in the United States. The opposite is argued by Joe R. Feagin and Hernan Vera in *White Racism: The Basics* (Routledge, 1995) and by Stephen Steinberg in *Turning Back* (Beacon Press, 1995). For international comparisons see Thomas Sowell, *Affirmative Action around the World: An Empirical Study* (Yale University Press, 2004).

ISSUE 10

Are Boys and Men Disadvantaged Relative to Girls and Women?

YES: Michelle Conlin, from "The New Gender Gap," *Business Week Online* (May 26, 2003)

NO: Joel Wendland, from "Reversing the 'Gender Gap'," *Political Affairs* (March 2004)

ISSUE SUMMARY

YES: Journalist Michelle Conlin reviews the many disadvantages of boys and men in school from kindergarten to grad school. Since education is the route to success, men will be less able to compete in the marketplace.

NO: Joel Wendland acknowledges the edge that females have over males today in education but argues that females are still disadvantaged in the marketplace.

America has always boasted of being the land of opportunity and there are many facts that support this claim. For centuries poor immigrants have come here and prospered or had their children prosper. Widespread public education enabled upward mobility for many in the lower classes. Merit plays a large role in hiring and pay. But America has also failed to give equal opportunity to women and selected minorities. As a result America failed to utilize all of the talent that was available to it, and therefore, developed slower than it could have. The black movement, the women's movement, the Civil Rights Act of 1964, and affirmative action policies have greatly improved the life chances of blacks and women. The changes have been great enough to lead some white males to now feel that they are being discriminated against. Of course, they focus on a single event where a women or black gets a position or a salary that they have good reasons to believe they themselves deserved. But they fail to take into account the many thousands of advantages their race and gender have given to them over their lifetime. If all those advantages were added up, they would greatly outweigh the disadvantage they experienced because of some affirmative action outcome. This issue can be brought into focus by asking "would males trade places with females and would whites trade places with blacks?"

There is one area where males have definitely lost their advantage and that is in education. This change can best be illustrated by looking at the gender distribution of college degrees over time. As recently as 1960 male college graduates outnumbered female by five to three. By 1980 they were equal and today women earn 57% of bachelor degrees. Obviously this radical a change needs to be explained. Is it because women are more intelligent and have been held back in the past by factors that have changed such as discrimination, differential treatment by teachers and parents, lower expectations, less ambition, and low career goals? Most scholars do not think that gender differences in intelligence are large enough to support this explanation. Is it because males are now being discriminated against in school? No way. Is it due to changing attitudes of both males and females toward education and careers? Perhaps. In the selection that follows Michelle Conlin provides a full explanation of this question.

The radical reversal in educational outcomes for males and females has caused some writers, such as Michelle Conlin in the first selection, to write about a new gender gap with males being disadvantaged. This implies that women's fight for equal rights has completely succeeded. In the second selection Joel Wendland argues that this is not the case. There is still the old gender gap with women disadvantaged in many ways.

YES ⤶

Michelle Conlin

The New Gender Gap

From kindergarten to grad school, boys are becoming the second sex.

Lawrence High is the usual fortress of manila-brick blandness and boxy 1960s architecture. At lunch, the metalheads saunter out to the smokers' park, while the AP types get pizzas at Marinara's, where they talk about—what else?—other people. The hallways are filled with lip-glossed divas in designer clothes and packs of girls in midriff-baring track tops. The guys run the gamut, too: skate punks, rich boys in Armani, and saggy-panted crews with their Eminem swaggers. In other words, they look pretty much as you'd expect.

But when the leaders of the Class of 2003 assemble in the Long Island high school's fluorescent-lit meeting rooms, most of these boys are nowhere to be seen. The senior class president? A girl. The vice-president? Girl. Head of student government? Girl. Captain of the math team, chief of the yearbook, and editor of the newspaper? Girls.

It's not that the girls of the Class of 2003 aren't willing to give the guys a chance. Last year, the juniors elected a boy as class president. But after taking office, he swiftly instructed his all-female slate that they were his cabinet and that he was going to be calling all the shots. The girls looked around and realized they had the votes, says Tufts University-bound Casey Vaughn, an Intel finalist and one of the alpha femmes of the graduating class. "So they impeached him and took over."

The female lock on power at Lawrence is emblematic of a stunning gender reversal in American education. From kindergarten to graduate school, boys are fast becoming the second sex. "Girls are on a tear through the educational system," says Thomas G. Mortenson, a senior scholar at the Pell Institute for the Study of Opportunity in Higher Education in Washington. "In the past 30 years, nearly every inch of educational progress has gone to them."

Just a century ago, the president of Harvard University, Charles W. Eliot, refused to admit women because he feared they would waste the precious resources of his school. Today, across the country, it seems as if girls have built a kind of scholastic Roman Empire alongside boys' languishing Greece. Although Lawrence High has its share of boy superstars—like this year's valedictorian—the gender takeover at some schools is nearly complete. "Every time I turn around, if something good is happening, there's a female in charge," says Terrill O. Stammler, principal of Rising Sun High School in Rising Sun, Md. Boys are missing from nearly every leadership position, academic honors slot, and student-activity post at the school. Even Rising Sun's girls' sports teams do better than the boys'.

At one exclusive private day school in the Midwest, administrators have even gone so far as to mandate that all awards and student-government positions be divvied equally between the sexes. "It's not just that boys are falling behind girls," says William S. Pollock, author of *Real Boys: Rescuing Our Sons from the Myths of Boyhood* and a professor of psychiatry at Harvard Medical School. "It's that boys themselves are falling behind their own functioning and doing worse than they did before."

It may still be a man's world. But it is no longer, in any way, a boy's. From his first days in school, an average boy is already developmentally two years behind the girls in reading and writing. Yet he's often expected to learn the same things in the same way in the same amount of time. While every nerve in his body tells him to run, he has to sit still and listen for almost eight hours a day. Biologically, he needs about four recesses a day, but he's lucky if he gets one, since some lawsuit-leery schools have banned them altogether. Hug a girl, and he could be labeled a "toucher" and swiftly suspended—a result of what some say is an increasingly anti-boy culture that pathologizes their behavior.

If he falls behind, he's apt to be shipped off to special ed, where he'll find that more than 70% of his classmates are also boys. Squirm, clown, or interrupt, and he is four times as likely to be diagnosed with attention deficit hyperactivity disorder. That often leads to being forced to take Ritalin or risk being expelled, sent to special ed, or having parents accused of negligence. One study of public schools in Fairfax County, Va., found that more than 20% of upper-middle-class white boys were taking Ritalin-like drugs by fifth grade.

Once a boy makes it to freshman year of high school, he's at greater risk of falling even further behind in grades, extracurricular activities, and advanced placement. Not even science and math remain his bastions. And while the girls are busy working on sweeping the honor roll at graduation, a boy is more likely to be bulking up in the weight room to enhance his steroid-fed Adonis complex, playing Grand Theft Auto: Vice City on his PlayStation2, or downloading rapper 50 Cent on his iPod. All the while, he's 30% more likely to drop out, 85% more likely to commit murder, and four to six times more likely to kill himself, with boy suicides tripling since 1970. "We get a bad rap," says Steven Covington, a sophomore at Ottumwa High School in Ottumwa, Iowa. "Society says we can't be trusted."

As for college—well, let's just say this: At least it's easier for the guys who get there to find a date. For 350 years, men outnumbered women on college campuses. Now, in every state, every income bracket, every racial and ethnic group, and most industrialized Western nations, women reign, earning an average 57% of all BAs and 58% of all master's degrees in the U.S. alone. There are 133 girls getting BAs for every 100 guys—a number that's projected to grow to 142 women per 100 men by 2010, according to the U.S. Education Dept. If current trends continue, demographers say, there will be 156 women per 100 men earning degrees by 2020.

Overall, more boys and girls are in college than a generation ago. But when adjusted for population growth, the percentage of boys entering college, master's programs, and most doctoral programs—except for PhDs in fields like engineering and computer science—has mostly stalled out, whereas for women it has continued to rise across the board. The trend is most pronounced among Hispanics, African Americans, and those from low-income families.

The female-to-male ratio is already 60–40 at the University of North Carolina, Boston University, and New York University. To keep their gender ratios 50–50, many Ivy League and other elite schools are secretly employing a kind of stealth affirmative action for boys. "Girls present better qualifications in the application process—better grades, tougher classes, and more thought in their essays," says Michael S. McPherson, president of Macalester College in St. Paul, Minn., where 57% of enrollees are women. "Boys get off to a slower start."

The trouble isn't limited to school. Once a young man is out of the house, he's more likely than his sister to boomerang back home and sponge off his mom and dad. It all adds up to the fact that before he reaches adulthood, a young man is more likely than he was 30 years ago to end up in the new and growing class of underachiever—what the British call the "sink group."

For a decade, British educators have waged successful classroom programs to ameliorate "laddism" (boys turning off to school) by focusing on teaching techniques that re-engage them. But in the U.S., boys' fall from alpha to omega status doesn't even have a name, let alone the public's attention. "No one wants to speak out on behalf of boys," says Andrew Sum, director of the Northeastern University Center for Labor Market Studies. As a social-policy or educational issue, "it's near nonexistent."

On the one hand, the education grab by girls is amazing news, which could make the 21st the first female century. Already, women are rapidly closing the M.D. and PhD gap and are on the verge of making up the majority of law students, according to the American Bar Assn. MBA programs, with just 29% females, remain among the few old-boy domains.

Still, it's hardly as if the world has been equalized: Ninety percent of the world's billionaires are men. Among the super rich, only one woman, Gap Inc. co-founder Doris F. Fisher, made, rather than inherited, her wealth. Men continue to dominate in the highest-paying jobs in such leading-edge industries as engineering, investment banking, and high tech—the sectors that still power the economy and build the biggest fortunes. And women still face sizable obstacles in the pay gap, the glass ceiling, and the still-Sisyphean struggle to juggle work and child-rearing.

But attaining a decisive educational edge may finally enable females to narrow the earnings gap, punch through more of the glass ceiling, and gain an equal hand in rewriting the rules of corporations, government, and society. "Girls are better able to deliver in terms of what modern society requires of people—paying attention, abiding by rules, being verbally competent, and dealing with interpersonal relationships in offices," says James Garbarino, a professor of human development at Cornell University and author of *Lost Boys: Why Our Sons Turn Violent and How We Can Save Them*.

Righting boys' problems needn't end up leading to reversals for girls. But some feminists say the danger in exploring what's happening to boys would be to mistakenly see any expansion of opportunities for women as inherently disadvantageous to boys. "It isn't a zero-sum game," says Susan M. Bailey, executive director of the Wellesley Centers for Women. Adds Macalester's McPherson: "It would be dangerous to even out the gender ratio by treating women worse. I don't think we've reached a point in this country where we are fully providing equal opportunities to women."

Still, if the creeping pattern of male disengagement and economic dependency continues, more men could end up becoming losers in a global economy that values mental powers over might—not to mention the loss of their talent and potential. The growing educational and economic imbalances could also create societal upheavals, altering family finances, social policies, and work-family practices. Men are already dropping out of the labor force, walking out on fatherhood, and disconnecting from civic life in greater numbers. Since 1964, for example, the voting rate in Presidential elections among men has fallen from 72% to 53%—twice the rate of decline among women, according to Pell's Mortenson. In a turnaround from the 1960s, more women now vote than men.

Boys' slide also threatens to erode male earnings, spark labor shortages for skilled workers, and create the same kind of marriage squeeze among white women that already exists for blacks. Among African Americans, 30% of 40- to 44-year-old women have never married, owing in part to the lack of men with the same academic credentials and earning potential. Currently, the never-married rate is 9% for white women of the same age. "Women are going to pull further and further ahead of men, and at some point, when they want to form families, they are going to look around and say, 'Where are the guys?'" says Mortenson.

Corporations should worry, too. During the boom, the most acute labor shortages occurred among educated workers—a problem companies often solved by hiring immigrants. When the economy reenergizes, a skills shortage in the U.S. could undermine employers' productivity and growth.

Better-educated men are also, on average, a much happier lot. They are more likely to marry, stick by their children, and pay more in taxes. From the ages of 18 to 65, the average male college grad earns $2.5 million over his lifetime, 90% more than his high school counterpart. That's up from 40% more in 1979, the peak year for U.S. manufacturing. The average college diploma holder also contributes four times more in net taxes over his career than a high school grad, according to Northeastern's Sum. Meanwhile, the typical high school dropout will usually get $40,000 more from the government than he pays in, a net drain on society.

Certainly, many boys continue to conquer scholastic summits, especially boys from high-income families with educated parents. Overall, boys continue to do better on standardized tests such as the scholastic aptitude test, though more low-income girls than low-income boys take it, thus depressing girls' scores. Many educators also believe that standardized testing's multiple-choice format favors boys because girls tend to think in broader, more complex terms. But that advantage is eroding as many colleges now weigh grades—where girls excel—more heavily than test scores.

Still, it's not as if girls don't face a slew of vexing issues, which are often harder to detect because girls are likelier to internalize low self-esteem through depression or the desire to starve themselves into perfection. And while boys may act out with their fists, girls, given their superior verbal skills, often do so with their mouths in the form of vicious gossip and female bullying. "They yell and cuss," says 15-year-old Keith Gates, an Ottumwa student. "But we always get in trouble. They never do."

Before educators, corporations, and policymakers can narrow the new gender gap, they will have to understand its myriad causes. Everything from absentee parenting to the lack of male teachers to corporate takeovers of lunch rooms with sugar-and-fat-filled food, which can make kids hyperactive and distractable, plays a role. So can TV violence, which hundreds of studies—including recent ones by Stanford University and the University of Michigan—have linked to aggressive behavior in kids. Some believe boys are responding to cultural signals—downsized dads cast adrift in the New Economy, a dumb-and-dumber dude culture that demeans academic achievement, and the glamorization of all things gangster that makes school seem so uncool. What can compare with the allure of a gun-wielding, model-dating hip hopper? Boys, who mature more slowly than girls, are also often less able to delay gratification or take a long-range view.

Schools have inadvertently played a big role, too, losing sight of boys—taking for granted that they were doing well, even though data began to show the opposite. Some educators believed it was a blip that would change or feared takebacks on girls' gains. Others were just in denial. Indeed, many administrators saw boys, rather than the way schools were treating them, as the problem.

Thirty years ago, educational experts launched what's known as the "Girl Project." The movement's noble objective was to help girls wipe out their weaknesses in math and science, build self-esteem, and give them the undisputed message: The opportunities are yours; take them. Schools focused on making the classroom more girl-friendly by including teaching styles that catered to them. Girls were also powerfully influenced by the women's movement, as well as by Title IX and the Gender & Equity Act, all of which created a legal environment in which discrimination against girls—from classrooms to the sports field—carried heavy penalties. Once the chains were off, girls soared.

Yet even as boys' educational development was flat-lining in the 1990s—with boys dropping out in greater numbers and failing to bridge the gap in reading and writing—the spotlight remained firmly fixed on girls. Part of the reason was that the issue had become politically charged and girls had powerful advocates. The American Association of University Women, for example, published research cementing into pedagogy the idea that girls had deep problems with self-esteem in school as a result of teachers' patterns, which included calling on girls less and lavishing attention on boys. Newspapers and TV newsmagazines lapped up the news, decrying a new confidence crisis among American girls. Universities and research centers sponsored scores of teacher symposiums centered on girls. "All the focus was on girls, all the grant monies, all the university programs—to get girls interested in science and math," says Steve Hanson, principal of Ottumwa High School in Iowa. "There wasn't a similar thing for reading and writing for boys."

Some boy champions go so far as to contend that schools have become boy-bashing laboratories. Christina Hoff Sommers, author of *The War Against Boys*, says the AAUW report, coupled with zero-tolerance sexual harassment laws, have hijacked schools by overly feminizing classrooms and attempting to engineer androgyny.

The "earliness" push, in which schools are pressured to show kids achieving the same standards by the same age or risk losing funding, is also far more damaging to boys, according to Lilian G. Katz, co-director of ERIC Clearinghouse on Elementary and Early Childhood Education. Even the nerves on boys' fingers develop later than girls', making it difficult to hold a pencil and push out perfect cursive. These developmental differences often unfairly sideline boys as slow or dumb, planting a distaste for school as early as the first grade.

Instead of catering to boys' learning styles, Pollock and others argue, many schools are force-fitting them into an unnatural mold. The reigning sit-still-and-listen paradigm isn't ideal for either sex. But it's one girls often tolerate better than boys. Girls have more intricate sensory capacities and bio-social aptitudes to decipher exactly what the teacher wants, whereas boys tend to be more anti-authoritarian, competitive, and risk-taking. They often don't bother with such details as writing their names in the exact place instructed by the teacher.

Experts say educators also haven't done nearly enough to keep up with the recent findings in brain research about developmental differences. "Ninety-nine-point-nine percent of teachers are not trained in this," says Michael Gurian, author of *Boys and Girls Learn Differently*. "They were taught 20 years ago that gender is just a social function."

In fact, brain research over the past decade has revealed how differently boys' and girls' brains can function. Early on, boys are usually superior spatial thinkers and possess the ability to see things in three dimensions. They are often drawn to play that involves intense movement and an element of make-believe violence. Instead of straitjacketing boys by attempting to restructure this behavior out of them, it would be better to teach them how to harness this energy effectively and healthily, Pollock says.

As it stands, the result is that too many boys are diagnosed with attention-deficit disorder or its companion, attention-deficit hyperactivity disorder. The U.S.—mostly its boys—now consumes 80% of the world's supply of methylphenidate (the generic name for Ritalin). That use has increased 500% over the past decade, leading some to call it the new K–12 management tool. There are school districts where 20% to 25% of the boys are on the drug, says Paul R. Wolpe, a psychiatry professor at the University of Pennsylvania and the senior fellow at the school's Center for Bioethics: "Ritalin is a response to an artificial social context that we've created for children."

Instead of recommending medication—something four states have recently banned school administrators from doing—experts say educators should focus on helping boys feel less like misfits. Experts are designing new developmentally appropriate, child-initiated learning that concentrates on problem-solving, not just test-taking. This approach benefits both sexes but especially boys, given that they tend to learn best through action, not just talk. Activities are geared toward the child's interest level and temperament. Boys, for example, can learn math through counting pinecones, biology through mucking around in a pond. They can read *Harry Potter* instead of *Little House on the Prairie*, and write about aliens attacking a hospital rather than about how to care for people in the hospital. If they get antsy, they can leave a teacher's lecture and go to an activity center replete with computers and manipulable objects that support the lesson plan.

Paying attention to boys' emotional lives also delivers dividends. Over the course of her longitudinal research project in Washington (D.C.) schools, University of Northern Florida researcher Rebecca Marcon found that boys who attend kindergartens that focus on social and emotional skills—as opposed to only academic learning—perform better, across the board, by the time they reach junior high.

Indeed, brain research shows that boys are actually more empathic, expressive, and emotive at birth than girls. But Pollock says the boy code, which bathes them in a culture of stoicism and reticence, often socializes those aptitudes out of them by the second grade. "We now have executives paying $10,000 a week to learn emotional intelligence," says Pollock. "These are actually the skills boys are born with."

The gender gap also has roots in the expectation gap. In the 1970s, boys were far more likely to anticipate getting a college degree—with girls firmly entrenched in the cheerleader role. Today, girls' expectations are ballooning, while boys' are plummeting. There's even a sense, including among the most privileged families, that today's boys are a sort of payback generation—the one that has to compensate for the advantages given to males in the past. In fact, the new equality is often perceived as a loss by many boys who expected to be on top. "My friends in high school, they just didn't see the value of college, they just didn't care enough," says New York University sophomore Joe Clabby. Only half his friends from his high school group in New Jersey went on to college.

They will face a far different world than their dads did. Without college diplomas, it will be harder for them to find good-paying jobs. And more and more, the positions available to them will be in industries long thought of as female. The services sector, where women make up 60% of employees, has ballooned by 260% since the 1970s. During the same period, manufacturing, where men hold 70% of jobs, has shrunk by 14%.

These men will also be more likely to marry women who outearn them. Even in this jobless recovery, women's wages have continued to grow, with the pay gap the smallest on record, while men's earnings haven't managed to keep up with the low rate of inflation. Given that the recession hit male-centric industries such as technology and manufacturing the hardest, native-born men experienced more than twice as much job loss as native-born women between 2000 and 2002.

Some feminists who fought hard for girl equality in schools in the early 1980s and '90s say this: So what if girls have gotten 10, 20 years of attention—does that make up for centuries of subjugation? Moreover, what's wrong with women gliding into first place, especially if they deserve it? "Just because girls aren't shooting 7-Eleven clerks doesn't mean they should be ignored," says Cornell's Garbarino. "Once you stop oppressing girls, it stands to reason they will thrive up to their potential."

Moreover, girls say much of their drive stems from parents and teachers pushing them to get a college degree because they have to be better to be equal—to make the same money and get the same respect as a guy. "Girls are more willing to take the initiative... they're not afraid to do the work," says Tara Prout, the Georgetown-bound senior class president at Lawrence High. "A lot of boys in my school are looking for credit to get into college to look good, but they don't really want to do the grunt work."

A new world has opened up for girls, but unless a symmetrical effort is made to help boys find their footing, it may turn out that it's a lonely place to be. After all, it takes more than one gender to have a gender revolution.

Joel Wendland  **NO**

Reversing the "Gender Gap"

"**B**oys are becoming the second sex" proclaimed *Business Week* last May in a cover story titled "The New Gender Gap." *Business Week's* article appeared as part of a spate of articles and television news segments on the subject of increased educational opportunities for women. The basics of the story are that in the education system, teachers have become so conscious of catering to the needs of girls and young women that boys are being left behind. Boys, they say, are being punished for "boyish" behavior. They are being put more often into special education programs or disciplinary classes, and the outcome is that boys have a negative educational experience. This trend translates into poorer high school performances and perhaps college as well.

According to statistics offered by *Business Week*, 57 percent of all new bachelor's degrees and 58 percent of master's degrees are awarded to women. This "education grab," according to the article, was the source of the "new gender gap." Though, the article did hint that even with the new trend in the numbers, women still had some ways to go in order to catch up after 350 years of being almost entirely excluded from the university.

Most observers of this situation will find such an article perplexing. Certainly most women will likely be skeptical of its major argument. That this "reverse gender gap" argument exists, however, is not surprising. Like its cousins in other areas of social life (reverse discrimination or reverse class warfare), it is being generated primarily by the ultra-right. The purpose is to stifle the struggle for equality by implying (or stating directly) that the gains made by women through struggle over the last 40 years have gone too far and have detrimentally affected society.

Some in this camp go so far as to suggest that women who demand equality are out to hurt men. At worst, it demonstrates that the right wants to twist the outcome of social progress to divide us. They say that a struggle between men and women for social goods is the fundamental source of social conflict and that women are winning—a situation that, for some, means reversed gender inequality and for others goes against natural laws of male supremacy invoked by God.

Any way you look at it, however, this picture is a distortion of reality. So what does the real gender gap look like?

Barbara Gault, director of research at the Institute for Women's Policy Research, recently told *Women'sWallStreet.com* that there are several explanations for and holes in the current data on the educational experiences of men and women. First, high-paying occupations that do not require college degrees, such as skilled trades, are still male dominated. Second, women need a college degree in order to earn roughly what men do with only high school diplomas, giving them stronger motives to make a special effort to obtain financial security. Third, among African Americans, where the difference between women and men earning college degrees is the widest among all racial or ethnic groups, it is clear that institutional racism directed at African American men plays a large role in keeping them out of college. Fourth, in the crucial field of information technology, women continue to earn only about one-third of the degrees awarded and get only about one-third of the jobs available. Finally, men continue to outpace women in completing doctoral and professional degrees (81 women for every 100 men), resulting in continued male dominance in corporate board rooms, the seats of political power, the highest positions in universities, etc.

The successes of the women's equality movement, progressive changes in attitudes about roles women can have and the implementation of affirmative action policies (which benefited women as a whole most) have had a tremendous positive impact on the access women have had in education. Just 30 years ago, women earned advanced or professional degrees at a rate of only 23 women per 100 men. In other arenas, such as the workforce or the political field, the gender gap, in sheer numbers, has largely narrowed. But the numbers still don't paint the whole picture.

While higher education is a major factor in gaining financial security, it is something that is only available to about one-fifth of the adult population. So for the vast majority of women, this supposed "new gender gap" means absolutely nothing. Other data on the condition of women's economic security paint another picture altogether. About eight of ten retired women are not eligible for pension benefits. When retired women do get a pension, it is typically far less than retired men get. Fifty percent of women who receive pension benefits get only about 60 cents for every dollar of male pensioners. On the average, retired women depend on Social Security for 71 percent of their income, and about 25 percent of retired women rely solely on Social Security for their income.

In the work force, women's pay averages only 76 percent of men's pay (at a cost of about $200 billion for working families annually). A report produced by the General Accounting Office last October shows that since 1983, the wage differential has actually increased. Sixty percent of all women earn less than $25,000 annually. Women are one-third more likely to live below the poverty level. Black women and Latinas are between two and three times more likely to live below the poverty line than men are. For women of color, facing the double oppression of racism and sexism, pay losses are even greater: 64 cents on the dollar at a loss of about $210 a week. The average woman, according to the AFL-CIO, will lose $523,000 in her lifetime due to unequal pay.

Even more costly to women, is the "price of motherhood," as journalist Ann Crittenden argues in her recent book of that title. In almost every case, women lose income, jobs, job experience and retirement income (while work hours increase) when they decide to have children. With some slight improvements, women remain the primary caregiver in nearly every family. For many mothers, single or married, the economic inequalities described above are exacerbated. For married women, dependence on men is heightened and the threat of economic hardship enforces interpersonal inequality and conflict. Divorced mothers and their children have among the highest rates of poverty of any demographic.

Crittenden argues that unless other sources of financial support for motherhood are made available institutionalized inequality will persist. She suggests retirement benefits for mothers, public funding for day care and health care for children and their caregivers, salaries for primary caregivers, expanded public education for pre-school children, equalized social security for spouses, increased financial contributions from husbands and fathers, increased educational and support resources for parents and equalization of living standards for divorced parents.

As for the fallacy of female supremacy, the gains made by women through struggle and implementation of policies such as affirmative action point to the necessity of broader systematic change. But if female supremacy is a fallacy, does this mean that men go unhurt by gender inequalities? No. Men and boys are hurt when their families suffer because pay inequity causes their mothers, grandmothers, sisters and aunts to lose income, get fired, face hiring discrimination, are refused pensions, don't have equal Social Security benefits, lose out on promotions or have limited access to higher education. Additionally, if the average woman loses $523,000 in income in her life, does this mean that the average man is enriched by $523,000 in his lifetime? If pay inequity costs women $200 billion yearly, does this mean that men are enriched by $200 billion? The answer is no. These billions are savings in labor costs to employers. Employers enjoy the profits of male supremacy and gendered divisions among working people. So it makes sense that the right tries to portray the benefits of progressive social change toward equality as bad. It cuts into their bottom line.

POSTSCRIPT

Are Boys and Men Disadvantaged Relative to Girls and Women?

Michelle Conlin establishes the fact that males are not doing as well in the education system as females and offers some plausible explanations why. The foremost reason offered is that K to 12 schools today are ill suited to boys. Upon entrance boys are developmentally behind girls but must handle tasks that they are not ready for. More importantly, boys are not biologically programmed for school life. As Conlin says "While every nerve in his body tells him to run, he has to sit still and listen for almost eight hours a day." The strong version of this argument is that today's schools have "an increasingly anti-boy culture that pathologizes their behavior." Others of the myriad of causes that she cites are the following: "Everything from absentee parenting to the lack of male teachers to corporate takeovers of lunch rooms with sugar-and-fat-filled food, which can make kids hyperactive and distractible, plays a role. So can TV violence, which hundreds of studies . . . have linked to aggressive behavior in kids. Some believe boys are responding to cultural signals—downsized dads cast adrift in the New Economy, a dumb-and-dumber dude culture that demeans academic achievement, and the glamorization of all things gangster that makes school seem so uncool. . . Boys who mature more slowly than girls, are also often less able to delay gratification or take a long-range view."

The gender gap debate is not over the differential educational outcomes for boys and girls, but over whether education and life is unfair to males and advantages females. If so, then the schools and other institutions should be altered to suit males as much as females. But first society would have to find a way to replace the dumb dude culture with a pro education and achievement culture for boys. The argument on the other side does not deny the superior educational achievement of females over males, but challenges the degree of unfairness in the educational system that needs to be corrected. If boys mature later than girls and tend to have a dumb dude culture, it is not the schools fault that they do badly and a pro boy reform may not be necessary. More importantly the female side of the argument points out that females are so much more disadvantaged in the rest of life, especially in employment, that having an advantage in education helps level the playing field. Perhaps it is fair to keep this one advantage.

There is considerable literature on inequality and discrimination against women in the workplace and very little on discrimination against men. The works that address discrimination against women include Nancy Maclean, *Freedom Is Not Enough: The Opening of the American Workplace*

(Russell Sage Foundation, 2006); Martha Burke, *Cult of Power: Sex Discrimination in Corporate America and What Can Be Done about It* (Scribner, 2005); Heidi Gottfried and Laura Reese, eds., *Equity in the Workplace: Gendering Workplace Policy Analysis* (Lexington Books, 2004); David Neumark, *Sex Differences in Labor Markets* (Routledge, 2004); Sandy Ruxton, ed., *Gender Equality and Men: Learning from Practice* (Oxfam, 2004); Evelyn F. Murphy, *Getting Even: Why Women Don't Get Paid Like Men—and What to Do about It* (Simon & Schuster, 2005); Judith Lorber, *Breaking the Bowls: Degendering and Feminist Change* (W.W. Norton, 2005) and *Gender Inequality: Feminist Theories and Politics,* 2nd ed. (Roxbury Pub., 2001); Phyllis Moen and Patricia Roehling, *The Career Mystique: Cracks in the American Dream* (Rowman and Littlefield, 2005); Jerry A. Jacobs and Kathleen Gerson, *The Time Divide: Work, Family, and Gender Inequality* (Harvard University Press, 2004); Linda Lavine and Charles V. Dale, *The Male-Female Wage Gap* (Novinka Books, 2003); and Michael S. Kimmel, *The Gendered Society* (Oxford University Press, 2000). For inequality in academia, see Susan K. Dyer, ed., *Tenure Denied: Cases of Sex Discrimination in Academia* (AAUW Educational Foundation, 2004). For worldwide sex discrimination, see Maria Charles, *Occupational Ghettoes: The Worldwide Segregation of Women and Men* (Stanford University Press, 2004) and Trudie M. Eklund, *Sisters around the World: The Global Struggle for Female Equality* (Hamilton Books, 2004).

Internet References . . .

Economic Report of the President

The Economic Report of the President Web site includes current and anticipated trends in the United States and annual numerical goals concerning topics such as employment, production, real income, and federal budget outlays. The database notes employment objectives for significant groups of the labor force, annual numeric goals, and a plan for carrying out program objectives.

```
http://www.gpoaccess.gov/eop/index.html
```

National Center for Policy Analysis

Through the National Center for Policy Analysis site you can read discussions that are of major interest in the study of American politics and government from a sociological perspective.

```
http://www.ncpa.org/
```

Speakout.com

The Speakout.com Web site contains a library of online information and links related to public policy issues, primarily those in the United States. The issues are organized into topics and subtopics for easy searching.

```
http://www.speakout.com/activism/issues/
```

Policy.com

Visit Policy.com, the site of the "policy community," to examine major issues related to social welfare, welfare reform, social work, and many other topics. The site includes substantial resources for researching issues online.

```
http://www.policy.com
```

Political Economy and Institutions

What is the proper role of government in the economy? Some believe that the government must correct for the many failures of the market, while others think that the government usually complicates the workings of the free market and reduces its effectiveness. The next debate concerns public policy: What is the impact of the end of the Federal AFDC program? The fourth issue examines alternative educational policies for significantly improving public education. Finally, the last issue in this part looks at the use of biotechnology to alter and enhance humans.

- Should Government Intervene in a Capitalist Economy?
- Has Welfare Reform Benefited the Poor?
- Is Competition the Reform that Will Fix Public Education?
- Should Biotechnology Be Used to Alter and Enhance Humans?

ISSUE 11

Should Government Intervene in a Capitalist Economy?

YES: Eliot Spitzer and Andrew G. Celli Jr., from "Bull Run: Capitalism with a Democratic Face," *The New Republic* (March 22, 2004)

NO: John Stossel, from "The Real Cost of Regulation," *Imprimis* (May 2001)

ISSUE SUMMARY

YES: Attorneys Eliot Spitzer and Andrew G. Celli Jr. argue that the government plays an essential role in enabling the market to work right. Capitalism runs amuck if it is not regulated to protect against abuse and ensure fairness.

NO: John Stossel, a TV news reporter and producer of one-hour news specials, argues that regulations have done immense damage and do not protect us as well as market forces.

$\mathbf{T}$he expression "That government is best which governs least" sums up a deeply rooted attitude of many Americans. From early presidents Thomas Jefferson and Andrew Jackson to America's most recent leaders, George Bush, Bill Clinton, and George W. Bush, American politicians have often echoed the popular view that there are certain areas of life best left to the private actions of citizens.

One such area is the economic sphere, where people make their living by buying, selling, and producing goods and services. The tendency of most Americans is to regard direct government involvement in the economic sphere as both unnecessary and dangerous. The purest expression of this view is the economic theory of *laissez-faire,* a French term meaning "let be" or "let alone." The seminal formulation of *laissez-faire* theory was the work of eighteenth-century Scottish philosopher Adam Smith, whose treatise *The Wealth of Nations* appeared in 1776. Smith's thesis was that each individual, pursuing his or her own selfish interests in a competitive market, will be "led by an invisible hand to promote an end which was no part of his intention." In other words, when people singlemindedly seek profit, they actually serve the community because sellers must keep prices down and quality up if they are to meet the competition of other sellers.

Laissez-faire economics was much honored (in theory, if not always in practice) during the nineteenth and early twentieth centuries. But as the nineteenth century drew to a close, the Populist Party sprang up. The Populists denounced eastern bankers, Wall Street stock manipulators, and rich "moneyed interests," and they called for government ownership of railroads, a progressive income tax, and other forms of state intervention. The Populist Party died out early in the twentieth century, but the Populist message was not forgotten. In fact, it was given new life after 1929, when the stock market collapsed and the United States was plunged into the worst economic depression in its history.

By 1932 a quarter of the nation's workforce was unemployed, and most Americans were finding it hard to believe that the "invisible hand" would set things right. Some Americans totally repudiated the idea of a free market and embraced socialism, the belief that the state (or "the community") should run all major industries. Most stopped short of supporting socialism, but they were now prepared to welcome some forms of state intervention in the economy. President Franklin D. Roosevelt, elected in 1932, spoke to this mood when he pledged a "New Deal" to the American people. "New Deal" has come to stand for a variety of programs that were enacted during the first eight years of Roosevelt's presidency, including business and banking regulations, government pension programs, federal aid to the disabled, unemployment compensation, and government-sponsored work programs. Side by side with the "invisible hand" of the marketplace was now the very visible hand of an activist government.

Government intervention in the economic sphere increased during World War II as the government fixed prices, rationed goods, and put millions to work in government-subsidized war industries. Activist government continued during the 1950s, but the biggest leap forward occurred during the late 1960s and early 1970s, when the federal government launched a variety of new welfare and regulatory programs: the multibillion-dollar War on Poverty, new civil rights and affirmative action mandates, and new laws protecting consumers, workers, disabled people, and the environment. These, in turn, led to a proliferation of new government agencies and bureaus, as well as shelves and shelves of published regulations. Proponents of the new activism conceded that it was expensive, but they insisted that activist government was necessary to protect Americans against pollution, discrimination, dangerous products, and other effects of the modern marketplace. Critics of government involvement called attention not only to its direct costs but also to its effect on business activity and individual freedom.

In the following selections, Eliot Spitzer and Andrew Calli Jr. are is aware that regulations can go too far, but over two decades of privatization, deregulation, and government downsizing has swung the pendulum too far, and tighter regulations or government interventions are needed for the public good and to make the market work right. John Stossel can only imagine greater harm coming from an expanded role of government if the past is our guide.

YES ↵

Eliot Spitzer and
Andrew G. Celli Jr.

Bull Run: Capitalism
with a Democratic Face

We are told we live in the New Economy, an economy of computers and fiber-optic cables, capital without borders, and competition on a global scale. This is mature market capitalism, and its promise for human advancement—when combined with democracy and individual freedom—is rightly touted at every turn. But, if our economy is a creature of the twenty-first century, our thinking about government's role in the economy is mired in the nineteenth.

Two essentially opposite viewpoints dominate today's debate. On one side are those who see market capitalism, loosely regulated and unencumbered by the artificial interventions of government, as perfection itself. They argue: Leave the markets alone, let them work, and efficiency, choice, and progress will follow. On the other side are those who argue that, as miraculous as the capitalist experiment has proved to be, free markets cannot be left unchecked. To maintain a just and equitable society, they say, markets must be protected from their natural tendency toward excesses that lead to monopolies and unfairness. In this scheme, government's role is to put the brakes on capitalism and to protect the public from market forces through its power to tax and regulate.

This conflict has often been reduced to caricature—heartless laissez-faire capitalists versus meddling government bureaucrats. But this characterization presents a false choice. If there is one lesson that can be gleaned from the New Economy, it is that the government's proper role is neither that of passive spectator nor lion tamer. The proper role of government is as market facilitator. Government should act to ensure that markets run cleanly as well as smoothly. It should prevent market failures and right them when they occur. And it should ensure that markets uphold the broad values of our culture rather than debase them. In this vision, government action is necessary for free markets to work as they are intended—in an open, competitive, and fair manner. In this vision, government helps to create, maintain, and expand competition, so the system as a whole can do what it does best: generate and broadly distribute wealth.

Where government has retreated from these core responsibilities, economic dislocation and decay have followed. Three recent examples make the point. We have chosen them not because they are the only or even the best available but because they reflect our practical experience over the past five years in New York state and because they illustrate three distinct rationales for market intervention: to enforce the rules to deal with market failures, and to uphold core American values. They show that the Bush administration's economic approach, while veiled in the rhetoric of free markets, actually subverts them. True free-marketers understand that free markets operate according to principles that must be enforced. But President George W. Bush has abdicated his responsibility to protect our markets, leaving a vacuum in which market failures are ignored or chalked up to "natural force" and the economy suffers shocks that could have been avoided or corrected by careful government intervention. By advocating smart government action and shifting the rhetorical paradigm, Democrats can provide voters with a coherent, pro-market justification for the policy objectives we share. It's good policy and good politics at the same time.

·◈·

Government has been effective and well received when it has acted to preserve (or restore) confidence in the fairness of the market itself. At a basic level, for a market to be truly free and efficient and have the full confidence of its participants, two things are required: integrity and transparency.

Integrity, in this context, is the idea that actors in the marketplace are what they purport to be: that those who claim to offer independent advice and analysis are not tainted by conflicts of interest; that those who are entrusted with protecting shareholders do so, rather than enriching themselves at shareholders' expenses; and that those who, by virtue of their wealth, power, or access, may be positioned to violate the rules do not. In a system where there is not, and cannot be, a cop on every metaphorical street corner, we rely on this integrity to give us confidence that the system is fair and genuinely competitive.

Just as actors must be what they claim to be, information in a free market must be accurate and truthful, freely flowing, disseminated in a timely way, and available to all. Transparency—implemented through disclosure requirements, institutional barriers to abuse, or widely accepted rules of conduct—is what makes meaningful choice possible. And choice by all actors in a rational market—be they investors or consumers, CEOs or shopkeepers—is what creates the competitive pressures that make the market more efficient and create wealth for us all.

Government is the institution best-suited to protect against corruption and abuse and to ensure that the economic playing field is level. But, in the 1990s, Wall Street experienced what can only be described as the "perfect storm" of government failure. It began with the consolidation of the financial-services sector—permitted by the repeal of the Glass-Steagall Act, a Depression-era statute requiring that commercial and investment banking be separated. The result was the formation of vast full-service enterprises that brought together many potentially conflicting lines of business, including commercial banking, investment banking, stock analysis, and retail brokerage. At the same time, we democratized the marketplace by (wisely) encouraging the American public at large to invest in the capital markets. The interface between mega-institutions and small investors was fraught with risk—risk met by a regulatory void. Indeed, Harvey Pitt, the first Securities and Exchange Commission (SEC) chair appointed by Bush, is a former industry lobbyist who promised the financial sector a "kinder, gentler SEC," an approach that led to a total breakdown in market enforcement. From Tyco to Enron to mutual funds to analyst compensation, the SEC simply was not attentive to the structural failures that were widely known to industry insiders.

With protections against conflicts of interest severely hobbled, integrity and transparency were soon sacrificed. As a result, research analysts whose compensation and career prospects depended upon the fortunes of their investment-banking partners pushed information about companies that was not just "imperfect," but false. In one infamous example, Merrill Lynch analyst Henry Blodget simultaneously helped pitch banking business to InfoSpace, a Web search company, and hyped the stock to investors, all the while telling his co-workers that the stock was a "piece of junk." In relying on corrupted advice like this, investors invested, corporate executives and investment bankers got rich, and companies that should have been market losers actually "succeeded."

But that success, which took the form of skyrocketing stock prices, options values, and compensation packages for corporate executives, was necessarily short-lived. The market had its revenge, as artificially pumped-up companies were unable to compete over the long term. Their business models failed and their stock prices plummeted. And yet abuses continued. Despite WorldCom's sinking fortunes, Citigroup analyst Jack Grubman kept promoting the stock, all the while receiving compensation that resulted from WorldCom's banking business with Citigroup. But, ultimately, he couldn't keep reality from catching up to WorldCom: Its share price dropped from $60 to 20 cents, wiping out $100 billion in market value.

The real victims were the companies' employees, the investing public, and the market itself. Not only had the public confidence essential to market performance been squandered, but the companies into which huge amounts of capital had been funneled were, from a long-term perspective, the wrong ones. Inefficient, unsound, and simply undeserving, these businesses failed to create meaningful jobs, growth, or lasting wealth. Couple these structural failures with the impact of other corporate scandals—such as Enron, Tyco, and Adelphia—and the result was grim. When the bubble burst in the late '90s, and the truth about overhyped companies came to light, stunned investors experienced the biggest drop in the S&P Index since the 1987 market crash—a drop with profound ripple effects throughout the national economy. A recession that was perhaps inevitable was deepened, and individuals who had set aside assets for education or retirement suddenly found these assets diminished or wiped out entirely.

So much had gone wrong in so short a time that government's ability to right the economy was limited. That said, the forceful reassertion of government's role as facilitator of the twin values of integrity and transparency has contributed powerfully to a sense that we are beginning to put our national economic house in order. With the acceptance of industry-wide codes of conduct by financial-services companies, new and more stringent disclosure and certification requirements under the Sarbanes-Oxley Act, and the aggressive policing of segments of the marketplace, the decline in investor confidence has been halted and perhaps even reversed.

‹⊙›

Government can also help facilitate the smooth functioning of markets when they are unable to appropriately distribute costs. The burdens of pollution provide a classic example. Where the market finds itself unable to allocate pollution costs efficiently and fairly, and where the federal government refuses to act, the intervention of others, including state governments like New York's, has become necessary.

Take air pollution in the Northeast caused by coal burning power plants in the Midwest. Corporate players, acting in their rational self-interest, have failed to bear or equitably spread the costs associated with their activity. Instead, they have shifted those costs to others, for whom there is no market recourse. In this case, the costs were acid rain and airborne pollutants, and their devastating effects on the environment and human health—not in the Midwest, where the plants generate and sell their energy, but hundreds of miles downwind, in the Northeast. Plant owners had purposely built smokestacks tall enough that pollutants would fall not on their consumers or those nearby but, quite literally, into someone else's backyard. The costs have been dear. Thousands of New York children suffer from asthma that is at least partially attributable to pollution sent East from power plants in states like Kentucky, Ohio, and West Virginia. And even the Bush administration's Environmental Protection Agency admits that, in New York's Adirondack Mountains, hundreds of lakes have acidity levels that could kill off certain aquatic species.

In a perfectly functioning market, the costs imposed by this conduct would be borne either by the producer in the form of reduced profits or by the consumer in the form of higher prices. Such costs would not be dumped on the doorstep of those who don't benefit from cheap Midwestern energy. But that is precisely what is happening: Northeasterners have been left holding the bag, and the market alone offers them no way to respond. They are stuck—unless and until government intervenes.

Alas, the Bush administration has refused to do that. Even as it spouts the rhetoric of free-market efficiency, the White House has allowed the polluters to avoid bearing the economic and health-related costs they have imposed. It has tried to reverse a long-standing interpretation of Clean Air Act regulations, which require power plants and other industrial facilities to install modern pollution controls when they are upgraded. This shift in environmental policy represents an abandonment of the market principle that costs should be borne by those who consume or pay for the product—an abandonment driven by a desire to benefit the energy industry. Indeed, the connection between administration policy and interest-group politics is direct and explicit: The shift in the Clean Air Act's interpretation—undertaken to protect Midwestern polluters from having to make expensive upgrades—grew directly out of Vice President Dick Cheney's industry-dominated Energy Task Force, through which energy producers effectively dictated the very policies that are supposed to regulate them.

Left with no other choice, the states and citizens suffering from Midwest-generated pollution have gone to court and successfully stopped the administration's attempted policy change. The point of this effort is neither to limit the availability of cheap energy to Midwest consumers, nor to shift the costs to them simply for the sake of doing so. Rather, it is to ensure, as an efficient market must, that the costs are borne by the parties responsible. Only by placing the costs where they belong can the market system as a whole assess whether the product is being efficiently created and appropriately priced vis-á-vis potential competitors. That is when the market, freed from its own failures, really works.

⟡

Lastly, our commitment to market capitalism cannot obscure one glaring and immutable fact: that, in a number of important ways, an unregulated market does not safeguard certain core American values. That's why our government—with broad bipartisan support—has instituted child-labor laws, minimum wage laws, anti-discrimination laws, and certain safety net protections designed to ensure that people do not fall below a basic level of sustenance. There is little debate today about the value of these measures. They are, in essence, what we are all about. Child labor is not forbidden in this country because it is inefficient (although it is): it is forbidden because it is wrong.

Unfortunately, our belief in the importance of equal opportunity and nondiscrimination is too often forgotten when it comes to the debate over whether and how to police the market for home mortgages. In poor and working-class communities across the nation, predatory mortgage lending has become a new scourge. Predatory lending is the practice of imposing inflated interest rates, fees, charges, and other onerous terms on home mortgage loans—not because the imperatives of the market require them, but because the lender has found a way to get away with them. These loans (which are often sold as refinance or home-improvement mechanisms) are foisted on borrowers who have no realistic ability to repay them and who face the loss of their hard-won home equity when the all-but-inevitable default and foreclosure occurs. When lenders systematically target certain low-income communities for loans of this sort, as they often do, the result is more insidious. Costs are imposed and burdens inflicted in a manner and to a degree that is discriminatory by race.

On the surface, predatory lenders are doing nothing more than seizing a "market opportunity" for refinancing or home-improvement loans in lower-income communities. To be sure, such communities desperately need credit. And it stands to reason that the prices and terms will be less favorable to borrowers whose financial circumstances are troubled or limited. In this sense, predatory loans are the natural outcome of a competitive market. In a policy debate bereft of values, this market rationale becomes a value unto itself—and values like equal opportunity disappear.

But, in our system, the market is there to serve our values, not the other way around. As study after study has shown, the overwhelming majority of people who fall prey to predatory loans would be better off with no loan at all.

Moreover, borrowers in this category often bear the same or similar financial characteristics—income levels, credit-worthiness, ability and willingness to repay—as their counterparts in the prime market. As a matter of economics, they actually qualify for good loans at good rates. What distinguishes them from borrowers who get credit at the right price, on the right terms, is their actual and perceived lack of options, their limited financial savvy, and, too often, the color of their skin—and sometimes their age or gender.

For a society devoted to fairness and nondiscrimination—as well as the quintessentially American goal of homeownership—the prices, terms, and over-all economic impact that we see in predatory home mortgage loans cannot be justified. They are just plain wrong. And, quite apart from the values issue, it is difficult to imagine a less rational, less efficient economic practice than lending of this sort. At the micro-level, it results in a gross misallocation of costs—imposing higher costs than the market requires on those least able to bear them. At the macro-level, it denies lower-cost capital to whole classes of persons who would otherwise qualify for it and to neighborhoods whose economic vitality depends on it.

In these circumstances, government must step in to curb predatory lending and encourage the flow of fairly priced capital to sectors where it is needed and will be well-used. Filling a gap left by federal inaction, state enforcement efforts in this arena have centered on identifying the valid economic criteria considered in mortgage underwriting and compelling lenders to focus on those factors—not on preconceptions, prejudices, or predatory instincts—in determining how to price home mortgage loans. The point is not to protect people from their own bad decisions or, conversely, to guarantee that mortgages be granted to specific persons or groups on specific terms—that would violate the principle of market freedom. The point is to support equal opportunity and to ensure that borrowers are charged rates and fees based upon their status and qualifications as economic actors in the mortgage market, not upon their diminished access or market savvy or their race. In taking action of this sort, state government regulators have upheld core national values and facilitated a fair and open market at the same time.

The Bush administration's reaction has been swift, predictable, and negative. The Treasury Department's Office of the Comptroller of the Currency has issued regulations stripping states of authority to stop predatory lending. It claims that continued state enforcement and regulatory authority will interfere with federal efforts to "regulate" national banks and, of course, with the free market in credit. In truth, the yawning gap between federal rhetoric and federal action in this area suggests a different rationale. Far from seeking to preserve federal prerogatives to regulate or to protect the market from state meddling, these efforts smack of a surrender to banking interests at the expense of market efficiency and the people capitalism is intended to serve.

⚜

In a period of severe budget constraints, complex and shifting global entanglements, and a failure of political will, one of our most difficult choices concerns what role government should play in an economy that on the whole has proved astonishingly durable, efficient, and successful. It is a choice we must make as members of a democratic polity, as citizens of a global economy, and as Democrats for whom the old answers no longer satisfy.

President Bush has helped frame that choice. By pursuing policies that are cloaked in free-market rhetoric but fail to facilitate fair markets, he has surrendered to corporate constituencies. He has shown that his party's rhetorical attachment to free markets is just that—a rhetorical attachment and nothing more. And he has done so at a time when it is clear that government nonintervention leads not to market freedom and a rising of all boats but to unrestrained corporatism, gross market distortions, inequitable accumulation of wealth, and economic stasis.

In trying to articulate a more constructive vision—one that is both fiscally and economically sound and that makes sense to the average American voter—Democrats should promote government as a supporter of free markets, not simply a check on them. Government action must be justified by its ability to define, catalyze, and facilitate the market's core mechanisms; to prevent it from faltering under the weight of its own imperfections; and to uphold the underlying values to which the system is, or ought to be, dedicated. It is a vision consistent with trust-busting and other progressive market measures first enunciated early in the last century by Theodore Roosevelt, who said, "We grudge no man a fortune which represents his own power and sagacity, when exercised with entire regard to the welfare of his fellows."

By taking up the mantle of efficient, forward-looking, and market-oriented government action, Democrats can move from being a party that simply opposes Bush's tainted version of laissez-faire to one that advocates for the progress that comes with real market freedom. It is a powerful argument, a true argument, and it is ours for the making.

John Stossel

→ **NO**

The Real Cost of Regulation

The following is an abridged version of Mr. Stossel's speech delivered on February 20, 2001, in Fort Myers, Florida, at a Hillsdale College seminar.

When I started 30 years ago as a consumer reporter, I took the approach that most young reporters take today. My attitude was that capitalism is essentially cruel and unfair, and that the job of government, with the help of lawyers and the press, is to protect people from it. For years I did stories along those lines—stories about Coffee Association ads claiming that coffee "picks you up while it calms you down," or Libby-Owens-Ford Glass Company ads touting the clarity of its product by showing cars with their windows rolled down. I and other consumer activists said, "We've got to have regulation. We've got to police these ads. We've got to have a Federal Trade Commission." And I'm embarrassed at how long it took me to realize that these regulations make things worse, not better, for ordinary people.

The damage done by regulation is so vast, it's often hard to see. The money wasted consists not only of the taxes taken directly from us to pay for bureaucrats, but also of the indirect cost of all the lost energy that goes into filling out the forms. Then there's the distraction of creative power. Listen to Jack Faris, president of the National Federation of Independent Business: "If you're a small businessman, you have to get involved in government or government will wreck your business." And that's what happens. You have all this energy going into lobbying the politicians, forming the trade associations and PACs, and trying to manipulate the leviathan that's grown up in Washington, D.C. and the state capitals. You have many of the smartest people in the country today going into law, rather than into engineering or science. This doesn't create a richer, freer society. Nor do regulations only depress the economy. They depress the spirit. Visitors to Moscow before the fall of communism noticed a dead-eyed look in the people. What was that about? I don't think it was about fear of the KGB. Most Muscovites didn't have intervention by the secret police in their daily lives. I think it was the look that people get when they live in an all-bureaucratic state. If you go to Washington, to the Environmental Protection Agency, I think you'll see the same thing.

One thing I noticed that started me toward seeing the folly of regulation was that it didn't even punish the obvious crooks. The people selling the breast-enlargers and the burn-fat-while-you-sleep pills got away with it.

Reprinted by permission from *Imprimis*, the national speech digest of Hillsdale College, www.hillsdale.edu., pp. 1, 3, 5. Copyright © 2001. SUBSCRIPTION FREE UPON REQUEST. ISSN 0277-8432. Imprimis trademark registered in U.S. Patent and Trade Office # 1563325.

The Attorney General would come at them after five years, they would hire lawyers to gain another five, and then they would change the name of their product or move to a different state. But regulation *did* punish *legitimate* businesses.

When I started reporting, all the aspirin companies were saying they were the best, when in fact aspirin is simply aspirin. So the FTC sued and demanded corrective advertising. Corrective ads would have been something like, "Contrary to our prior ads, Excedrin does not relieve twice as much pain." Of course these ads never ran. Instead, nine years of costly litigation finally led to a consent order. The aspirin companies said, "We don't admit doing anything wrong, but we won't do it again." So who won? Unquestionably the lawyers did. But did the public? Aspirin ads are more honest now. They say things like, "Nothing works better than Bayer"—which, if you think about it, simply means, "We're all the same." But I came to see that the same thing would have happened without nearly a decade of litigation, because markets police themselves. I can't say for certain *how* it would have happened. I think it's a fatal conceit to predict how markets will work. Maybe Better Business Bureaus would have gotten involved. Maybe the aspirin companies would have sued each other. Maybe the press would have embarrassed them. But the truth would have gotten out. The more I watched the market, the more impressed I was by how flexible and reasonable it is compared to government-imposed solutions.

Market forces protect us even where we tend most to think we need government. Consider the greedy, profit-driven companies that have employed me. CBS, NBC, and ABC make their money from advertisers, and they've paid me for 20 years to bite the hand that feeds them. Bristol-Myers sued CBS and me for $23 million when I did the story on aspirin. You'd think CBS would have said, "Stossel ain't worth that." But they didn't. Sometimes advertisers would pull their accounts, but still I wasn't fired. Ralph Nader once said that this would never happen except on public television. In fact the opposite is true: Unlike PBS, almost every local TV station has a consumer reporter. The reason is capitalism: More people watch stations that give honest information about their sponsors' products. So although a station might lose some advertisers, it can charge the others more. Markets protect us in unexpected ways.

Alternatives to the Nanny State

People often say to me, "That's okay for advertising. But when it comes to health and safety, we've got to have OSHA, the FDA, the CPSC" and the whole alphabet soup of regulatory agencies that have been created over the past several decades. At first glance this might seem to make sense. But by interfering with free markets, regulations almost invariably have nasty side effects. Take the FDA, which saved us from thalidomide—the drug to prevent morning sickness in pregnant women that was discovered to cause birth defects. To be accurate, it wasn't so much that the FDA saved us, as that it was so slow in studying thalidomide that by the end of the approval process, the drug's awful effects were being seen in Europe. I'm glad for this. But since the thalidomide scare, the FDA has grown ten-fold in size, and I believe it now does more harm than good. If you want to get a new drug approved today, it costs about $500 million and takes about ten years. This means that there are drugs currently in existence that would improve or even save lives, but that are being withheld from us because of a tiny chance they contain carcinogens. Some years ago, the FDA held a press conference to announce its long-awaited approval of a new beta-blocker, and predicted it would save 14,000 American lives per year. Why didn't anybody stand up at the time and say, "Excuse me, doesn't that mean you killed 14,000 people last year by not approving it?" The answer is, reporters don't think that way.

Why, in a free society, do we allow government to perform this kind of nanny-state function? A reasonable alternative would be for government to serve as an information agency. Drug companies wanting to submit their products to a ten-year process could do so. Those of us who choose to be cautious could take only FDA-approved drugs. But others, including people with terminal illnesses, could try non-approved drugs without sneaking off to Mexico or breaking the law. As an added benefit, all of us would learn something valuable by their doing so. I'd argue further that we don't need the FDA to perform this research. As a rule, government agencies are inefficient. If we abolished the FDA, private groups like the publisher of *Consumer Reports* would step in and do the job better, cheaper, and faster. In any case, wouldn't that be more compatible with what America is about? Patrick Henry never said, "Give me absolute safety or give me death!"

Lawyers and Liability

If we embrace the idea of free markets, we have to accept the fact that trial lawyers have a place. Private lawsuits could be seen as a supplement to Adam Smith's invisible hand: the invisible fist. In theory they should deter bad behavior. But because of how our laws have evolved, this process has gone horribly wrong. It takes years for victims to get their money, and most of the money goes to lawyers. Additionally, the wrong people get sued. A Harvard study of medical malpractice suits found that most of those getting money don't deserve it, and that most people injured by negligence don't sue. The system is a mess. Even the cases the trial lawyers are most proud of don't really make us safer. They brag about their lawsuit over football helmets, which were thin enough that some kids were getting head injuries. But now the helmets are so thick that kids are butting each other and getting other kinds of injuries. Worst of all, they cost over $100 each. School districts on the margin can't afford them, and as a result some are dropping their football programs. Are the kids from these schools safer playing on the streets? No.

An even clearer example concerns vaccines. Trial lawyers sued over the Diphtheria-Pertussis-Tetanus Vaccine, claiming that it wasn't as safe as it might have been. Although I suspect this case rested on junk science, I don't know what the truth is. But assuming these lawyers were right, and that they've made the DPT vaccine a little safer, are we safer? When they sued, there were twenty companies in America researching and making vaccines.

Now there are four. Many got out of the business because they said, "We don't make that much on vaccines. Who needs this huge liability?" Is America better off with four vaccine makers instead of twenty? No way.

These lawsuits also disrupt the flow of information that helps free people protect themselves. For example, we ought to read labels. We should read the label on tetracycline, which says that it won't work if taken with milk. But who reads labels anymore? I sure don't. There are 21 warning labels on stepladders—"Don't dance on stepladders wearing wet shoes," etc.—because of the threat of liability. Drug labels are even crazier. If anyone were actually to read the two pages of fine print that come with birth control pills, they wouldn't need to take the drug. My point is that government and lawyers don't make us safer. Freedom makes us safer. It allows us to protect *ourselves*. Some say, "That's fine for us. We're educated. But the poor and the ignorant need government regulations to protect them." Not so. I sure don't know what makes one car run better or safer than another. Few of us are automotive engineers. But it's hard to get totally ripped off buying a car in America. The worst car you can find here is safer than the best cars produced in planned economies. In a free society, not everyone has to be an expert in order for markets to protect us. In the case of cars, we just need a few car buffs who read car magazines. Information gets around through word-of-mouth. Good companies thrive and bad ones atrophy. Freedom protects the ignorant, too.

Admittedly there are exceptions to this argument. I think we need some environmental regulation, because now and then we lack a market incentive to behave well in that area. Where is the incentive for me to keep my waste-treatment plant from contaminating your drinking water? So we need some rules, and some have done a lot of good. Our air and water are cleaner thanks to catalytic converters. But how much regulation is enough? President Clinton set a record as he left office, adding 500,000 new pages to the Federal Register—a whole new spiderweb of little rules for us to obey. How big should government be? For most of America's history, when we grew the fastest, government accounted for five percent or less of GDP. The figure is now 40 percent. This is still less than Europe. But shouldn't we at least have an intelligent debate about how much government should do? The problem is that to have such a debate, we need an informed public. And here I'm embarrassed, because people in my business are not helping that cause.

Fear-Mongering: A Risky Business

A turning point came in my career when a producer came into my office excited because he had been given a story by a trial lawyer—the lazy reporter's best friend—about Bic lighters spontaneously catching fire in people's pockets. These lighters, he told me, had killed four Americans in four years. By this time I'd done some homework, so I said, "Fine. I'll do the exploding lighter story after I do stories on plastic bags, which kill 40 Americans every four years, and five-gallon buckets, which kill 200 Americans (mostly children) every four years." This is a big country, with 280 million people. Bad things happen to some of them. But if we frighten all the rest about ant-sized dangers, they won't be prepared when an elephant comes along. The producer stalked off angrily and got Bob Brown to do the story. But several years later, when ABC gave me three hour-long specials a year in order to keep me, I insisted the first one be called, "Are We Scaring Ourselves to Death?" In it, I ranked some of these risks and made fun of the press for its silliness in reporting them.

Risk specialists compare risks not according to how many people they kill, but according to how many days they reduce the average life. The press goes nuts over airplane crashes, but airplane crashes have caused fewer than 200 deaths per year over the past 20 years. That's less than one day off the average life. There is no proof that toxic-waste sites like Love Canal or Times Beach have hurt anybody at all, despite widely reported claims that they cause 1,000 cases of cancer a year. (Even assuming they do, and assuming further that all these cancer victims die, that would still be less than four days off the average life.) House fires account for about 4,500 American deaths per year— 18 days off the average life. And murder, which leads the news in most towns, takes about 100 days off the average life. But to bring these risks into proper perspective, we need to compare them to far greater risks like driving, which knocks 182 days off the average life. I am often asked to do scare stories about flying—"The Ten Most Dangerous Airports" or "The Three Most Dangerous Airlines"—and I refuse because it's morally irresponsible. When we scare people about flying, more people drive to Grandma's house, and more are killed as a result. This is statistical murder, perpetuated by regulators and the media.

Even more dramatic is the fact that Americans below the poverty line live seven to ten fewer years than the rest of us. Some of this difference is self-induced: poor people smoke and drink more. But most of it results from the fact that they can't afford some of the good things that keep the rest of us alive. They drive older cars with older tires; they can't afford the same medical care; and so on. This means that when bureaucrats get obsessed about flying or toxic-waste sites, and create new regulations and drive up the cost of living in order to reduce these risks, they shorten people's lives by making them poorer. Bangladesh has floods that kill 100,000 people. America has comparable floods and no one dies. The difference is wealth. Here we have TVs and radios to hear about floods, and cars to drive off in. Wealthier is healthier, and regulations make the country poorer. Maybe the motto of OSHA should be: "To save four, kill ten."

Largely due to the prevalence of misleading scare stories in the press, we see in society an increasing fear of innovation. Natural gas in the home kills 200 Americans a year, but we accept it because it's old. It happened before we got crazy. We accept coal, which is awful stuff, but we're terrified of nuclear power, which is probably cleaner and safer. Swimming pools kill over 1,000 Americans every year, and I think it's safe to say that the government wouldn't allow them today if they didn't already exist. What about vehicles that weigh a ton and are driven within inches of pedestrians by 16-year-olds, all while spewing noxious exhaust? Cars, I fear, would never make it off the drawing board in 2001.

What's happened to America? Why do we allow government to make decisions for us as if we were children? In a free society we should be allowed to take risks, and to learn from them. The press carps and whines about our exposure to dangerous new things—invisible chemicals, food additives, radiation, etc. But what's the result? We're living longer than ever. A century ago, most people my age were already dead. If we were better informed, we'd realize that what's behind this longevity is the spirit of enterprise, and that's what gives us this spirit—what makes America thrive—isn't regulation. It's freedom.

POSTSCRIPT

Should Government Intervene in a Capitalist Economy?

As with most good debates, the issue of the rightness of government intervention is difficult to decide. Part of the difficulty is that it involves the trade-off of values that are in conflict in real situations, and part of the difficulty is that it involves uncertain estimations of the future consequences of policy changes. Both experts and interested parties can differ greatly on value trade-offs and estimations of impacts. Government regulations and other interventions cost money for both administration and compliance. Nevertheless, Spitzer and Celli argue that certain government actions will provide benefits that greatly exceed the costs, and Stossel argues the contrary view that the costs will be far greater than Spitzer and Celli expect and probably will have net negative results. Part of the strength of Stossel's argument is that regulations often fail to do what they are designed to do. Part of the strength of Spitzer and Celli argument is that there are many observable problems that need to be addressed, and for some of these government action seems to be the only viable option.

One aspect of the issue is the morality of businesses. Most commentators have a low opinion of business ethics and the way corporations use their power, and point to the recent corporate scandals as confirmation. Thus it is easy to conclude that since they will not do what is right, they must be made to do what is right. For support of this view see Joel Bakan, *The Corporation: The Pathological Pursuit of Profit and Power* (Free Press, 2004); Justin O"Brien, *Wall Street on Trial: A Corrupted State?* (Wiley, 2003); Steve Tombs and Dave Whyte, *Unmasking the Crimes of the Powerful: Scrutinizing States and Corporations* (P. Lang, 2003); Jamie Court, *Corporateering: How Corporate Power Steals Your Personal Freedom—and What You Can Do about It* (Jeremy P. Tarcher/Putnam, 2003); Kenneth R. Gray et al., *Corporate Scandels: The Many Faces of Greed: The Great Heist, Financial Bubbles, and the Absence of Virtue* (Paragon House, 2005); and Victor Perlo, *Superprofits and Crisis: Modern U.S. Capitalism* (International Publishers, 1988). Some commentators, however, defend businesses in a competitive capitalistic market.

Philosopher Michael Novak contends that the ethic of capitalism transcends mere moneymaking and is (or can be made) compatible with Judeo-Christian morality. See *The Spirit of Democratic Capitalism* (Madison Books, 1991) and *The Catholic Ethic and the Spirit of Capitalism* (Free Press, 1993). Another broad-based defense of capitalism is Peter L. Berger's *The Capitalist Revolution: Fifty Propositions About Prosperity, Equality and Liberty* (Basic Books, 1988). For a feminist critique of capitalism, see J. K. Gibson-Graham, *The End of Capitalism (As We Know It): A Feminist Critique of Political Economy* (Blackwell, 1996). For a mixed view of capitalism, see Charles Wolf, Jr., *Markets or Governments: Choosing Between Imperfect Alternatives* (MIT Press, 1993). A strong attack on government interventions in the market is Jonathan Rauch, *Demosclerosis: The Silent Killer of American Government* (Times Books, 1994).

For an in-depth understanding of the way that markets work and the role that institutions maintained by the state, including property rights, function to maintain markets, see Neil Fligstein, *The Architecture of Markets: An Economic Sociology of Twenty-First Century Capitalist Societies* (Princeton University Press, 2001). An interesting role of government is its bailing-out failed corporations. See *Too Big to Fail: Policies and Practices in Government Bailouts* edited by Benton E. Gup (Praeger, 2004) and David G. Mayes et al. *Who Pays for Bank Insolvency?* (Palgrave Macmillan, 2004). Often self-regulation is better than government regulation. See Virgina Haufler, *A Public Role for the Private Sector: Industry Self-Regulation in a Global Economy* (Carnegie Endowment for International Peace, 2001).

ISSUE 12

Has Welfare Reform Benefited the Poor?

YES: David Coates, from *A Liberal Toolkit: Progressive Responses to Conservative Arguments* (Praeger, 2007)

NO: David Coates, from *A Liberal Toolkit: Progressive Responses to Conservative Arguments* (Praeger, 2007)

ISSUE SUMMARY

YES: David Coates presents the argument for welfare reform, which is that most poverty is self-induced, the previous welfare program created poverty and many other problems; and the reform reduces poverty, improves the lives of the people who left welfare, and solves other problems.

NO: David Coates also presents a counter-argument saying that most poverty is not self-induced, many of the old welfare programs worked fairly well, and welfare-to-work programs are hampered by extremely low wages.

$\mathbf{I}$n his 1984 book *Losing Ground: American Social Policy, 1950–1980* (Basic Books), policy analyst Charles Murray recommends abolishing Aid to Families with Dependent Children (AFDC), the program at the heart of the welfare debate. At the time of the book's publication, this suggestion struck many as simply a dramatic way for Murray to make some of his points. However, 14 years later this idea became the dominant idea in Congress. In 1996, President Bill Clinton signed into law the Work Opportunity Reconciliation Act and fulfilled his 1992 campaign pledge to "end welfare as we know it." Murray's thesis that welfare hurt the poor had become widely accepted. In "What to Do About Welfare," *Commentary* (December 1994), Murray argues that welfare contributes to dependency, illegitimacy, and the number of absent fathers, which in turn can have terrible effects on the children involved. He states that workfare, enforced child support, and the abolition of welfare would greatly reduce these problems. One reason why Congress ended AFDC was the emergence of a widespread backlash against welfare recipients. Much of the backlash, however, was misguided. It often rested on the assumptions that welfare is generous and that most people on welfare are professional loafers. In fact, over the previous two decades, payments to families with dependent children eroded considerably relative to the cost of living. Furthermore, most women with dependent children on welfare had intermittent periods of work, were elderly, or were disabled. Petty fraud may be common because welfare payments are insufficient to live on in many cities, but "welfare queens" who cheat the system for spectacular sums are so rare that they should not be part of any serious debate on welfare issues. The majority of people on welfare are those whose condition would become desperate if payments were cut off. Although many believe that women on welfare commonly bear children in order to increase their benefits, there is no conclusive evidence to support this conclusion.

Not all objections to AFDC can be easily dismissed, however. There does seem to be evidence that in some cases AFDC reduces work incentives and increases the likelihood of family breakups. But there is also a positive side to AFDC—it helped many needy people get back on their feet. When all things are considered together, therefore, it is not clear that welfare, meaning AFDC, was bad enough to be abolished. But it was abolished on July 1, 1997, when the Work Opportunity Reconciliation Act went into effect. Now the question is whether the new policy is better than the old policy.

It is too soon to obtain an accurate assessment of the long-term impacts of the Act. Nevertheless, AFDC rolls have declined since the Act was passed, so many conclude that it is a success rather than a failure. Of course, the early leavers are the ones with the best prospects of succeeding in the work world; the welfare-to-work transition gets harder as the program works with the more difficult cases. The crucial question is whether or not the reform will benefit those it affects. Already many working former welfare recipients are better off. But what about the average or more vulnerable recipient?

In the readings that follow, David Coates presents a fair summary of the case for the benefits of welfare reform and then presents his own counter-argument. The two sides disagree on the extent of poverty, the role of the poor in their poverty, the negative effects of welfare programs, and the limits of the welfare-to-work approach.

YES ↵

David Coates

Cutting "Welfare" to Help the Poor

Welfare states in the modern world aren't very old—60 or 70 years at most. Some parts are older—the German social insurance system started with Bismarck—but in general the provision of government help to the poor, the sick, the disabled, and the elderly is a recent phenomenon. Not all governments make that provision even now, but most do. Certainly in recent times, all governments in the advanced democracies have taken on a major welfare role, and that includes federal and state authorities here in the United States.

Yet in this, as in so much else, the United States has proved to be unique. Unique in coverage: No universal system of health care, free at the point of use, emerged here in the late 1940s as it did in much of Western Europe. Unique in delivery system: From the early 1950s, pensions and health care were tied directly to wage settlements here, in wage-and-benefit packages with few foreign parallels. Unique in timing: The United States set the pace in the 1930s with the New Deal, and again in the late 1960s with its own War on Poverty. Unique in vocabulary: The U.S. state pension system is known as *social security* and the term *welfare* is restricted to payments to the poor, giving it a stigma it lacks in much of Western Europe. And unique in fragility: The United States is the only major industrial democracy formally committed to the "ending of welfare as we know it," through the 1996 Personal Responsibility and Work Opportunity Reconciliation Act.

The result has been the consolidation in the United States of a publicly financed welfare system, which, in comparative terms, in now both residual and modest. It's residual in that it leaves the bulk of provision for the sick and the old to the private sector. It's modest in that the public provision made available (pensions apart) is less generous than that now commonplace in Western Europe and Japan. For many American liberals, there's something profoundly embarrassing about the richest country on earth getting by with the most limited welfare system in the advanced industrial world. But that's not how the Conservative Right sees it. On the contrary, having a residual and modest welfare state is, for them, one of the key reasons why the United States is the richest country on earth. Protecting that economic success then requires U.S. welfare provision to be made ever more residual and modest over time. In a manner and scale without precedence elsewhere, *cutting welfare*—either to the bone, or away completely—is regularly and seriously canvassed by conservative forces in the United States as the best way to help the poor. . . .

⋅⦿⋅

A Liberal Response

Oh, if it was only that simple. But, for the following reasons at least, it's not. . . .

There's More Poverty Out There Than You Might Think

12.7 percent of all Americans now live on incomes that fall at or below the official poverty lines. Even worse, of the 37 million people living in officially defined poverty in 2004, 13 million were children. That's equivalent to the entire populations of Sweden and Norway. The poverty rate for very young children in the United States in the first half-decade of the twenty-first century was slightly over 20 percent: that's one preschool child in every five. And around them are what the Economic Policy Institute (EPI) calls "the twice-poor," that is, Americans living on or below-incomes that are only twice the officially defined level for their family size. Amazingly, more than 89 million Americans fell into that broader category in 2003—all close to poverty and all accordingly obliged to watch every penny. Collectively, the poor and the twice-poor now constitute 31 percent of the population—that's 3 in every 10 Americans. That's a lot of people in or near the poverty margin, no matter what Congress is or isn't being told by the people in suits.

What they experience is real poverty, in both the absolute and relative senses of the term. Currently, 39 million Americans are classified as "food insecure" and 40 percent of all those using food banks live in families in which at least one adult is working. . . . It doesn't help them—or indeed us—to be told that most of them have cars. Of course they do. Given the absence of adequate systems of public transport in vast swathes of the United States, how else are they meant to get to shops or to the food bank? A car in the United States isn't a luxury. It's a necessity; an extra financial burden that can't be avoided if doing the ordinary things of life is not to become nearly impossible. The Western European poor don't need cars to anything like the same degree, because the scale of public provision—the size of the social wage that everyone enjoys regardless of income—is so much larger in those countries.

That's one reason why it's simply untrue to claim that the American poor are better off than most ordinary Europeans and better off than the entirety of the Western European poor. Sadly, they're not. On the contrary, the child poverty rate in the United States is currently *four* times that of northern

Europe. There are *only three* Western European countries whose poor children have a lower living standard than do poor children in the United States. . . .

If All This Poverty Is Self-Inflicted, Then Masochism in the United States is Amazingly Rife

This is why there's something particularly offensive about the speed and case with which so many commentators on the American Right, instead of probing beneath the surface for the underlying causes of the "pathologies" of poverty they so dislike, move instead to demonize the poor, endlessly blaming them for making "bad choices" as though good ones were plentiful and immediately at hand. Telling young black women to marry the fathers of their children, for example, carries with it the premise that the men are there to be married. Yet "twelve percent of all black men between eighteen and thirty-four are [currently] in jail," a bigger proportion of "men away" than the United States as a whole experienced during the entirety of World War II. Unemployment rates among young black men are double those among their white contemporaries. "The problem is not that the nation's poorest women have systematically passed up good jobs and good marriage partners. The problem is that there are significant economic and cultural inadequacies in the choices available to them. They, like the rest of America, value children; but unlike the rest of America, they cannot easily support them. . . .

Given a Chance, Welfare Works Better Than is Claimed

The payment of welfare stands accused by many on the American Right of creating poverty and damaging those to whom it is given. With one important caveat—welfare traps—to which we will come later, the claim is literally ludicrous. Welfare did not create poverty in America. Poverty was here long before the New Deal and long before Johnson's "war." Neither set of welfare initiatives created their clienteles. They simply responded to their prior existence. The poverty of the 1930s was of a mass kind, the product of a general economic collapse that was rectified not by welfare programs but by the United States' mobilization for war. Within it, however, were categories of the poor that had existed before 1929 and that continued to exist after 1941—the temporarily unemployed, the genetically infirm, widows, and the elderly. By the 1960s, those categories of the poor had been joined by another, one explicitly excluded from the coverage of the original New Deal. To get any sort of legislative package through a Congress whose committees were dominated by southern Democrats, Roosevelt had excluded black workers in the south. Servants and agricultural workers gained no benefits from the core programs of the New Deal. They survived instead in the invisible southern poverty, poverty which—as prosperity returned with the war—then drew them out of the south into the cities and industries of the northeast and the midwest. In the first half of the postwar period. African Americans increasingly exchanged *invisible* southern rural poverty for its *visible* urban northern equivalent. It was an exchange to which the welfare programs of the 1960s were a belated response.

So it was a case of poverty first, and welfare second, and not the other way around. It was also a case of a welfare response that, when properly funded, took the rate of poverty *down* not up: a response that over time definitely improved the lives of many categories of the American poor. The official poverty rate in 1959—the first year in the United States that it was taken—was 22.4 percent: By 1973, with the War on Poverty at its height, that rate had halved. Then, as programs were cut back in the 1970s and 1980s, the rate grew again. It was back to 14.5 percent by 1992, although it's slightly lower now, as we've seen. . . .

The Charity Illusion

Unless, of course, as the Cato people would have it, private charity would have stepped into the breach and done a better job. But there's just no evidence to sustain that claim. There's certainly no evidence that private charity could, or did, scratch more than the surface of the poverty experienced by the old, the infirm, and the widowed before the New Deal. And of the nature of things, no evidence can sustain the claim that if welfare was entirely removed (and tax levels cut accordingly), those benefiting from the tax cuts would then redirect all or most of their extra income into charitable endeavors. American altruism—although impressive by international standards—is not without limit, and because it isn't, the private sector can't be treated as a reliable and problem-free alternative to existing welfare programs. Charity-based welfare contains no mechanisms to guard against unevenness of provision, moralizing in the terms set for aid given, or the onset of "gift exhaustion" over time. The gathering of funds by private charities is in any case always time-consuming, intrusive, and administratively inefficient; and the distribution of funds as private handouts only serves to reinforce—for those who receive them—the very sense of dependency and impotence that conservatives are apparently so keen to avoid. . . .

The Fallacy of the Incompetent State

In any event, in making the pitch for the full privatization of welfare, the Charles Murrays and Michael Tanners of this world are not comparing like with like. They're also generalizing from an extraordinarily parochial base. They advocate the replacement of the American welfare system by an idealized and untested network of private charities, using as their evidence inadequacies in American public welfare policy since the 1970s. With few exceptions, they don't appear to have looked in any systematic way at Western Europe, where states have run welfare systems successfully for years. Nor have they engaged with—indeed have they even read—the fabulous and extensive scholarly literature on comparative welfare systems. If they had, they'd quickly have come to see that the great tragedy of Lyndon Johnson's War on Poverty was not that poverty won, but that the war itself was not pursued with sufficient consistency and zeal.

All governments—European and American alike—distribute income and dispense welfare. They're all, in James Galbraith's telling term, "transfer states," and inequality always shows what he called "the fingerprints of state policy." The War on Poverty required those fingerprints to distribute income downward, and initially it did. General poverty levels fell. But command of the war then shifted. Under Reagan and the two Bush administrations, the fingerprints were deployed differently. Income was consciously moved upward. Welfare systems can always be made to fail, if inadequately financed and led. An agency such as Federal Emergency Management Agency (FEMA) will always fail if it's led by cronies and managed by fools. But by the same token, welfare systems can always be made to work well if supplied with sufficient funds and commitment. Indeed, take a welfare system up to about 40 percent of gross domestic product (GDP)—when it's servicing the entire community and not just the poor—and popular support for it will rise, not fall. That's been the universal Western European experience. . . .

The Limits of Welfare-to-Work Programs in a World of Low Pay

The 1996 Act is the Republicans ace card in their attempt to roll back the American welfare state, and they have one huge piece of evidence going in their favor: the dramatic fall in the number of people—especially young single mothers—in receipt of welfare since its passing. But the figures on caseload reduction, although real, are also deceptive, and we need to say so. They're deceptive in a *causal* sense: in that the full implementation of the Act coincided with a significant period of job growth in the American economy. When that growth stalled, so too did the rate of job take-up by single mothers. The figures on caseload reduction are deceptive, too, in a *social* sense. People came off welfare, but then ran into a whole series of new problems that the figures don't catch. Women fleeing domestic violence lost a vital source of autonomy from the men who had violated them. Young women with small children lost a significant percentage of their new wages on child care and transport costs; and the children themselves—whose enhanced well-being was, after all, a key aim of the new legislation—often found themselves in inadequate child care, looked after by undertrained and underpaid female staff. Women didn't stop providing child care. They simply stopped providing their own. And, overwhelmingly; the figures on caseload reduction are deceptive in an *economic* sense. Going off welfare, although it reduced the numbers, did not reduce the scale and rate of poverty among those who previously had been in receipt of aid. The Cato Institute's Michael Tanner has conceded as much, noting that "self-sufficiency appears to be eluding the grasp of many, if not most, former recipients." And of course it is, because (quite predictably) the vast majority of the jobs into which former welfare recipients were moved turned out to be *low-paid* jobs. Welfare-to-work moved people from government-sponsored poverty to private sector-based poverty, adding to their transport and child care costs as it did so. Workfare changed the source of poverty; but not the poverty itself. . . .

The "Welfare Poor" and the "Working Poor" Are on the Same Side

Republicans likes to present themselves as champions of the working poor against the welfare poor, implying that the interests of the two groups are in tension and painting the Democratic Party into a "tax-and-spend" corner as they do so. But the argument is false in both of its premises: The interests of the two are not in tension and the Republicans are not the defenders of the real interests of the working poor.

The existence of a large group of full-time workers—paid so little that they themselves are on the margin of poverty—actually traps the welfare poor a second time. If you're on welfare, you're poor. If you get out of welfare and into work, you'll still be poor, because the move will only take you into the bottom tier of the poorly paid. If the people in that low-pay group are then financially pressed—and they definitely are—it's not because of the weight of any welfare taxation that they carry. It's because their wages are low. It's not taxes that make them poor, but the lack of income growth. What really hurts the low paid is not the poverty of the people below them but the greed of the people above them. As we read in chapter 3, the truly unique feature of the recent American income story is the proportion of total income growth taken by the ultrarich. You remember, 24 percent of all income growth in the U.S. economy between 1997 and 2001 was taken by just 1 percent of the population, and it was taken at the end of a quarter-century in which wages remained flat for the majority of working Americans. What the working poor need is not welfare retrenchment but higher wages. They *and* the welfare poor need the creation of a high-wage, high-growth economy to ease the burden of poverty on them both. They both need full employment and rising wages in an economy in which there is a fair distribution of rewards. That's the kind of economy that the Republicans always promise in the run-up to elections, but it's also the kind of economy that after the elections, for 80 million Americans at least, the party regularly fails to deliver. . . .

Welfare Doesn't Trap the Poor in an Underclass—We Do

Welfare critics are right on at least this: There is a welfare trap, work disincentive issue in any welfare system. As people come off welfare and lose benefits, the effective tax rate on their own earnings can be extraordinarily high. Depending on the rules, in the move from welfare to work you might lose 60 cents of welfare provision for every dollar you earn, and effectively be only 40 cents better off—a rate of taxation against which the rich regularly howl when experiencing it themselves. So there is a problem of "disincentives to work" associated with welfare, one on which the Right regularly latch. But it's not the only, or indeed the main, problem currently facing young mothers in search of good jobs in America's inner cities. Good jobs are scarce because the middle-class workers have left those cities, taking the jobs with them. Available child care is poor because the programs have been cut. Young men are scarce because incarceration rates have been systematically ratcheted up. Suburban flight, welfare retrenchment, drugs, and the rise of a prison economy are the real villains here. As Barack Obama said, "the people of New Orleans just weren't abandoned during the Hurricane. They were abandoned long ago—to murder and mayhem in the streets, to sub-standard schools, to dilapidated housing, to inadequate health care, to a pervasive sense of hopelessness." Underclasses don't create themselves. They're created. You can't be trapped unless somebody does the trapping.

The great thing about traps, however, is that they can be sprung. The solution to the disincentive effect of welfare payments is to phase in benefit reductions slowly—allowing people to earn and receive benefits in parallel until their incomes reach a tolerable level. . . .

Poverty is a Matter of Choice—It's Just Not a Choice Made by the Poor

The ultimate irony here is that poverty, as the Republican Right regularly claims, is indeed a matter of choice. It's just not a choice that the poor themselves are called on to make. It's a choice made by the rest of us. In the main, for most of us, by how we vote, and for those who govern us, by how they legislate. They and us, not the poor, have the power to choose. We can choose, as an economy and a society, to meet the arrival of intensified global competition by outsourcing production, lowering American wages, and increasing income inequality. Or we can choose to reset the way we organize the economy and regulate trade to pull jobs back to the United States and to improve the quality of work and levels of remuneration attached to them. There is a choice to be made. If we take the first route, we'll create new sources of poverty for those low-skilled American workers currently in employment and extra barriers for those trying to move into work from welfare dependency. If we take the second, we'll have to dismantle much of the hidden welfare state now going to the rich, and perhaps not just to them. A proper system of rent subsidy for people on low incomes, for example, may have to be financed by phasing out the enormous tax subsidy currently provided to those of us fortunate enough to be buying rather than renting our houses. But at least the more affluent among us have a choice. The poor do not. Or perhaps more accurately, the affluent have the choice of making a big difference by making a small sacrifice. The poor, by contrast, have to labor mightily just to change their individual circumstances by merely an inch.

"Poor people and investment bankers have one thing in common. They both spend considerable energy thinking about money." Which is why, on this topic at least, the Republicans are both right and wrong. They're right: when discussing poverty, policy is ultimately a matter of making right choices. But they're also wrong. Over and over again, the choices they make are the wrong ones—and we need to say so.

David Coates

Cutting "Welfare" to Help the Poor

There's Not as Much Poverty in America as Liberals Like to Claim

The liberal media are way too quick to exaggerate and at times misreport the data on poverty in the United States. We have to be very careful here. "For most Americans, the word 'poverty' suggests destitution," but in truth only a tiny portion of the 37 million people reported as living in poverty by the Census Bureau are poor in any meaningful sense of that term. "Overall, the living standards of most poor Americans are far higher than is generally appreciated." Most of them have a fridge, a stove, a television—normally two, both color—a microwave, air conditioning, and a car. The bulk of the American poor has basic but decent housing and access to food and health care. In fact, "the average poor American has more living space than the average individual living in Paris . . . and other cities throughout Europe." This is not poverty by world standards. It's in Asia and Africa that poverty stunts the growth of children. Not the United States. What poverty there is in the United States is often short lived. "More than half of all poverty 'spells' (time spent in poverty) last less than four months, and about 80 percent last less than a year." There's a lot of upward *and* downward social mobility in the United States. One household in three escapes poverty within three years; and one rich family in three slips down into a lower income bracket during that same period. "In fact, very few people—only about 2 percent of the total population—are chronically poor in America, as defined by living in poverty for four years or more," and all societies have a stratum of folk like that. Poverty, after all, is natural. The poor are always with us, so it's ridiculous to criticize the United States for simply being like all the rest. We're not denying that there is real hardship for roughly one poor house-hold in three. We're simply saying that "even those households would be judged to have high living standards compared to most people in the world." So we need to keep a sense of proportion when discussing poverty—a sense of proportion that, on this as on so much else, liberals normally lack.

What Poverty There Is in the United States Is Almost Entirely Self-Induced

America is still a society in which, by hard work and personal effort, all things are possible. You don't have to be poor. Poverty is, in that sense, a question of choice. If you want to stay out of poverty, make sure that you stay first at school and then in work; make sure, too, that you don't have children until you've established a stable and well-funded relationship. School, work, and marriage are the great barriers to poverty here, and all three are readily available if you look for them.

So if you don't, that tells us something, not about the society in which you're poor, but about you as someone who remains poor when you don't need to. Why are you still there, trapped in your own poverty? Perhaps it's because you don't have the right skills or the willingness to acquire them. Or, perhaps it's because you blew off school and now are paying the price. There might even be an intelligence issue here. Or, perhaps it is simply that you moved too quickly into casual and careless sex and are now looking for support from people less feckless than yourself. Not that everyone is guilty here, of course. There are innocents caught up in poverty, too—widows, the genetically infirm, and overwhelmingly the children you so casually bred—innocents who, if not helped, will find themselves trapped in a culture of poverty from which it is hard to escape. We know that "nearly two-thirds of poor children reside in single-parent families," but we also know that "if poor mothers married the fathers of their children, nearly 75 percent would immediately be lifted out of poverty."

So there are things that can be done, and there is a role for public policy. But it has to be policy anchored in a clear recognition of at least three things. First, that, in the main, people put themselves into poverty, rather than being put there. Policy therefore has to be designed primarily to stop them doing that. Second, that it's not the rich who cause poverty, but the poor themselves. Tax the rich into oblivion—play class politics—and you'll end up with even more poverty. And, third, that public policy can only do so much and can easily overreach itself. "The government can force your parents to send you to school, but it can't force you to learn." There's a matter of personal responsibility here. "If you do not educate yourself or develop a marketable skill, the chances are you will be poor and powerless," and that will be nobody's fault but your own.

The Big Thing That's Wrong with Liberal Welfare Programs Is That They Create More Poverty Than They Remove

The liberal welfare programs of the 1960s were designed on the premise that what the poor lacked, more than anything else, was money and skills. Liberal-minded politicians threw trillions of tax dollars into the urban ghettos, offering what they termed "a hand but not a handout." In the main, this largesse was well intentioned, although some of it, it should be said, did reflect a Democratic Party desire to build up a dependent client base. Even when welfare policy was well intentioned, it was entirely counterproductive. It got nowhere near the real causes of poverty, rooted as those are in illegitimacy and idleness. It simply transferred hard-earned resources from the working poor to the nonworking poor, in the process sending out entirely the wrong message about effort and personal responsibility, and squeezing the very people whose industry and personal morality were and remain the backbone of the American success story.

In designing their welfare programs, liberals ignored the warning, given long ago by Franklin D. Roosevelt himself, that "continued dependence on relief induces a spiritual and moral disintegration fundamentally destructive to the national fiber." They choose instead to dole out ever larger quantities of that relief—to administer what he'd called in 1935 "a narcotic, a subtle destroyer of the human spirit"—tolerating as they did so the existence of far too many "welfare queens." The relief they doled out so indiscriminately to both the deserving and the undeserving poor then literally cost a fortune—$8.3 trillion since 1973 alone—but failed entirely to remove the poverty it was designed to end. Even Jimmy Carter admitted as much: the liberal welfare system was "anti-work, anti-family, inequitable in its treatment of the poor and wasteful of the taxpayers dollars." But like all Democrats, he never tackled its inadequacies. He had far too many dependent constituencies to service to be able to match his understanding of the system's defects with policy adequate for its reform.

Many of Today's Social Ills Can and Must Be Laid at the Door of Welfare Itself

The War on Poverty was a disaster, and because it was, the liberal establishment in Washington stills bears a huge responsibility for the level and scale of deprivation in America's inner cities. As Ronald Reagan said in his last State of the Union Address. "Some years ago the federal government declared war on poverty, and poverty won." Like all welfare states, the War on Poverty, made it "profitable to be poor." In doing so, it "degrade[d] the tradition of work, thrift and neighborliness that enabled a society to work at the outset," and then spawned "social and economic problems that it [was] powerless to solve." What had started as a "safety net" quickly became nothing less than a "hammock."

The incentive structures in its programs locked people into the very poverty on which the war was being waged. Welfare programs developed in the late 1960s and early 1970s made it far too easy for young men to shirk their parental responsibilities and for young women to have children without being able to afford them. "One out-of-wedlock birth every 35 seconds," Robert Rector told Congress in February 2005. Those same programs built in powerful disincentives to work, reducing the potential U.S. labor supply by nearly 5 percent and lowering the work effort of welfare recipients by as much as 30 percent. They also helped to consolidate a culture of instant gratification and moral fecklessness among welfare recipients that ran counter to the work ethic that had lifted previous generations of the poor into their contemporary affluence. Far from raising living standards in America's urban heartlands, the War on Poverty created an *underclass* of people excluded by their welfare dependency from full participation in the values and practices of mainstream American life; and at the core of that underclass, this well-meaning but ill-informed expansion of welfare programs then marooned in poverty a whole generation of ghetto kids.

Suffer the little children . . .

It was, and still is, these children of the poor who are welfares greatest casualties. These are the kids who lack the guidance of an ever-present and hard-working father. They're the ones who, in consequence, are disproportionately exposed to "emotional and behavioral problems, school failure, drug and alcohol abuse, crime and incarceration." It's they who face the bleakest future, because "the longer a child remains on [welfare] in childhood the lower will be his earnings as an adult" and the greater will be the likelihood of dropping out of school and ending up back on welfare when older. The driver here is *not* poverty. It's welfare itself. It's welfare, not poverty, that produces dependency; and it's dependency that lowers a child's IQ. Hold everything else constant—income, race, parental IQ, everything you want—and then test for cognitive capacity in kids on welfare and kids who are not. You'll find a 20 percent drop in cognitive capacity among kids who've spent at least a sixth of their life on welfare. "The traditional welfare state's core dilemma." Robert Rector has written, "is that profligate spending intended to alleviate *material* poverty" actually "led to a dramatic increase in *behavioral* poverty . . . dependency and an eroded work ethic, lack of educational aspirations and achievement, inability or unwillingness to control one's children, increased single parenthood and illegitimacy, criminal activity, and drug and alcohol abuse." The liberals' welfare programs did more than simply fail to solve poverty. They also damaged those for whom they were created.

Fortunately, There Is a Better Way Out of Poverty Than Welfare

Once the true answers to poverty (school, work, and marriage) were recognized by the Republicans who swept to power in Congress in 1994, the solution was obvious. Instead of handouts and entitlements, the Gingrich Contract with America ushered in an era of personal responsibility, workfare, and the promotion of responsible parenthood. The 1996 Act took away entitlements to permanent welfare support, replacing the New Deal's Aid to Families with Dependent Children with a new Temporary Assistance to Needy Families program that linked welfare to a commitment to work or seek work. The Act set a firm time limit—five years—on the receipt of welfare and established targets for the percentage of recipients in work or job training schemes by 2001 and 2002, triggering a move from welfare to work. It also began systematically to reinforce the institution of marriage, by encouraging states to establish paternity and collect child support, and by obliging teenage mothers to remain in school and to live with an adult. According to its advocates, the 1996 Act worked. Contrary to the fears of increased poverty expressed by liberals at the time, there were 2.3 million fewer children in poverty in 2001 than in 1996, the rates of poverty among African American children and among families headed by single mothers were at all-time lows, welfare caseloads were significantly down, the growth rate of illegitimate births had slowed, and employment among single mothers was up by anything between 50 and 100 percent. With Earned Income Tax Credit and noncash benefits from the remaining 69 federal welfare programs added in, the number of people in poverty in the United States actually *fell* between 1996 and 2001 by more than 4 million—a rate of poverty down in just five years from 10.2 percent to 8.8.

One section of the Republican coalition—anchored in the Heritage Foundation and in sections of the Christian Right—now wants a second round of welfare reform, focusing on a stricter and wider application of the work rules established in 1996 and on a more powerful advocacy of marriage. They want work rules added to the other main welfare programs—public housing and food stamps. They support the president's "healthy marriage initiative" and want to see it augmented by a wider advocacy of sexual abstinence before marriage. Their argument is that the 1996 Act was a step in the right direction. It began a welfare revolution that must now be carried forward—on the certain conviction that "by increasing work and marriage, our nation can virtually eliminate remaining child poverty" within our lifetime.

The more Libertarian elements within the Republican coalition, however—those closer to the Cato Institute—are less comfortable with *state* orchestration of marriage voews than are those close to the Heritage Foundation. They remain convinced that even the 1996 reform failed to reduce out-of-wedlock births on any significant scale. Not did it enable welfare recipients to become self-sustaining. They don't believe that even Republican-inspired welfare reforms can ever adequately do either of those things. So they favor a different tack: initially, the complete removal of welfare benefits from "young women who continue to make untenable life decision," the return of all welfare funds from the federal government to the states, and eventually the replacement of *all* welfare payments with a negative income tax and the complete privatization of welfare. Charities are so much better than governments, they insist, in dealing with poverty. They're more responsive to their donors and to their clients, more flexible, more efficient, and more effective. The federal government should therefore return "responsibility for the poor first to the states, then to the private sector." Cato-based Libertarians see the 1996 Act as a mixed blessing—as a necessary first step, but one freezing the policy debate in the wrong place—by implying that, if properly designed, welfare can be made to work. No it can't, they say. Welfare will only work by being totally abolished. "When it comes to welfare," as Michael Tanner has written, "we should end it, not mend it.

POSTSCRIPT

Has Welfare Reform Benefited the Poor?

There was considerable national agreement that the old welfare system had to be changed so that it would encourage people to find jobs and achieve self-sufficiency. Much success has been gained regarding this goal so far, but some state that numerous problems still remain. Coates focuses on these problems, especially the inadequate supports for welfare-to-work mothers. The main problem, however, is the large number of poor-paying jobs for the bottom quarter of the labor force. If that problem was solved, the welfare-to-work program would be a great success. In fact, few would need welfare in the first place.

Michael B. Katz, in *The Undeserving Poor: From the War on Poverty to the War on Welfare* (Pantheon Books, 1989), traces the evolution of welfare policies in the United States from the 1960s through the 1980s. Charles Noble traces the evolution of welfare policies into the late 1990s and argues that the structure of the political economy has greatly limited the welfare state in *Welfare as We Knew It: A Political History of the American Welfare State* (Oxford University Press, 1997). Joel F. Handler carries the historical analysis of welfare in the United States to the present in *Blame Welfare, Ignore Poverty and Inequality* (Cambridge University Press, 2007). Bruce S. Johnson criticizes welfare policies in the United States since the 1930s in *The Sixteen-Trillion-Dollar Mistake: How the U.S. Bungled Its National Priorities from the New Deal to the Present* (Columbia University Press, 2001). For discussions of welfare reform, see Jeff Groggen and Lynn A. Karoly, *Welfare Reform: Effects of a Decade of Change* (Harvard University Press, 2005); Ron Haskins, *Work Over Welfare: The Inside Story of the 1996 Welfare Reform Law* (Brookings Institution Press, 2006); Mary Reintsma, *The Political Economy of Welfare Reform in the United States (Edward Elgar, 2007);* Harrell R. Rodgers, Jr., *American Poverty in a New Era of Reform* (M.E. Sharpe, 2006); Sharon Hayes, *Flat Broke with Children: Women in the Age of Welfare Reform* (Oxford University Press, 2003); and *Work, Welfare and Politics: Confronting Poverty in the Wake of Welfare,* edited by Frances Fox Piven et al. (University of Oregon Press, 2002). A great deal of information can be obtained from the reauthorization hearings in the House Committee on Education and the Workforce, *Welfare Reform: Reauthorization of Work and Child Care* (March 15, 2005). A new emphasis in current welfare policy involves faith-based programs, which are discussed in Mary Jo Bane and Lawrence M. Mead, *Lifting Up the Poor: A Dialogue on Religion, Poverty, and Welfare Reform* (Brookings Institution Press, 2003) and John P. Bartkowski, *Charitable Choices: Religion, Race, and Poverty in the Post-Welfare Era* (New York

University, 2003). Most assessments of the 1996 welfare reform are positive. Two works that explore the negative consequences of this bill are Jane Henrici ed., *Doing Without: Women and Work after Welfare Reform* (University of Arizona Press, 2006) and Kathleen M. Shaw, et al., *Putting Poor People to Work: How the Work-First Idea Eroded College Access for the Poor* (Russell Sage Foundation). Many recognize that the key to reducing welfare rolls is to make work profitable. To understand welfare from this perspective, see *Making Work Pay: America after Welfare: A Reader,* edited by Robert Kuttner (New York Press, 2002) and Dave Hage, *Reforming Welfare by Rewarding Work: One State's Successful Experiment* (University of Minnesota Press, 2004). Two books that offer explanations as to why welfare provision is so minimal in the United States are Frank Stricker, *Why America Lost the War on Poverty—and How to Win It* (University of North Carolina Press, 2007) and Linda Gordon, *Pitied but Not Entitled: Single Mothers and the History of Welfare* (Free Press, 1994).

ISSUE 13

Is Competition the Reform That Will Fix Education?

YES: Clint Bolick, from "The Key to Closing the Minority Schooling Gap: School Choice," *The American Enterprise* (April/May 2003)

NO: Ron Wolk, from "Think the Unthinkable," *Educational Horizons* (Summer 2004)

ISSUE SUMMARY

YES: Clint Bolick, vice president of the Institute for Justice, presents the argument for school choice that competition leads to improvements and makes the case that minorities especially need school choice to improve their educational performance.

NO: Educator and businessman Ron Wolk argues that school choice and most other educational reforms can only be marginally effective because they do not get at the heart of the educational problem, which is the way students learn. Too much attention is directed to the way teachers teach when the attention should be placed on how to stimulate students to learn more. Wolk advocates giving students more responsibility for their education.

T he quality of American public schooling has been criticized for several decades. Secretary of Education Richard Riley said in 1994 that some American schools are so bad that they "should never be called schools at all." The average school year in the United States is 180 days, while Japanese children attend school 240 days of the year. American schoolchildren score lower than the children of many other Western countries on certain standardized achievement tests. In 1983 the National Commission on Excellence in Education published *A Nation at Risk,* which argued that American education was a failure. Critics of *A Nation at Risk* maintain that the report produced very little evidence to support its thesis, but the public accepted it anyway. Currently, much of the public still thinks that the American school system is failing and needs to be fixed. The solution most frequently proposed today is some form of competition from charter schools to a voucher system.

Today 99 percent of children ages 6 to 13 are in school. In 1900 only about 7 percent of the appropriate age group graduated from high school, but in 1990, 86 percent did. Another success is the extraordinary improvement in the graduation rates for blacks since 1964, when it was 45 percent, to 1987, when it was 83 percent. Now this rate is almost at parity with white graduation rates. And over two-thirds of the present American population has a high school degree. No other nation comes close to these accomplishments. Nevertheless, most voices are very critical of American education.

American education reforms of the past 40 years have focused on quality and on what is taught. In the late 1950s the Soviet Union's launch of the first space satellite convinced the public of the need for more math and science in the curriculum. In the late 1960s and 1970s schools were criticized for rigid authoritarian teaching styles, and schools were made less structured. They became more open, participatory, and individualized in order to stimulate student involvement, creativity, and emotional growth. In the 1980s a crusade for the return to basics was triggered by the announcement that SAT scores had declined since the early 1960s. In the 1990s the continued problems of public schools led many to call for their restructuring by means of school choice, that is, competition.

The debate today is whether or not competition will finally make American schools succeed. The answer depends on whether or not the current structure of schools is the main reason why schools seem to be failing. Many other trends have also affected school performance, so the structure of the school system may not be the key to the problem. For example, many argue that curricula changes away from basics, new unstructured teaching techniques, and the decline of discipline in the classroom have contributed to perceived problems. Perhaps the quality of teachers needs to be raised. There is evidence that those who go into teaching score far lower on SATs than the average college student. In addition, societal trends outside the school may significantly impact school performance. Increasing breakdown of the family, more permissive childrearing, the substantial decline in the amount of time that parents spend with children, and the increased exposure of children to television are trends that many believe are adversely affecting school performance.

In the selections that follow, the costs and the benefits of school choice are debated. Clint Bolick argues that school choice applies to college education and U.S. higher education is the envy of the world. The role of competition in producing excellence in business, sports, and elsewhere is well-known. And from the moral point of view, the parents should have the right to choose. Wolk argues that most educational reforms, including school choice, do not get at the heart of the educational problem, which is the way students are taught. Too much emphasis is placed on better teaching and not where it belongs, which is on students' learning. Wolk advocates shifting considerable responsibility from teachers to the students for their education.

YES ↵

Clint Bolick

The Key to Closing the Minority Schooling Gap: School Choice

In a nation supposedly committed to free enterprise, consumer choice, and equal educational opportunities, school choice should be routine. That it is not demonstrates the clout of those dedicated to preserving the government's monopoly over public education. To listen to the education establishment, one would think that school choice is a radical, scary, alien concept. Indeed, the defenders of the status quo have convinced many voters that school choice is a threat to American society.

But school choice is not threatening, and it is not new. To the contrary, it is the norm in most modern nations. . . . Even in the U.S., non-government schools have long played a key educational role, often using public funds. America's college system—the world's envy—is built on school choice: Students can use the G.I. Bill, Pell Grants, and other forms of government aid to attend either public or private schools, including religious institutions. At the other end of the age spectrum, parents of preschoolers can use child care vouchers in private and religious settings. And under federal law, tens of thousands of disabled elementary and high school age children receive schooling in private schools at public expense. It is only mainstream K-12 schools in which the government commands a monopoly over public funds.

Thomas Paine, the most prescient of our founding fathers, is credited with first suggesting a voucher system in the United States. He wanted an educated, enlightened citizenry, but the idea that the government should operate schools was an alien concept to him and his generation. Instead, Paine proposed providing citizens with financial support that they could use to purchase education in private schools.

The great portion of early American "public" education took place in private schools. Even when states started creating government schools, the teachers often were ministers. The concept of "separation of church and state" is not in the U.S. Constitution, and was certainly never applied to education.

In 1869, Vermont adopted a school choice program for communities that did not build their own public schools, and Maine followed suit in 1873. To this day, both states will pay tuition for children to attend private schools, or public schools in neighboring communities. In Vermont, 6,500 children from 90 towns attend private schools at government expense; in Maine, 5,600 children

From *The American Enterprise*, April/May 2003, pp. 30–33. Copyright © 2003 by American Enterprise Institute. Reprinted by permission. www.TAE.com

from 55 towns do so. Those programs, in existence for more than a century and a quarter, have not destroyed the local public schools; to the contrary, both states boast a well-educated population.

But the goal of universal common schooling, fueled by the ideas of Horace Mann, helped make government schools the norm in the late nineteenth century. Thereafter, private schools typically served two groups: the elite, and those seeking a religious immersion different from the Protestant theology that dominated public schools. The latter, of course, were primarily Catholic immigrants.

The rise of Catholic schools bitterly annoyed Protestant public school advocates like Senator James Blaine (R-ME). Blaine struck back in 1876. His proposed amendment to the U.S. Constitution to prohibit any government aid to religious schools came just short of securing passage in Congress. His allies, however, lobbied state legislatures and succeeded in attaching "Blaine amendments" to approximately 37 state constitutions which prohibited expenditure of public funds in "support" of sectarian (i.e., Catholic) schools. Anti-Catholic bigotry crested in an Oregon law, secured by the Ku Klux Klan, which *required* all children to attend government schools.

In the landmark 1925 decision *Pierce v. Society of Sisters,* the U.S. Supreme Court struck down that Oregon law, declaring that "The fundamental theory of liberty upon which all governments in this Union repose excludes any general power of the State to standardize its children by forcing them to accept instruction from public teachers only. The child is not the mere creature of the State; those who nurture him and direct his destiny have the right, coupled with the high duty, to recognize and prepare him for additional obligations." This principle of parental sovereignty remains a cornerstone of American law today. Though it remains constantly under attack, it continues to keep private educational options (among other rights) open to parents.

The modern case for school vouchers was first made by the Nobel laureate economist Milton Friedman in 1955. Instead of providing education as a monopoly supplier, Friedman suggested, government should just finance it. Every child would be given a voucher redeemable at a school of the parent's choice, public or private. Schools would compete to attract the vouchers. Friedman's proposal contained two insights that formed the intellectual foundations of the contemporary school choice movement: that parents, rather than government, should decide where children attend school, and that the economic rules which yield good services and products are not suspended at the schoolhouse door.

Support for school choice began to expand and diversify in the 1970s, when two liberal Berkeley law professors, Jack Coons and Steven Sugarman, began to consider school choice as a means of delivering educational equity. If forced busing plans had failed, Coons and Sugarman argued, why not give vouchers to poor and minority parents so they could choose the best education for their children? Coons and Sugarman adapted Friedman's proposal to their own ends: While Friedman advocated universal vouchers, Coons and Sugarman wanted to target them to disadvantaged populations. Friedman preferred a lightly regulated system, while Coons and Sugarman called for substantial government oversight. Still, there was the beginning of an alliance between freedom-seeking conservatives on the one hand and equality-seeking liberals on the other. That alliance eventually made the school choice programs of the 1990s a reality.

The main force generating support for vouchers, however, was the alarming decline in urban public schools. During the 1960s and 1970s, most urban public schools were ruined. Whites and middle-class blacks fled to the suburbs, leaving poor and mostly minority populations in rapidly worsening city public schools.

The problems of urban public schools were connected to a broader decline in public education. The 1983 study A *Nation at Risk* warned that large doses of mediocrity and failure had crept into American public schools. Meanwhile, starting in the 1980s, social scientists like James Coleman began showing that private and religious schools were succeeding in educating the very same poor, minority schoolchildren that government schools were failing. Many corroborating studies followed.

Also helping set the stage for a school choice movement was the 1990 Brookings Institution study by John Chubb and Terry Moe, *Politics, Markets & America's Schools*. Chubb and Moe set out to discover why suburban public schools and inner-city private schools generally produced good academic outcomes, while inner-city public schools were disasters. They found that whereas the first two types of schools were characterized by strong leaders with a clear mission and a high degree of responsiveness to parents, inner-city schools were not. Instead, urban public school districts were run by bloated bureaucracies whose principal constituencies were not parents, but politicians and unions.

A crucial factor distinguishing the successful and unsuccessful schools was the element of choice: Suburban parents could send their children to private schools, or move to different communities, if they were dissatisfied with their public schools. Private schools, obviously, were entirely dependent on satisfied parents. But inner-city public school parents were captives: They had no choice except to send their children to whatever the local government school offered. In school districts with tens or hundreds of thousands of students, they were powerless to do anything about the system.

Introducing choice in inner-city public schools, Chubb and Moe concluded—particularly giving parents the power to exit the public system altogether—would force the bureaucracy to respond to its customers rather than to politicians and special-interest groups. These findings created a scholarly foundation for school choice as a way not merely of helping children in failing government schools, but also as an essential prerequisite for reforming public school systems.

When the current school choice movement started to come together a decade or two ago, its leading protagonists could have met comfortably in a telephone booth. In an amazingly short period, it has grown into a sophisticated, passionate, and ecumenical movement. There are philanthropists, activists, public officials, clergy, lawyers, and parents, all willing to put aside ideological differences in pursuit of a common cause.

The movement's core argument is that parents, not government, should have the primary responsibility and power to determine where and how their children are educated. That this basic principle should require a vicious fight is testimony to the strength, determination, and ferocity of the reactionary forces defending today's educational status quo. Teacher unions, which form the cornerstone of our education establishment, are the most powerful special-interest group in America today. At the national level, they essentially own the Democratic Party. At the state level, they wield enormous influence over elected officials in both parties. At the local level, they frequently control school boards. They and their education allies dedicated all the resources at their disposal to defeat meaningful school choice anywhere it has presented itself.

For the education establishment, this battle is about preserving their monopolistic vise grip on American schooling. For parents—and our society—the stakes are much higher. Nearly 50 years after *Brown v. Board of Education*, vast numbers of black and Hispanic children do not graduate from high school. Many of those who do still lack the most basic skills needed for even entry-level jobs. As a result, many children in inner-city schools wind up on welfare or in jail. Children who most need the compensations of a quality education are instead regulated to dysfunctional schools. In climbing out of this morass we should not worry about whether a particular reform is too radical; we should worry about whether it is radical enough.

The school choice movement is not only a crusade to improve American education. It is also a true civil rights struggle. It is critical to the real lives of real people. The system has written off many of the people who most need choice—both the parents and their children. Minority citizens may be offered welfare payments, or racial preferences, but little is done to help them become productive, self-supporting citizens. Government schools and their liberal patrons implicitly assume that low-income children are incapable of learning. With little expected of these children, that becomes a self-fulfilling prophecy.

Meanwhile, conditions are different in most inner-city private schools. Not because they have greater resources than their public school counterparts (they typically have far fewer), or because they are selective (they usually accept all applicants), but rather because the operating philosophy is markedly different. At non-government schools, parents are not discouraged from involvement, they are *required* to play a role in the school and in their children's education. The children are expected to behave. They are expected to achieve. And research shows that they do.

Ultimately, we want school choice programs that are large and accessible enough to give government schools a serious run for their money. But initially, even a small program—publicly or privately funded—can begin to introduce inner-city parents to the previously unknown concept that there is an alternative to failure. That creates a constituency for a larger program.

Any functioning program, no matter how small, will change the debate from one about hypotheticals to one about realities. When we can show that competition helps public schools, and that families are choosing good schools rather than, say, witch-craft schools, we can begin to debunk the myths of choice adversaries. In Milwaukee, where school choice has been pioneered, public opinion polls show that support for choice is stronger the closer one is to the program. Not only inner-city parents but also suburban parents now support school choice there.

Actual experience has shown that school choice programs do not "skim the cream" of students, as our detractors like to say, leaving only hard cases in the public schools. Instead (not surprisingly), school choice programs usually attract children who are experiencing academic or disciplinary problems in government schools. Many such children are on a downward trajectory. Just arresting that trajectory is an accomplishment, even if it doesn't show up immediately in improved test scores.

Academic research by Harvard's Paul Peterson and others shows that academic gains are modest in the first year or two of a school choice program, and begin to accelerate afterward. Longitudinal studies tracking choice students over many years seem likely to find higher high school graduation and college enrollment rates, plus other measures of success. If that happens, the debate over the desirability of school choice will be over. The pioneers of school choice will have shown how to rescue individuals from otherwise dark futures, as well as how to force our larger system of public education to improve itself for the good of all students.

Ron Wolk

NO

Think the Unthinkable

For more than two decades, the United States has been struggling to improve public education. In April 1983 the federal report *A Nation at Risk* stunned the nation with its dire warning that "a rising tide of mediocrity" was swamping our schools. A spate of articles and editorials on the occasion of its twentieth anniversary last spring concluded that the schools today are not much better than they were then.

Five years after *A Nation at Risk,* in 1988, the first President Bush and the nation's governors, with much fanfare, set lofty education goals to be met by the year 2000, including the goals that every child would be ready for school and that the U.S. would be first in the world in math and science by the dawn of the new millennium. We didn't even come close to meeting any of the goals.

Now we have "No Child Left Behind," the sweeping and intrusive new federal law that more than doubles the amount of standardized testing. It promises, among other things, that a highly qualified teacher will be in every classroom by 2006 and that all children will be proficient in a dozen years. It, too, will inevitably fall well short of its noble objectives.

How could a country with such knowledge, wealth, and power and such stellar accomplishments in every other field of human endeavor try so hard and still be so far behind in education that it ranks among Third World nations?

The Wrong Questions Encourage the Wrong Answers

After pondering that conundrum for many years, I've come to believe it is because we are seeking answers to the wrong questions. In the current school-reform movement—and in every previous one—we have asked:

- How do we fix our broken public schools?
- How do we raise student achievement (meaning test scores)?

Not surprisingly, the answers to those questions nearly always focus on the school. We always accept the school as a given, which means we are essentially stuck with all the conventions and sacred cows of the traditional school. It almost guarantees that we will not be able, as they say, to "think outside the box."

From *Educational Horizons,* Summer 2004, pp. 268–279. Copyright © 2004 by Ron Wolk. Reprinted by permission.

The questions we should be asking are:

- How do we guide our kids through their very challenging formative years so that they emerge as responsible young adults with the skills and attitudes they need to function and thrive in a rapidly changing world?
- What do we want every child to achieve?

The answers to those questions must focus on a lot more than just school. Three short sketches from where I live—Providence, Rhode Island—make the point.

Jesse the Janitor.   Sixteen-year-old Jesse lived with his widowed mother and attended Coventry High School in Rhode Island. Bored to death and "fed up" with school, Jesse told the principal he intended to drop out. Although Jesse had been labeled "troubled," the principal knew Jesse liked to work and considered him to be a bright, mature young man. So he offered Jesse a deal: if Jesse would attend classes in the morning, he could work as a janitor in the afternoons for five dollars an hour.

Jesse accepted, and in the following months the school was never cleaner. Jesse got grass to grow where it hadn't grown before and even inspired his classmates to cease littering almost completely. Jesse now wants to go on to community college to study computer programming. Says his principal: "This kid is going to be a productive citizen someday, and I would not have been able to say that months ago."

Following Footsteps.   Michelle and Tiffany were sophomores at the Met school in Providence, perhaps the most unconventional high school in the nation. Students at the Met spend a couple of days a week out of school, working with mentors on term projects in the community. Each student has a personalized curriculum worked out in consultation with the parent, teacher (known as "adviser"), and mentor. Michelle and Tiffany decided that for their term project they would join a group of adults and retrace Martin Luther King Jr.'s Alabama Freedom March from Selma to Montgomery.

They read biographies of King, studied contemporary accounts of the march in newspapers and magazines, and plotted their day-by-day itinerary. Then, with their adviser's help, they arranged to stay with families along the route. The girls traveled for three weeks, interviewing civil rights leaders and participants in the march.

When the girls returned to school, they wrote a detailed account of their adventure. Michelle said she had never understood before all the fuss about voting, but she learned during that trip that people died so she could vote, and she vowed that her vote would never be wasted.

Learning Leadership.   To be admitted to Classical High School (arguably Providence's best), students must pass an examination. On her first day as a freshman, Maria, nervous and scared, sat in the auditorium as the principal told students to look to their left and right. One of those kids would not be there at graduation, he warned. As the months passed, Maria found school boring and irrelevant. She wondered if she might be one of the absent ones four years later.

Then Maria heard about a community organization called "Youth in Action" and joined. Suddenly she was immersed in meaningful and interesting work—designing an AIDS curriculum, gathering data for a local environmental-justice campaign, working with troubled children, speaking to groups, planning events, raising money. Maria became an officer and a member of the board of Youth in Action.

After graduating from high school and beginning college, Maria returned to Providence to speak at a meeting on educational opportunities for American adolescents. Poised, passionate, and articulate, she talked more about her work in the community than her high school experience. When she finished, she was complimented on her accomplishments and asked how much of her success she attributed to attending Classical and how much to participating in Youth in Action. Without hesitation, she said that the youth group was responsible for 95 percent of her growth.

Jesse was fortunate that his principal was perceptive enough and flexible enough to adapt to his needs and skills. Michelle and Tiffany learned about history and the meaning of citizenship by following their own interests. Maria blossomed through doing real work in the real world.

America Wasn't Listening

For those youngsters and millions like them, the conventional school with its rigid academic curriculum and inflexible procedures is neither the only way nor the best way to become educated—that is, if we accept Webster's definition of educate, which means "to rear, to develop mentally and morally." If our primary goal is to help children become competent and responsible adults, then the conventional school, at least after grade six, may be counterproductive.

That same message was delivered to the nation by a panel of researchers assembled by the White House Science Advisory Committee almost a decade before *A Nation at Risk*. Led by the noted sociologist James S. Coleman, the panel in 1974 published "Youth: Transition to Adulthood." The report began with this profound observation:

> As the labor of children has become unnecessary to society, school has been extended for them. With every decade, the length of schooling has increased, until a thoughtful person must ask whether society can conceive of no other way for youth to come into adulthood.
>
> If schooling were a complete environment, the answer would probably be that no amount of school is too much, and increased schooling for the young is the best way for the young to spend their increased leisure and society its increased wealth.

Coleman and his colleagues concluded, however, that schooling was far from a complete environment, and called for a "serious examination" of the institutional framework in which young people develop into adults. They argued, "The school is not the world, and is not perceived by students as 'real.'" The panel recommended that high school play a lesser role in the lives of adolescents and that their learning be transferred to a variety of sites in the community where they can develop the skills and attitudes which society expects of responsible young adults.

If that 175-page report had galvanized the nation the way *A Nation at Risk* did, the past twenty-five years of education reform probably would have been much different and, arguably, much more productive.

Two years before Coleman's report appeared, a colleague of his, the sociologist Christopher Jencks, published his landmark study *Inequality: A Reassessment of the Effect of Family and Schooling in America*. Jencks found that not only is school not the complete environment, but he discovered no evidence that "school reform can be expected to bring about significant social changes outside of schools." The research showed that the outcomes of school depend largely on what goes in: i.e., the students. Middle- and upper-class kids tend to perform adequately; poor kids tend to do poorly. The schools that kids from affluent families attend do relatively well; the schools that poor kids attend do poorly.

That remains true today. The quality of a child's education in the United States depends mainly on where he lives, the color of her skin, and the socio-economic status of the family. . . .

The Good Old Days

There was a time when the responsibility for transforming kids into competent young adults was mainly the job of the family, shared by the church and, for six or eight years of children's lives, the public school. The responsibility was more easily fulfilled in the simpler era of the nineteenth century because the distractions were far fewer than they are in this cacophonous age of mass media. Today, neither the family nor the church wields the kind of influence on the young that it once did. That has left the school as the primary institution charged with shaping our young.

The school might have successfully filled the vacuum left by family and church had it changed as dramatically and continually as the rest of the world, but it didn't. The core of the school remains essentially as it was a century ago, even though the students and the world have changed radically. As a consequence, schools are declining in influence and effectiveness at the very time that kids are facing greater and more demanding challenges. Restoring the family and the church to their long-lost cultural dominance is unlikely. And because the school is in decline, we are leaving much of the social and intellectual development of our children to their peers, the media, and popular culture.

Needed: A New Education Strategy

It is not productive to criticize schools or to blame them for not changing over the decades or for not solving a problem they are not now equipped to solve. The rational course of action is to recognize where we are, what the main task is, and how to accomplish it. Our paramount goal should be to help kids progress successfully into adulthood. To accomplish that, our priorities should include, at least, the following:

- To help youngsters acquire the skills and knowledge they will need to function in a continually changing world. That means nourishing in them the motivation and ability to continue educating themselves.
- To guide them as they develop a system of positive values and ethics that will govern their day-to-day behavior and their relationships with others.
- To assist them in understanding their rights and responsibilities as members of a community and a democratic society.
- To give them the opportunity to explore the world of work and to recognize their obligation to support themselves and their families.

Schools have an important role to play in the development of the young, but it is not their only—or even the dominant—role. If we want children to become responsible adults, we need to forge an alternative or parallel system that offers a range of choices to young people and allows them to make decisions and change directions as they grow into adults.

The elements of such a new system already exist in some schools and communities across the country. Certainly, there are enough models available for states and municipalities to construct a system that addresses the varied needs of young people and offers them choices at critical times in their development. The challenge to policymakers in statehouses and school-district offices is to create some open space in the present system for new educational opportunities.

Here is a glimpse of what that system might look like and how it might come to be.

Proposed: A Parallel System to Educate the Young

On the premise that it is easier to make significant change by starting something new than by trying to reform something old, I would argue that each state should charter a nongeographic district that could include institutions located anywhere in the state. The charter district would be led by a superintendent with a relatively small administrative staff. The superintendent would be appointed by, and accountable to, a board, whose members would in turn be elected by the individual schools in the charter district. The state would exempt the charter district from all regulations governing public schools except those involving safety and civil rights.

The role of the district would be largely to coordinate and support innovation and experimentation in education and youth development. It would offer educational alternatives to the conventional schools. The charter district might be viewed as the research and development arm of the state's educational system. There would be two kinds of learning institutions in the charter district. Children from age five to age thirteen would attend "primary" schools, and children ages thirteen and over would enroll in secondary learning centers.

The primary schools could be new schools established by the state, schools chartered by nonprofit organizations (the way charter schools are today in most states), or existing innovative elementary schools that opt into the new charter district. Like many of the innovative elementary schools, the primary schools in the charter district could be organized around a theme or a particular pedagogy. All primary schools in the charter district would focus significantly on literacy, numeracy, and the arts. Students would be exposed to the disciplines—science, history, literature, biography, geography, and civics—through reading in those disciplines. The emphasis would be on reading and comprehension of concepts and ideas in those disciplines, not on coverage and memorization of enormous amounts of trivia. In addition, the primary school would nourish children's curiosity and inculcate good habits of mind and behavior.

To be admitted to a secondary learning center or school in the charter district, students would have to demonstrate mastery of reading comprehension and basic mathematics. The secondary learning centers would not be schools as such, but rather community-based organizations created by the state or operated under contract with the state by existing organizations. Their primary functions would be supervising young people and helping them manage their education. Secondary learning centers would be limited to about 200 "students."

In addition to the new secondary learning centers, the charter district could include innovative secondary schools that already exist in virtually every state. The Bill and Melinda Gates Foundation funds some of the more innovative schools, such as the New Country School in Minnesota, High Tech High in San Diego, the Met in Providence, and Best Practices High School in Chicago. Schools like those would add strength and diversity to the charter district. In addition, they would find the sanctuary and support that they often lack as outliers in the conventional system. (For additional examples of innovative schools, see Timothy J. Dyer, *Breaking Ranks: Changing an American Institution,* DIANE Publishing, November 1999, ISBN 0788183559,and Thomas Toch, *High Schools on a Human Scale: How Small Schools Can Transform American Education,* Beacon Press, April 2003, ISBN 080703245X.)

New Institutions and New Roles for Teachers and Students.   In the new secondary learning centers, the roles of teachers and students would change. Students would assume much more responsibility for their own education and would be assigned to an adult adviser: a teacher in most cases. Although advisers would teach, their primary function would be supervising fifteen to twenty students and helping them manage their learning and their time. The adviser and his or her students would remain together during the students' stay at the learning center. In schools practicing that model, students and advisers tend to become "families," forging close and productive relationships.

Personalized Curricula.   In consultation with advisers and parents, students would formulate personalized curricula. Each year they would choose from a menu of opportunities. Periodically, as they progressed, they would be able to change directions if they were so inclined. For example, they could participate in apprenticeships and internships with adult mentors in businesses, hospitals, government agencies, and other employers where they could experience the workplace and see the need for punctuality, attention to detail, and teamwork. They could volunteer to perform social and human services or work for worthy causes where they would observe democratic practices and politics in action.

Educational Travel.   Youngsters would have opportunities for educational travel in the United States and abroad, both individually and in groups. Programs like Americorps could provide opportunities for high- school-age kids. Programs like Outward Bound could help young people test themselves and develop self-confidence. Previous efforts such as the Civilian Conservation Corps of the New Deal era could provide a useful model for such programs.

Extracurricular Activities.   As the role of high schools diminished, extracurricular activities would have to be provided largely through out-of-school clubs, teams, and youth organizations, perhaps coordinated by the secondary learning center. Many graduates attest that their most rewarding experiences in high school were activities such as chorus, band, debate, and athletics. To the extent that those activities met student needs, they would continue to command a significant amount of time and resources. However, because students would be spending much of their time in real-world situations, they might come to rely less on extracurricular activities to develop a sense of self-worth and to learn the values of teamwork, performance, effort, and proficiency.

Just-in-Time Instruction.   All the activities the students chose would be constructed to involve learning at several levels, including academic instruction. Students would have available "just-in-time" instruction: e.g., a student interning in a hospital might need to take a course in biology or anatomy; an intern in a bank might require instruction in math or accounting; a student apprenticing in a restaurant might need chemistry instruction. The secondary learning centers could make such instruction available both in person and online.

Technology.   A modest investment in research and development and a little imagination could produce software programs to provide "just-in-time" instruction. Simulations, computer games, chat rooms, CDs, Internet courses, and the like enable students to do almost everything that they could in a classroom: dissect a frog on the computer, conduct physics experiments, learn languages, study poetry read aloud by the poets themselves, conduct research, and carry on extensive discussions about issues. The infrastructure is already there: most schools in nearly every state already are wired to the Internet. Indeed, following the lead of the University of Phoenix, many of the nation's top universities and nearly seventy charter schools now offer online courses and degrees.

In-person Instruction.   Technology by itself would not encompass the complete environment that students need to learn and grow. Secondary learning centers would offer live instruction either by contracting with a conventional school, arranging for courses in community or four-year colleges, or arranging for tutoring.

Flexible Scheduling.   Whether online or in person, instruction would not necessarily be delivered in semester courses of several classes a week. For example, an adviser and a small group of students might spend every day for two weeks in intense study of the Constitution, an area of mathematics, or the geography of the United States, but the decision to do so would arise from the needs and desires of the students— not from a pre-set curriculum.

The great philosopher and mathematician Alfred North Whitehead described the challenge this way: "The result of teaching small parts of a large number of subjects is the passive reception of disconnected ideas; not illumined with any spark of vitality. Let the main ideas which are introduced into a child's education be few and important and let them be thrown into every combination possible. The child should make them his own, and should understand their application here and now in the circumstances of his actual life."

Students at the Met School in Providence constantly demonstrate how effective and committed kids can be when they are working on something that interests them, which they have chosen. For example:

A play of her own: A young woman in her junior year wrote a play for her term project. When she finished it, she decided to produce it. She selected the cast, designed the set, directed the play, rented the hall, printed and distributed announcements, sold the tickets, and played the lead. She symbolizes the independence and conscientiousness of students who engage in self-education, and she is not unusual.

His father's war: A young man had long been intrigued by the fact that his father had served in Vietnam, but the father always declined to talk about his experience. The boy decided he had to visit Vietnam and he desperately wanted to take his father with him. He studied the history and geography of the country and read widely about the war; then he wrote a proposal that helped him raise enough money to cover travel expenses. He and his father spent several weeks visiting places in Vietnam where his father had been stationed. When they returned, the student wrote a detailed and thoughtful report about the experience and what he had learned about his father and himself.

"This is who I am":   Met students must write a seventy-five-page autobiography to graduate. Many students moan and resist. One student in particular insisted that he couldn't do it, that it was cruel and unusual punishment. When he walked across the stage to collect his diploma, that student's adviser noted that the young man had submitted a 100-page autobiography with the comment, "Until I wrote that paper, I didn't really know who I was."

In such projects, students learn a great deal and it becomes part of them, not just something to regurgitate on a test and forget. Doing real work in the real world—whether interning with a chef, a glassblower, or a hospital technician—requires some knowledge in a number of disciplines. Youngsters pursue that knowledge and assimilate it because they need it to do their work. Equally important, the work helps them to mature, gain confidence, and understand the power of learning. And their success in one endeavor tends to fuel their curiosity and lead to broader learning. . . .

It's the Students' Work, Stupid!   Students' work and accomplishments are at the heart of the new system. Common norm-referenced and criterion-referenced standardized testing would not be used. For diagnostic purposes and to assess value added, the charter district would use computer-adaptive online testing. In all the students' activities, teachers, mentors, and other adults would view the students' work and accomplishments to determine progress. Evaluating the work would be more complicated but far richer than assigning test scores. The evaluations of advisers and mentors would reveal infinitely more about a student's ability, attitude, and effort than simple letter grades.

At age sixteen, each student would have three options: continuing in the system for two more years; leaving to enroll in postsecondary education; or leaving to take a job, which could include the military, the Peace Corps, and other such occupations (which today is usually considered dropping out). If students left school at age sixteen for any reason, they would have the right to return to the system for two years before they turned twenty-one.

Instead of receiving a high school diploma, which tells an employer or a college admission officer virtually nothing about who a student is and what he or she has accomplished, students would receive a certificate of completion and a dossier. The dossier would list the courses they took, the internships they served, their volunteer work, and the organizations to which they belonged, along with the evaluations submitted by their adult supervisors. It would include selected samples of their work. Employers are much more likely to be satisfied with such an evaluation than colleges, suggesting that higher education needs to reassess admission requirements and find more substantive ways to evaluate student ability.

POSTSCRIPT

Is Competition the Reform
That Will Fix Education?

Since school reformers have focused on school choice, the literature on it has mushroomed. The choice proposal first gained public attention in 1955 when Milton Friedman wrote about vouchers in "The Role of Government in Education," in Robert Solo, ed., *Economics and the Public Interest* (Rutgers University Press). More recent school choice advocates include Harry Brighouse, *School Choice and Social Justice* (Oxford University Press, 2000); Mark Schneider, *Choosing Schools: Consumer Choice and the Quality of American Schools* (Princeton University Press, 2000); Philip A. Woods, *School Choice and Competition: Markets in the Public Interest* (Routledge, 1998); Sol Stern, *Breaking Free: Public School Lessons and the Imperative of School Choice* (Encounter Books, 2003); Clint Bolick, *Voucher Wars: Waging the Legal Battle over School Choice* (Cato Institute, 2003); Clive R. Belfield and Henry M. Levin, *Privatizing Educational Choice* (Paradigm Publishers, 2005); James G. Dwyer, *Vouchers within Reason: A Child-Centered Approach to Education Reform* (Cornell University Press, 2002); and Emily Van Dunk, *School Choice and the Question of Accountability: The Milwaukee Experience* (Yale University Press, 2003). School choice is most strongly advocated for inner-city schools. See Frederick M. Hess, *Revolution at the Margins: The Impact of Competition on Urban School Systems* (Brookings Institution Press, 2002) and William G. Howell, *The Education Gap: Vouchers and Urban Schools* (Brookings Institution Press, 2002). For discussions between school choice systems, see *Public School Choice vs. Private School Vouchers,* edited by Richard D. Kahlenberg (Century Foundation, 2003). For a less partisan view see Joseph P. Viteritti, *Choosing Equality: School Choice, the Constitution, and Civil Society* (Brookings Institute Press, 1999). For comparisons of school choice with other reforms, see Margaret C. Wang and Herbert J. Walberg, eds., *School Choice or Best Systems: What Improves Education?* (L. Erlbaum Associates, 2001). Some advocates of choice would limit the choices in major ways. TimothyW. Young and Evans Clinchy, in *Choice in Public Education* (Teachers College Press, 1992), contend that there is already considerable choice in public education so they argue against a voucher system, which they feel will divert badly needed financial resources from the public schools to give further support to parents who can already afford private schools.

Important critiques of school choice include Albert Shanker and Bella Rosenberg, *Politics, Markets, and America's Schools: The Fallacies of Private School Choice* (American Federation of Teachers, 1991); Kevin B. Smith and Kenneth J. Meier, *The Case Against School Choice: Politics, Markets, and Fools* (M. E. Sharpe, 1995); Seymour Bernard Sarason, *Questions You Should Ask about Charter*

Schools and Vouchers (Heinemann, 2002); Lois H. André Buchely, *Could It Be Otherwise? Parents and the Inequities of Public School Choice* (Routledge, 2005); Gary Miron and Christopher Nelson, *What's Public about Charter Schools?: Lessons Learned about Choice and Accountability* (Corwin Press, 2002); R. Kenneth Godwin and Frand R. Kemerer, *School Choice Tradeoff: Liberty, Equity, and Diversity* (University of Texas Press, 2002); *School Choice: The Moral Debate,* edited by Alan Wolfe (Princeton University Press, 2003); Ronald G. Corwin and E. Joseph Schneider, *The School Choice Hoax: Fixing American's Schools* (Praeger, 2005).

ISSUE 14

Should Biotechnology Be Used to Alter and Enhance Humans?

YES: Ronald Bailey, from *Liberation Biology* (Prometheus Books, 2006)

NO: Michael J. Sandel, from *The Case Against Perfectionism* (Belknap Press, 2007)

ISSUE SUMMARY

YES: Ronald Bailey, science editor for *Reason* magazine, discusses and advocates all the beneficial things that biotechnology can do for humans.

NO: Political science professor Michael J. Sandel is very cautionary on the use of biotechnology to alter and enhance humans. He praises many other uses of biotechnology, but he condemns using biotechnology to alter and enhance humans. In these activities, humans play God and attempt to inappropriately remake nature.

$\mathbf{A}$s a sociologist I feel that I am on relatively firm ground discussing the 19 other issues in this book. I am not on firm ground discussing the issue of how biotechnology should or should not be used. And I am not alone. The nation does not know what to think about this issue, at least not in a coherent way. But the discussion must begin because the issue is coming at us like a tornado. Already America is debating the use of drugs to enhance athletic performance. Athletes and body builders want to use them to build muscle, strength, and/or endurance, but much of the public does not approve. Drug use has been outlawed for competitive sports and users have been publicly discredited.

Soon, however, parents will be able to pay for genetic engineering to give their children the bodies to be good athletes and perhaps even great athletes. Will that also be illegal? This is only the tip of the iceberg. Thousands of difficult questions will arise as the technology for designing babies will become more and more powerful. Stem cell research is currently a divisive issue. Are we blocking the development of technologies that can save thousands of lives by severely limiting stem cell research?

The classic expression of this issue is in the stories and legends of a very learned sixteenth-century German doctor named Faust. According to legend, he sold his soul to the devil in exchange for knowledge and magical power. The first printed version of the legend, written by Johann Spiess, was later used by Christopher Marlow as the basis for his famous play, *Dr. Faustus* (1593). Speiss and Marlow presented Faust as a scoundrel who deserved damnation. Some of the other representations of Faust made him a heroic figure who strived for knowledge and power for good. This theme was continued by the most famous Faust legend of all, written by Johann Wolfgang von Goethe in both a poem and a play. In the beginning, Faust's bargain with the Devil was for a moment of perfect happiness or contentment. The Devil, however, could not deliver this to Faust. More elements are added to the story, including women's love. In the end, Faust finds a moment of perfect contentment and happiness in helping others and dies because of the wager. But Goethe gives the story a Hollywood ending and Faust, the hero, goes to heaven.

Many of the issues in the biotechnology debate are found in the Faust legends. Both are focused on the search for knowledge and its use. Is the knowledge-seeking Faust a scoundrel or a saint? Will his knowledge be used for selfish or altruistic purposes? Is mankind better off with it or without it? If powerful new biotechnologies are able to make our babies safe from diseases and defects, certainly we should use them. By the same logic, we should also use them when they can enhance our children's physical and mental powers. Continuing the same logic we should also use them to enhance our physical and mental powers as adults. Sooner or later, however, we must face the Faustian myth, which suggests that at some point, mankind's reach for knowledge may transcend man's proper role in the universe and be devilish. But this question takes us into realms where I get quickly lost. How do I discuss mankind's proper role in the universe? The wise thing for me to do is not to try and to leave it to you and the readings.

Ronald Bailey presents the reasons for using biotechnology to alter and enhance humans. They are simply the many benefits that biotechnology can produce. Michael J. Sandel, on the other hand, argues against using biotechnology for altering and enhancing humans. Sandel is passionately against going down this road.

YES

Liberation Biology: The Scientific and Moral Case for the Biotech Revolution

Introduction Biopolitics

Fight of the Century

By the end of the twenty-first century, the typical American may attend a family reunion in which five generations are playing together. And great-great-great grandma, at 150 years old, will be as vital, with muscle tone as firm and supple, skin as elastic and glowing, as the thirty-year-old great-great-grandson with whom she's playing touch football.

After the game, while enjoying a plate of greens filled with not only a solid day's worth of nutrients, but medicines she needs to repair damage to her aging cells, she'll be able to chat about some academic discipline she stud-ied in the 1980s with as much acuity and depth of knowledge and memory as her fifty-year-old great-granddaughter who is studying it right now.

No one in her extended family will have ever caught a cold. They will have been from birth immune to such shocks as diabetes and Parkinson's dis-ease. Their bodies will be as athletic as a human is capable of being, with brains as clever and capable of learning and retaining knowledge and training as human brains can be.

Her granddaughter, who recently suffered an unfortunate transport acci-dent, will be sporting new versions of the arm and lung that got damaged in the wreck. She'll join in the touch football game, as skilled and energetic as anyone else there. Infectious diseases that terrifed us in the early twenty-first century, such as HIV/AIDS and severe acute respiratory syndrome (SARS), will be horrific historical curiosities for the family to chat about over their plates of superfat farm-raised salmon, as tasty and nutritious as any fish any human has ever eaten. Surrounding them, though few of them will think much of it with all their health, vitality, and riches, will be a world that's greener and cleaner, more abundant in natural vegetation, with less of an obvious human footprint, than the one we live in now. And it's not only this family that will enjoy all these benefits—nearly everyone they work with, socialize with, or ever meet will enjoy them as well. It will be a remarkably peaceful and pleasant world even beyond their health and wealth—antisocial tendencies, crippling depression, will all be managed—by individual choice—through new biotech pharmaceuticals and even genetic treatments.

This idyllic fantasy is more than realistic, given reasonably expected breakthroughs and extensions of our knowledge of human, plant, and animal biology, and mastery of the techniques—known as biotechnology—to manipulate and adjust those biologies to meet human needs and desires.

Although this vision would strike most people of goodwill and hope as encouraging, and devoutly to be wished for, an extraordinary political and intellectual coalition of left-wing and right-wing bioconservatives has come together to resist the biotechnological progress that could make that vision a reality for the whole human race. . . .

Immortality When?

So what are your chances of living forever? First, the bad news. As Hayflick says, "There is no intervention that has been proven to slow, stop, or reverse aging. Period." A position statement on human aging issued in 2002 by fifty-one of the world's leading researchers in the field of aging declared that "claim[s] that it is now possible to slow, stop or reverse aging through existing medical and scientific interventions . . . are as false today as they were in the past."

Now the good news: Despite this, researchers are making a lot of progress. Even the fifty-one skeptical researchers agreed: "Most biogerontologists believe that our rapidly expanding scientific knowledge holds the promise that means may eventually be discovered to slow the rate of aging. If successful, these interventions are likely to postpone age-related diseases and disorders and extend the period of healthy life." . . .

Final Victory Over Disease?

Building Humanity's Extended Immune System

"I certainly am happy to still be in the land of the living," declares Bernis Teaters, a five-year survivor of lung cancer from Friendswood, Texas. "It's wonderful," agrees Alfredo Gonzalvo, another five-year lung cancer survivor. Both are alive today thanks to a pioneering anticancer gene therapy. In 1999 researchers at the M. D. Anderson Cancer Center in Houston, Texas, injected their lung tumors with a vaccine of deactivated viruses containing the cancer-killing p53 gene while they underwent radiation treatments. The p53 gene in the anticancer vaccine instructed their tumor cells to commit suicide. As a result, the two are cancer free today. A similar vaccine is already available in China and will soon be approved for use in the United States. . . .

Since 1990 only a few thousand patients have been treated with any forms of gene therapy, and successes are still disappointingly few. As with any new technology, there is generally a lot of hype in the early stages. Still, therapies based on replacing faulty genes with healthy ones are just the first halting baby steps of a revolution in biomedicine leading, if all goes well, to the creation of humanity's extended immune system.

The notion of an extended immune system is adapted from evolutionary theorist Richard Dawkins's idea of an extended phenotype. Dawkins observed that genes not only mold the bodies of organisms, but also shape their behaviors. Some of those behaviors result in the creation of inanimate objects—technologies, if you will—that help organisms to survive and reproduce, such as beaver dams and bird nests. Nothing could be more natural to human beings than striving to use our technological prowess to liberate ourselves from our biological constraints. Biotechnologists are now turning humanity's technological prowess from the outside world to the intimate inner worlds of our bodies, tissues, and cells. Our immune systems protect our bodies from foreign substances and pathogenic organisms by producing the immune response. Our immune systems also guard our bodies against cells, such as cancer cells, that betray the body. The immune response results from an integrated system of organs, tissues, cells, and cell products such as antibodies.

Thanks to the development of a whole suite of new diagnostics and therapies, human intelligence is extending our technological control to our immune systems, much as we have extended and enlarged the effects of our bodies in the world by means of our tools. Over the next several decades, biomedical technologies will enable us to better protect our bodies against foreign invaders and traitorous cells.

Progress is moving so rapidly and on so many fronts that we can only touch on a few of the fascinating breakthrough that are enabling humanity to construct its extended immune system. These include gene transfer and replacement therapies, gene therapies aimed at preventing and curing cancer, medicines to prevent and cure infectious diseases, and new techniques to turn genes on and off as a way to defeat disease. We will also see how maintaining scientific openness and the development of a robust biotechnological capability are vital to protecting humanity against the threat of bioterrorism. . . .

Research so far has concentrated on devising gene therapy fixes for single broken genes, but most common diseases such as heart disease, cancer, and diabetes are caused by a combination of many genes interacting with environmental influences. Researchers are busy poring over the human genome to find the variations that make each individual different from all other persons. They are looking not just for gene variants for traits such as hair and eye color, but also for gene variants associated with disease propensities. Constellations of certain genes are associated with heightened propensities for specific diseases. As difficult as it currently is to fix single gene defects, using small vectors to try to install several genes to reduce a patient's risk of a heart attack would be even more challenging.

One way around the problem might be to insert artificial chromosomes loaded up with the proper suite of genes to counteract those associated with common diseases. Such artificial chromosomes have already been developed by Chromos Molecular Systems of Burnaby, British Columbia, and Athersys in Cleveland, Ohio. Someday, the gene variants that allow some people to eat all the foie gras and pizza they want and still have clean-as-a-whistle coronary arteries will be identified. People who are not so fortunate as to have been born with those heart-protective genes might someday have an artificial chromosome inserted that contains genes optimized for coronary longevity—the foie gras genes, if you will. . . .

Hooray for Designer Babies!

In a near-future world, parents may well be able to spare their children the agony of diseases such as cystic fibrosis and muscular dystrophy. Even more wonderfully, they may be able to better ensure that their children will be smart, skilled in certain respects, and less prone to depression. As paradisiacal as this world might sound, a variety of influential thinkers and bioethicists want to keep us from it—by any means necessary.

The beginnings of this world are already upon us. A mother was able to spare her infant daughter the horror of losing her mind by age forty by means of genetic testing. Specifically, a married thirty-year-old genetics counselor who will almost certainly suffer from early-onset Alzheimer's disease by age forty chose to test her embryos in vitro for the gene that causes the ailment. She then implanted into her womb only embryos without that disease gene.

The result was the birth of a healthy baby girl—one who will not suffer Alzheimer's in her forties. The mother in this case certainly knows what would face any child of hers born with the disease gene. Her father, a sister, and a brother have all already succumbed to early Alzheimer's.

To achieve this miracle, the mother used the services of the Reproductive Genetics Institute (RGI) in Chicago, a private fertility clinic that's a pioneer of this type of testing, called preimplantation genetic diagnosis (PGD). PGD is being used by more and more parents who want to avoid passing on devastating genetic diseases to their progeny. Diseases tested for include cystic fibrosis, Tay-Sachs, various familial cancers, early-onset Alzheimer's sickle-cell disease, hemophilia, neurofibromatosis, muscular dystrophy, and Fanconi anemia. . . .

Thus, preimplementation genetic diagnosis (PGD) is just the first step toward allowing parents to enhance their children genetically. The next steps in reproductive technologies will be toward repairing genetic diseases and genetically enhancing existing human capacities. Instead of selecting healthy embryos, researchers believe that it will be possible to correct disease genes such as those for sickle cell anemia, muscular dystrophy, and Tay-Sachs in embryos, so that the resulting children will be born healthy. . . .

These so-called germline interventions would be permanent genetic changes made in the embryos, and they would be passed on to future generations. These techniques not only cure one baby but all of that baby's potential descendants as well.

Any technology that can safely correct disease genes can also be used to introduce "enhanced" genes into embryos. Someday parents using biotechnology will be able to ensure that their children have stronger immune systems, higher intelligence, and more athletic bodies than they otherwise would have.

For example, possibly just over the horizon are artificial chromosomes containing genes that protect against HIV, diabetes, prostate and breast cancer, and Parkinson's disease, all of which could be introduced into a developing human embryo. Already, Chromos Molecular Systems, based in Vancouver, British Columbia, makes a mammalian artificial chromosome that allows bio-technologists to plug in new genes just as new computer chips can be plugged into a motherboard. These artificial chromosomes, which have been developed for both mice and humans, offer exquisite control over what genes will be introduced into an organism and how they will operate. Artificial chromosomes carrying genes selected by parents could be inserted into an embryo at the one-cell stage. Once the artificial chromosomes were incorporated into the embryo's genome, the selected genes would spread normally. They would be in every cell of the enhanced child's body when he or she was born.

When born, a child carrying such an artificial chromosome could have, for example, a souped-up immune system. Even more remarkably, artificial chromosomes could be designed with "hooks" or "docking stations," so that new genetic upgrades could later be slotted into the chromosomes and expressed when the child becomes an adult. Artificial chromosomes could also be arranged to replicate only in somatic cells, which form only the tissues that make up the body, and not in the germ cells involved in reproduction. As a result, genetically enhanced parents would not pass those enhancements on to their children; they could choose new or different enhancements for their children, or have them born without the benefit of any new genetic technologies at all. . . .

Sex Selection

Parents are already able to use PGD to select some of the traits they want in their children. A political debate now facing us is over what limits, if any, should be placed on the traits parents are allowed to select. Sex is the easiest trait to select using PGD. Such attempts have a long history, from the herbal nostrums recommended by traditional healers to more recent therapists' advice about which forms of intercourse are allegedly likely to produce girls or boys. Sex selection is becoming a national crisis in India and China, where cheap mobile ultrasound clinics travel the countryside testing pregnant women. Women in these countries who discover their fetus is female often opt for legal abortions. The natural sex ratio is about 105 boys per 100 girls, but in India it is now 113 boys per 100 girls and as high as 156 boys per 100 girls in some regions. In China the sex ratio in recent years has been just shy of 120 boys per 100 girls. Such results have led both China and India to ban ultrasound testing for sex selection purposes.

In the United States, abortion is very rarely used for sex selection. A variety of new techniques do exist, though, that can help parents select their next child's sex. Consider flow cytometry, a method for sex selection in farm animals that fertility specialists have now adapted for human beings. This technology tags sperm bearing X chromosomes (those that determine females) and sperm bearing Y chromosomes (those that determine males) with a fluorescent dye so they can be segregated into different batches. The dye harmlessly attaches to the DNA molecules that make up genes. Female-determining X chromosomes are much bigger than male-determining Y chromosomes, which means that human sperm carrying X chromosomes have 2.8 percent more DNA than do sperm with Y chromosomes. Thus, sperm with X chromosomes soak up more of the fluorescent dye and glow more brightly. This difference in brightness allows flow cytometry machines to separate the X-bearing sperm from the Y-bearing sperm.

Once the sperm have been segregated, they may be used in either artificial insemination or in vitro fertilization to produce a child of the desired sex. Using sex-segregated sperm in artificial insemination also sidesteps the contentious debate over the moral status of embryos, since fertilization takes place directly in the would-be mothers' wombs. . . .

Sex selection is the first example of genetic selection for a nondisease trait. Being a boy or girl is not a disease. Few aspects of human development are more significant than one's sex; it's a central fact of one's identity. If it is ethically permissible for parents to make that choice, the case for letting them make less significant genetic choices, including ones aimed at genetic enhancement, is already made. . . .

Conclusion

The Age of Liberation Biology

"The age of biotechnology is not so much about technology itself as it is about *human beings empowered by biotechnology*," emphasizes the President's Council on Bioethics in its report *Beyond Therapy*. The report adds, "The dawning age of biotechnology" is providing humanity "greatly augmented power . . . not only for gaining better health but also for improving our natural capacities and pursuing our own happiness." The council also acknowledges that the fondest hopes of biotechnology proponents are likely to be realized: "We have every reason to expect exponential increases in biotechnologies and, therefore, in their potential uses in all aspects of human life."

Yet this prospect of biological liberation must be rejected, say influential bioconservatives on both the political Left and Right. They fear that the biotech revolution will undermine their devoutly held beliefs about the proper order of society and the goals of human life. So at the beginning of the twenty-first century we find ourselves in the remarkable position of having many of our leading intellectuals and policymakers arguing that their fellow citizens should be denied access to technologies they know will enable them and their families to live healthier, saner, and longer lives. These bioconservatives argue that a life span of seventy years is enough; that human freedom lies in randomly inheriting genes; that people should not be allowed to use assisted reproductive technologies to guarantee the health of their offspring; that deriving stem cells from five-day-old embryos is the moral equivalent of ripping the heart out of a thirty-year-old woman; that biotech crops are a danger to human health and the natural environment; and that drugs to improve memory and mood should be forbidden. . . .

To the extent that new biotechnologies need regulation, agencies should be limited to deciding, as they have traditionally done, only questions about safety and efficacy. Regulatory agencies also certainly have an important role in protecting research subjects and patients from force and fraud by requiring that researchers obtain their informed consent. But when people of goodwill deeply disagree on moral issues that do not involve the prevention of force or fraud, it is not appropriate to submit their disagreement to a panel of political appointees.

The genius of a liberal society is that its citizens have wide scope to pursue their own visions of the good without excessive hindrance by their fellow citizens. In the United States we honor the free expression of moral diversity. Consequently, the federal government does not force Roman Catholic hospitals to provide abortions or contraception to their patients. Similarly, we recognize the right of adult Jehovah's Witnesses to refuse blood products and of Christian Scientists to refuse all medical treatments. . . .

The bioconservatives claim they want "wise public policy" to guide decisions about cloning and other biotechnologies. History has shown that truly wise public policy allows people, including biomedical researchers, maximum scope to pursue the good and the true in their own ways, in conformity with the dictates of their own consciences. The benefits of biotechnology are well known—the cure of diseases and disabilities for millions of sufferers; the production of more nutritious food with less damage to the natural environment; the enhancement of human physical and intellectual capacities—and all can be easily foreseen. It is the alleged dangers of biotechnology that are, in fact, vague, ill defined, and nebulous.

So what will the next fifty years of liberation biology hold? I foresee a convergence between science and art as the Promethean possibilities of genetic research become more widely available. The future will see miracles, cures, ecological restoration, vivid new art forms, and a greater understanding of the wellsprings of human compassion. But what can liberate can also tyrannize if misused. Evil minds may indeed try to pervert the gifts of bioscience by creating such monstrosities as designer plagues or a caste of genetic slaves. But history has shown that with vigilance—not with blanket prohibitions—humanity can secure the benefits of science for posterity while minimizing the tragic results of any possible abuse.

Nobody said the future would be risk free and the moral choices easy, but the future also brings wondrous new opportunities to cure disease, alleviate suffering, end hunger, and lengthen healthy lives. We would be less than human not to seize those opportunities.

Michael J. Sandel

NO

The Case Against Perfection: Ethics in the Age of Genetic Engineering

The Ethics of Enhancement

A few years ago, a couple decided they wanted to have a child, preferably a deaf one. Both partners were deaf, and proudly so. Like others in the deaf-pride community, Sharon Duchesneau and Candy McCullough considered deafness a cultural identity, not a disability to be cured. "Being deaf is just a way of life," said Duchesneau. "We feel whole as deaf people and we want to share the wonderful aspects of our deaf community—a sense of belonging and connectedness—with children. We truly feel we live rich lives as deaf people."

In hopes of conceiving a deaf child, they sought out a sperm donor with five generations of deafness in his family. And they succeeded. Their son Gauvin was born deaf.

The new parents were surprised when their story, which was reported in the *Washington Post*, brought widespread condemnation. Most of the outrage focused on the charge that they had deliberately inflicted a disability on their child. Duchesneau and McCullough (who are lesbian partners) denied that deafness is a disability and argued that they had simply wanted a child like themselves. "We do not view what we did as very different from what many straight couples do when they have children," said Duchesneau.

Is it wrong to make a child deaf by design? If so, what makes it wrong—the deafness or the design? Suppose, for the sake of argument, that deafness is not a disability but a distinctive identity. Is there still something wrong with the idea of parents picking and choosing the kind of child they will have? Or do parents do that all the time, in their choice of mate and, these days, in their use of new reproductive technologies? . . .

Articulating Our Unease

Breakthroughs in genetics present us with a promise and a predicament. The promise is that we may soon be able to treat and prevent a host of debilitating diseases. The predicament is that our new-found genetic knowledge may also enable us to manipulate our own nature—to enhance our muscles, memories, and moods; to choose the sex, height, and other genetic traits of our children; to improve our physical and cognitive capacities; to make ourselves "better

From *The Atlantic Monthly*, April 2004. pp. 50–62. Copyright © 2004 by Michael J. Sandel, Ph. D. Reprinted by permission of the author.

than well." Most people find at least some forms of genetic engineering disquieting. But it is not easy to articulate the source of our unease. The familiar terms of moral and political discourse make it difficult to say what is wrong with reengineering our nature. . . .

When science moves faster than moral understanding, as it does today, men and women struggle to articulate their unease. In liberal societies, they reach first for the language of autonomy, fairness, and individual rights. But this part of our moral vocabulary does not equip us to address the hardest questions posed by cloning, designer children, and genetic engineering. That is why the genomic revolution has induced a kind of moral vertigo. To grapple with the ethics of enhancement, we need to confront questions largely lost from view in the modern world—questions about the moral status of nature, and about the proper stance of human beings toward the given world. Since these questions verge on theology, modern philosophers and political theorists tend to shrink from them. But our new powers of biotechnology make them unavoidable.

Genetic Engineering

To see how this is so, consider four examples of bioengineering already on the horizon: muscle enhancement, memory enhancement, height enhancement, and sex selection. In each case, what began as an attempt to treat a disease or prevent a genetic disorder now beckons as an instrument of improvement and consumer choice.

Muscles

Everyone would welcome a gene therapy to alleviate muscular dystrophy and to reverse the debilitating muscle loss that comes with old age. But what if the same therapy were used to produce genetically altered athletes? Researchers have developed a synthetic gene that, when injected into the muscle cells of mice, makes muscles grow and prevents them from deteriorating with age. The success bodes well for human applications. Dr. H. Lee Sweeney, who leads the research, hopes his discovery will cure the immobility that afflicts the elderly. But Dr. Sweeney's bulked-up mice have already attracted the attention of athletes seeking a competitive edge. The gene not only repairs injured muscles but also strengthens healthy ones. Although the therapy is not yet approved for human use, the prospect of genetically enhanced weight lifters, home-run sluggers, linebackers, and sprinters is easy to imagine. The widespread use of steroids and other performance-enhancing drugs in professional sports suggests that many athletes will be eager to avail themselves of genetic enhancement. The International Olympic Committee has already begun to worry about the fact that, unlike drugs, altered genes cannot be detected in urine or blood tests.

The prospect of genetically altered athletes offers a good illustration of the ethical quandaries surrounding enhancement. Should the IOC and professional sports leagues ban genetically enhanced athletes, and if so, on what grounds? The two most obvious reasons for banning drugs in sports are safety and fairness: Steroids have harmful side effects, and to allow some to boost their performance by incurring serious health risks would put their competitors at an unfair disadvantage. But suppose, for the sake of argument, that muscle-enhancing gene therapy turned out to be safe, or at least no riskier than a rigorous weight-training regime. Would there still be a reason to ban its use in sports? There is something unsettling about the specter of genetically altered athletes lifting SUVs or hitting 650-foot home runs or running a three-minute mile. But what exactly is troubling about these scenarios? Is it simply that we find such superhuman spectacles too bizarre to contemplate, or does our unease point to something of ethical significance? . . .

Designer Children, Designing Parents

The ethic of giftedness, under siege in sports, persists in the practice of parenting. But here, too, bioengineering and genetic enhancement threaten to dislodge it. To appreciate children as gifts is to accept them as they come, not as objects of our design, or products of our will, or instruments of our ambition. Parental love is not contingent on the talents and attributes the child happens to have. We choose our friends and spouses at least partly on the basis of qualities we find attractive. But we do not choose our children. Their qualities are unpredictable, and even the most conscientious parents cannot be held wholly responsible for the kind of child they have. That is why parenthood, more than other human relationships, teaches what the theologian William F. May calls an "openness to the unbidden."

Molding and Beholding

May's resonant phrase describes a quality of character and heart that restrains the impulse to mastery and control and prompts a sense of life as gift. It helps us see that the deepest moral objection to enhancement lies less in the perfection it seeks than in the human disposition it expresses and promotes. The problem is not that the parents usurp the autonomy of the child they design. (It is not as if the child could otherwise choose her genetic traits for herself.) The problem lies in the hubris of the designing parents, in their drive to master the mystery of birth. Even if this disposition does not make parents tyrants to their children, it disfigures the relation between parent and child, and deprives the parent of the humility and enlarged human sympathies that an openness to the unbidden can cultivate.

To appreciate children as gifts or blessings is not to be passive in the face of illness or disease. Healing a sick or injured child does not override her natural capacities but permits them to flourish. Although medical treatment intervenes in nature, it does so for the sake of health, and so does not represent a boundless bid for mastery and dominion. Even strenuous attempts to treat or cure disease do not constitute a Promethean assault on the given. The reason is that medicine is governed, or at least guided, by the norm of restoring and preserving the natural human functions that constitute health.

Medicine, like sports, is a practice with a purpose, a telos, that orients and constraints it. Of course what counts as good health or normal human functioning is open to argument; it is not only a biological question. People disagree, for example, about whether deafness is a disability to be cured or a form of community and identity to be cherished. But even the disagreement proceeds from the assumption that the point of medicine is to promote health and cure disease.

Some people argue that a parent's obligation to heal a sick child implies an obligation to enhance a healthy one, to maximize his or her potential for success in life. But this is true only if one accepts the utilitarian idea that health is not a distinctive human good, but simply a means of maximizing happiness or well-being. Bioethicist Julian Savulescu argues, for example, that "health is not intrinsically valuable," only "instrumentally valuable," a "resource" that allows us to do what we want. This way of thinking about health rejects the distinction between healing and enhancing. According to Savulescu, parents not only have a duty to promote their children's health; they are also "morally obliged to genetically modify their children." Parents should use technology to manipulate their children's "memory, temperament, patience, empathy, sense of humor, optimism," and other characteristics in order to give them "the best opportunity of the best life."

But it is a mistake to think of health in wholly instrumental terms, as a way of maximizing something else. Good health, like good character, is a constitutive element of human flourishing. Although more health is better than less, at least within a certain range, it is not the kind of good that can be maximized. No one aspires to be a virtuoso at health (except, perhaps, a hypochondriac). During the 1920s, eugenicists held health contests at state fairs and awarded prizes to the "fittest families." But this bizarre practice illustrates the folly of conceiving health in instrumental terms, or as a good to be maximized. Unlike the talents and traits that bring success in a competitive society, health is a bounded good; parents can seek it for their children without risk of being drawn into an ever-escalating arms race.

In caring for the health of their children, parents do not cast themselves as designers or convert their children into products of their will or instruments of their ambition. The same cannot be said of parents who pay large sums to select the sex of their child (for nonmedical reasons) or who aspire to bioengineer their child's intellectual endowments or athletic prowess. Like all distinctions, the line between therapy and enhancement blurs at the edges. (What about orthodontics, for example, or growth hormone for very short kids?) But this does not obscure the reason the distinction matters: parents bent on enhancing their children are more likely to overreach, to express and entrench attitudes at odds with the norm of unconditional love.

Of course, unconditional love does not require that parents refrain from shaping and directing the development of their child. To the contrary, parents have an obligation to cultivate their children, to help them discover and develop their talents and gifts. As May points out, parental love has two aspects: accepting love and transforming love. Accepting love affirms the being of the child, whereas transforming love seeks the well-being of the child. Each side of parental love corrects the excesses of the other: "Attachment becomes too quietistic if it slackens into mere acceptance of the child as he is." Parents have a duty to promote their child's excellence.

These days, however, overly ambitious parents are prone to get carried away with transforming love—promoting and demanding all manner of accomplishments from their children, seeking perfection. "Parents find it difficult to maintain an equilibrium between the two sides of love," May observes. "Accepting love, without transforming love, slides into indulgence and finally neglect. Transforming love, without accepting love, badgers and finally rejects." May finds in these competing impulses a parallel with modern science; it, too, engages us in beholding the given world, studying and savoring it, and also in molding the world, transforming and perfecting it.

The mandate to mold our children, to cultivate and improve them, complicates the case against enhancement. We admire parents who seek the best for their children, who spare no effort to help them achieve happiness and success. What, then, is the difference between providing such help through education and training and providing it by means of genetic enhancement? Some parents confer advantages on their children by enrolling them in expensive schools, hiring private tutors, sending them to tennis camp, providing them with piano lessons, ballet lessons, swimming lessons, SAT prep courses, and so on. If it is permissible, even admirable, for parents to help their children in these ways, why isn't it equally admirable for parents to use whatever genetic technologies may emerge (provided they are safe) to enhance their child's intelligence, musical ability, or athletic skill?

Defenders of enhancement argue that there is no difference, in principle, between improving children through education and improving them through bioengineering. Critics of enhancement insist there is all the difference in the world. They argue that trying to improve children by manipulating their genetic makeup is reminiscent of eugenics, the discredited movement of the past century to improve the human race through policies (including forced sterilization and other odious measures) aimed at improving the gene pool. These competing analogies help clarify the moral status of genetic enhancement. Is the attempt of parents to enhance their children through genetic engineering more like education and training (a presumably good thing) or more like eugenics (a presumably bad thing)?

The defenders of enhancement are right to this extent: Improving children through genetic engineering is similar in spirit to the heavily managed, high-pressure child-rearing practices that have become common these days. But this similarity does not vindicate genetic enhancement. On the contrary, it highlights a problem with the trend toward hyperparenting. . . .

The Pressure to Perform

Grubman's willingness to move heaven and earth, and even the market, to get his two-year-olds into a fancy nursery school is a sign of the times. It tells of mounting pressures in American life that are changing the expectations parents have for their children and increasing the demands placed on children to perform. When preschoolers apply to private kindergartens and elementary schools, their fate depends on favorable letters of recommendation and a standardized test intended to measure their intelligence and development. Some parents have their four-year-olds coached to prepare for the test. . . .

Some see a bright line between genetic enhancement and other ways that people seek improvement in their children and themselves. Genetic manipulation seems somehow worse—more intrusive, more sinister—than other ways of enhancing performance and seeking success. But morally speaking, the difference is less significant than it seems.

Those who argue that bioengineering is similar in spirit to other ways ambitious parents shape and mold their children have a point. But this similarity does not give us reason to embrace the genetic manipulation of children. Instead, it gives us reason to question the low-tech, high-pressure child-rearing practices we commonly accept. The hyperparenting familiar in our time represents an anxious excess of mastery and dominion that misses the sense of life as gift. This draws it disturbingly close to eugenics. . . .

Although liberal eugenics finds support among many Anglo-American moral and political philosophers, Jürgen Habermas, Germany's most prominent political philosopher, opposes it. Acutely aware of Germany's dark eugenic past, Habermas argues against the use of embryo screening and genetic manipulation for nonmedical enhancement. His case against liberal eugenics is especially intriguing because he believes it rests wholly on liberal premises and need not invoke spiritual or theological notions. His critique of genetic engineering "does not relinquish the premises of postmeta-physical thinking," by which he means it does not depend on any particular conception of the good life. Habermas agrees with John Rawls that, since people in modern pluralist societies disagree about morality and religion, a just society should not take sides in such disputes but should instead accord each person the freedom to choose and pursue his or her own conception of the good life.

Genetic intervention to select or improve children is objectionable, Habermas argues, because it violates the liberal principles of autonomy and equality. It violates autonomy because genetically programmed persons cannot regard themselves as "the sole authors of their own life history." And it undermines equality by destroying "the essentially symmetrical relations between free and equal human beings" across generations. One measure of this asymmetry is that, once parents become the designers of their children, they inevitably incur a responsibility for their children's lives that cannot possibly be reciprocal.

Habermas is right to oppose eugenic parenting, but wrong to think that the case against it can rest on liberal terms alone. The defenders of liberal eugenics have a point when they argue that designer children are no less autonomous with respect to their genetic traits that children born the natural way. It is not as if, absent eugenic manipulation, we can choose our genetic inheritance for ourselves. As for Habermas's worry about equality and reciprocity between the generations, defenders of liberal eugenics can reply that this worry, though legitimate, does not apply uniquely to genetic manipulation. The parent who forces her child to practice the piano incessantly from the age of three, or to hit tennis balls from dawn to dusk, also exerts a kind of control over the child's life that cannot possibly be reciprocal. The question, liberals insist, is whether the parental intervention, be it eugenic or environmental, undermines the child's freedom to choose her own life plan.

An ethic of autonomy and equality cannot explain what is wrong with eugenics. But Habermas has a further argument that cuts deeper, even as it points beyond the limits of liberal, or "postmeta-physical" considerations. This is the idea that "we experience our own freedom with reference to something which, by its very nature, is not at our disposal." To think of ourselves as free, we must be able to ascribe our origins "to a beginning which eludes human disposal," a beginning that arises from "something—like God or nature—that is not at the disposal of some *other* person." Habermas goes on to suggest that birth, "being a natural fact, meets the conceptual requirement of constituting a beginning we cannot control. Philosophy has but rarely addressed this matter." An exception, he observes, is found in the work of Hannah Arendt, who sees "natality," the fact that human beings are born not made, as a condition of their capacity to initiate action.

Habermas is onto something important, I think, when he asserts a "connection between the contingency of a life's beginning that is not at our disposal and the freedom to give one's life an ethical shape." For him, this connection matters because it explains why a genetically designed child is beholden and subordinate to another person (the designing parent) in a way that a child born of a contingent, impersonal beginning is not. But the notion that our freedom is bound up with "a beginning we cannot control" also carries a broader significance: Whatever its effect on the autonomy of the child, the drive to banish contingency and to master the mystery of birth diminishes the designing parent and corrupts parenting as a social practice governed by norms of unconditional love.

This takes us back to the notion of giftedness. Even if it does not harm the child or impair its autonomy, eugenic parenting is objectionable because it expresses and entrenches a certain stance toward the world—a stance of mastery and dominion that fails to appreciate the gifted character of human powers and achievements, and misses the part of freedom that consists in a persisting negotiation with the given.

Mastery and Gift

The problem with eugenics and genetic engineering is that they represent the one-sided triumph of willfulness over giftedness, of dominion over reverence, of molding over beholding. But why, we may wonder, should we worry about this triumph? Why not shake off our unease with enhancement as so much superstition? What would be lost if biotechnology dissolved our sense of giftedness?

Humility, Responsibility, and Solidarity

From the standpoint of religion, the answer is clear: To believe that our talents and powers are wholly our own doing is to misunderstand our place in creation, to confuse our role with God's. But religion is not the only source of reasons to care about giftedness. The moral stakes can also be described in secular terms. If the genetic revolution erodes our appreciation for the gifted character of human powers and achievements, it will transform three key features of our moral landscape—humility, responsibility, and solidarity.

In a social world that prizes mastery and control, parenthood is a school for humility. That we care deeply about our children, and yet cannot choose the kind we want, teaches parents to be open to the unbidden. Such openness is a disposition worth affirming, not only within families but in the wider world as well. It invites us to abide the unexpected, to live with dissonance, to reign in the impulse to control. A *Gattaca*-like world, in which parents became accustomed to specifying the sex and genetic traits of their children, would be a world inhospitable to the unbidden, a gated community writ large. . . .

It is sometimes thought that genetic enhancement erodes human responsibility by overriding effort and striving. But the real problem is the explosion, not the erosion, of responsibility. As humility gives way, responsibility expands to daunting proportions. We attribute less to chance and more to choice. Parents become responsible for choosing, or failing to choose, the right traits for their children. Athletes become responsible for acquiring, or failing to acquire, the talents that will help their team win.

One of the blessings of seeing ourselves as creatures of nature, God, or fortune is that we are not wholly responsible for the way we are. The more we become masters of our genetic endowments, the greater the burden we bear for the talents we have and the way we perform. Today when a basketball player misses a rebound, his coach can blame him for being out of position. Tomorrow the coach may blame him for being too short.

Even now, the growing use of performance-enhancing drugs in professional sports is subtly transforming the expectations players have for one another. In the past when a starting pitcher's team scored too few runs to win, he could only curse his bad luck and take it in stride. These days, the use of amphetamines and other stimulants is so wide-spread that players who take the field without them are criticized for "playing naked." A recently retired major league outfielder told *Sports Illustrated* that some pitchers blame teammates who play unenhanced: "If the starting pitcher knows that you're going out there naked, he's upset that you're not giving him [everything] you can. The big-time pitcher wants to make sure you're beaning up before the game." . . .

The Promethean impulse is contagious. In parenting as in sports, it unsettles and erodes the gifted dimension of human experience. When performance-enhancing drugs become commonplace, unenhanced ballplayers find themselves "playing naked." When genetic screening becomes a routine part of pregnancy, parents who eschew it are regarded as "flying blind" and are held responsible for whatever genetic defect befalls their child. . . .

If genetic engineering enabled us to override the results of the genetic lottery, to replace chance with choice, the gifted character of human powers and achievements would recede, and with it, perhaps, our capacity to see ourselves as sharing a common fate. The successful would become even more likely than they are now to view themselves as self-made and self-sufficient, and hence wholly responsible for their success. Those at the bottom of society would be viewed not as disadvantaged, and so worthy of a measure of compensation, but as simply unfit, and so worthy of eugenic repair. The meritocracy, less chastened by chance, would become harder, less forgiving. As perfect genetic knowledge would end the simulacrum of solidarity in insurance markets, perfect genetic control would erode the actual solidarity that arises when men and women reflect on the contingency of their talents and fortunes. . . .

There is something appealing, even intoxicating, about a vision of human freedom unfettered by the given. It may even be the case that the allure of that vision played a part in summoning the genomic age into being. It is often assumed that the powers of enhancement we now possess arose as an inadvertent by-product of biomedical progress—the genetic revolution came, so to speak, to cure disease, but stayed to tempt us with the prospect of enhancing our performance, designing our children, and perfecting our nature. But that may have the story backward. It is also possible to view genetic engineering as the ultimate expression of our resolve to see ourselves astride the world, the masters of our nature. But that vision of freedom is flawed. It threatens to banish our appreciation of life as a gift, and to leave us with nothing to affirm or behold outside our own will. . . .

POSTSCRIPT

Should Biotechnology Be Used to Alter and Enhance Humans?

The most often-cited arguments in favor of using biotechnologies for altering and enhancing humans are the benefits of protecting children from diseases, preventing handicaps and deficiencies, and enhancing physical and mental abilities. The main arguments against using biotechnology are the fear that something awful will happen and the moral arguments against playing God and too mightily interfering in nature. But what about the possibility of making people more moral in the sense of more caring, compassionate, cooperative, trusting, and helpful and less uncooperative, unsympathetic, and easily irritated? A number of scientists believe that these characteristics are fairly closely related to genes, so the moral improvement of the human race could be assisted by bioengineering. Furthermore, chemical treatments could help adults become less selfish and aggressive and become more altruistic and cooperative.

Thus, the moral argument can be used in favor of biotechnologies. In some sense, this is an old debate as the Faust legend indicates. Nevertheless, it is only recently that science has brought us to the doorstep of the bioengineering of humans. Two books from the mid-1980s serve as classics in this field. Jeremy Rivkin and Nicanor Perlas warn against bioengineering in *Algeny* (Penguin Books, 1984). They argue that biotechnology's destructive power far exceeds its potential benefits. Johnathan Glover reverses the weights for benefits and costs and champions bioengineering in *What Sort of People Should there Be?* (Penguin Books, 1984). More recent works that are opposed to bioengineering include Jeremy Rivkin, *The Biotech Century* (Tarcher/Putnam, 1998); Francis Fukuyama, *Our Posthuman Future* (Farrar, Strauss, and Giroux, 2002); and Bill McKibben, *Enough* (Henry Holt, 2003). More positive views of genetic engineering are found in the following: Eric S. Grace, *Biotechnology Unzipped: Promises and Realities* (Joseph Henry Press, 2006); Ramex Naam, *More Than Human: Embracing the Promise of Biological Enhancement* (Broadway Books, 2005); Gregory Stock, *Redesigning Humans: Our Inevitable Genetic Future* (Houghton Mifflin, 2002); Allan Buchanan et al., *From Chance to Choice: Genetics and Justice* (Cambridge University Press, 2000); and Emirates Center for Strategic Studies and Research, *Biotechnology and the Future of Society: Challenges and Opportunities* (Emirates Center for Strategic Studies and Research, 2004). For works that present multiple views, see Bernard E. Rollin, *Science and Ethics* (Cambridge University Press, 2006); Lori P. Knowles and Gregory E. Kaebnick eds., *Reprogenetics: Law, Policy, and Ethical Issues* (Johns Hopkins University Press, 2007); Rose M. Morgan, *The Genetics Revolution: History, Fears, and Future of a Life-Altering*

Science (Greenwood Press, 2006); Pete Shanks, *Human Genetic Engineering: A Guide for Activists, Skeptics, and the Very Perplexed* (Nation Books, 2005); Gerald Magill, ed., *Genetics and Ethics: An Interdisciplinary Study* (Saint Louis University Press, 2004); Audrey R. Chapman and Mark S. Frankel, eds., *Designing Our Descendants: The Promises and Perils of Genetic Modifications* (Johns Hopkins University Press, 2003); Scott Gilbert et al., *Bioethics and the New Embryology: Springboards for Debate* (W.H. Freeman, 2005); Howard W. Baillie and Timothy K. Casey, eds., *Is Human Nature Obsolete?: Genetics, Bioengineering, and the Future of the Human Condition* (MIT Press, 2005); and Rose M. Morgan, *The Genetic Revolution: History, Fears, and Future of a Life-Altering Science* (Greenwood Press, 2006). For discussions of human cloning, see Martha C. Nusbaum and Cass R. Sunstein, eds., *Clones and Clones: Facts and Fantasies about Human Cloning* (W.W. Norton, 1998) and President's Council on Bioethics, *Human Cloning and Human Dignity: An Ethical Inquiry* (Government Printing Office, 2002).

We leave to Colin Tudge ("The Future of Humanity," *New Statesman*, April 8, 2002) the final word on this subject. "On present knowledge, or even with what we are likely to know in the next two centuries, it would be as presumptuous to try to improve on the genes of a healthy human baby as it would be to edit sacred verse in medieval Chinese if all we had to go on was a bad dictionary. So all in all, human beings are likely to remain as they are, genetically speaking . . . and there doesn't seem to be much that meddling human beings can do about it. This, surely, is a mercy. We may have been shaped blindly by evolution. We may have been guided on our way by God. Whichever it was, or both, the job has been done a million times better than we are ever likely to do. Natural selection is far more subtle than human invention. "What a piece of work is a man!" said Hamlet. "How beauteous mankind is!" said Miranda. Both of them were absolutely right."

Internet References . . .

American Society of Criminology

The American Society of Criminology Web site is an excellent starting point for studying all aspects of criminology and criminal justice. This page provides links to sites on criminal justice in general, international criminal justice, juvenile justice, courts, the police, and the government.

http://www.asc41.com/

Crime Times

This Crime Times site lists research reviews and other information regarding the causes of criminal and violent behavior. It is provided by the nonprofit Wacker Foundation, publishers of Crime Times.

http://www.crimetimes.org/

Justice Information Center (JIC)

Provided by the National Criminal Justice Reference Service, the Justice Information Center (JIC) site connects to information about corrections, courts, crime prevention, criminal justice, statistics, drugs and crime, law enforcement, and victims, among other topics.

http://www.ncjrs.gov/

Crime and Social Control

*A*ll societies label certain hurtful actions as crimes and punish those who commit them. Other harmful actions, however, are not defined as crimes, and the perpetrators are not punished. Today the definition of crime and the appropriate treatment of criminals is widely debated. Some of the major questions are: Does street crime pose more of a threat to the public's well-being than white-collar crime? Billions of dollars have been spent on the "war on drugs," but who is winning? Would legalizing some drugs free up money that could be directed to other types of social welfare programs, such as the rehabilitation of addicts?

- Is Street Crime More Harmful Than White-Collar Crime?
- Should Marijuana Be Legalized?
- Does the Threat of Terrorism Warrant Curtailment of Civil Liberties?

ISSUE 15

Is Street Crime More Harmful Than White-Collar Crime?

YES: David A. Anderson, from "The Aggregate Burden of Crime," *Journal of Law and Economics* XLII (2) (October 1999)

NO: Jeffrey Reiman, from *The Rich Get Richer and the Poor Get Prison: Ideology, Class, and Criminal Justice*, 5th ed. (Allyn & Bacon, 1998)

ISSUE SUMMARY

YES: David A. Anderson estimates the total annual cost of crime including law enforcement and security services. The costs exceed one trillion, with fraud (mostly white collar crime) causing about one-fifth of the total. His calculations of the full costs of the loss of life and injury comes to about half of the total costs. It is right, therefore, to view personal and violent crime as the big crime problem.

NO: Professor of philosophy Jeffrey Reiman argues that the dangers posed by negligent corporations and white-collar criminals are a greater menace to society than are the activities of typical street criminals.

The word *crime* entered the English language (from the Old French) around A.D. 1250, when it was identified with "sinfulness." Later, the meaning of the word was modified: crime became the kind of sinfulness that was rightly punishable by law. Even medieval writers, who did not distinguish very sharply between church and state, recognized that there were some sins for which punishment was best left to God; the laws should punish only those that cause harm to the community. Of course, their concept of harm was a very broad one, embracing such offenses as witchcraft and blasphemy. Modern jurists, even those who deplore such practices, would say that the state has no business punishing the perpetrators of these types of offenses.

What, then, should the laws punish? The answer depends in part on our notion of harm. We usually limit the term to the kind of harm that is tangible and obvious: taking a life, causing bodily injury or psychological trauma, and destroying property. For most Americans today, particularly those who live in cities, the word *crime* is practically synonymous with street crime.

Anyone who has ever been robbed or beaten by street criminals will never forget the experience. The harm that these criminals cause is tangible, and the connection between the harm and the perpetrator is very direct.

But suppose the connection is not so direct. Suppose, for example, that A hires B to shoot C. Is that any less a crime? B is the actual shooter, but is A any less guilty? Of course not, we say; he may even be more guilty, since he is the ultimate mover behind the crime. A would be guilty even if the chain of command were much longer, involving A's orders to B, and B's to C, then on to D, E, and F to kill G. Organized crime kingpins go to jail even when they are far removed from the people who carry out their orders. High officials of the Nixon administration, even though they were not directly involved in the burglary attempt at the Democratic National Committee headquarters at the Watergate Hotel complex in 1972, were imprisoned.

This brings us to the topic of white-collar crime. The burglars at the Watergate Hotel were acting on orders that trickled down from the highest reaches of political power in the United States. Other white-collar criminals are as varied as the occupations from which they come. They include stock-brokers who make millions through insider trading, as Ivan Boesky did; members of Congress who take payoffs; and people who cheat on their income taxes, like hotel owner and billionaire Leona Helmsley. Some, like Helmsley, get stiff prison sentences when convicted, though many others (like most of the officials in the Watergate scandal) do little or no time in prison. Do they deserve stiffer punishment, or are their crimes less harmful than the crimes of street criminals?

Although white-collar criminals do not directly cause physical harm or relieve people of their wallets, they can still end up doing considerable harm. The harm done by Nixon's aides threatened the integrity of the U.S. electoral system. Every embezzler, corrupt politician, and tax cheat exacts a toll on our society. Individuals can be hurt in more tangible ways by decisions made in corporate boardrooms: Auto executives, for example, have approved design features that have caused fatalities. Managers of chemical companies have allowed practices that have polluted the environment with cancer-causing agents. And heads of corporations have presided over industries wherein workers have been needlessly killed or maimed.

Whether or not these decisions should be considered crimes is debatable. A crime must always involve "malicious intent," or what the legal system calls *mens rea*. This certainly applies to street crime—the mugger obviously has sinister designs—but does it apply to every decision made in a boardroom that ends up causing harm? And does that harm match or exceed the harm caused by street criminals? In the following selections, David A. Anderson tries to calculate all the costs of all crimes. His message is that crime costs society far more than we realize. But for the debate on the relative costs of street vs. white collar crime, his study shows that street crime costs society more than white collar crime. According to Jeffrey Reiman, white-collar crime does more harm than is commonly recognized. By his count, white-collar crime causes far more deaths, injuries, illnesses, and financial loss than street crime. In light of this, he argues, we must redefine our ideas about what crime is and who the criminals are.

The Aggregate Burden of Crime

Introduction

Distinct from previous studies that have focused on selected crimes, regions, or outcomes, this study attempts an exhaustively broad estimation of the crime burden. . . .

Overt annual expenditures on crime in the United States include $47 billion for police protection, $36 billion for corrections, and $19 billion for the legal and judicial costs of state and local criminal cases. (Unless otherwise noted, all figures are adjusted to reflect 1997 dollars using the Consumer Price Index.) Crime victims suffer $876 million worth of lost workdays, and guns cost society $25 billion in medical bills and lost productivity in a typical year. Beyond the costs of the legal system, victim losses, and crime prevention agencies, the crime burden includes the costs of deterrence (locks, safety lighting and fencing, alarm systems and munitions), the costs of compliance enforcement (non-gendarme inspectors and regulators), implicit psychic and health costs (fear, agony, and the inability to behave as desired), and the opportunity costs of time spent preventing, carrying out, and serving prison terms for criminal activity.

This study estimates the impact of crime taking a comprehensive list of the repercussions of aberrant behavior into account. While the standard measures of criminal activity count crimes and direct costs, this study measures the impact of crimes and includes indirect costs as well. Further, the available data on which crime cost figures are typically based is imprecise. Problems with crime figures stem from the prevalence of unreported crimes, inconsistencies in recording procedures among law enforcement agencies, policies of recording only the most serious crime in events with multiple offenses, and a lack of distinction between attempted and completed crimes. This research does not eliminate these problems, but it includes critical crime-prevention and opportunity costs that are measured with relative precision, and thus places less emphasis on the imprecise figures used in most other measures of the impact of crime. . . .

Previous Studies

Several studies have estimated the impact of crime; however, none has been thorough in its assessment of the substantial indirect costs of crime and the

From *Journal of Law and Economics*, vol. 42, October 1999, pp. 611–642. Copyright © 1999 by David A. Anderson. Reprinted by permission of the author.

Table 1

Previous Study	Focus	Not Included	$ (billions)
Colins (1994)	General	Opportunity Costs, Miscellaneous Indirect Components	728
Cohen, Miller, and Wiersema (1995)	Victim Costs of Violent and Property Crimes	Prevention, Opportunity, and Indirect Costs	472
U.S. News (1974)	General	Opportunity Costs, Miscellaneous Indirect Components	288
Cohen, Miller, Rossman (1994)	Cost of Rape, Robbery, and Assault	Prevention, Opportunity, and Indirect Costs	183
Zedlewski (1985)	Firearms, Guard Dogs, Victim Losses, Commercial Security	Residential Security, Opportunity Costs, Indirect Costs	160
Cohen (1990)	Cost of Personal and Household Crime to Victims	Prevention, Opportunity, and Indirect Costs	113
President's Commission on Law Enforcement (1967)	General	Opportunity Costs, Miscellaneous Indirect Components	107
Klaus (1994)	National Crime and Victimization Survey Crimes	Prevention, Opportunity, and Indirect Costs	19

crucial consideration of private crime prevention expenditures. The FBI Crime Index provides a measure of the level of crime by counting the acts of murder, rape, robbery, aggravated assault, burglary, larceny, motor vehicle theft, and arson each year. The FBI Index is purely a count of crimes and does not attempt to place weights on various criminal acts based on their severity. If the number of acts of burglary, larceny, motor vehicle theft, or arson decreases, society might be better off, but with no measure of the severity of the crimes, such a conclusion is necessarily tentative. From a societal standpoint what matters is the extent of damage inflicted by these crimes, which the FBI Index does not measure.

Over the past three decades, studies of the cost of crime have reported increasing crime burdens, perhaps more as a result of improved understanding and accounting for the broad repercussions of crime than due to the increase in the burden itself. Table 1 summarizes the findings of eight previous studies. . . .

The Effects of Crime

The effects of crime fall into several categories depending on whether they constitute the allocation of resources due to crime that could otherwise be used more productively, the production of ill-favored commodities, transfers from victims to criminals, opportunity costs, or implicit costs associated with risks to life and health. This section examines the meaning and ramifications of each of these categories of crime costs.

Crime-Induced Production

Crime can result in the allocation of resources towards products and activities that do not contribute to society except in their association with crime. Examples include the production of personal protection devices, the trafficking of drugs, and the operation of correctional facilities. In the absence of crime, the time, money, and material resources absorbed by the provision of these goods and services could be used for the creation of benefits rather than the avoidance of harm. The foregone benefits from these alternatives represent a real cost of crime to society. (Twenty dollars spent on a door lock is twenty dollars that cannot be spent on groceries.) Thus, expenditures on crime-related products are treated as a loss to society.

Crimes against property also create unnecessary production due to the destruction and expenditure of resources, and crimes against persons necessitate the use of medical and psychological care resources. In each of these cases, crime-related purchases bid-up prices for the associated items, resulting in higher prices for all consumers of the goods. In the absence of crime, the dollars currently spent to remedy and recover from crime would largely be spent in pursuit of other goals, bidding-up the prices of alternative categories of goods. For this reason, the *net* impact of price effects is assumed to be zero in the present research.

Opportunity Costs

As the number of incarcerated individuals increases steadily, society faces the large and growing loss of these potential workers' productivity. . . . Criminals are risk takers and instigators—characteristics that could make them contributors to society if their entrepreneurial talents were not misguided. Crimes also take time to conceive and carry out, and thus involve the opportunity cost of the criminals' time regardless of detection and incarceration. For many, crime is a full-time occupation. Society is deprived of the goods and services a criminal would have produced in the time consumed by crime and the production of "bads" if he or she were on the level. Additional opportunity costs arise due to victims' lost workdays, and time spent securing assets, looking for keys, purchasing and installing crime prevention devices, and patrolling neighborhood-watch areas.

The Value of Risks to Life and Health

The implicit costs of violent crime include the fear of being injured or killed, the anger associated with the inability to behave as desired, and the agony of being a crime victim. Costs associated with life and health risks are perhaps the most difficult to ascertain, although a considerable literature is devoted to their estimation. The implicit values of lost life and injury are included in the list of crime costs below; those not wishing to consider them can simply subtract these estimates from the aggregate figure.

Transfers

One result of fraud and theft is a transfer of assets from victim to criminal. . . .

Numerical Findings

Crime-Induced Production

. . . Crime-induced production accounts for about $400 billion in expenditures annually. Table 2 presents the costs of goods and services that would not have to be produced in the absence of crime. Drug trafficking accounts for an estimated $161 billion in expenditure. With the $28 billion cost of pre-natal drug exposure and almost $11 billion worth of federal, state, and local drug control efforts (including drug treatment, education, interdiction, research, and intelligence), the combined cost of drug-related activities is about $200 billion. Findings that over half of the arrestees in 24 cities tested positive for recent drug use and about one-third of offenders reported being under the influence of drugs at the time of their offense suggest that signifi-cant portions of the other crime-cost categories may result indirectly from drug use.

Table 2

Crime-Induced Production	$ (millions)
Drug Trafficking	160,584
Police Protection	47,129
Corrections	35,879
Prenatal Exposure to Cocaine and Heroin	28,156
Federal Agencies	23,381
Judicial and Legal Services—State & Local	18,901
Guards	17,917
Drug Control	10,951
DUI Costs to Driver	10,302
Medical Care for Victims	8,990
Computer Viruses and Security	8,000
Alarm Systems	6,478
Passes for Business Access	4,659
Locks, Safes, and Vaults	4,359
Vandalism (except Arson)	2,317
Small Arms and Small Arms Ammunition	2,252
Replacements due to Arson	1,902
Surveillance Cameras	1,471
Safety Lighting	1,466
Protective Fences and Gates	1,159
Airport Security	448
Nonlethal weaponry, e.g., Mace	324
Elec. Retail Article Surveillance	149
Theft Insurance (less indemnity)	96
Guard Dogs	49
Mothers Against Drunk Driving	49
Library Theft Detection	28
Total	**397,395**

About 682,000 police and 17,000 federal, state, special (park, transit, or county) and local police agencies account for $47 billion in expenditures annually. Thirty-six billion dollars is dedicated each year to the 895 federal and state prisons, 3,019 jails, and 1,091 state, county, and local juvenile detention centers. Aside from guards in correctional institutions, private expenditure on guards amounts to more than $18 billion annually. Security guard agencies employ 55 percent of the 867,000 guards in the U.S.; the remainder are employed in-house. While guards are expected and identifiable at banks and military complexes, they have a less conspicuous presence at railroads, ports, golf courses, laboratories, factories, hospitals, retail stores, and other places of business. The figures in this paper do not include receptionists, who often play a duel role of monitoring unlawful entry into a building and providing information and assistance. . . .

Opportunity Costs

In their study of the costs of murder, rape, robbery, and aggravated assault, Cohen, Miller, and Rossman estimate that the average incarcerated offender costs society $5,700 in lost productivity per year. Their estimate was based on the observation that many prisoners did not work in the legal market prior to their offense, and the opportunity cost of those prisoners' time can be considered to be zero. The current study uses a higher estimate of the opportunity cost of incarceration because unlike previous studies, it examines the relative savings from a *crime-free* society. It is likely that in the absence of crime including drug use, some criminals who are not presently employed in the legal workforce would be willing and able to find gainful employment. This assumption is supported by the fact that many criminals are, in a way, motivated entrepreneurs whose energy has taken an unfortunate focus. In the absence of more enticing underground activities, some of the same individuals could apply these skills successfully in the legal sector. . . .

The Value of Risks to Life and Health

Table 3 presents estimates of the implicit costs of violent crime. The value of life and injury estimates used here reflect the amounts individuals are willing to accept to enter a work environment in which their health state might change. The labor market estimates do not include losses covered by workers' compensation, namely health care costs (usually provided without dollar or time limits) and lost earnings (within modest bounds, victims or their spouses typically receive about two thirds of lost earnings for life or the duration of the injury). The values do capture perceived risks of pain, suffering,

Table 3

The Value of Risks to Life and Health	$ (millions)
Value of Lost Life	439,880
Value of Injuries	134,515
Total	**574,395**

and mental distress associated with the health losses. If the risk of involvement in violent crime evokes more mental distress than the risk of occupational injuries and fatalities, the labor market values represent conservative estimates of the corresponding costs of crime. Similar estimates have been used in previous studies of crime costs. . . .

The average of 27 previous estimates of the implicit value of human life as reported by W. Kip Viscusi is 7.1 million. Removing two outlying estimates of just under $20 million about which the authors express reservation, the average of the remaining studies is $6.1 million. Viscusi points out that the majority of the estimates fall between $3.7 and $8.6 million ($3 and $7 million in 1990 dollars), the average of which is again $6.1 million. The $6.1 million figure was multiplied by the 72,111 crime-related deaths to obtain the $440 billion estimate of the value of lives lost to crime. Similarly, the average of 15 studies of the implicit value of non-fatal injuries, $52,637, was multiplied by the 2,555,520 reported injuries resulting from drunk driving and boating, arson, rape, robbery, and assaults to find the $135 billion estimate for the implicit cost of crime-related injuries.

Transfers

More than $603 billion worth of transfers result from crime. After the $204 billion lost to occupational fraud and the $123 billion in unpaid taxes, the $109 billion lost to health insurance fraud represents the greatest transfer by more than a factor of two, and the associated costs amount to almost ten percent of the nations' health care expenditures. Robberies, perhaps the classic crime, ironically generate a smaller volume of transfers ($775 million) than any other category of crime. The transfers of goods and money resulting from fraud and theft do not necessarily impose a net burden on society, and may in fact increase social welfare to the extent that those on the receiving end value the goods more than those losing them. Nonetheless, as Table 4 illustrates, those on the losing side bear a $603 billion annual burden. . . .

There are additional cost categories that are not included here, largely because measures that are included absorb much of their impact. Nonetheless, several are worth noting. Thaler, Hellman and Naroff, and Rizzo estimate the erosion of property values per crime. An average of their figures, $2,024, can be multiplied by the total number of crimes reported in 1994, 13,992, to estimate an aggregate housing devaluation of $28 billion. Although this figure should reflect the inability to behave as desired in the presence of crime, it also includes psychic and monetary costs imposed by criminal behavior that are already included in this [article].

Julie Berry Cullen and Stephen D. Levitt discuss urban flight resulting from crime. They report a nearly one-to-one relationship between serious crimes and individuals parting from major cities. The cost component of this is difficult to assess because higher commuting costs must be measured against lower property costs in rural areas, and the conveniences of city living must be compared with the amenities of suburbia. Several other categories of crime costs receive incomplete representation due to insufficient data, and

Table 4

Transfers	$ (millions)
Occupational Fraud	203,952
Unpaid Taxes	123,108
Health Insurance Fraud	108,610
Financial Institution Fraud	52,901
Mail Fraud	35,986
Property/Casualty Insurance Fraud	20,527
Telemarketing Fraud	16,609
Business Burglary	13,229
Motor Vehicle Theft	8,913
Shoplifting	7,185
Household Burglary	4,527
Personal Theft	3,909
Household Larceny	1,996
Coupon Fraud	912
Robbery	775
Total	**603,140**

therefore make the estimates here conservative. These include the costs of unreported crimes (although the National Crime Victimization Survey provides information beyond that reported to the police), lost taxes due to the underground economy, and restrictions of behavior due to crime.

When criminals' costs are estimated implicitly as the value of the assets they receive through crime, the gross cost of crime (including transfers) is estimated to exceed $2,269 billion each year, and the net cost is an estimated $1,666 billion. When criminals' costs are assumed to equal the value of time spent planning and committing crimes and in prison, the estimated annual gross and net costs of crime are $1,705 and $1,102 billion respectively. Table 5 presents the aggregate costs of crime based on the more conservative, time-based estimation method. The disaggregation of this and the previous tables facilitates the creation of customized estimates based on the reader's preferred assumptions. Each of the general studies summarized in Table 1 included transfers, so the appropriate comparison is to the gross cost estimate in the current study. As the result of a more comprehensive treatment of

Table 5

The Aggregate Burden of Crime	$ (billions)
Crime-Induced Production	397
Opportunity Costs	130
Risks to Life and Health	574
Transfers	603
Gross Burden	**$1,705**
Net of Transfers	**$1,102**
Per Capita (in dollars)	**$4,118**

repercussions, the cost of crime is now seen to be more than twice as large as previously recognized.

Conclusion

Previous studies of the burden of crime have counted crimes or concentrated on direct crime costs. This paper calculates the aggregate burden of crime rather than absolute numbers, includes indirect costs, and recognizes that transfers resulting from theft should not be included in the net burden of crime to society. The accuracy of society's perspective on crime costs will improve with the understanding that these costs extend beyond victims' losses and the cost of law enforcement to include the opportunity costs of criminals' and prisoners' time, our inability to behave as desired, and the private costs of crime deterrence.

As criminals acquire an estimated $603 billion dollars worth of assets from their victims, they generate an additional $1,102 billion worth of lost productivity, crime-related expenses, and diminished quality of life. The net losses represent an annual per capita burden of $4,118. Including transfers, the aggregate burden of crime is $1,705 billion. In the United States, this is of the same order of magnitude as life insurance purchases ($1,680 billion), the outstanding mortgage debt to commercial banks and savings institutions ($1,853 billion), and annual expenditures on health ($1,038 billion).

As the enormity of this negative-sum game comes to light, so, too, will the need for countervailing efforts to redefine legal policy and forge new ethical standards. Periodic estimates of the full cost of crime could speak to the success of national strategies to encourage decorum, including increased expenditures on law enforcement, new community strategic approaches, technological innovations, legal reform, education, and the development of ethics curricula. Economic theory dictates that resources should be devoted to moral enhancement until the benefits from marginal efforts are surpassed by their costs. Programs that decrease the burden of crime by more than the cost of implementation should be continued, while those associated with negligible or positive net increments in the cost of crime should be altered to better serve societal goals.

Jeffrey Reiman

 **NO**

A Crime by Any Other Name . . .

If one individual inflicts a bodily injury upon another which leads to the death of the person attacked we call it manslaughter; on the other hand, if the attacker knows beforehand that the blow will be fatal we call it murder. Murder has also been committed if society places hundreds of workers in such a position that they inevitably come to premature and unnatural ends. Their death is as violent as if they had been stabbed or shot. . . . Murder has been committed if society knows perfectly well that thousands of workers cannot avoid being sacrificed so long as these conditions are allowed to continue. Murder of this sort is just as culpable as the murder committed by an individual.

—Frederick Engels
The Condition of the Working Class in England

What's In a Name?

If it takes you an hour to read this chapter, by the time you reach the last page, three of your fellow citizens will have been murdered. *During that same time, at least four Americans will die as a result of unhealthy or unsafe conditions in the workplace!* Although these work-related deaths could have been prevented, they are not called murders. Why not? Doesn't crime by any other name still cause misery and suffering? What's in a name?

The fact is that the label "crime" is not used in America to name all or the worst of the actions that cause misery and suffering to Americans. It is primarily reserved for the dangerous actions of the poor.

In the February 21, 1993, edition of the *New York Times*, an article appears with the headline: "Company in Mine Deaths Set to Pay Big Fine." It describes an agreement by the owners of a Kentucky mine to pay a fine for safety misconduct that may have led to "the worst American mining accident in nearly a decade." Ten workers died in a methane explosion, and the company pleaded guilty to "a pattern of safety misconduct" that included falsifying reports of methane levels and requiring miners to work under unsupported roofs. The company was fined $3.75 million. The acting foreman at the mine was the only individual charged by the federal government, and for his cooperation with the investigation, prosecutors were recommending that he receive the minimum sentence: probation to six months in prison. The company's president expressed regret for the tragedy that occurred. And the U.S. attorney said he hoped the case "sent a clear message that violations of Federal safety and health regulations that endanger the lives of our citizens will not be tolerated."

Compare this with the story of Colin Ferguson, who prompted an editorial in the *New York Times* of December 10, 1993, with the headline: "Mass Murder on the 5:33." A few days earlier, Colin had boarded a commuter train in Garden City, Long Island, and methodically shot passengers with a 9-millimeter pistol, killing 5 and wounding 18. Colin Ferguson was surely a murderer, maybe a mass murderer. My question is, Why wasn't the death of the miners also murder? Why weren't those responsible for subjecting ten miners to deadly conditions also "mass murderers"?

Why do ten dead miners amount to an "accident," a "tragedy," and five dead commuters a "mass murder"? "Murder" suggests a murderer, whereas "accident" and "tragedy" suggest the work of impersonal forces. But the charge against the company that owned the mine said that they "repeatedly exposed the mine's work crews to danger and that such conditions were frequently concealed from Federal inspectors responsible for enforcing the mine safety act." And the acting foreman admitted to falsifying records of methane levels only two months before the fatal blast. Someone was responsible for the conditions that led to the death of ten miners. Is that person not a murderer, perhaps even a *mass murderer?*

These questions are at this point rhetorical. My aim is not to discuss this case but rather to point to the blinders we wear when we look at such an "accident." There was an investigation. One person, the acting foreman, was held responsible for falsifying records. He is to be sentenced to six months in prison (at most). The company was fined. But no one will be tried for *murder.* No one will be thought of as a murderer. *Why not?. . .*

Didn't those miners have a right to protection from the violence that took their lives? *And if not, why not?*

Once we are ready to ask this question seriously, we are in a position to see that the reality of crime—that is, the acts we label crime, the acts we think of as crime, the actors and actions we treat as criminal—is *created*: It is an image shaped by decisions as to *what* will be called crime and *who* will be treated as a criminal.

The Carnival Mirror

. . . The American criminal justice system is a mirror that shows a distorted image of the dangers that threaten us—an image created more by the shape of the mirror than by the reality reflected. What do we see when we look in the criminal justice mirror? . . .

He is, first of all, a *he*. Out of 2,012,906 persons arrested for FBI Index crimes [which are criminal homicide, forcible rape, robbery, aggravated assault, burglary, larceny, and motor vehicle theft] in 1991, 1,572,591, or 78 percent, were males. Second, he is a *youth*. . . . Third, he is predominantly *urban*. . . . Fourth, he is disproportionately *black*—blacks are arrested for Index crimes at a rate three times that of their percentage in the national population. . . . Finally, he is *poor*: Among state prisoners in 1991, 33 percent were unemployed prior to being arrested—a rate nearly four times that of males in the general population. . . .

This is the Typical Criminal feared by most law-abiding Americans. Poor, young, urban, (disproportionately) black males make up the core of the enemy forces in the war against crime. They are the heart of a vicious, unorganized guerrilla army, threatening the lives, limbs, and possessions of the law-abiding members of society—necessitating recourse to the ultimate weapons of force and detention in our common defense.

. . . The acts of the Typical Criminal are not the only acts that endanger us, nor are they the acts that endanger us the most. As I shall show . . . , we have as great or sometimes even a greater chance of being killed or disabled by an occupational injury or disease, by unnecessary surgery, or by shoddy emergency medical services than by aggravated assault or even homicide! Yet even though these threats to our well-being are graver than those posed by our poor young criminals, they do not show up in the FBI's Index of serious crimes. The individuals responsible for them do not turn up in arrest records or prison statistics. *They never become part of the reality reflected in the criminal justice mirror, although the danger they pose is at least as great and often greater than the danger posed by those who do!*

Similarly, the general public loses more money *by for* . . . from price-fixing and monopolistic practices and from consumer deception and embezzlement than from all the property crimes in the FBI's Index combined. Yet these far more costly acts are either not criminal, or if technically criminal, not prosecuted, or if prosecuted, not punished, or if punished, only mildly . . . *Their faces rarely appear in the criminal justice mirror, although the danger they pose is at least as great and often greater than that of those who do. . . .*

The criminal justice system is like a mirror in which society can see the face of the evil in its midst. Because the system deals with some evil and not with others, because it treats some evils as the gravest and treats some of the gravest evils as minor, the image it throws back is distorted like the image in a carnival mirror. Thus, the image cast back is false not because it is invented out of thin air but because the proportions of the real are distorted. . . .

If criminal justice really gives us a carnival-mirror of "crime," we are doubly deceived. First, we are led to believe that the criminal justice system is protecting us against the gravest threats to our well-being when, in fact, the system is protecting us against only some threats and not necessarily the gravest ones. We are deceived about how much protection we are receiving and thus left vulnerable. The second deception is just the other side of this one. If people believe that the carnival mirror is a true mirror—that is, if they believe the criminal justice system simply *reacts* to the gravest threats to their well-being—they come to believe that whatever is the target of the criminal justice system must be the greatest threat to their well-being. . . .

A Crime by Any Other Name . . .

Think of a crime, any crime. Picture the first "crime" that comes into your mind. What do you see? The odds are you are not imagining a mining company executive sitting at his desk, calculating the costs of proper safety precautions and deciding not to invest in them. Probably what you do see with your mind's eye is one person physically attacking another or robbing something from another via the threat of physical attack. Look more closely. What does the attacker look like? It's a safe bet he (and it is a *he*, of course) is not wearing a suit and tie. In fact, my hunch is that you—like me, like almost anyone else in America—picture a young, tough lower-class male when the thought of crime first pops into your head. You (we) picture someone like the Typical Criminal described above. The crime itself is one in which the Typical Criminal sets out to attack or rob some specific person.

It is important to identify this model of the Typical Crime because it functions like a set of blinders. It keeps us from calling a mine disaster a mass murder even if ten men are killed, even if someone is responsible for the unsafe conditions in which they worked and died. I contend that this particular piece of mental furniture so blocks our view that it keeps us from using the criminal justice system to protect ourselves from the greatest threats to our persons and possessions.

What keeps a mine disaster from being a mass murder in our eyes is that it is not a one-on-one harm. What is important in one-on-one harm is not the numbers but the *desire of someone (or ones) to harm someone (or ones) else.* An attack by a gang on one or more persons or an attack by one individual on several fits the model of one-on-one harm; that is, for each person harmed there is at least one individual who wanted to harm that person. Once he selects his victim, the rapist, the mugger, the murderer all want this person they have selected to suffer. A mine executive, on the other hand, does not want his employees to be harmed. He would truly prefer that there be no accident, no injured or dead miners. What he does want is something legitimate. It is what he has been hired to get: maximum profits at minimum costs. If he cuts corners to save a buck, he is just doing his job. If ten men die because he cut corners on safety, we may think him crude or callous but not a murderer. He is, at most, responsible for an *indirect harm*, not a one-on-one harm. For this, he may even be criminally indictable for violating safety regulations—but not for murder. The ten men are dead as an unwanted consequence of his (perhaps overzealous or undercautious) pursuit of a legitimate goal. So, unlike the Typical Criminal, he has not committed the Typical Crime—or so we generally believe. As a result, ten men are dead who might be alive now if cutting corners of the kind that leads to loss of life, whether suffering is specifically aimed at or not, were treated as murder.

This is my point. Because we accept the belief . . . that the model for crime is one person specifically trying to harm another, we accept a legal system that leaves us unprotected against much greater dangers to our lives and well-being than those threatened by the Typical Criminal. . . .

According to the FBI's *Uniform Crime Reports,* in 1991, there were 24,703 murders and nonnegligent manslaughters, and 1,092,739 aggravated assaults. In 1992, there were 23,760 murders and nonnegligent manslaughters, and 1,126,970 aggravated assaults. . . . Thus, as a measure of the physical harm done by crime in the beginning of the 1990s, we can say that reported crimes lead to roughly 24,000 deaths and 1,000,000 instances of serious bodily injury short of death a year. As a measure of monetary loss due to property crime, we can use $15.1 billion—the total estimated dollar losses due to property crime in 1992 according to the UCR. Whatever the shortcomings of these reported crime statistics, they are the statistics upon which public policy has traditionally been based. Thus, I will consider any actions that lead to loss of life, physical harm, and property loss comparable to the figures in the UCR as actions that pose grave dangers to the community comparable to the threats posed by crimes. . . .

In testimony before the Senate Committee on Labor and Human Resources, Dr. Philip Landrigan, director of the Division of Environmental and Occupational Medicine at the Mount Sinai School of Medicine in New York City, stated that

> [I]t may be calculated that occupational disease is responsible each year in the United States for 50,000 to 70,000 deaths, and for approximately 350,000 new cases of illness.

. . . The BLS estimate of 330,000 job-related illnesses for 1990 roughly matches Dr. Landrigan's estimates. For 1991, BLS estimates 368,000 job-related illnesses. These illnesses are of varying severity. . . . Because I want to compare these occupational harms with those resulting from aggravated assault, I shall stay on the conservative side here too, as with deaths from occupational diseases, and say that there are annually in the United States approximately 150,000 job-related serious illnesses. Taken together with 25,000 deaths from occupational diseases, how does this compare with the threat posed by crime?

Before jumping to any conclusions, note that the risk of occupational disease and death falls only on members of the labor force, whereas the risk of crime falls on the whole population, from infants to the elderly. Because the labor force is about half the total population (124,810,000 in 1990, out of a total population of 249,900,000), to get a true picture of the *relative* threat posed by occupational diseases compared with that posed by crimes, we should *halve* the crime statistics when comparing them with the figures for industrial disease and death. Using the crime figures for the first years of the 1990s, . . . we note that the *comparable* figures would be

	Occupational Hazard	Crime (halved)
Death	25,000	12,000
Other physical harm	150,000	500,000

. . . Note . . . that the estimates in the last chart are *only* for occupational *diseases* and deaths from those diseases. They do not include death and disability from work-related injuries. Here, too, the statistics are gruesome. The National Safety Council reported that in 1991, work-related accidents caused 9,600 deaths and 1.7 million disabling work injuries, a total cost to the economy of $63.3 billion. This brings the number of occupation-related deaths to 34,600 a year and other physical harms to 1,850,000. If, on the basis of these additional figures, we recalculated our chart comparing occupational harms from both disease and accident with criminal harms, it would look like this:

	Occupational Hazard	Crime (halved)
Death	34,600	12,000
Other physical harm	1,850,000	500,000

Can there be any doubt that workers are more likely to stay alive and healthy in the face of the danger from the underworld than in the work-world? . . .

To say that some of these workers died from accidents due to their own carelessness is about as helpful as saying that some of those who died at the hands of murderers asked for it. It overlooks the fact that where workers are careless, it is not because they love to live dangerously. They have production quotas to meet, quotas that they themselves do not set. If quotas were set with an eye to keeping work at a safe pace rather than to keeping the production-to-wages ratio as high as possible, it might be more reasonable to expect workers to take the time to be careful. Beyond this, we should bear in mind that the vast majority of occupational deaths result from disease, not accident, and disease is generally a function of conditions outside a worker's control. Examples of such conditions are the level of coal dust in the air ("260,000 miners receive benefits for [black lung] disease, and perhaps as many as 4,000 retired miners die from the illness or its complications each year"; about 10,000 currently working miners "have X-ray evidence of the beginnings of the crippling and often fatal disease") or textile dust . . . or asbestos fibers . . . or coal tars . . .; (coke oven workers develop cancer of the scrotum at a rate five times that of the general population). Also, some 800,000 people suffer from occupationally related skin disease each year. . . .

To blame the workers for occupational disease and deaths is to ignore the history of governmental attempts to compel industrial firms to meet safety standards that would keep dangers (such as chemicals or fibers or dust particles in the air) that are outside the worker's control down to a safe level. This has been a continual struggle, with firms using everything from their own "independent" research institutes to more direct and often questionable forms of political pressure to influence government in the direction of loose standards and lax enforcement. So far, industry has been winning because OSHA [Occupational Safety and Health Administration] has been given neither the personnel nor the mandate to fulfill its purpose. It is so understaffed that, in 1973, when 1,500 federal sky marshals guarded the nation's airplanes from hijackers, only 500 OSHA inspectors toured the nation's workplaces. By 1980, OSHA employed 1,581 compliance safety and health officers, but this still enabled inspection of only roughly 2 percent of the 2.5 million establishments covered by OSHA. The *New York Times* reports that in 1987 the number of OSHA inspectors was down to 1,044. As might be expected, the agency performs fewer inspections that it did a dozen years ago. . . .

According to a report issued by the AFL-CIO [American Federation of Labor and Congress of Industrial Organizations] in 1992, "The median penalty paid by an employer during the years 1972–1990 following an incident resulting in death or serious injury of a worker was just $480." The same report claims that the federal government spends $1.1 billion a year to protect fish and wildlife and only $300 million a year to protect workers from health and safety hazards on the job. . . .

Is a person who kills another in a bar brawl a greater threat to society than a business executive who refuses to cut into his profits to make his plant a safe place to work? By any measure of death and suffering the latter is by far a greater danger than the former. Because he wishes his workers no harm, because he is only indirectly responsible for death and disability while pursuing legitimate economic goals, his acts are not called "crimes." Once we free our imagination from the blinders of the one-on-one model of crime, can there be any doubt that the criminal justice system does *not* protect us from the gravest threats to life and limb? It seeks to protect us when danger comes from a young, lower-class male in the inner city. When a threat comes from an upper-class business executive in an office, the criminal justice system looks the other way. This is in the face of growing evidence that for every three American citizens murdered by thugs, at least four American workers are killed by the recklessness of their bosses and the indifference of their government.

Health Care May Be Dangerous to Your Health

. . . On July 15, 1975, Dr. Sidney Wolfe of Ralph Nader's Public Interest Health Research Group testified before the House Commerce Oversight and Investigations Subcommittee that there "were 3.2 million cases of unnecessary surgery performed each year in the United States." These unneeded operations, Wolfe added, "cost close to $5 billion a year and kill as many as 16,000 Americans.". . .

In an article on an experimental program by Blue Cross and Blue Shield aimed at curbing unnecessary surgery, *Newsweek* reports that

> a Congressional committee earlier this year [1976] estimated that more than 2 million of the elective operations performed in 1974 were not only unnecessary—but also killed about 12,000 patients and cost nearly $4 billion.

Because the number of surgical operations performed in the United States rose from 16.7 million in 1975 to 22.4 million in 1991, there is reason to believe that at least somewhere between . . . 12,000 and . . . 16,000 people a year still die from unnecessary surgery. In 1991, the FBI reported that 3,405 murders were committed by a "cutting or stabbing instrument." Obviously, the FBI does not include the scalpel as a cutting or stabbing instrument. If they did, they would have had to report that between 15,405 and 19,405 persons were killed by "cutting or stabbing" in 1991. . . . No matter how you slice it, the scalpel may be more dangerous than the switchblade. . . .

Waging Chemical Warfare Against America

One in 4 Americans can expect to contract cancer during their lifetimes. The American Cancer Society estimated that 420,000 Americans would die of cancer in 1981. The National Cancer Institute's estimate for 1993 is 526,000 deaths from cancer. "A 1978 report issued by the President's Council on Environmental Quality (CEQ) unequivocally states that 'most researchers agree that 70 to 90 percent of cancers are caused by environmental influences and are hence theoretically preventable.'" This means that a concerted national effort could result in saving 350,000 or more lives a year and reducing each individual's chances of getting cancer in his or her lifetime from 1 in 4 to 1 in 12 or fewer. If you think this would require a massive effort in terms of money and personnel, you are right. How much of an effort, though, would the nation make to stop a foreign invader who was killing a thousand people and bent on capturing one-quarter of the present population?

In face of this "invasion" that is already under way, the U.S. government has allocated $1.9 billion to the National Cancer Institute (NCI) for fiscal year 1992, and NCI has allocated $219 million to the study of the physical and chemical (i.e., environmental) causes of cancer. Compare this with the (at least) $45 billion spent to fight the Persian Gulf War. The simple truth is that the government that strove so mightily to protect the borders of a small, undemocratic nation 7,000 miles away is doing next to nothing to protect us against the chemical war in our midst. This war is being waged against us on three fronts:

- Pollution
- Cigarette smoking
- Food additives

. . . The evidence linking *air pollution* and cancer, as well as other serious and often fatal diseases, has been rapidly accumulating in recent years. In 1993, the *Journal of the American Medical Association* reported on research that found "'robust' associations between premature mortality and air pollution levels." They estimate that pollutants cause about 2 percent of all cancer deaths (at least 10,000 a year). . . .

A . . . recent study . . . concluded that air pollution at 1988 levels was responsible for 60,000 deaths a year. The Natural Resources Defense Council sued the EPA [Environmental Protection Agency] for its foot-dragging in implementation of the Clean Air Act, charging that "One hundred million people live in areas of unhealthy air."

This chemical war is not limited to the air. The National Cancer Institute has identified as carcinogens or suspected carcinogens 23 of the chemicals commonly found in our drinking water. Moreover, according to one observer, we are now facing a "new plague—toxic exposure.". . .

The evidence linking *cigarette smoking* and cancer is overwhelming and need not be repeated here. The Centers for Disease Control estimates that cigarettes cause 87 percent of lung cancers—approximately 146,000 in 1992.

Tobacco continues to kill an estimated 400,000 Americans a year. Cigarettes are widely estimated to cause 30 percent of all cancer deaths. . . .

This is enough to expose the hypocrisy of running a full-scale war against heroin (which produces no degenerative disease) while allowing cigarette sales and advertising to flourish. It also should be enough to underscore the point that once again there are threats to our lives much greater than criminal homicide. The legal order does not protect us against them. Indeed, not only does our government fail to protect us against this threat, it promotes it! . . .

Based on the knowledge we have, there can be no doubt that air pollution, tobacco, and food additives amount to a chemical war that makes the crime wave look like a football scrimmage. Even with the most conservative estimates, it is clear that *the death toll in this war is far higher than the number of people killed by criminal homicide!*

Summary

Once again, our investigations lead to the same result. The criminal justice system does not protect us against the gravest threats to life, limb, or possessions. Its definitions of crime are not simply a reflection of the objective dangers that threaten us. The workplace, the medical profession, the air we breathe, and the poverty we refuse to rectify lead to far more human suffering, far more death and disability, and take far more dollars from our pockets than the murders, aggravated assaults, and thefts reported annually by the FBI. What is more, this human suffering is preventable. A government really intent on protecting our well-being could enforce work safety regulations, police the medical profession, require that clean air standards be met, and funnel sufficient money to the poor to alleviate the major disabilities of poverty—but it does not. Instead we hear a lot of cant about law and order and a lot of rant about crime in the streets. It is as if our leaders were not only refusing to protect us from the major threats to our well-being but trying to cover up this refusal by diverting our attention to crime—as if this were the only real threat.

POSTSCRIPT

Is Street Crime More Harmful Than White-Collar Crime?

It is important to consider both the suffering and the wider ramifications caused by crimes. Anderson captures many of these dimensions and gives a full account of the harms of street crime. Today the public is very concerned about street crime, especially wanton violence. However, it seems relatively unconcerned about white-collar crime. Reiman tries to change that perception. By defining many harmful actions by managers and professionals as crimes, he argues that white-collar crime is worse than street crime. He says that more people are killed and injured by "occupational injury or disease, by unnecessary surgery, and by shoddy emergency medical services than by aggravated assault or even homicide!" But are shoddy medical services a crime? In the end, the questions remain: What is a crime? Who are the criminals?

A set of readings that support Reiman's viewpoint is *Corporate Violence: Injury and Death for Profit* edited by Stuart L. Hills (Rowman & Littlefield, 1987); *Unmasking the Crimes of the Powerful: Scrutinizing States and Corporations,* edited by Steve Tombs and Dave Whyte (P. Lang, 2003); Joel Bakan, *The Corporation: The Pathological Pursuit of Profit and Power* (Free Press, 2004); Hazel Croall, *Understanding White Collar Crime* (Open University Press, 2001); Stephen M. Rosoff et el, *Looting, America: Greed, Corruption, Villians, and Victims* (Prentice Hall, 2003) *Readings in White-Collar Crime,* edited by David Shichor et al. (Waveland Press, 2002); and David Weisburd, *White-Collar Crime and Criminal Career* (Cambridge University Press, 2001). Most works on crime deal mainly with theft, drugs, and violence and the injury and fear that they cause including Leslie Williams Reid, *Crime in the City: A Political and Economic Analysis of Urban Crime* (LFB Scholarly Pub., 2003); Walter S. DeKeseredy, *Under Seige: Poverty and Crime in a Public Housing Community* (Lexington Books, 2003); Alex Alverez and Ronet Bachman, *Murder American Style* (Wadsworth, 2003); Claire Valier, *Crime and Punishment in Contemporary Culture* (Routledge, 2004); Matthew B. Robinson, *Why Crime?: An Integrated Systems Theory of Antisocial Behavior* (Pearson, 2004); Ronald B. Flowers, *Male Crime and Deviance: Exploring Its Causes, Dynamics, and Nature* (C.C. Thomas, 2003); and Meda Chesney-Lind and Lisa Pasko, *The Female Offender: Girls, Women, and Crime,* 2nd edition (Sage, 2004). Two works on gangs, which are often connected with violent street crime, are Martin Sanchez Jankowski, *Islands in the Street: Gangs and American Urban Society* (University of California Press, 1991) and Felix M. Padilla, *The Gang as an American Enterprise* (Rutgers University Press, 1992). William J. Bennett, John J. DiIulio, and John P. Walters, in *Body Count: Moral Poverty—and How to Win America's War Against*

Crime and Drugs (Simon & Schuster, 1996), argue that moral poverty is the root cause of crime (meaning street crime). How applicable is this thesis to white-collar crime? One interesting aspect of many corporate, or white-collar, crimes is that they involve crimes of obedience, as discussed in Herman C. Kelman and V. Lee Hamilton, *Crimes of Obedience: Toward a Social Psychology of Authority and Responsibility* (Yale University Press, 1989).

For recent effort to calculate the costs of crime and law enforcement see Mark A. Cohen, *The Costs of Crime and Justice* (Routledge, 2005). Finally, there is a new type of crime that is increasingly troublesome: digital crime and terrorism. This is thoroughly examined by Robert W. Taylor et al., in *Digital Crime and Digital Terrorism* (Pearson/Prentice Hall, 2006).

ISSUE 16

Should Marijuana Be Legalized?

YES: Ethan A. Nadelmann, from "An End to Marijuana Prohibition," *National Review* (July 12, 2004)

NO: John P. Walters, from "No Surrender," *National Review* (July 12, 2004)

ISSUE SUMMARY

YES: Ethan A. Nadelmann, director of the Lindesmith Center, a drug policy research institute, argues that marijuana laws do not make sense. It is doubtful that marijuana should be outlawed since the majority of Americans want it treated like alcohol—illegal for children and regulated for adults. It is not nearly as harmful as a number of legal substances, so why is so much energy and money wasted in enforcing this unpopular law?

NO: John P. Walters, director of the Office of National Drug Control Policy, argues that marijuana is the most socially harmful of the illegal drugs. Its legalization would greatly increase addiction to it.

$\mathbf{A}$ century ago, drugs of every kind were freely available to Americans. Laudanum, a mixture of opium and alcohol, was popularly used as a pain-killer. One drug company even claimed that it was a very useful substance for calming hyperactive children, and the company called it "Mother's Helper." Morphine came into common use during the Civil War. Heroin, developed as a supposedly less-addictive substitute for morphine, began to be marketed at the end of the nineteenth century. By that time, drug paraphernalia could be ordered through Sears and Roebuck catalogues; and Coca-Cola, which contained small quantities of cocaine, had become a popular drink.

Public concerns about addiction and dangerous patent medicines, and an active campaign for drug laws waged by Dr. Harvey Wiley, a chemist in the U.S. Department of Agriculture, led Congress to pass the first national drug regulation act in 1906. The Pure Food and Drug Act required that medicines containing certain drugs, such as opium, must say so on their labels. The Harrison Narcotic Act of 1914 went much further and cut off completely the supply of legal opiates to addicts. Since then, ever-stricter drug laws have been passed by Congress and by state legislatures.

Drug abuse in America again came to the forefront of public discourse during the 1960s, when heroin addiction started growing rapidly in inner city neighborhoods. Also, by the end of the decade, drug experimentation had spread to the middle class—affluent baby boomers who were then attending college. Indeed, certain types of drugs began to be celebrated by some of the leaders of the counterculture. Heroin was still taboo, but other drugs, notably marijuana and LSD (a psychedelic drug), were regarded as harmless and even spiritually transforming. At music festivals like Woodstock in 1969, marijuana and LSD were used openly and associated with love, peace, and heightened sensitivity. Much of this enthusiasm cooled over the next 20 years as baby boomers entered the workforce full-time and began their careers. With the Reagan presidency, the country became more conservative and public attitudes and public policies emphasized law-and-order toughness.

The drug decriminalization issue is especially interesting to sociologists because it raises basic questions about what should be socially sanctioned or approved, what is illegal or legal, and what is immoral or moral. An aspect of the basic value system of America is under review. The process of value change may be taking place in front of our eyes. As part of this debate, Ethan A. Nadelmann argues that the present policy toward marijuana use is harsh and criminalizes behavior that is not harmful or immoral. John P. Walters stands firmly behind the law. He argues that this law saves lives and stops much harm.

YES ↵

Ethan A. Nadelmann

An End To Marijuana Prohibition

Never before have so many Americans supported decriminalizing and even legalizing marijuana. Seventy-two percent say that for simple marijuana possession, people should not be incarcerated but fined: the generally accepted definition of "decriminalization." Even more Americans support making marijuana legal for medical purposes. Support for broader legalization ranges between 25 and 42 percent, depending on how one asks the question. Two of every five Americans—according to a 2003 Zogby poll—say "the government should treat marijuana more or less the same way it treats alcohol: It should regulate it, control it, tax it, and only make it illegal for children."

Close to 100 million Americans—including more than half of those between the ages of 18 and 50—have tried marijuana at least once. Military and police recruiters often have no choice but to ignore past marijuana use by job seekers. The public apparently feels the same way about presidential and other political candidates. Al Gore, Bill Bradley, and John Kerry all say they smoked pot in days past. So did Bill Clinton, with his notorious caveat. George W. Bush won't deny he did. And ever more political, business, religious, intellectual, and other leaders plead guilty as well.

The debate over ending marijuana prohibition simmers just below the surface of mainstream politics, crossing ideological and partisan boundaries. Marijuana is no longer the symbol of Sixties rebellion and Seventies permissiveness, and it's not just liberals and libertarians who say it should be legal, as William F. Buckley Jr. has demonstrated better than anyone. As director of the country's leading drug-policy-reform organization, I've had countless conversations with police and prosecutors, judges and politicians, and hundreds of others who quietly agree that the criminalization of marijuana is costly, foolish, and destructive. What's most needed now is principled conservative leadership. Buckley has led the way, and New Mexico's former governor, Gary Johnson, spoke out courageously while in office. How about others?

A Systemic Overreaction

Marijuana prohibition is unique among American criminal laws. No other law is both enforced so widely and harshly and yet deemed unnecessary by such a substantial portion of the populace.

From *National Review*, July 12, 2004, pp. 28–33. Copyright © 2004 by Ethan Nadelmann. Reprinted by permission of the author. www.drugpolicy.org

Police make about 700,000 arrests per year for marijuana offenses. That's almost the same number as are arrested each year for cocaine, heroin, methamphetamine, Ecstasy, and all other illicit drugs combined. Roughly 600,000, or 87 percent, of marijuana arrests are for nothing more than possession of small amounts. Millions of Americans have never been arrested or convicted of any criminal offense except this. Enforcing marijuana laws costs an estimated $10-15 billion in direct costs alone.

Punishments range widely across the country, from modest fines to a few days in jail to many years in prison. Prosecutors often contend that no one goes to prison for simple possession— but tens, perhaps hundreds, of thousands of people on probation and parole are locked up each year because their urine tested positive for marijuana or because they were picked up in possession of a joint. Alabama currently locks up people convicted three times of marijuana *possession* for 15 years to life. There are probably— no firm estimates exist—100,000 Americans behind bars tonight for one marijuana offense or another. And even for those who don't lose their freedom, simply being arrested can be traumatic and costly. A parent's marijuana use can be the basis for taking away her children and putting them in foster care. Foreign-born residents of the U.S. can be deported for a marijuana offense no matter how long they have lived in this country, no matter if their children are U. S. citizens, and no matter how long they have been legally employed. More than half the states revoke or suspend driver's licenses of people arrested for marijuana possession even though they were not driving at the time of arrest. The federal Higher Education Act prohibits student loans to young people convicted of any drug offense; all other criminal offenders remain eligible.

This is clearly an overreaction on the part of government. No drug is perfectly safe, and every psychoactive drug can be used in ways that are problematic. The federal government has spent billions of dollars on advertisements and anti-drug programs that preach the dangers of marijuana—that it's a gateway drug, and addictive in its own right, and dramatically more potent than it used to be, and responsible for all sorts of physical and social diseases as well as international terrorism. But the government has yet to repudiate the 1988 finding of the Drug Enforcement Administration's own administrative law judge, Francis Young, who concluded after extensive testimony that "marijuana in its natural form is one of the safest therapeutically active substances known to man."

Is marijuana a gateway drug? Yes, insofar as most Americans try marijuana before they try other illicit drugs. But no, insofar as the vast majority of Americans who have tried marijuana have never gone on to try other illegal drugs, much less get in trouble with them, and most have never even gone on to become regular or problem marijuana users. Trying to reduce heroin addiction by preventing marijuana use, it's been said, is like trying to reduce motorcycle fatalities by cracking down on bicycle riding. If marijuana did not exist, there's little reason to believe that there would be less drug abuse in the U.S.; indeed, its role would most likely be filled by a more dangerous substance.

Is marijuana dramatically more potent today? There's certainly a greater variety of high-quality marijuana available today than 30 years ago. But anyone who smoked marijuana in the 1970s and 1980s can recall smoking pot that was just as strong as anything available today. What's more, one needs to take only a few puffs of higher-potency pot to get the desired effect, so there's less wear and tear on the lungs.

Is marijuana addictive? Yes, it can be, in that some people use it to excess, in ways that are problematic for themselves and those around them, and find it hard to stop. But marijuana may well be the least addictive and least damaging of all commonly used psychoactive drugs, including many that are now legal. Most people who smoke marijuana never become dependent. Withdrawal symptoms pale compared with those from other drugs. No one has ever died from a marijuana overdose, which cannot be said of most other drugs. Marijuana is not associated with violent behavior and only minimally with reckless sexual behavior. And even heavy marijuana smokers smoke only a fraction of what cigarette addicts smoke. Lung cancers involving only marijuana are rare.

The government's most recent claim is that marijuana abuse accounts for more people entering treatment than any other illegal drug. That shouldn't be surprising, given that tens of millions of Americans smoke marijuana while only a few million use all other illicit drugs. But the claim is spurious nonetheless. Few Americans who enter "treatment" for marijuana are addicted. Fewer than one in five people entering drug treatment for marijuana do so voluntarily. More than half were referred by the criminal-justice system. They go because they got caught with a joint or failed a drug test at school or work (typically for having smoked marijuana days ago, not for being impaired), or because they were caught by a law-enforcement officer—and attending a marijuana "treatment" program is what's required to avoid expulsion, dismissal, or incarceration. Many traditional drug-treatment programs shamelessly participate in this charade to preserve a profitable and captive client stream.

Even those who recoil at the "nanny state" telling adults what they can or cannot sell to one another often make an exception when it comes to marijuana—to "protect the kids." This is a bad joke, as any teenager will attest. The criminalization of marijuana for adults has not prevented young people from having better access to marijuana than anyone else. Even as marijuana's popularity has waxed and waned since the 1970s, one statistic has remained constant: More than 80 percent of high-school students report it's easy to get. Meanwhile, the government's exaggerations and outright dishonesty easily backfire. For every teen who refrains from trying marijuana because it's illegal (for adults), another is tempted by its status as "forbidden fruit." Many respond to the lies about marijuana by disbelieving warnings about more dangerous drugs. So much for protecting the kids by criminalizing the adults.

The Medical Dimension

The debate over medical marijuana obviously colors the broader debate over marijuana prohibition. Marijuana's medical efficacy is no longer in serious dispute. Its use as a medicine dates back thousands of years. Pharmaceutical products containing marijuana's central ingredient, THC, are legally sold in the U.S., and more are emerging. Some people find the pill form satisfactory, and others consume it in teas or baked products. Most find smoking the easiest and most effective way to consume this unusual medicine, but non-smoking consumption methods, notably vaporizers, are emerging.

Federal law still prohibits medical marijuana. But every state ballot initiative to legalize medical marijuana has been approved, often by wide margins—in California, Washington, Oregon, Alaska, Colorado, Nevada, Maine, and Washington, D.C. State legislatures in Vermont, Hawaii, and Maryland have followed suit, and many others are now considering their own medical-marijuana bills—including New York, Connecticut, Rhode Island, and Illinois. . . .

Majorities in virtually every state in the country would vote, if given the chance, to legalize medical marijuana. . . . State and local governments are increasingly involved in trying to regulate medical marijuana, notwithstanding the federal prohibition. California, Oregon, Hawaii, Alaska, Colorado, and Nevada have created confidential medical-marijuana patient registries, which protect bona fide patients and caregivers from arrest or prosecution. Some municipal governments are now trying to figure out how to regulate production and distribution. In California, where dozens of medical-marijuana programs now operate openly, with tacit approval by local authorities, some program directors are asking to be licensed and regulated. Many state and local authorities, including law enforcement, favor this but are intimidated by federal threats to arrest and prosecute them for violating federal law.

The drug czar and DEA spokespersons recite the mantra that "there is no such thing as medical marijuana," but the claim is so specious on its face that it clearly undermines federal credibility. The federal government currently provides marijuana—from its own production site in Mississippi—to a few patients who years ago were recognized by the courts as bona fide patients. . . .

What support there is for marijuana prohibition would likely end quickly absent the billions of dollars spent annually by federal and other governments to prop it up. All those anti-marijuana ads pretend to be about reducing drug abuse, but in fact their basic purpose is sustaining popular support for the war on marijuana. What's needed now are conservative politicians willing to say enough is enough: Tens of billions of taxpayer dollars down the drain each year. People losing their jobs, their property, and their freedom for nothing more than possessing a joint or growing a few marijuana plants. And all for what? To send a message? To keep pretending that we're protecting our children? Alcohol Prohibition made a lot more sense than marijuana prohibition does today—and it, too, was a disaster. . . .

The Future of An Illusion

I am grateful for John Walters's ill-considered rejoinder to my article, mostly because it demonstrates so well the disregard for science, lack of intellectual rigor, and passion for partisan insult that characterize the drug czar and his failure of a drug-control policy. (My original article, with extensive footnotes, can be found at . . .

Let's start with Walters's paragraph on medical marijuana, which might best be summarized as "Who are you going to believe: me or your own lying eyes?" Dozens of scientific studies now confirm the medical utility of marijuana. (Interested readers can go to the National Library of Medicine site . . . and enter the search term "therapeutic cannabis.") Thousands of doctors have recommended marijuana to tens of thousands of patients in the ten states whose laws allow such recommendations. A pharmaceutical product containing marijuana's essential ingredient, THC, is FDA-approved and widely prescribed—but scientific studies as well as thousands of doctor and patient reports indicate that most patients find it less effective than marijuana itself. In Canada, marijuana for medicinal purposes is provided by the government. And, as I noted in my original article, the same is true in this country, with a handful of patients still receiving a monthly supply of joints from the government's marijuana-production facility in Mississippi.

Marijuana remains in Schedule I for reasons that are entirely political, not scientific. In 1988, the DEA's administrative-law judge, Francis Young, recommended after extensive hearings that marijuana be placed in Schedule II, noting both its medicinal value and its relatively low potential for abuse compared with other drugs. That recommendation was rejected by the agency's director on political grounds. Consider that Schedule II, a less restrictive category, includes cocaine, amphetamine, and various opioid drugs responsible for thousands of overdose fatalities each year. No overdose fatality has ever been attributed to marijuana.

One might say that Walters's views on medical marijuana are still stuck in the Dark Ages—except that evidence keeps emerging of marijuana's having been used for medicinal purposes in the so-called Dark Ages and even earlier.

With respect to the broader issue of marijuana policy, Walters's broadside essentially amounts to a hodgepodge of mistakes, distortions, and crude attacks. He ignores overwhelming evidence that most people who smoke marijuana do no harm to their health. He implies that alcohol's greater popularity relative to marijuana is mostly a function of marijuana prohibition, ignoring historical and other evidence to the contrary. He slips back and forth between claims about marijuana and claims about more dangerous illicit drugs, presumably hoping to score a few cheap debating points. He analogizes simple possession of a marijuana joint to drunk driving.

From *The National Review*, September 21, 2004, pp. 42–43. Copyright © 2004 by Ethan Nadelmann. Reprinted by permission.

"The truth is," Walters says, "there are laws against marijuana because marijuana is harmful." Consider the implications of this statement. Does he mean to imply that anything that is harmful—or as harmful as marijuana—should be prohibited? The list would be endless given the relative safety margin of marijuana compared with thousands of legal drugs, food products, sports activities, and means of transportation. His criteria for prohibition, applied more broadly, represent not a conservative vision but a potentially totalitarian one, in which the nanny state criminalizes whatever offends its tastes and prejudices.

"A case can be made," Walters says, "that marijuana does the most social harm of any illegal drug." That is an extraordinary claim. Misuse of cocaine, methamphetamine, heroin, and illegally diverted pharmaceutical drugs results in tens of thousands of deaths each year. Many people addicted to these drugs steal to support their habits and some become violent while under the influence. Hundreds of thousands have contracted HIV/AIDS, hepatitis, and other infectious diseases. Keep in mind, too, that alcohol is an illegal drug for people under the age of 21; its misuse is powerfully associated with injuries and fatalities on the roads as well as violent and reckless sexual behavior. Marijuana can be harmful in all sorts of ways, as I noted in my article, but it is absurd to equate its harms with those of other illegal drugs.

"In several states," Walters notes, "marijuana smoking exceeds tobacco smoking among young people." This may be the ultimate indictment of marijuana prohibition. Young people have better access to marijuana than anyone else, notwithstanding decades of criminal enforcement, and many are tempted by its status as a "forbidden fruit." But consumption of cigarettes, which remains legal for adults, has dropped dramatically among young people over the past few decades. If ever a case could be made for preferring a policy of honest education and high taxation over zero tolerance and criminal prohibition, this is it. (Keep in mind that criminal prohibition represents the ultimate high-tax policy, except that the bloated "prohibition tax" benefits black-market entrepreneurs rather than the public treasury.)

The real question here is not what one thinks of marijuana, or whether one wishes it could be eradicated from our society, but rather what the government should do about it. Even as Walters grossly exaggerates marijuana's harms, he ignores entirely the harms occasioned by marijuana prohibition: billions of taxpayer dollars down the drain each year; 700,000 people arrested annually; private properties confiscated; and other basic freedoms violated by government agents futilely trying to enforce paternalistic laws. Millions of Americans who don't like marijuana nonetheless support an end to marijuana prohibition for precisely these reasons. When a government prohibition proves ineffective, unreasonably costly, and substantially more harmful than the supposed evil it was intended to cure, that prohibition merits repeal—just as alcohol prohibition did 70 years ago.

Let me offer, finally, a few words regarding Walters's style of argumentation and repeated attacks on George Soros. It seems a cheap shot to target George Soros in the pages of NATIONAL REVIEW for supporting me and the growing drug-policy reform movement. Walters might just as well have insulted William F. Buckley Jr., Richard Brookhiser, Milton Friedman, George Shultz,

Grover Norquist, Congressman Dana Rohrabacher, former New Mexico Governor Gary Johnson, and dozens of other prominent Republicans and conservatives who have criticized the war on drugs and supported alternative policies, including an end to marijuana prohibition.

The principled conservative believes in restricting the reach of government into the lives and homes of its citizens. He respects the rights of states and local communities to regulate their own affairs free from federal overreach. He rejects wasteful government expenditures. And he requires intellectual rigor in refuting the arguments of opponents and advancing his own views. It should therefore come as no surprise that so many principled conservatives oppose the war on drugs.

But there's another point worth making about George Soros. There is probably no private individual who played a greater role than George Soros in hastening the downfall of Communism in Central and Eastern Europe, and in trying to assist the subsequent transformation of those states into democratic, capitalist open societies. He has contributed close to $2 billion over the past two decades toward this end. His commitment to this goal was motivated by many of the same principles that readers of NATIONAL REVIEW hold dear.

Soros saw in America's drug war many of the same political and intellectual traits that had made him hate Communism and fascism: political indoctrination substituted for education; bureaucratic apparatchiks disfiguring scientific evidence to serve the state's agenda; massive deployment of police agents and their informants in ever more intrusive ways; politicians mouthing stupid clichés without the slightest hint of embarrassment; official spokesmen responding to substantive criticisms of government policy not in kind but instead by impugning the motivations and characters of their critics; and the arrest and incarceration of millions for engaging in personal tastes and vices, as well as capitalist transactions, prohibited by the state for reasons it can no longer clearly recall.

John Walters needs to get out of his drug-war bunker and venture beyond the closed venues in which he attacks his critics without ever daring to engage us directly. The vitality of our democracy depends in part on the willingness of government officials to defend their policies in open and honest debate, but Walters has fled from one opportunity after another. If the federal government's drug policy is defensible, he should dare to defend it, and defend it honestly. And if he's unable or unwilling to defend it against informed critics, it's time for him to resign or be replaced.

John P. Walters

No Surrender: The Drug War Saves Lives

The prospect of a drug-control policy that includes regulated legalization has enticed intelligent commentators for years, no doubt because it offers, on the surface, a simple solution to a complex problem. Reasoned debate about the real consequences usually dampens enthusiasm, leaving many erstwhile proponents feeling mugged by reality; not so Ethan Nadelmann, whose version of marijuana legalization ("An End to Marijuana Prohibition," NR, July 12) fronts for a worldwide political movement, funded by billionaire George Soros, to embed the use of all drugs as acceptable policy. Unfortunately for Nadelmann, his is not a serious argument. Nor is it attached to the facts.

To take but one example, Nadelmann's article alleges the therapeutic value of smoked marijuana by claiming: "Marijuana's medical efficacy is no longer in serious dispute." But he never substantiates this sweeping claim. In fact, smoked marijuana, a Schedule I controlled substance (Schedule I is the government's most restrictive category), has no medical value and a high risk of abuse. The Food and Drug Administration notes that marijuana has not been approved for any indication, that scientific studies do not support claims of marijuana's usefulness as a medication, and that there is a lack of accepted safety standards for the use of smoked marijuana.

The FDA has also expressed concern that marijuana use may worsen the condition of those for whom it is prescribed. Legalization advocates such as Nadelmann simply ignore these facts and continue their promotion, the outcome of which will undermine drug-prevention and treatment efforts, and put genuinely sick patients at risk.

The legalization scheme is also unworkable. A government-sanctioned program to produce, distribute, and tax an addictive intoxicant creates more problems than it solves.

First, drug use would increase. No student of supply-and demand curves can doubt that marijuana would become cheaper, more readily available, and more widespread than it currently is when all legal risk is removed and demand is increased by marketing.

Second, legalization will not eliminate marijuana use among young people any more than legalizing alcohol eliminated underage drinking. If you think we can tax marijuana to where it costs more than the average teenager can afford, think again. Marijuana is a plant that can be readily grown by anyone. If law enforcement is unable to distinguish "legal" marijuana from illegal, growing marijuana at home becomes a low-cost (and low-risk) way to supply your neighborhood and friends. "Official marijuana" will not drive out the black market, nor will it eliminate the need for tough law enforcement. It will only make the task more difficult.

In debating legalization, the burden is to consider the costs and benefits both of keeping strict control over dangerous substances and of making them more accessible. The Soros position consistently overstates the benefits of legalizing marijuana and understates the risks. At the same time, drug promoters ignore the current benefits of criminalization while dramatically overstating the costs.

Government-sanctioned marijuana would be a bonanza for trial lawyers (the government may wake up to find that it has a liability for the stoned trucker who plows into a school bus). Health-care and employment-benefits costs will increase (there is plenty of evidence that drug-using employees are less productive, and less healthy), while more marijuana use will further burden our education system.

The truth is, there are laws against marijuana because marijuana is harmful. With every year that passes, medical research discovers greater dangers from smoking it, from links to serious mental illness to the risk of cancer, and even dangers from in utero exposure.

In fact, given the new levels of potency and the sheer prevalence of marijuana (the number of users contrasted with the number of those using cocaine or heroin), a case can be made that marijuana does the most social harm of any illegal drug. Marijuana is currently the leading cause of treatment need: Nearly two-thirds of those who meet the psychiatric criteria for needing substance-abuse treatment do so because of marijuana use. For youth, the harmful effects of marijuana use now exceed those of all other drugs combined. Remarkably, over 40 percent of youths who are current marijuana smokers meet the criteria for abuse or dependency. In several states, marijuana smoking exceeds tobacco smoking among young people, while marijuana has become more important than alcohol as a factor in treatment for teenagers.

Legalizers assert that the justice system arrests 700,000 marijuana users a year, suggesting that an oppressive system is persecuting the innocent. This charge is a fraud. Less than 1 percent of those in prison for drug violations are low-level marijuana offenders, and many of these have "pled down" to the marijuana violation in the face of other crimes. The vast majority of those in prison on drug convictions are true criminals involved in drug trafficking, repeat offenses, or violent crime.

The value of legal control is that it enables judicial discretion over offenders, diverting minor offenders who need it into treatment while retaining the authority to guard against the violent and incorrigible. Further, where the sanction and supervision of a court are present, the likelihood of recovery is greatly increased. Removing legal sanction endangers the public and fails to help the offender.

Proponents of legalization argue that because approximately half of the referrals for treatment are from the criminal-justice system, it is the law and not marijuana that is the problem. Yet nearly half of all referrals for alcohol treatment likewise derive from judicial intervention, and nobody argues that drunk drivers do not really have a substance-abuse problem, or that it is the courts that are creating the perception of alcoholism. Marijuana's role in emergency-room cases has tripled in the past decade. Yet no judge is sending people to emergency rooms. They are there because of the dangers of the drug, which have greatly increased because of soaring potency.

Legalization advocates suggest that youth will reduce their smoking because of this new potency. But when tobacco companies were accused of deliberately "spiking" their product with nicotine, no one saw this as a public-health gesture intended to reduce cigarette consumption. The deliberate effort to increase marijuana potency (and market it to younger initiates) should be seen for what it is—a steeply increased threat of addiction.

Proponents of legalization argue that the fact that 100 million Americans admit on surveys that they have tried marijuana in their lifetime demonstrates the public's acceptance of the drug. But the pertinent number tells a different story. There are approximately 15 million Americans, mostly young people, who report using marijuana on a monthly basis. That is, only about 6 percent of the population age twelve and over use marijuana on a regular basis.

To grasp the impact of legal control, contrast that figure with the number of current alcohol users (approximately 120 million). Regular alcohol use is eight times that of marijuana, and a large part of the difference is a function of laws against marijuana use. Under legalization, which would decrease the cost (now a little-noticed impediment to the young) and eliminate the legal risk, it is certain that the number of users would increase. Can anyone seriously argue that American democracy would be strengthened by more marijuana smoking?

The law itself is our safeguard, and it works. Far from being a hopeless battle, the drug-control tide is turning against marijuana. We have witnessed an 11 percent reduction in youth marijuana use over the last two years, while perceptions of risk have soared.

Make no mistake about what is going on here: Drug legalization is a worldwide movement, the goal of which is to make drug consumption—including heroin, cocaine, and methamphetamine—an acceptable practice. Using the discourse of rights without responsibilities, the effort strives to establish an entitlement to addictive substances. The impact will be devastating.

Drug legalizers will not be satisfied with a limited distribution of medical marijuana, nor will they stop at legal marijuana for sale in convenience stores. Their goal is clearly identifiable: tolerated addiction. It is a travesty to suggest, as Ethan Nadelmann has done, that it is consistent with conservative principles to abandon those who could be treated for their addiction, to create a situation in which government both condones and is the agent of drug distribution, and to place in the hands of the state the power to grant or not grant access to an addictive substance. This is not a conservative vision. But it is the goal of George Soros.

POSTSCRIPT

Should Marijuana Be Legalized?

The analogy often cited by proponents of drug legalization is the ill-fated attempt to ban the sale of liquor in the United States, which lasted from 1919 to 1933. Prohibition has been called "an experiment noble in purpose," but it was an experiment that greatly contributed to the rise of organized crime. The repeal of Prohibition brought about an increase in liquor consumption and alcoholism, but it also deprived organized crime of an important source of income. Would marijuana legalization similarly strike a blow at the drug dealers? Possibly, and such a prospect is obviously appealing. But would marijuana legalization also greatly increase the problems that Walters cites?

Much of the literature on this issue deals with drug laws and drug use generally. For a comprehensive overview of the history, effects, and prevention of drug use, see Mike Gray, *Drug Crazy: How We Got Into This Mess and How We Can Get Out* (Random House, 1998). For a textbook treatment of the drug issue, see Eric Goode, *Drugs in American Society 7th Edition* (McGraw-Hill, 2008). For a balanced review of drug policies, see Douglas Husak and Peter de Marneffe, *The Legalization of Drugs* (Cambridge University Press, 2005). Terry Williams describes the goings-on in a crackhouse in *Crackhouse: Notes From the End of the Zone* (Addison-Wesley, 1992). Works that examine the connection of drugs with predatory crime include Charles Bowden, *Down by the River: Drugs, Money, Murder, and Family* (Simon & Schuster, 2002); Philip Bean, *Drugs and Crime* (Willan, 2002); and Pierre Kipp, *Political Economy of Illegal Drugs* (Routledge, 2004). Works that advocate or debate legalizing drugs are Gary L. Fisher, *Rethinking Our War on Drugs: Candid Talk About Controversial Issues* (Praeger, 2006); Douglas N. Husak, *Legalize This!: The Case for Decriminalizing Drugs* (Verso, 2002); Jacob Sullum, *Saying Yes: In Defense of Drug Use* (J.P. Tarcher, 2003); Eric Goode, *Between Politics and Reason: The Drug Legalization Debate* (St. Martin's Press, 1997); and *The Drug Legalization Debate*, edited by James A. Inciardi (Sage, 1999). On legalizing marijuana, see Rudolph Gerber, *Legalizing Marijuana: Drug Policy Reform and Prohibition Politics* (Praeger, 2004). William O. Walker III, ed., *Drug Control Policy* (Pennsylvania State University Press, 1992), critically evaluates drug policies from historical and comparative perspectives.

ISSUE 17

Does the Threat of Terrorism Warrant Curtailment of Civil Liberties?

YES: Robert H. Bork, from "Liberty and Terrorism: Avoiding a Police State," *Current* (December 2003)

NO: Larry Cox, from "The War on Human Rights," *Vital Speeches of the Day* (April 2007)

ISSUE SUMMARY

YES: Robert H. Bork, senior fellow at the American Enterprise Institute, recognizes that the values of security and civil rights must be balanced while we are at war against terrorism, but he is concerned that some commentators would hamstring security forces in order to protect nonessential civil rights. For example, to not use ethnic profiling of Muslim or Arab persons would reduce the effectiveness of security forces, while holding suspected terrorists without filing charges or allowing them council would increase their effectiveness.

NO: Larry Cox, Executive Director of Amnesty International USA, accuses the United States of making "the most serious attack on the idea of human rights" today. The record of rights abuses include torture and degrading treatment, suspension of habeas corpus, denial of legal representation, and secret detention.

America was very optimistic at the end of the twentieth century. The cold war had ended, and the 1990s brought the longest economic boom in American history. The only danger on the horizon was the Y2K problem, and that vanished like the mist. September 11, 2001, changed everything. Now Americans live in fear of terrorism, and this fear led the government to launch two wars—the first against the Taliban and Al Qaeda in Afghanistan and the second against Saddam Hussein's regime in Iraq. The United States has also aggressively pursued international terrorists throughout the world and pushed many countries to aid in the capture of known terrorists. All of these efforts have been quite successful in specific strategic objectives but not in reducing our fear of terrorism. The number of terrorists dedicated to mass terrorist events in America has even increased in the past five years, because hatred of America has increased greatly.

The German sociologist and political leader Ralph Dahrendorf, who was a child when Hitler came to power in his country, said that fear is antithetical to democracy. In fearful times, the public wants the government to do whatever it must to solve the crisis, whether the crisis is economic failure, social disorder, or danger from criminals, terrorists, or foreign powers. Some civil rights are often the first things sacrificed. During the economic crisis of the 1930s, Germany turned to Hitler and Italy turned to Mussolini. Democracy was sacrificed for the hope of a more prosperous economy.

Fortunately, during the Great Depression the United States turned to President Franklin D. Roosevelt, not to a dictator. But in other dangerous times our history has proven to be less democratic. In the 1860s, President Abraham Lincoln suspended habeas corpus and detained hundreds of suspected confederate sympathizers. The chief justice of the Supreme Court ruled Lincoln's suspension of habeas corpus as unconstitutional, but Lincoln ignored the ruling. There were widespread violations of civil liberties during World War I and again during World War II, including the shameful internment of Japanese-American citizens in concentration camps. Civil liberties were diminished again during the McCarthy era in the 1950s, a time when a witch-hunt atmosphere occurred due to anti-communist hysteria. American history caused civil rights advocates to become quite concerned when Attorney General John Ashcroft said after September 11th, "We should strengthen our laws to increase the ability of the Department of Justice and its component agencies to identify, prevent, and punish terrorism." Of course he is right, but the question is whether the government will go too far in policing us and whether the newly authorized powers will be badly abused. Senator Joseph Biden, Jr. remarked that "if we alter our basic freedom, our civil liberties, change the way we function as a democratic society, then we will have lost the war before it has begun in earnest." As of this writing, the Patriot Act has been passed and expanded in an attempt to give the government the power it needs to better protect citizens from terrorism. Does this Act go too far? Will its results be shameful?

One of the great aspects of America is our freedom to debate issues such as this one. This gives us the hope that through passionate and/or reasoned dialogue, we will work toward the right balance between the values of security and civil rights. The articles that have been selected to debate this issue are both passionate and well-reasoned. Robert H. Bork discusses many of the provisions of the Patriot Act and explains how useful they are in the war against terrorism. He also argues that the Act contains safeguards, such as judicial approval, that should adequately protect against abuse. Larry Cox is greatly distressed by the current laws that have supported the incarceration and torture of many hundreds of people for years without charging them with crimes. Our civil liberties are under attack.

YES ⬅

Robert H. Bork

Liberty and Terrorism: Avoiding a Police State

When a nation faces deadly attacks on its citizens at home and abroad, it is only reasonable to expect that its leaders will take appropriate measures to increase security. And, since security inevitably means restrictions, it is likewise only reasonable to expect a public debate over the question of how much individual liberty should be sacrificed for how much individual and national safety.

That, however, is not the way our national debate has shaped up. From the public outcry over the Bush administration's measures to combat terrorism, one might suppose that America is well on the way to becoming a police state. A full-page newspaper ad by the American Civil Liberties Union (ACLU), for instance, informs us that the Patriot Act, the administration's major security initiative, goes "far beyond fighting terrorism" and has "allowed government agents to violate our civil liberties—tapping deep into the private lives of innocent Americans." According to Laura W. Murphy, director of the ACLU's Washington office, Attorney General John Ashcroft has "clearly abused his power," "systematically erod[ing] free-speech rights, privacy rights, and due-process rights." From the libertarian Left, Anthony Lewis in the *New York Times Magazine* has charged President Bush with undermining safeguards for the accused in a way that Lewis "did not believe was possible in our country," while from the libertarian Right, William Safire has protested the administration's effort to realize "the supersnoop's dream" of spying on all Americans.

The charge that our civil liberties are being systematically dismantled must be taken seriously. America has, in the past, overreacted to perceived security threats; the Palmer raids after World War I and the internment of Japanese-Americans during World War II are the most notorious examples. Are we once again jeopardizing the liberties of all Americans while also inflicting particular harm on Muslims in our midst? . . .

Security and Ethnic Profiling

According to Ibrahim Hooper, a spokesman for the Council on American-Islamic Relations, American Muslims have already lost many of their civil rights. "All Muslims are now suspects," Hooper has protested bitterly.

The most salient outward sign of this is said to be the ethnic profiling that now occurs routinely in this country, particularly at airports but elsewhere as well—a form of discrimination widely considered to be self-evidently evil.

For most of us, airport security checks are the only first-hand experience we have with counter-measures to terrorism, and their intrusiveness and often seeming pointlessness have, not surprisingly, led many people to question such measures in general. But minor vexations are not the same as an assault on fundamental liberties. As for ethnic profiling, that is another matter, and a serious one. It is serious, however, not because it is rampant but because it does not exist.

That profiling is wicked *per se* is an idea that seems to have originated in connection with police work, when black civil-rights spokesmen began to allege that officers were relying on race as the sole criterion for suspecting someone of criminal activity. Profiling, in other words, equaled racism by definition. Yet, as Heather MacDonald has demonstrated in *Are Cops Racist?*, the idea rests on a false assumption—namely, that crime rates are constant across every racial and ethnic component of our society. Thus, if blacks, who make up 11 percent of the population, are subject to 20 percent of all police stops on a particular highway, racial bias must be at fault.

But the truth is that (to stick to this particular example) blacks do speed more than whites, a fact that in itself justifies a heightened awareness of skin color as one of several criteria in police work. Of course, there is no excuse for blatant racism; but, as MacDonald meticulously documents in case after case around the country, there is by and large no evidence that police have relied excessively on ethnic or racial profiling in conducting their normal investigations.

The War on Terror

The stigma attached to profiling where it hardly exists has perversely carried over to an area where it should exist but does not: the war against terrorism. This war, let us remember, pre-dates 9/11. According to MacDonald, when a commission on aviation security headed by then-Vice President Al Gore was considering a system that would take into account a passenger's national origin and ethnicity—by far the best predictors of terrorism—both the Arab lobby and civil libertarians exploded in indignation. The commission duly capitulated—which is why the final Computer-Assisted Passenger Prescreening System (CAPPS) specified that such criteria as national origin, religion, ethnicity, and even gender were not to be taken into consideration.

This emasculated system did manage, even so, to pinpoint two of the September 11 terrorists on the day of their gruesome flight, but prevented any action beyond searching their luggage. As MacDonald points out, had the system been allowed to utilize all relevant criteria, followed up by personal searches, the massacres might well have been averted.

Ironically, it is the very randomness of the new security checks that has generated so much skepticism about their efficacy. Old ladies, children, Catholic priests—all have been subject to searches of San Quentin-like thoroughness despite being beyond rational suspicion. According to the authorities, this randomness is itself a virtue, preventing would-be terrorists from easily predicting who or what will draw attention. But it is far more probable that frisking unlikely persons has nothing to do with security and everything to do with political correctness. Frightening as the prospect of terrorism may be, it pales, in the minds of many officials, in comparison with the prospect of being charged with racism.

Ethnic Profiling

Registration, Tracking, and Detention of Visitors

Ethnic Profiling, it is charged, is also responsible for the unjustified harassment and occasional detention of Arab and Muslim visitors to the United States. This is said to be an egregious violation not only of the rights of such persons but of America's traditional hospitality toward foreign visitors.

An irony here is that the procedures being deplored are hardly new, although they are being imposed with greater rigor. The current system has its roots in the 1950's in the first of a series of statutes ordering the Immigration and Naturalization Service (INS) to require aliens from countries listed as state sponsors of terrorism, as well as from countries with a history of breeding terrorists, to register and be fingerprinted, to state where they will be while in the U.S., and to notify the INS when they change address or leave the country.

Historically, however, the INS has been absurdly lax about fulfilling its mandate. When a visitor with illegal status—someone, for example, thought to have overstayed a student visa or committed a crime—is apprehended, the usual practice of immigration judges has been to release him upon the posting of a bond, unless he is designated a "person of interest." In the latter case, he is held for deportation or criminal prosecution and given a handbook detailing his rights, which include access to an attorney. It is a matter of dispute whether the proceedings before an immigration judge can be closed, as authorities prefer, or whether they must be open; the Supreme Court has so far declined to review the practice.

The procedures are now being adhered to more strictly, and this is what has given rise to accusations of ethnic or religious profiling. But such charges are as beside the point as in the case of domestic police work, if not more so. There is indeed a correlation between detention and ethnicity or religion, but that is because most of the countries identified as state sponsors or breeders of terrorism are, in fact, populated by Muslims and Arabs.

Stricter enforcement has also led to backlogs, as the Justice Department has proved unable to deal expeditiously with the hundreds of illegal immigrants rounded up in the aftermath of September 11. A report by the department's inspector general, released in early June, found "significant problems" with the processing of these cases. There is no question that, in an ideal world, many of them would have been handled with greater dispatch, but it is also hardly surprising that problems that have long plagued our criminal justice system should reappear in the context of the fight against terrorism. In any case, the department has already taken steps to ameliorate matters. The only way for the problems to vanish would be for the authorities to cease doing their proper job; we have tried that route, and lived to regret it.

Discovery, Detention, and Prosecution of Suspected Terrorists

According to civil libertarians, the constitutional safeguards that normally protect individuals suspected of criminal activity have been destroyed in the case of persons suspected of links with terrorism. This accusation reflects an ignorance both of the Constitution and of long-established limits on the criminal-justice system.

History

Prior to 1978, and dating back at least to World War II, attorneys general of the United States routinely authorized warrantless FBI surveillance, wire taps, and break-ins for national-security purposes. Such actions were taken pursuant to authority delegated by the President as commander-in-chief of the armed forces and as the officer principally responsible for the conduct of foreign affairs. The practice was justified because obtaining a warrant in each disparate case resulted in inconsistent standards and also posed unacceptable risks. (In one notorious instance, a judge had read aloud in his courtroom from highly classified material submitted to him by the government; even under more conscientious judges, clerks, secretaries, and others were becoming privy to secret materials.)

Attorneys general were never entirely comfortable with these warrantless searches, whose legality had never been confirmed by the Supreme Court. The solution in 1978 was the enactment of the Foreign Intelligence Surveillance Act (FISA). Henceforth, sitting district court judges would conduct secret hearings to approve or disapprove government applications for surveillance.

A further complication arose in the 1980's, however, when, by consensus of the Department of Justice and the FISA court, it was decided that the act authorized the gathering of foreign intelligence only for its own sake ("primary purpose"), and not for the possible criminal prosecution of any foreign agent. The effect was to erect a "wall" between the gathering of intelligence and the enforcement of criminal laws. But last year, the Foreign Intelligence Surveillance Court of Review held that the act did not, in fact, preclude or limit the government's use of that information in such prosecutions. In the opinion of the court, arresting and prosecuting terrorist agents or spies might well be the best way to inhibit their activities, as the threat of prosecution might persuade an agent to cooperate with the government, or enable the government to "turn" him.

When the wall came down, Justice Department prosecutors were able to learn what FBI intelligence officials already knew. This contributed to the arrest of Sami al-Arian, a professor at the University of South Florida, on charges that he raised funds for Palestinian Islamic Jihad and its suicide bombers. Once the evidence could be put at the disposition of prosecutors, al-Arian's longstanding claim that he was being persecuted by the authorities as an innocent victim of anti-Muslim prejudice was shattered.

Treatment of Captured Terrorists

According, by depriving certain captured individuals of access to lawyers, and by holding them without filing charges, the government is violating the Geneva Convention's protections of lawful combatants or prisoners of war. This is nonsense.

Lawful Combatants

Four criteria must be met to qualify a person as a lawful combatant. He must be under the command of a person responsible for his subordinates; wear a fixed distinctive emblem recognizable at a distance; carry arms openly; and conduct operations in accordance with the laws and customs of war. The men the United States has captured and detained so far do not meet these criteria.

The government's policy is as follows: if a captured unlawful enemy combatant is believed to have further information about terrorism, he can be held without access to legal counsel and without charges being filed. Once the government is satisfied that it has all the relevant information it can obtain, the captive can be held until the end of hostilities, or be released, or be brought up on charges before a criminal court. . . .

The Terrorist Information Awareness Program

Among Menaces to American liberty, this has been widely held to be the most sinister of all. Here is William Safire:

Every purchase you make with a credit card, every magazine subscription you buy and medical prescription you fill, every website you visit and e-mail you send or receive, every academic grade you receive, every bank deposit you make, every trip you book and every event you attend—all these transactions and communications will go into what the Defense Department describes as "a virtual, centralized grand database."

To this computerized dossier on your private life from commercial sources, add every piece of information that government has about you—passport application, driver's license and bridge toll records, judicial and divorce records, complaints from nosy neighbors to the F.B.I., your lifetime paper trail plus the latest hidden camera surveillance—and you have the supersnoop's dream.

Information Awareness

What is the reality? The Terrorist Information Awareness program (TIA) is still only in a developmental stage; we do not know whether it can even be made to work. If it can, it might turn out to be one of the most valuable weapons in America's war with terrorists.

In brief, the program would seek to identify patterns of conduct that indicate terrorist activity. This entails separating small sets of transactions from a vast universe of similar transactions. Since terrorists use the same avenues of communication, commerce, and transportation that everybody else uses, the objective is to build a prototype of an intelligence system whose purpose would be to find terrorists' signals in a "sea of noise." Taking advantage of the integrative power of computer technology, the system would allow the government to develop hypotheses about possible terrorist activity, basing itself entirely on data that are *already legally available*.

But we may never find out whether the program's objective can be achieved, since TIA has been effectively gutted in advance. Impressed, no doubt, by the ideological breadth of the opposition to TIA, Congress was led to adopt a vague prohibition, sponsored by Democratic Senator Ron Wyden, draining TIA of much of its value. The amendment specifies that the program's technology may be used for military operations outside the U.S. and for "lawful foreign intelligence activities conducted wholly against non-United States persons." By inference, TIA may therefore *not* be used to gather information about U.S. citizens or resident aliens—despite the clear fact that significant number of persons in these categories have ties to terrorist groups. . . .

Possible Safeguards

Are there techniques that could be devised to prevent TIA from becoming the playground of Safire's hypothetical supersnoop without disabling it altogether? In domestic criminal investigations, courts require warrants for electronic surveillances. As we have seen, the Foreign Intelligence Surveillance Act also requires judicial approval of surveillances for intelligence and counterintelligence purposes. While there would be no need for a warrant-like requirement in initiating a computer search, other safeguards can be imagined for TIA. Among them, according to Taylor, might be "software designs and legal rules that would block human agents from learning the identities of people whose transactions are being 'data-mined' by TIA computers unless the agents can obtain judicial warrants by showing something analogous to the 'probable cause' that the law requires to justify a wiretap." . . .

The benefits of the TIA program are palpable, and potentially invaluable; the hazards are either hyped or imaginary. There is nothing to prevent Congress from replacing the Wyden amendment with oversight provisions, or from requiring reasonable safeguards that would preserve the program's efficacy.

What Remains to Be Done

The fact that opponents of the Bush administration's efforts to protect American security have resorted to often shameless misrepresentation and outright scare-mongering does not mean those efforts are invulnerable to criticism. They are indeed vulnerable—for not going far enough.

In addition to the lack of properly targeted security procedures at airports, and the failure to resist the gutting of TIA, a truly gaping deficiency in our arrangements is the openness of our northern and southern borders to illegal entrants. In the south, reportedly, as many as 1,000 illegal aliens *a day* enter through Arizona's Organ Pipe National Monument park. . . .

There is, in short, plenty of work to go around. The war we are in, like no other we have ever faced, may last for decades rather than years. The enemy blends into our population and those of other nations around the world, attacks without warning, and consists of men who are quite willing to die in order to kill us and destroy our civilization. Never before has it been possible to imagine one suicidal individual, inspired by the promise of paradise and armed with a nuclear device, able to murder tens or even hundreds of thousands of Americans in a single attack. Those facts justify what the administration has already done, and urgently require more. . . .

Larry Cox NO

The War on Human Rights

Thank you very much. It's great to be here. I have to let you know that I escaped the New York weather a little too late so I arrived and brought to Los Angeles a very severe head cold which I'm told nobody in Los Angeles ever gets. I'll do my very best today because the topic is a very important one—the global fight for human rights. The global fight for the rights that belong, that are inherent in every one of us that are in this room and that belong to every human being on the planet and we are, as I speak here, at a very critical moment in that fight. This is not just because around the globe human rights are being violated—human rights have sadly always been violated around the globe, but what makes the fight so critical right now is that the idea of human rights has begun to be put into question and come under attack. This idea, this revolutionary idea that all people, no matter who they are, no matter what they believe or no matter what they've done, have certain rights that are rooted in the inherent dignity of the human being that cannot be violated for any reason by any power, even a superpower. This is the idea that has been one of the most powerful weapons ever seen in reducing human suffering, in advancing human dignity and freedom and transforming our world for the better. And this is the idea that is now under attack as never before. What makes that attack so disturbing and so serious and so damaging is that it's coming not just from those who've always demonstrated their contempt for human rights, but it's coming from the most unexpected of places, from a nation that has long seen itself and been seen by people all around the world as the champion of human rights.

In 2007, the most serious attack on the idea of human rights is coming from the United States of America, from the country that we love and believe in. I don't say that sentence lightly or easily. I have the privilege of being, as you've just heard, the executive director of Amnesty International USA, an organization that for more than four decades has been documenting and mobilizing public pressure around the world against some of the cruelest abuses that human beings can inflict on other human beings. These include jailing people for reasons of their beliefs indefinitely without charges or trial, sentencing people to many years or even death after trials which are unfair, disappearing people, kidnapping people and sending them to secret prisons so that even their families or even the Red Cross cannot know where they are or what's being done to them and of course using torture and other cruel, inhuman

From *Vital Speeches of the Day*, April 2007, pp. 153–157. Copyright © 2007 by Larry Cox. Reprinted by permission of Larry Cox.

and degrading treatments; a practice that can destroy the spirit of those who suffer it and the humanity of those who inflict it. While Amnesty has been documenting these cases always in other countries it's always had concerns about what's happening in the United States including cases of unfair trials, racial discrimination and the widespread use of the death penalty. And we've always documented and we've always fought against the U.S. role in condoning or in some cases even encouraging torture and other serious violations of human rights by our supposed allies. But if we're honest, even in our most pessimistic and discouraged moments, none of us ever expected to live to see the day when precisely these kinds of gross violations of human rights would be carried out openly and would be publicly defended by the highest elected officials in the land, including the president and the vice president, and then ratified by the U.S. Congress. And yet we know—anyone who simply reads the newspaper knows—that this is what is now happening.

We have locked up hundreds and hundreds of individuals, not for days or months, but years, more than four or five years in places like Guantanamo Bay without charging them, let alone trying them for a crime. We are told that we can do this because these are the worst and most dangerous people on the earth and some of them may well be, but many we know are not, among other reasons, because the U.S. authorities have let hundreds of them go free. People like Murat Kurnaz, a Turkish national arrested in Afghanistan in November 2001, and his family. His mother began to campaign for his release when they learned about in three or four months later, and it was only four years and eight months after that when he was finally reunited with his family never having been charged with a crime, never tried and receiving no compensation for what was done to him. Because there are no trials, because those being held have no access to a court, we can't know for sure how many others are as innocent as Murat Kurnaz. But we do know the way that many have been treated. Listen to this description of what was observed in Guantanamo: "On a couple of occasions I entered interview rooms with a detainee chained hand and foot in a fetal position to the floor with no chair, food or water. Most times they had urinated or defecated on themselves and had been left there for 18 or 24 hours or more. On one occasion the air conditioning had been turned down so far and the temperature was so cold in the room that the bare-footed detainee was shaking with cold. On another occasion the air conditioning had been turned off making the temperature in the unventilated room probably well over 100 degrees. The detainee was almost unconscious on the floor with a pile of hair next to him. He had apparently been literally pulling his own hair out throughout the night." Now this is not the testimony of another detainee or of a bleeding heart human rights advocate like me. This is the testimony of an agent of the FBI, and what he is reporting are techniques that when they are used by other countries, the United States calls them by their proper name—which is torture.

We also know that we are outsourcing torture, using what is called "extraordinary rendition." This means we seize individuals and we send them to countries where it's known they will also be subjected to torture. Maher Arar, a Canadian citizen, was changing planes in JFK airport in New York when he was taken into custody by FBI and other officials, denied a lawyer and then after a week in detention he was taken in the middle of night to New Jersey. He was put on a plane and taken to Jordan where he was chained and beaten and then driven across the border to Syria where he was placed in a filthy underground cell about the size of a grave where once again he was beaten with cables until he told them falsely—because that's what they had wanted to hear—that he had been in Afghanistan. He was held in those conditions for more than 10 months until the Syrians let him go, acknowledging that they could find no evidence that he was ever involved in terrorism. Others have been kidnapped and sent to U.S. secret detention sites somewhere in Europe or Asia where they've been subjected to torture also. Khaled El-Masri—he's a German national—he was on vacation in Macedonia when he was abducted, handcuffed and hooded and sent to a secret CIA prison in Afghanistan where for months he says he was shackled, beaten, injected with drugs and he was released after five months of this torture allegedly by a direct order from Condoleezza Rice when she was told that a mistake had been made. He had been confused with someone with a similar name. Just last week you may have read in *The New York Times* or elsewhere that a German court issued an arrest warrant for 13 CIA agents who were part of his abduction team, part of his disappearance team. We know, we have other testimonies that there are many others who have been treated like El-Masri, but we don't know exactly how many, we don't know the size, location and exactly what happens in these secret prisons because that information is being withheld from all of us. The president in September did proudly announce to the world that these secret prisons exist where what he called "alternative techniques" are used and he said that he would fight as hard as he could fight on any issue to make sure those prisons continued to function. His biggest obstacle—and it should be a source of pride I think to all of us—have been the courts.

In June the Supreme Court ruled that the so-called military commissions set up to eventually try some of the prisoners in Guantanamo—that those military commissions were unconstitutional, that they had not been authorized by Congress, they violated international law and it also ruled that the Geneva Conventions, which among other things prohibit torture or humiliating or degrading treatment, applied to all detainees held by the United States. That gave the U.S. Congress an opportunity to put the United States back on the road to respecting and protecting human rights. Instead, our Congress took bad policy and turned it into even worse law. It passed something called the Military Commissions Act of 2006 which states that the president has the power to designate almost any non-citizen as an illegal enemy combatant and that allows them to be held indefinitely without charges or trial, to be tried if they ever are tried, not by a court but by a military commission which will hear evidence that would not be allowed in an ordinary court. It also stripped them of habeas corpus, the longest standing form of protection of prisoners which goes back 800 years to the Magna Carta. Congress did nothing to challenge the idea of secret detention sites. It did, in the end, uphold the Geneva Conventions, but it gave to the president the authority to decide what exactly constitutes humiliating and degrading treatment and the administration has said this will allow it to continue to use so-called alternative techniques, which so far it has declined to describe. With this act the U.S. Congress officially in the name of all of us carried out an assault on the very idea of human rights.

Now why does this matter so much? Of course it matters to the individuals who have suffered directly and immensely and their families, because of these acts. But there are, it must be said, many countries whose abuse of human rights is both more massive and more egregious than that of the United States. The problem is there is no country whose example is more powerful than that of the United States. What makes the U.S. attack on the idea of human rights so serious—it's not that we are worse than other countries but that we have always aspired to be so much better, that we have proclaimed to the world that we are better. So when the world's superpower, when the world's greatest democracy openly defends its own violation of human rights it sends a powerful message to dictators and killers around the world helping them to justify what is unjustifiable. It encourages repressive policies by our allies and perhaps most seriously it undermines the difficult and dangerous work carried out by brave men and women who are fighting around the world against acts of cruelty and tyranny. We see this every single day in our work in places like Egypt, Zimbabwe, China and Russia, among others. We see the acts of U.S. government being used as a cover for cruelty. Those who know this best are those who have suffered the most from it. Recently I had the chance to speak with a remarkable man named Hassan Bility, a courageous journalist who was arrested and severely tortured seven times in Liberia by the notorious gangster president Charles Taylor. He told me the last time he was arrested Charles Taylor informed him, "You know, you have no rights because you are an enemy combatant." And Hassan said he never heard the expression "enemy combatant" before and Taylor explained to him that Liberia had learned from the United States. The point here is not that repressive governments and groups would not commit these acts without the help or the example of the United States—they don't need our help to violate human rights. The point is that the United States can hardly play a leading role in working against these acts when we have by our deeds and words provided the rationale for them. . . .

The first step is to begin to understand how we got here, how did we reach the point where this country is openly defying international law and human rights and where we are actually debating how much torture is all right to use? The simple answer, and perhaps it's a simplistic answer for our collective human rights failure, is 9/11, the horrific attacks that killed 3,000 people and made it painfully clear that the United States of America is no longer safe from the kind of terror that has been used throughout the rest of the world. No one should try to downplay the extremely serious threat that those attacks represent and it's a threat that will continue for many years to come. The attacks of 9/11 were massive crimes against humanity and they were carried out by people who do not feel bound by any way or any notion of human rights, who believe they have the right to kill who-ever they choose to kill and openly celebrate those killings. So no one, certainly no one who cares about human rights, should fail to take with the utmost seriousness the need to find a way to combat this ideology of death or should question that we needed to mount a strong response to those attacks. But what is in question is the way we responded in our anger, in our fear because it was not the inevitable or the only possible response. This is, after all, hardly the first time in our history that we have been attacked including being attacked on our own soil by people determined to destroy us in the name of a superior ideology. There was a time when no one could question that we were engaged in a true battle for civilization, a time when the United States and its allies were engaged in a fight against foes whose leaders were not hiding in caves in Afghanistan but had seats in the capitols of some of the world's most powerful military states and whose ideology of racial superiority led to the deaths not of thousands but of millions, and the conquest and brutal occupation of country after country. In the face of this threat to our very existence, the United States of course responded militarily. But what changed the course of history, what changed the history of the human race is the U.S. response to the challenge of fascism was not simply military. We understood that what we needed was a larger vision, an idea around which we could build a strong international alliance and it was our president, Franklin Roosevelt, who in a remarkable speech on January 6, 1941, gave words to that idea saying that the world we were fighting for would be built on four fundamental freedoms and he defined freedom in that speech as "the supremacy of human rights everywhere." This is the idea that seven years later would be embodied in the Universal Declaration of Human Rights, putting in motion forces that have led to some of humanity's greatest victories.

Yet after 9/11 we did not respond to the new threat we faced by embracing this powerful idea of human rights. We didn't strengthen the mechanisms created to advance human rights, we didn't affirm human rights by bringing to justice those responsible for crimes against humanity, and we did not use human rights to try and isolate those who celebrate death and to win over others to life by advancing economic and social rights around the world. Instead, sadly, we responded not by fighting fear but by giving in to it, indeed by exploiting it. Declaring that we were in a new kind of a war and that therefore we had to have a new way to fight, but it turned out the new way of fighting was a very old way of fighting, one which rolled back the lessons of World War II, declared that the Geneva Conventions were quaint and obsolete and began as we have seen to chip away at this core notion of human rights. What's been the result? There is little if any evidence that the creation of secret detention sites, or the abandonment of habeas corpus, or the use of indefinite detention, or the use of torture and cruel and degrading treatment has bought those who committed acts of terror to justice or reduced the numbers of those who want to carry out new acts of terror. In fact, as you may know our numerous intelligence agencies have agreed that there are now more people using terror, more organizations using terror and more acts of terror than ever before. Instead of presenting to potential sympathizers of terror an alternative way, a better way to obtain justice and a better life, places like Guantanamo and the terrible acts committed at Abu Ghraib have become the very face of America.

We may be, as the president says, in a global battle for civilization but to fight it we first have to resolve the battle for civilization inside the United States and I'm here today speaking to you because Amnesty International believes this is a battle we have to win and that we can win. We believe we can win it not because of who we are but because of who we have always aspired and fought to become, because the truth is there have always been two Americas. There's the America we live in, that's an America that if we're honest has always fallen short of its ideals. That's the America that, after all, began with genocide against indigenous people, the America that built its wealth with slaves and long after slavery was gone continued with a system of racial apartheid. That's the America that has learned to live with massive poverty and a lack of healthcare for millions. It's the America of too many in inadequate schools, jails and death rows. It's the America of Guantanamo and Abu Ghraib, but there has always been, thank god, another America and that's the America we believe in, the America that all of us, Republican or Democrat, liberal or conservative, young or old, rich or poor, all of us were taught to believe in that America. That's the America we took a pledge to. You all remember the pledge; it was a pledge to liberty and justice for all. That's the America that as Jimmy Carter once said did not invent human rights but was invented by human rights. The America that began with a declaration that said all people are created equal with certain inalienable rights, the America that a lot of people have fought and died to realize, fought to abolish slavery and racial apartheid, fought to win the vote for women, fought to seek better labor conditions and better education for all. This is the America than millions of people around the world have looked to for help and hope because this is the America that's a leader for and not a violator of human rights. Amnesty International has launched a campaign to get people to sign a new pledge, a pledge to this America and to join us in presenting those pledges to the administration and to the new Congress as we seek to end secret detentions and indefinite imprisonment without charges—secondhand justice—and to guarantee that never again will this country ever engage in torture or cruel, inhumane and degrading treatment of detainees. To do this we need the help of every American of every political stripe who believes in the America we believe in. . . .

POSTSCRIPT

Does the Threat of Terrorism Warrant Curtailment of Civil Liberties?

Since September 11th, books and articles on terrorism have increased greatly. Some recent notable general works on terrorism include Paul J. Smith, *The Terrorism Ahead: Confronting Transnational Violence in the Twenty-first Century* (M.E. Sharpe, 2008); Brian T. Bennett, *Understanding, Assessing, and Responding to Terrorism* (Wiley-Interscience, 2007); Joseph H. Compos, *The State and Terrorism* (Ashgate, 2007); Ann E. Robertson, *Terrorism and Global Security* (Facts on File, 2007); Philip P. Purpura, *Terrorism and Homeland Security* (Butterworth-Heinemann, 2007); Thomas R. Mockaitis, *The New Terrorism* (Praeger, 2007); Cindy C. Combs, *Encyclopedia of Terrorism* (Facts on Fine, 2007); Clifford E. Simonsen and Jeremy R. Spindlove, *Terrorism Today: The Past, the Players, the Future,* 2d ed. (Prentice Hall, 2004); Cindy C. Combs, *Terrorism in the Twenty- First Century,* 3rd ed. (Prentice Hall, 2003); Pamala Griset and Sue Mahan, *Terrorism in Perspective* (Sage Publications, 2003); Gus Martin, *Understanding Terrorism: Challenges, Perspectives, and Issues* (Sage Publications, 2003); Vincent Burns and Kate Dempsey Peterson, *Terrorism: A Documentary and Reference Guide* (Greenwood Press, 2005); Bard E. O'Neill, *Insurgency and Terrorism: From Revolution to Apocalypse,* 2nd edition (Potomac Books, 2005); James M. and Benda J. Lutz, *Terrorism: Origins and Evolution* (Palgrave Macmillan, 2005); and Leonard Weinberg, *Global Terrorism: A Beginner's Guide* (Oneworld, 2005). Works that focus on the motives for terrorism include Robert A. Pape, *Dying to Win: The Strategic Logic of Suicide Terrorism* (Random House, 2005); Talal Asad, *On Suicide Bombing* (Columbia University Press, 2007); Bruce Bonger et al., *Psychology of Terrorism* (Oxford University Press, 2007); David M. Rosen, *Armies of the Young: Child Soldiers in War and Terrorism* (Rutgars University Press, 2005); and Bruce Wilshire, *Get 'em All! Kill 'em!: Genocide, Terrorism, Righteous Communities* (Lexington Books, 2005). Terrorism with weapons of mass destruction has been labeled "the new terrorism," and an extensive literature on it has rapidly formed, including Walter Laqueur, *No End to War: Terrorism in the Twenty-First Century* (Continuum, 2003); Nadine Gurr and Benjamin Cole, *The New Face of Terrorism: Threats From Weapons of Mass Destruction* (St. Martin's Press, 2000); Paul Gilbert, *New Terror, New Wars* (Georgetown University Press, 2003); and Peter Brookes, *A Devil's Triangle: Terrorism, Weapons of Mass Destruction, and Rogue States* (Rowman & Litlefield, 2005). Another threatening aspect of terrorism is the terrorists' willingness to commit suicide. To explore this issue, see Christopher Reuter, *My Life as a Weapon: A Modern History of Suicide Bombing* (Princeton University Press, 2004).

The critical issue is how the United States deals with the terrorist threat. Richard A. Clark provides an insider's revelation of the U.S. response in *Against All Enemies: Inside America's War on Terror* (Free Press, 2004). See also Michael Ignatieff, *The Lesser Evil: Political Ethics in an Age of Terror* (Princeton University Press, 2004); *The Politics of Terror: The U.S. Response to 9/11*, edited by William Crotty (Northwestern University Press, 2004); Lawrence Freedman, ed., *Superterrorism: Policy Responses* (Blackwell Publishers, 2002); Dilip K. Das and Peter C. Kratcoski, eds., *Meeting the Challenges of Global Terrorism: Prevention, Control, and Recovery* (Lexington, 2003); Hayim Granot and Jay Levinson, *Terror Bombing: The New Urban Threat: Practical Approaches for Response Agencies and Security* (Dekel, 2002); Mark A. Sauter and James Jay Carafano, *Homeland Security: A Complete Guide to Understanding, Preventing, and Surviving Terrorism* (McGraw-Hill, 2005); Russell D. Howard et al. (eds.), *Homeland Security and Terrorism* (McGraw-Hill, 2006); Joel Leson, *New Realities: Assessing and Managing the Terrorism Threat* (U.S. Department of Justice, 2005); John Davis (ed.), *The Global War on Terrorism: Assessing the American Response* (Nova Science Publishers, 2005); Medea Benjamin and Jodie Evans, eds., *Stop the Next War Now: Effective Responses to Violence and Terrorism* (Inner Ocean Publishers, 2005); and Amy Sterling Casil, *Coping With Terrorism* (Rosen, 2004). Works that discuss the issue of balancing the need for greater police powers and the desire for strong civil rights include *National Security: Opposing Viewpoints*, edited by Helen Cothern (Greenhaven Press, 2004); *American National Security and Civil Liberties in an Age of Terrorism*, edited by David B. Cohen and John W. Wells (Palgrave Macmillan, 2004); Richard Ashby Wilson, ed., *Human Rights in the 'War on Terror'* (Cambridge University Press, 2005); and Raneta Lawson Mack and Michael J. Kelly, *Equal Justice in the Balance: America's Legal Responses to the Emerging Terrorist Threat* (University of Michigan Press, 2004). Three works that criticize the U.S. legal response are *Lost Liberties: Ashcroft and the Assault on Personal Freedom*, edited by Cynthia Brown (New Press, 2003); Thomas E. Baker and John F. Stack, Jr., eds., *At War with Civil Rights and Civil Liberties* (Rowman & Littlefield Publishers, 2006); and Jeffrey Rosen, *The Naked Crowd: Reclaiming Security and Freedom in an Anxious Age* (Random House, 2004). Another side of the story is provided by Alan M. Dershowitz in *Why Terrorism Works* (Yale University Press, 2002).

Internet References . . .

United Nations Environment Program (UNEP)

The United Nations Environment Program (UNEP) Web site offers links to environmental topics of critical concern to sociologists. The site will direct you to useful databases and global resource information.

http://www.unep.ch

Worldwatch Institute Home Page

The Worldwatch Institute is dedicated to fostering the evolution of an environmentally sustainable society in which human needs are met without threatening the health of the natural environment. This site provides access to World Watch Magazine and State of the World 2000.

http://www.worldwatch.org

William Davidson Institute

The William Davidson Institute at the University of Michigan Business School is dedicated to the understanding and promotion of economic transition. Consult this site for discussions of topics related to the changing global economy and the effects of globalization on society.

http://www.wdi.bus.umich.edu

World Future Society

The World Future Society is an educational and scientific organization for those interested in how social and technological developments are shaping the future.

http://www.wfs.org

Population Division: Department of Economic and Social Affairs

The Department of Economic and Social Affairs, Population Division, is responsible for monitoring and appraisal of the broad range of areas in the field of population.

http://www.un.org/esa/population/aboutpop.htm

The Future: Population/ Environment/Society

*T*he leading issues for the beginning of the twenty-first century include global warming, environmental decline, and globalization. The state of the environment and the effects of globalization produce strong arguments concerning what can be harmful or beneficial. Technology has increased enormously in the last 100 years, as have worldwide population growth, consumption, and new forms of pollution that threaten to undermine the world's fragile ecological support system. Although all nations have a stake in the health of the planet, many believe that none are doing enough to protect its health. Will technology itself be the key to controlling or accommodating the increase of population and consumption, along with the resulting increase in waste production? Perhaps so, but new policies will also be needed. Technology is driving the process of globalization, which can be seen as both good and bad. Those who support globalization theory state that globalization increases competition, production, wealth, and the peaceful integration of nations. However, not everyone agrees. This section explores what is occurring in our environment and in our current global economy.

- Is Humankind Dangerously Harming the Environment?

- Is Globalization Good for Mankind?

- Is America Dominated by Big Business?

- Are Barriers to Women's Success as Leaders Due to Societal Obstacles?

- Is the World a Victim of American Cultural Imperialism?

ISSUE 18

Is Humankind Dangerously Harming the Environment?

YES: Lester R. Brown, from "Pushing Beyond the Earth's Limits," *The Futurist* (May/June 2005)

NO: Bjorn Lomborg, from "The Truth About the Environment," *The Economist* (August 4, 2001)

ISSUE SUMMARY

YES: Lester R. Brown, founder of the Worldwatch Institute, and now president of the Earth Policy Institute, argues the population growth and economic development are placing increasing harmful demands on the environment for resources and to grow food for improving diets.

NO: Bjorn Lomborg, a statistician at the University of Aarhus, Denmark, presents evidence that population growth is slowing down, natural resources are not running out, species are disappearing very slowly, the environment is improving in some ways, and assertions about environmental decline are exaggerated.

$\mathbf{M}$uch of the literature on socioeconomic development in the 1960s was premised on the assumption of inevitable material progress for all. It largely ignored the impacts of development on the environment and presumed that the availability of raw materials would not be a problem. The belief was that all societies would get richer because all societies were investing in new equipment and technologies that would increase productivity and wealth. Theorists recognized that some poor countries were having trouble developing, but they blamed those problems on the deficiencies of the values and attitudes of those countries and on inefficient organizations.

In the late 1960s and early 1970s an intellectual revolution occurred. Environmentalists had criticized the growth paradigm throughout the 1960s, but they were not taken very seriously at first. By the end of the 1960s, however, marine scientist Rachel Carson's book *Silent Spring* (Alfred A. Knopf, 1962) had worked its way into the public's consciousness. Carson's book traces the noticeable loss of birds to the use of pesticides. Her book made the middle and upper classes in the United States realize that pollution affects complex ecological systems in ways that put even the wealthy at risk.

In 1968 Paul Ehrlich, a professor of population studies, published *The Population Bomb* (Ballantine Books), which states that overpopulation is the major problem facing mankind. This means that population has to be controlled or the human race might cause the collapse of the global ecosystems and the deaths of many humans. Ehrlich explained why he thought the devastation of the world was imminent:

> Because the human population of the planet is about five times too large, and we're managing to support all these people—at today's level of misery—only by spending our capital, burning our fossil fuels, dispersing our mineral resources and turning our fresh water into salt water. We have not only overpopulated but overstretched our environment. We are poisoning the ecological systems of the earth—systems upon which we are ultimately dependent for all of our food, for all of our oxygen and for all of our waste disposal.

In 1973 *The Limits to Growth* (Universe) by Donella H. Meadows et al. was published. It presents a dynamic systems computer model for world economic, demographic, and environmental trends. When the computer model projected trends into the future, it predicted that the world would experience ecological collapse and population die-off unless population growth and economic activity were greatly reduced. This study was both attacked and defended, and the debate about the health of the world has been heated ever since.

Let us examine the population growth rates for the past, present, and future. At about A.D. 1, the world had about one-quarter billion people. It took about 1,650 years to double this number to one-half billion and 200 years to double the world population again to 1 billion by 1850. The next doubling took only about 80 years, and the last doubling took about 45 years (from 2 billion in 1930 to about 4 billion in 1975). The world population may double again to 8 billion sometime between 2015 and 2025. At the same time that population is growing people are trying to get richer, which means consuming more, polluting more, and using more resources. Are all these trends threatening the carrying capacity of the planet and jeopardizing the prospects for future generations?

In the following selections, Lester R. Brown warns that the population growth and the sevenfold expansion of the economy in the past half century is placing demands on the environment that exceeds the earth's natural capacity. As a result we face many environmental problems. The one that Brown focuses on is the difficulty of increasing food production enough to feed growing populations with better diets and with declining natural resources. Bjorn Lomborg counters that the evidence supports optimism—not environmental pessimism. He maintains that resources are becoming more abundant, food per capita is increasing, the extinction of species is at a very slow rate, and environmental problems are transient and will get better.

YES ↵

Lester R. Brown

Pushing Beyond the Earth's Limits

During the last half of the twentieth century, the world economy expanded sevenfold. In 2000 alone, its growth exceeded that of the entire nineteenth century. Economic growth, now the goal of governments everywhere, has become the status quo. Stability is considered a departure from the norm.

As the economy grows, its demands are outgrowing the earth, exceeding many of the planet's natural capacities. While the world economy multiplied sevenfold in just 50 years, the earth's natural life-support systems remained essentially the same. Water use tripled, but the capacity of the hydrological system to produce fresh water through evaporation changed little. The demand for seafood increased fivefold, but the sustainable yield of oceanic fisheries was unchanged. Fossil-fuel burning raised carbon dioxide (CO_2) emissions fourfold, but the capacity of nature to absorb it changed little, leading to a buildup of CO_2 in the atmosphere and a rise in the earth's temperature. As human demands surpass the earth's natural capacities, expanding food production becomes more difficult.

Losing Agricultural Momentum

Environmentalists have been saying for years that, if the environmental trends of recent decades continued, the world would one day be in trouble. What was not clear was what form the trouble would take and when it would occur. Now it has become increasingly clear that tightening food supplies will be our greatest trouble and that it will emerge within the next few years. In early 2004, China's forays into the world market to buy 8 million tons of wheat marked what could be the beginning of the global shift from an era of grain surpluses to one of grain scarcity.

World grain production is a basic indicator of dietary adequacy at the individual level and of overall food security at the global level. After nearly tripling from 1950 to 1996, the grain harvest stayed flat for seven years in a row, through 2003, showing no increase at all. And production fell short of consumption in each of the last four of those years. The shortfalls of nearly 100 million tons in 2002 and again in 2003 were the largest on record.

Consumption exceeded production for four years, leading world grain stocks to drop to the lowest level in 30 years. The last time stocks were this

From *The Futurist*, May/June 2005, pp. 18–24. Copyright © 2005 by World Future Society. Reprinted by permission.

low, in 1972–1974, wheat and rice prices doubled. Importing countries competed vigorously for inadequate supplies. A politics of scarcity emerged, and some countries, such as the United States, restricted exports.

In 2004, a combination of stronger grain prices at planting time and the best weather in a decade yielded a substantially larger harvest for the first time in eight years. Yet even with a harvest that was up 124 million tons from that in 2003, the world still consumed all the grain it produced, leaving none to rebuild stocks. If stocks cannot be rebuilt in a year of exceptional weather, when can they?

From 1950 to 1984, world grain production expanded faster than population, raising the grain produced per person per year from 250 kilograms to the historic peak of 339 kilograms—an increase of 34%. This positive development initially reflected recovery from the disruption of World War II, and then later solid technological advances. The rising tide of food production lifted all ships, largely eradicating hunger in some countries and substantially reducing it in many others.

But since 1984, growth in grain harvests has fallen behind growth in population. The amount of grain produced per person fell to 308 kilograms in 2004.

Africa is suffering the most, with a decline in grain produced per person that is unusually steep and taking a heavy human toll. Soils are depleted of nutrients, and the amount of grainland per person has been shrinking steadily due to population growth in recent decades. But in addition, Africa must now contend with the loss of adults to AIDS, which is depleting the rural workforce and undermining agriculture. In two of the last three years, grain production per person in sub-Saharan Africa has been below 120 kilograms—dropping to a level that leaves millions of Africans on the edge of starvation.

Several long-standing environmental trends are contributing to the global loss of agricultural momentum. Among these are the cumulative effects of soil erosion on land productivity, the loss of cropland to desertification, and the accelerating conversion of cropland to nonfarm uses. All are taking a toll, although their relative roles vary among countries.

In addition, farmers are seeing fewer new technologies to dramatically boost production. The high-yielding varieties of wheat, rice, and corn that were developed a generation or so ago doubled and tripled yields, but there have not been any dramatic advances in the genetic yield potential of grains since then.

Similarly, the use of fertilizer has now plateaued or even declined slightly in key food-producing countries. The rapid growth in irrigation that characterized much of the last half century has also slowed. Indeed, in some countries the irrigated area is shrinking.

And now, two newer environmental trends are slowing the growth in world food production: falling water tables and rising temperatures. The bottom line is that it is now more difficult for farmers to keep up with the growing demand for grain. The rise in world grainland productivity, which averaged over 2% a year from 1950 to 1990, fell to scarcely 1% a year in the last decade of the twentieth century. This will likely drop further in the years immediately ahead.

If the rise in land productivity continues to slow and if population continues to grow by 70 million or more per year, governments may begin to define national security in terms of food shortages, rising food prices, and the emerging politics of scarcity. Food insecurity may soon eclipse terrorism as the overriding concern of national governments.

Food Challenges Go from Local to Global

The world economy is making excessive demands on the earth. Evidence of this can be seen in collapsing fisheries, shrinking forests, expanding deserts, rising CO^2 levels, eroding soils, rising temperatures, falling water tables, melting glaciers, deteriorating grasslands, rising seas, rivers that are running dry, and disappearing species.

Nearly all of these environmentally destructive trends contribute to global food insecurity. For example, even a modest rise of 1°F in temperature in mountainous regions can substantially increase rainfall and decrease snowfall. The result is more flooding during the rainy season and less snowmelt to feed rivers during the dry season, when farmers need irrigation water.

Or consider the collapse of fisheries and the associated leveling off of the oceanic fish catch. During the last half century, the fivefold growth in the world fish catch that satisfied much of the growing demand for animal protein pushed oceanic fisheries to their limits and beyond. Now, in this new century, we cannot expect any growth at all in the catch. The Food and Agriculture Organization warns that all future growth in animal protein supplies can only come from that produced on land, not the sea, putting even more pressure on the earth's land and water resources.

Until recently, the economic effects of environmental trends, such as overfishing, overpumping, and overplowing, were largely local. Among the many examples are the collapse of the cod fishery off Newfoundland from overfishing that cost Canada 40,000 jobs, the halving of Saudi Arabia's wheat harvest as a result of aquifer depletion, and the shrinking grain harvest of Kazakhstan as wind erosion claimed half of its cropland.

Now, if world food supplies tighten, we may see the first global economic effect of environmentally destructive trends. Rising food prices could be the first economic indicator to signal serious trouble in the deteriorating relationship between the global economy and the earth's ecosystem. The short-lived 20% rise in world grain prices in early 2004 may turn out to be a warning tremor before the quake.

Two New Challenges

As world demand for food has tripled, so too has the use of water for irrigation. As a result, the world is incurring a vast water deficit. But the trend is largely invisible because the deficit takes the form of aquifer overpumping and falling water tables. Falling water levels are often not discovered until wells go dry.

The world water deficit is a relatively recent phenomenon. Only within the last half century have powerful diesel and electrically driven pumps given us the pumping capacity to deplete aquifers. The worldwide spread of these pumps since the late 1960s and the drilling of millions of wells have in many cases pushed water withdrawal beyond the aquifers' recharge from rainfall. As a result, water tables are now falling in countries that are home to more than half of the world's people, including China, India, and the United States—the three largest grain producers.

Groundwater levels are falling throughout the northern half of China. Under the North China Plain, they are dropping 1–3 meters (3–10 feet) a year. In India, they are falling in most states, including the Punjab, the country's breadbasket. And in the United States, water levels are falling throughout the southern Great Plains and the Southwest. Overpumping creates a false sense of food security: It enables us to satisfy growing food needs today, but it almost guarantees a decline in food production tomorrow when the aquifer is depleted.

It takes a thousand tons of water to produce a single ton of grain, so food security is closely tied to water security. Seventy percent of world water use is for irrigation, 20% is used by industry, and 10% is for residential purposes. As urban water use rises while aquifers are being depleted, farmers are faced with a shrinking share of a shrinking water supply.

Meanwhile, temperatures are rising and concern about climate change is intensifying. Scientists have begun to focus on the precise relationship between temperature and crop yields. Crop ecologists at the International Rice Research Institute in the Philippines and at the U.S. Department of Agriculture (USDA) have jointly concluded that each 1°C rise in temperature during the growing season cuts 10% off the yields of wheat, rice, and corn.

Over the last three decades, the earth's average temperature has climbed by nearly 0.7°C; the four warmest years on record came during the last six years. In 2002, record-high temperatures and drought shrank grain harvests in both India and the United States. In 2003, Europe bore the brunt of the intense heat. The record-breaking August heat wave claimed 35,000 lives in eight nations and withered grain harvests in virtually every country from France to Ukraine.

In a business-as-usual scenario, the earth's average temperature will rise by 1.4°–5.8°C (2°–10°F) during this century, according to the Intergovernmental Panel on Climate Change. These projections are for the earth's average temperature, but the rise is expected to be much greater over land than over the oceans, in the higher latitudes than in the equatorial regions, and in the interior of continents than in the coastal regions. This suggests that increases far in excess of the projected average are likely for regions such as the North American breadbasket—the region defined by the Great Plains of the United States and Canada and the U.S. corn belt. Today's farmers face the prospect of temperatures higher than any generation of farmers since agriculture began.

The Japan Syndrome

When studying the USDA world grain database more than a decade ago, I noted that, if countries are already densely populated when they begin to industrialize rapidly, three things happen in quick succession to make them heavily dependent on grain imports: Grain consumption climbs as incomes rise, grainland area shrinks, and grain production falls. The rapid industrialization that drives up demand simultaneously shrinks the cropland area. The inevitable result is that grain imports soar. Within a few decades, countries can go from being essentially self-sufficient to importing 70% or more of their grain. I call this the "Japan syndrome" because I first recognized this sequence of events in Japan, a country that today imports 70% of its grain.

In a fast-industrializing country, grain consumption rises rapidly. Initially, rising incomes permit more direct consumption of grain, but before long the growth shifts to the greater indirect consumption of grain in the form of grain-intensive livestock products, such as pork, poultry, and eggs.

Once rapid industrialization is under way, the grainland area begins to shrink within a few years. As a country industrializes and modernizes, cropland gets taken over by industrial and residential developments and by roads, highways, and parking lots to accommodate more cars and drivers. When farmers are left with fragments of land that are too small to be cultivated economically, they often simply abandon their plots, seeking employment elsewhere.

As rapid industrialization pulls labor out of the countryside, it often leads to less double cropping, a practice that depends on quickly harvesting one grain crop once it is ripe and immediately preparing the seedbed for the next crop. With the loss of workers as young people migrate to cities, the capacity to do this diminishes.

As incomes rise, diets diversify, generating demand for more fruits and vegetables. This in turn leads farmers to shift land from grain to these more profitable, high-value crops.

Japan was essentially self-sufficient in grain when its grain harvested area peaked in 1955. Since then the grainland area has shrunk by more than half. The multiple-cropping index has dropped from nearly 1.4 crops per hectare per year in 1960 to scarcely one crop today. Some six years after Japan's grain area began to shrink, the shrinkage overrode the rise in land productivity and overall production began to decline. With grain consumption climbing and production falling, grain imports soared. By 1983, imports accounted for 70% of Japan's grain consumption, a level they remain at today.

South Korea and Taiwan are tracing Japan's pattern. In both cases, the decline in grain area was followed roughly a decade later by a decline in production. Perhaps this should not be surprising, since the forces at work in the two countries are exactly the same as in Japan. And, like Japan, both South Korea and Taiwan now import some 70% of their total grain supply.

Based on the sequence of events in these three countries that affected grain production, consumption, and imports—the Japan syndrome—it was easy to anticipate the precipitous decline in China's grain production that began in 1998. The obvious question now is which other countries will enter a period of declining grain production because of the same combination of forces. Among those that come to mind are India, Indonesia, Bangladesh, Pakistan, Egypt, and Mexico.

Of particular concern is India, with a population of nearly 1.1 billion now and growing by 18 million a year. In recent years, India's economic growth has accelerated, averaging 6%-7% a year. This growth, only slightly slower than that of China, is also beginning to consume cropland. In addition to the grainland shrinkage associated with the Japan syndrome, the extensive overpumping of aquifers in India—which will one day deprive farmers of irrigation water—will also reduce grain production.

Exactly when rapid industrialization in a country that is densely populated will translate into a decline in grain production is difficult to anticipate. Once crop production begins to decline, countries often try to reverse the trend. But the difficulty of achieving this can be seen in Japan, where a rice support price that is four times the world market price has failed to expand production.

The China Factor

China—the most-populous country in the world—is now beginning to experience the Japan syndrome. The precipitous fall in China's grain production since 1998 is perhaps the most alarming recent world agricultural event. After an impressive climb from 90 million tons in 1950 to a peak of 392 million tons in 1998, China's grain harvest fell in four of the next five years, dropping to 322 million tons in 2003. For perspective, this decline of 70 million tons exceeds the entire grain harvest of Canada. . . .

If smaller countries like Japan, South Korea, and Taiwan import 70% or more of their grain, the impacts on the global economy are not so dramatic. But if China turns to the outside world to meet even 20% of its grain needs—which would be close to 80 million tons—it will create a huge challenge for grain exporters. The resulting rise in world grain prices could destabilize governments in low-income, grain-importing countries. The entire world thus has a stake in China's efforts to stabilize its agricultural resource base.

The Challenge Ahead

We must not underestimate the challenges that the world faces over the next half century. There will be a projected 3 billion more people to feed, and 5 billion who will want to improve their diets by eating more meat, which requires more grain (as livestock feed) to produce. Meanwhile, the world's farmers will still be fighting soil erosion and the loss of cropland to nonfarm uses, as well as newer challenges, such as falling water tables, the diversion of irrigation water to cities, and rising temperatures. . . .

In a world where the food economy has been shaped by an abundance of cheap oil, tightening world oil supplies will further complicate efforts to eradicate hunger. Modern mechanized agriculture requires large amounts of fuel for tractors, irrigation pumps, and grain drying. Rising oil prices may soon translate into rising food prices.

Feeding the World

If grain imports continue to grow in Asia, where half the world's people live, and if harvests continue to shrink in Africa, the second-most populous continent, we have to ask where tomorrow's grain will come from. The countries that dominated world grain exports for the last half century—the United States, Canada, Australia, and Argentina—may not be able to export much beyond current levels.

The United States has produced as much as 350 million tons of grain a year several times over the last two decades, though never much more than this. The country exported about 100 million tons of grain a year two decades ago, but only an average of 80 million tons in recent years, as demand has increased domestically. The potential for expanding grain production and export in both Canada and Australia is constrained by relatively low rainfall in their grain-growing regions. Argentina's grain production has actually declined over the last several years as land has shifted to soybeans, principally used for feeding livestock rather than people.

By contrast, Russia and Ukraine should be able to expand their grain exports, at least modestly, as population has stabilized or is declining. There is also some unrealized agricultural production potential in these countries. But northern countries heavily dependent on spring wheat typically have lower yields, so Russia is unlikely to become a major grain exporter. Ukraine has a somewhat more promising potential if it can provide farmers with the economic incentives they need to expand production. So, too, do Poland and Romania.

Yet, the likely increases in exports from these countries are small compared with the prospective import needs of China and, potentially, India. It is worth noting that the drop in China's grain harvest of 70 million tons over five years is equal to the grain exports of Canada, Australia, and Argentina combined.

Argentina can expand its already large volume of soybean exports, but its growth potential for grain exports is limited by the availability of arable land. The only country that has the potential to substantially expand the world's grainland area is Brazil, with its vast cerrado—a savannah-like region on the southern edge of the Amazon basin. Because its soils require the heavy use of fertilizer and because transporting grain from Brazil's remote interior to distant world markets is costly, it would likely take substantially higher world grain prices for Brazil to emerge as a major exporter. Beyond this, would a vast expansion of cropland in Brazil's interior be sustainable? Or is its vulnerability to soil erosion likely to prevent it from making a long-term contribution? And what will be the price paid in the irretrievable loss of ecosystems and plant and animal species?

In sum, ensuring future food security is a formidable, multifaceted problem. To solve it, the world will need to:

- Check the HIV epidemic before it so depletes Africa's adult population that starvation stalks the land.
- Arrest the steady shrinkage in grainland area per person.

- Eliminate the overgrazing that is converting grasslands to desert.
- Reduce soil erosion losses to below the natural rate of new soil formation.
- Halt the advancing deserts that are engulfing cropland.
- Check the rising temperature that threatens to shrink harvests.
- Arrest the fall in water tables.
- Protect cropland from careless conversion to nonfarm uses.

Bjorn Lomborg

➡ **NO**

The Truth About the Environment

Ecology and economics should push in the same direction. After all, the "eco" part of each word derives from the greek word for "home", and the protagonists of both claim to have humanity's welfare as their goal. Yet environmentalists and economists are often at loggerheads. For economists, the world seems to be getting better. For many environmentalists, it seems to be getting worse.

These environmentalists, led by such veterans as Paul Ehrlich of Stanford University, and Lester Brown of the Worldwatch Institute, have developed a sort of "litany" of four big environmental fears:

- Natural resources are running out.
- The population is ever growing, leaving less and less to eat.
- Species are becoming extinct in vast numbers: forests are disappearing and fish stocks are collapsing.
- The planet's air and water are becoming ever more polluted.

Human activity is thus defiling the earth, and humanity may end up killing itself in the process.

The trouble is, the evidence does not back up this litany. First, energy and other natural resources have become more abundant, not less so since the Club of Rome published "The Limits to Growth" in 1972. Second, more food is now produced per head of the world's population than at any time in history. Fewer people are starving. Third, although species are indeed becoming extinct, only about 0.7% of them are expected to disappear in the next 50 years, not 25–50%, as has so often been predicted. And finally, most forms of environmental pollution either appear to have been exaggerated, or are transient—associated with the early phrases of industrialisation and therefore best cured not by restricting economic growth, but by accelerating it. One form of pollution—the release of greenhouse gases that causes global warming—does appear to be a long-term phenomenon, but its total impact is unlikely to pose a devastating problem for the future of humanity. A bigger problem may well turn out to be an inappropriate response to it.

Can Things Only Get Better?

Take these four points one by one. First, the exhaustion of natural resources. The early environmental movement worried that the mineral resources on which modern industry depends would run out. Clearly, there must be some limit to the amount of fossil fuels and metal ores that can be extracted from the earth: the planet, after all, has a finite mass. But that limit is far greater than many environmentalists would have people believe.

Reserves of natural resources have to be located, a process that costs money. That, not natural scarcity, is the main limit on their availability. However, known reserves of all fossil fuels, and of most commercially important metals, are now larger than they were when "the Limits to Growth" was published. In the case of oil, for example, reserves that could be extracted at reasonably competitive prices would keep the world economy running for about 150 years at present consumption rates. Add to that the fact that the price of solar energy has fallen by half in every decade for the past 30 years, and appears likely to continue to do so into the future, and energy shortages do not look like a serious threat either to the economy or to the environment.

The development for non-fuel resources has been similar. Cement, aluminum, iron, copper, gold, nitrogen and zinc account for more than 75% of global expenditure on raw materials. Despite an increase in consumption of these materials of between two- and ten-fold over the past 50 years, the number of years of available reserves has actually grown. Moreover, the increasing abundance is reflected in an ever-decreasing price: *The Economist's* index of prices of industrial raw materials has dropped some 80% in inflation-adjusted terms since 1845.

Next, the population explosion is also turning out to be a bugaboo. In 1968, Dr Ehrlich predicted in his best selling book, "The Population Bomb", that "the battle to feed humanity is over. In the course of the 1970s the world will experience starvation of tragic proportions—hundreds of millions of people will starve to death."

That did not happen. Instead, according to the United Nations, agricultural production in the developing world has increased by 52% per person since 1961. The daily food intake in poor countries has increased from 1,932 calories, barely enough for survival, in 1961 to 2,650 calories in 1998, and is expected to rise to 3,020 by 2030. Likewise, the proportion of people in developing countries who are starving has dropped from 45% in 1949 to 18% today, and is expected to decline even further to 12% in 2010 and just 6% in 2030. Food, in other words, is becoming not scarcer but ever more abundant. This is reflected in its price. Since 1800 food prices have decreased by more than 90%, and in 2000, according to the World Bank, prices were lower than ever before.

Modern Malthus

Dr Ehrlich's prediction echoes that made 170 years earlier by Thomas Malthus. Malthus claimed that, if unchecked, human population would expand exponentially, while food production could increase only linearly, by bringing new land into cultivation. He was wrong. Population growth has turned out to have an internal check: as people grow richer and healthier, they have smaller families. Indeed, the growth rate of the human population reached its peak, of more than 2% a year, in the early 1960s. The rate of

Figure 1

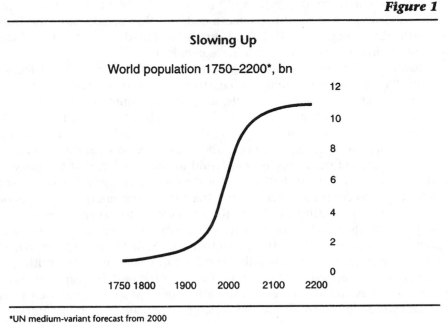

Slowing Up

World population 1750–2200*, bn

*UN medium-variant forecast from 2000
Source: UNPD

increase has been declining ever since. It is now 1.26%, and is expected to fall to 0.46% in 2050. The United Nations estimates that most of the world's population growth will be over by 2100, with the population stabilising at just below 11 billion (see Figure 1).

Malthus also failed to take account of developments in agricultural technology. These have squeezed more and more food out of each hectare of land. It is this application of human ingenuity that has boosted food production, not merely in line with, but ahead of, population growth. It has also, incidentally, reduced the need to take new land into cultivation, thus reducing the pressure on biodiversity.

Third, that threat of biodiversity loss is real, but exaggerated. Most early estimates used simple island models that linked a loss in habitat with a loss of biodiversity. A rule-of-thumb indicated that loss of 90% of forest meant a 50% loss of species. As rainforests seemed to be cut at alarming rates, estimates of annual species loss of 20,000–100,000 abounded. Many people expected the number of species to fall by half globally within a generation or two.

However, the data simply does not bear out these predictions. In the eastern United States, forests were reduced over two centuries to fragments totalling just 1–2% of their original area, yet this resulted in the extinction of only one forest bird. In Puerto Rico, the primary forest area has been reduced over the past 400 years by 99%, yet "only" seven of 60 species of bird has become extinct. All but 12% of the Brazilian Atlantic rainforest was cleared in the 19th century, leaving only scattered fragments. According to the rule-of-thumb, half of all its species should have become extinct. Yet, when the World

Figure 2

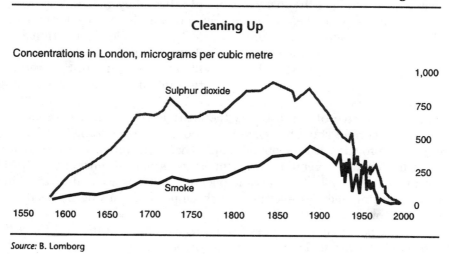

Cleaning Up

Concentrations in London, micrograms per cubic metre

Source: B. Lomborg

Conservation Union and the Brazilian Society of Zoology analysed all 291 known Atlantic forest animals, none could be declared extinct. Species, therefore, seem more resilient than expected. And tropical forests are not lost at annual rates of 2.4%, as many environmentalists have claimed: the latest UN figures indicate a loss of less than 0.5%.

Fourth, pollution is also exaggerated. Many analyses show that air pollution diminishes when a society becomes rich enough to be able to afford to be concerned about the environment. For London, the city for which the best data are available, air pollution peaked around 1890 (see Figure 2). Today, the air is cleaner than it has been since 1585. There is good reason to believe that this general picture holds true for all developed countries. And, although air pollution is increasing in many developing countries, they are merely replicating the development of the industrialised countries. When they grow sufficiently rich they, too, will start to reduce their air pollution.

All this contradicts the litany. Yet opinion polls suggest that many people, in the rich world, at least, nurture the belief that environmental standards are declining. Four factors cause this disjunction between perception and reality.

Always Look on the Dark Side of Life

One is the lopsidedness built into scientific research. Scientific funding goes mainly to areas with many problems. That may be wise policy, but it will also create an impression that many more potential problems exist than is the case.

Secondly, environmental groups need to be noticed by the mass media. They also need to keep the money rolling in. Understandably, perhaps, they sometimes exaggerate. In 1997, for example, the Worldwide Fund for Nature issued a press release entitled, "Two-thirds of the world's forests lost forever". The truth turns out to be nearer 20%.

Though these groups are run overwhelmingly by selfless folk, they nevertheless share many of the characteristics of other lobby groups. That would matter less if people applied the same degree of scepticism to environmental lobbying as they do to lobby groups in other fields. A trade organisation arguing for, say, weaker pollution controls is instantly seen as self-interested. Yet a green organisation opposing such a weakening is seen as altruistic, even if a dispassionate view of the controls in question might suggest they are doing more harm than good.

A third source of confusion is the attitude of the media. People are clearly more curious about bad news than good. Newspapers and broadcasters are there to provide what the public wants. That, however, can lead to significant distortions of perception. An example was America's encounter with El Niño in 1997 and 1998. This climatic phenomenon was accused of wrecking tourism, causing allergies, melting the ski-slopes and causing 22 deaths by dumping snow in Ohio.

A more balanced view comes from a recent article in the *Bulletin of the American Meteorological Society.* This tries to count up both the problems and the benefits of the 1997–98 Niño. The damage it did was estimated at $4 billion. However, the benefits amounted to some $19 billion. These came from higher winter temperatures (which saved an estimated 850 lives, reduced heating costs and diminished spring floods caused by meltwaters, and from the well-documented connection between past Niños and fewer Atlantic hurricanes. In 1998, America experienced no big Atlantic hurricanes and thus avoided huge losses. These benefits were not reported as widely as the losses.

The fourth factor is poor individual perception. People worry that the endless rise in the amount of stuff everyone throws away will cause the world to run out of places to dispose of waste. Yet, even if America's trash output continues to rise as it has done in the past, and even if the American population doubles by 2100, all the rubbish America produces through the entire 21st century will still take up only the area of a square, each of whose sides measures 28 km (18 miles). That is just one-12,000th of the area of the entire United States.

Ignorance matters only when it leads to faulty judgments. But fear of largely imaginary environmental problems can divert political energy from dealing with real ones. The table, showing the cost in the United States of various measures to save a year of a person's life, illustrates the danger. Some environmental policies, such as reducing lead in petrol and sulphur-dioxide emissions from fuel oil, are very cost-effective. But many of these are already in place. Most environmental measures are less cost-effective than interventions aimed at improving safety (such as installing air-bags in cars) and those involving medical screening and vaccination. Some are absurdly expensive.

Yet a false perception of risk may be about to lead to errors more expensive even than controlling the emission of benzene at tyre plants. Carbon-dioxide emissions are causing the planet to warm. The best estimates are that the temperature will rise by some 2°–3°C in this century, causing considerable problems, almost exclusively in the developing world, at a total cost of $5,000 billion. Getting rid of global warming would thus seem to be a

Table 1

The Price of a Life

Cost of saving one year of one person's life – 1993$

Passing laws to make seat-belt use mandatory	69
Sickle-cell anaemia screening for black new-borns	240
Mammography for women aged 50	810
Pneumonia vaccination for people aged over 65	2,000
Giving advice on stopping smoking to people who smoke more than one packet a day	9,800
Putting men aged 30 on a low-cholesterol diet	19,000
Regular leisure-time physical activity, such as jogging for men aged 35	38,000
Making pedestrians and cyclists more visible	73,000
Installing air-bags (rather than manual lap belts) in cars	120,000
Installing arsenic emission-control at glass-manufacturing plants	51,000,000
Setting radiation emission standards for nuclear-power plants	180,000,000
Installing benzene emission control at rubber-tyre manufacturing plants	20,000,000,000

Source: T. Tengs et al, *Risk Analysis*, June 1995

good idea. The question is whether the cure will actually be more costly than the ailment.

Despite the intuition that something drastic needs to be done about such a costly problem, economic analyses clearly show that it will be far more expensive to cut carbon-dioxide emissions radically than to pay the costs of adaptation to the increased temperatures. The effect of the Kyoto Protocol on the climate would be minuscule, even if it were implemented in full. A model by Tom Wigley, one of the main authors of the reports of the UN Climate Change Panel, shows how an expected temperature increase of 2.1°C in 2100 would be diminished by the treaty to an increase of 1.9°C instead. Or, to put it another way, the temperature increase that the planet would have experienced in 2094 would be postponed to 2100.

So the Kyoto agreement does not prevent global warming, but merely buys the world six years. Yet, the cost of Kyoto, for the United States alone, will be higher than the cost of solving the world's single most pressing health problems: providing universal access to clean drinking water and sanitation. Such measures would avoid 2m deaths every year, and prevent half a billion people from becoming seriously ill.

And that is the best case. If the treaty were implemented inefficiently, the cost of Kyoto could approach $1 trillion, or more than five times the cost of worldwide water and sanitation coverage. For comparison, the total global-aid budget today is about $50 billion a year.

To replace the litany with facts is crucial if people want to make the best possible decisions for the future. Of course, rational environmental management and environmental investment are good ideas—but the costs and benefits of such investments should be compared to those of similar investments in all the other important areas of human endeavour. It may be costly to be overly optimistic—but more costly still to be too pessimistic.

POSTSCRIPT

Is Humankind Dangerously Harming the Environment?

Though a number of works (see below) support Lomborg's argument, his evidence has come under heavy attack (see Richard C. Bell, "How Did *The Skeptical Environmentalist* Pull the Wool Over the Eyes of So Many Editors?" *WorldWatch* [March–April 2002] and *Scientific American* [January 2002]). The issue of the state of the environment and prospects for the future have been hotly debated for over 30 years with little chance of ending soon. Two key issues are the potential impacts of global warming and the net effects of future agricultural technologies, which will be used to feed growing populations with richer diets. On the former, see Douglas Long, *Global Warming* (Facts on File, 2004); Robert Hunter, *Thermageddon: Countdown to 2030* (Arcade Pub., 2003); John Theodore Houghton, *Global Warming: The Complete Briefing*, 3rd edition (Cambridge University, 2004); Andrew Simms et al., *Up in Smoke?: Threats from, and Responses to, the Impact of Global Warming on Human Development* (New Economic Foundation, 2004); and the journal *The Ecologist* (March 2002). Ronald Bailey and others debunk the global warming "scare" in his edited book, *Global Warming and Other Eco-Myths: How the Environmental Movement Uses False Science to Scare Us to Death* (Prima, 2002). See also Patrick J. Michaels, *Meltdown: The Predicatable Distortion of Global Warming by Scientists, Politicians, and the Media* (Cato Institue, 2004). On food production issues and agriculture technologies, see Lester R. Brown, *Outgrowing the Earth: The Food Security Challenge in the Age of Falling Water Tables and Rising Temperatures* (Earth Policy Institute, 2004); Bread for the World, *Are We on Track to End Hunger?: 14th Annual Report on the State of World Hunger* (Bread for the World Institution, 2004); and On agricultural technologies, see Vaclav Smil, *Feeding the World: A Challenge for the Twenty-First Century* (MIT Press, 2000).

Paul R. Ehrlich and Anne H. Ehrlich wrote *Betrayal of Science and Reason: How Anti-Environmental Rhetoric Threatens Our Future* (Island Press, 1996) to refute statements by those who do not agree with the messages of the concerned environmentalists. Julian Lincoln Simon counters with *Hoodwinking the Nation* (Transaction, 1999). For a debate on this issue see Norman Myers and Julian L. Simon, *Scarcity or Abundance? A Debate on the Environment* (W. W. Norton, 1994).

Publications that are optimistic about the availability of resources and the health of the environment include Ronald Bailey, ed., *The True State of the Planet* (Free Press, 1995) and Gregg Easterbrook, *A Moment on the Earth: The Coming Age of Environmental Optimism* (Viking, 1995). Publications by some who believe that population growth and human interventions in the environment have dangerous consequences for the future of mankind include Joseph Wayne Smith, Graham Lyons, and Gary Sauer-Thompson, *Healing a Wounded World* (Praeger, 1997); Douglas E. Booth, *The Environmental Consequences of Growth* (Routledge, 1998); and Kirill Kondratyev et al., *Stability of Life on Earth: Principal Subject of Scientific Research in the 21st Century* (Springer 2004); and James Gustive Speth, *Red Sky at Morning: America and the Crisis of the Global Environment* (Yale University Press, 2004).

Several works relate environmental problems to very severe political, social, and economic problems, including Michael Renner, *Fighting for Survival* (W. W. Norton, 1996); Michael N. Dobkowski and Isidor Wallimann, eds., *The Coming Age of Scarcity: Preventing Mass Death and Genocide in the Twenty-First Century* (Syracuse University Press, 1998); and one with a long timeframe, Sing C. Chew, *World Ecological Degradation: Accumulation, Urbanization, and Deforestation, 3000BC–AD2000* (Roman and Littlefield, 2001). An important series of publications on environmental problems is by the World-watch Institute, including two annuals: *State of the World* and *Vital Signs*.

ISSUE 19

Is Globalization Good for Humankind?

YES: Johan Norberg, from "Three Cheers for Global Capitalism," *The American Enterprise* (June 2004)

NO: Martin Hart-Landsberg, from "Neoliberalism: Myths and Reality," *Monthly Review* (April 2006)

ISSUE SUMMARY

YES: Author Johan Norberg argues that globalization is overwhelmingly good. Consumers throughout the world get better-quality goods at lower prices because the competition forces producers to be more creative, efficient, and responsive to consumers' demands. Even most poor people benefit greatly.

NO: Martin Hart-Landsberg, Professor of Economics at Lewis and Clark College, argues that globalization has "enhanced transnational capitalist power and profits at the cost of growing economic instability and deteriorating working and living conditions."

Globalization, which stands for worldwide processes, activities, and institutions, is a really big issue today. It involves world markets, world finance, world communications, world media, world religions, world popular culture, world rights movements, world drug trade, etc. The focus of most commentators is on the world economy, which many believe promises strong growth in world wealth. Critics focus on the world economy's negative impacts on workers' wages, environmental protections and regulations, and national and local cultures. Many say that it is easy for Americans to feel positive toward globalization because America and its businesses, media, and culture are at the center of the globalized world, which ensures that America gains more than its proportional share of the benefits. But the real debate is whether or not globalization benefits all mankind. When the whole world is considered, there may be far more minuses to be weighed against the pluses. It is hard to settle this debate because so many different dimensions that are incomparable must be included in the calculation of the cost-benefit ratio.

The concept of globalization forces us to think about many complicated issues at the same time. There are technological, economic, political, cultural, and ethical aspects of globalization. Technological developments make possible the communication, transportation, coordination, and organization that make economic globalization possible. Political factors have made this a relatively free global economy. Restrictions on trade and production have been greatly reduced, and competition has greatly increased. The results have been increased production and wealth and celebration in financial circles. But competition creates losers as well as winners, so peoples throughout the world are protesting and resisting economic globalization. Many are also resisting cultural globalization because their own cultures are threatened. They feel that the global culture is materialistic, sexualized, secular, and egocentric—and they may be right. But many also consider the strengths of the global culture, such as championing human rights, democracy, and justice.

In the selections that follow, Johan Norberg reports on the benefits of the global economy and counters many of the arguments against globalization. His main argument is that the global economy stimulates faster economic growth, which improves the standard of living of all groups. Martin Hart-Landsberg opposes globalization because it adversely impacts workers, the environment, and the poor. To establish his argument, he attacks its theoretical underpinning on globalization—which is that free trade enhances economic growth that benefits everyone.

YES

Johan Norberg

Three Cheers for Global Capitalism

Under what is rather barrenly termed "globalization"—the process by which people, information, trade, investments, democracy, and the market economy tend more and more to cross national borders—our options and opportunities have multiplied. We don't have to shop at the big local company; we can turn to a foreign competitor. We don't have to work for the village's one and only employer; we can seek alternative opportunities. We don't have to make do with local cultural amenities; the world's culture is at our disposal. Companies, politicians, and associations have to exert themselves to elicit interest from people who have a whole world of options. Our ability to control our own lives is growing, and prosperity is growing with it.

Free markets and free trade and free choices transfer power to individuals at the expense of political institutions. Because there is no central control booth, it seems unchecked, chaotic. Political theorist Benjamin Barber speaks for many critics when he bemoans the absence of "viable powers of opposing, subduing, and civilizing the anarchic forces of the global economy." "Globalization" conjures up the image of an anonymous, enigmatic, elusive force, but it is actually just the sum of billions of people in thousands of places making decentralized decisions about their own lives. No one is in the driver's seat precisely because all of us are steering.

No company would import goods from abroad if we didn't buy them. If we did not send e-mails, order books, and download music every day, the Internet would wither and die. We eat bananas from Ecuador, order magazines from Britain, work for export companies selling to Germany and Russia, vacation in Thailand, and save money for retirement by investing in South America and Asia. These things are carried out by businesses only because we as individuals want them to. Globalization takes place from the bottom up.

A recent book about the nineteenth-century Swedish historian Erik Geijer notes that he was able to keep himself up to date just by sitting in Uppsala reading the *Edinburgh Review* and the *Quarterly Review*. That is how simple and intelligible the world can be when only a tiny elite in the capitals of Europe makes any difference to the course of world events. How much more complex and confusing everything is now, with ordinary people having a say over their own lives. Elites may mourn that they have lost power, but everyday life has vastly improved now that inexpensive goods and outside information and different employment opportunities are no longer blocked by political barriers.

From *American Enterprise*, June 2004, pp. 20–27. Copyright © 2004 by American Enterprise Institute. Reprinted by permission.

To those of us in rich countries, more economic liberty to pick and choose may sound like a trivial luxury, even an annoyance—but it isn't. Fresh options are invaluable for all of us. And the existence from which globalization delivers people in the Third World—poverty, filth, ignorance, and powerlessness—really is intolerable. When global capitalism knocks at the door of Bhagant, an elderly agricultural worker and "untouchable" in the Indian village of Saijani, it leads to his house being built of brick instead of mud, to shoes on his feet, and clean clothes—not rags—on his back. Outside Bhagant's house, the streets now have drains, and the fragrance of tilled earth has replaced the stench of refuse. Thirty years ago Bhagant didn't know he was living in India. Today he watches world news on television. The stand that we in the privileged world take on the burning issue of globalization can determine whether or not more people will experience the development that has taken place in Bhagant's village.

Critics of globalization often paint a picture of capitalist marauders secretly plotting for world mastery, but this notion is completely off the mark. It has mostly been pragmatic, previously socialist, politicians who fanned globalization in China, Latin America, and East Asia—after realizing that government control-freakery had ruined their societies. Any allegation of runaway capitalism has to be tempered by the observation that today we have the largest public sectors and highest taxes the world has ever known. The economic liberalization measures of the last quarter century may have abolished some of the recent past's centralist excesses, but they have hardly ushered in a system of laissez-faire.

What defenders of global capitalism believe in, first and foremost, is man's capacity for achieving great things by means of the combined force of market exchanges. It is not their intention to put a price tag on everything. The important things—love, family, friendship, one's own way of life—cannot be assigned a monetary value. Principled advocates of global economic liberty plead for a more open world because that setting unleashes individual creativity as none other can. At its core, the belief in capitalist freedom among nations is a belief in mankind. . . .

Today, we hear that life is increasingly unfair amidst the market economy: "The rich are getting richer, and the poor are getting poorer." But if we look beyond the catchy slogans, we find that while many of the rich have indeed grown richer, so have most of the poor. Absolute poverty has diminished, and where it was greatest 20 years ago—in Asia—hundreds of millions of people have achieved a secure existence, even affluence, previously undreamed of. Global misery has diminished, and great injustices have started to unravel. . . .

◦◦◦

This progress is all very well, many critics of globalization will argue, but even if the majority are better off, gaps have widened and wealthy people and countries have improved their lot more rapidly than others. The critics point out that 40 years ago the combined per capita GDP of the 20 richest countries was 15 times greater than that of the 20 poorest, and is now 30 times greater.

There are two reasons why this objection to globalization does not hold up. First, if everyone is better off, what does it matter that the improvement comes faster for some than for others? Only those who consider wealth a greater problem than poverty can find irritation in middle-class citizens becoming millionaires while the previously poverty-stricken become middle class.

Second, the allegation of increased inequality is simply wrong.

The notion that global inequality has increased is largely based on figures from the U.N.'s 1999 *Human Development Report*. The problem with these figures is that they don't take into account what people can actually buy with their money. Without that "purchasing power" adjustment, the figures only show what a currency is worth on the international market, and nothing about local conditions. Poor people's actual living standards hinge on the cost of their food, their clothing, their housing—not what their money would get them while vacationing in Europe. That's why the U.N. uses purchasing-power-adjusted figures in other measures of living standards. It only resorts to the unadjusted figures, oddly, in order to present a theory of inequality.

A report from the Norwegian Institute for Foreign Affairs investigated global inequality by means of figures adjusted for purchasing power. Their data show that, contrary to conventional wisdom, inequality between countries has continuously *declined* ever since the end of the 1970s. This decline has been especially rapid since 1993, when globalization really gathered speed.

More recently, similar research by Columbia University development economist Xavier Sala-i-Martin has confirmed those findings. He found that when U.N. figures are adjusted for purchasing power, they point to a sharp decline in world inequality. Sala-i-Martin and co-author Surjit Bhalla also found independently that if we focus on inequality between *persons*, rather than inequality between *countries*, global inequality at the end of 2000 was at its lowest point since the end of World War II.

Estimates that compare countries rather than individuals, both authors note, grossly overestimate real inequality because they allow gains for huge numbers of people to be outweighed by losses for far fewer. For instance, country aggregates treat China and Grenada as data points of equal weight, even though China's population is 12,000 times Grenada's. Once we shift our focus to people rather than nations, the evidence is overwhelming that the past 30 years have witnessed a strong shift toward global equalization.

⌒◉⌒

One myth about trade is the notion that exports to other countries are a good thing, but that imports are somehow a bad thing. Many believe that a country grows powerful by selling much and buying little. The truth is that our standard of living will not rise until we use our money to buy more and cheaper things. One of the first trade theorists, James Mill, rightly noted in 1821 that "The benefit which derives from exchanging one commodity for another arises in all cases from the commodity received, not the commodity given." The only point of exports, in other words, is to enable us to get imports in return. . . .

Trade is not a zero-sum game in which one party loses what the other party gains. There would *be* no exchange if both parties did not feel that they benefited. The really interesting yardstick is not the "balance of trade" (where a "surplus" means that we are exporting more than we are importing) but the *quantity* of trade, since both exports and imports are gains. Imports are often feared as a potential cause of unemployment: If we import cheap toys and clothing from China, then toy and garment manufacturers here will have to scale down. But by obtaining cheaper goods from abroad, we save resources in the United States and can therefore invest in new industries and occupations.

જ⊙ર

Free trade brings freedom: freedom for people to buy and sell what they want. As an added benefit, this leads to the efficient use of resources. A company, or country, specializes where it can generate the greatest value.

Economic openness also leads to an enduring effort to improve production, because foreign competition forces firms to be as good and cheap as possible. As production in established industries becomes ever more efficient, resources are freed up for investment in new methods, inventions, and products. Foreign competition brings the same benefits that we recognize in economic competition generally; it simply extends competition to a broader field.

One of the most important but hard to measure benefits of free trade is that a country trading a great deal with the rest of the world imports new ideas and new techniques in the bargain. If the United States pursues free trade, our companies are exposed to the world's best ideas. They can then borrow those ideas, buy leading technology from elsewhere, and hire the best available manpower. This compels the companies to be more dynamic themselves.

The world's output today is six times what it was 50 years ago, and world trade is 16 times greater. There is reason to believe that the trade growth drove much of the production growth. One comprehensive study of the effects of trade was conducted by Harvard economists Jeffrey Sachs and Andrew Warner. They examined the trade policies between 1970 and 1989 of 117 countries. The study reveals a statistically significant connection between free trade and economic growth. Growth was between three and six times *higher* in free-trade countries than in protectionist ones. Factors like improved education turned out to be vastly less important than trade in increasing economic progress.

Over those two decades, developing countries that practiced free trade had an average annual growth rate of 4.5 percent, while developing countries that practiced protectionism grew by only 0.7 percent. Among industrial countries, the free traders experienced annual growth of 2.3 percent, versus only 0.7 percent among the protectionists. It must be emphasized that this is not a matter of countries earning more because *others* opened to *their* exports. Rather, these countries earned more by keeping their own markets open.

જ⊙ર

If free trade is constantly making production more efficient, won't that result in the disappearance of job opportunities? When Asians manufacture our cars and South Americans produce our meat, auto workers and farmers in the

United States lose their jobs and unemployment rises. Foreigners and developing countries will increasingly produce the things we need, until we don't have any jobs left. If increasing automation means everything we consume today will be able to be made by half the U.S. labor force in 20 years, doesn't that mean that the other half will be out of work? Such are the horror scenarios depicted in many anti-globalization writings.

The notion that a colossal unemployment crisis is looming began to grow popular in the mid 1970s. Since then, production has been streamlined and internationalized more than ever. Yet far more jobs have been created than have disappeared. We have more efficient production than ever before, but also more people at work. Between 1975 and 1998, employment in countries like the United States, Canada, and Australia rose by 50 percent.

And it is in the most internationalized economies, making the most use of modern technology, that employment has grown fastest. Between 1983 and 1995 in the United States, 24 million more job opportunities were created than disappeared. And those were not low-paid, unskilled jobs, as is often alleged. On the contrary, 70 percent of the new jobs carried a wage above the American median level. Nearly half the new jobs belonged to the most highly skilled, a figure which has risen even more rapidly since 1995.

So allegations of progressively fewer people being needed in production have no empirical foundation. And no wonder, for they are wrong in theory too. Imagine a pre-industrial economy where most everyone is laboring to feed himself. Then food production is improved by new technologies, new machines, foreign competition, and imports. That results in a lot of people being forced to leave the agricultural sector. Does that mean there is nothing for them to do, that consumption is constant? Of course not; the manpower which used to be required to feed the population shifts to clothing it, and providing better housing. Then improved transport, and entertainment. Then newspapers, telephones, and computers.

The notion that the quantity of employment is constant, that a job gained by one person is always a job taken from someone else, has provoked a variety of foolish responses. Some advocate that jobs must be shared. Others smash machinery. Many advocate raising tariffs and excluding immigrants. But the whole notion is wrong. The very process of a task being done more efficiently, thus allowing jobs to be shed, enables new industries to grow, providing people with new and better jobs.

꿍◉ꕤ

Efficiency does, of course, have a flip side. Economist Joseph Schumpeter famously described a dynamic market as a process of "creative destruction," because it destroys old solutions and industries, with a creative end in view. As the word "destruction" suggests, not everyone benefits from every market transformation in the short term. The process is painful for those who have invested in or are employed by less-efficient industries. Drivers of horse-drawn cabs lost out with the spread of automobiles, as did producers of paraffin lamps when electric light was introduced. In more modern times, manufacturers of typewriters were put out of business by the computer, and LP records were superseded by CDs.

Painful changes of this kind happen all the time as a result of new inventions and methods of production. Unquestionably, such changes can cause trauma for those affected. But the most foolish way to counter such problems is to try to prevent them. It is generally fruitless; mere spitting into the wind. Besides, without "creative destruction," we would *all* be stuck with a lower standard of living. . . .

A review of more than 50 surveys of adjustments after trade liberalization in different countries shows clearly that adjustment problems are far milder than the conventional debate suggests. For every dollar of trade adjustment costs, roughly $30 is harvested in the form of welfare gains. A study of trade liberalization in 13 different countries showed that in all but one, industrial employment had already increased just one year after the liberalization. The process turns out to be far more creative than destructive.

If there are problems resulting from unshackled capitalism, they ought to be greatest in the United States, with its constant swirling economic transformations. But our job market is a bit like the Hydra in the legend of Hercules. Every time Hercules cuts off one of the beast's heads, two new ones appear. The danger of having to continue changing jobs all one's life is exaggerated: The average length of time an American stays in a particular job actually increased between 1983 and 1995, from 3.5 years to 3.8. Nor is it true, as many people believe, that more jobs are created in the United States only because real wages have stagnated or fallen since the 1970s. A growing proportion of wages is now paid in non-money forms, such as health insurance, stocks, 401(k) contributions, day care, and so forth, to avoid taxation. When these benefits are included, American wages have risen right along with productivity. Among poor Americans, the proportion of consumption devoted to food, clothing, and housing has fallen since the 1970s from 52 to 37 percent, which clearly shows that they have money to spare for much more than the bare necessities of life. . . .

⋅⊶⊙⊷⋅

Advocates of protectionism often complain of "sweatshops" allegedly run by multinational corporations in the Third World. Let's look at the evidence: Economists have compared the conditions of people employed in American-owned facilities in developing countries with those of people employed elsewhere in the same country. In the poorest developing countries, the average employee of an American-affiliated company makes *eight times* the average national wage! In middle income countries, American employers pay *three times* the national average. Even compared with corresponding modern jobs in the same country, the multinationals pay about 30 percent higher wages. Marxists maintain that multinationals exploit poor workers. Are much higher wages "exploitation"?

The same marked difference can be seen in working conditions. The International Labor Organization has shown that multinationals, especially in the footwear and garment industries, are leading the trend toward better working conditions in the Third World. When multinational corporations accustom workers to better-lit, safer, and cleaner factories, they raise the general standard. Native firms then also have to offer better conditions, otherwise no one will work for them. Zhou Litai, one of China's foremost labor attorneys, has pointed out that Western consumers are the principal driving force behind the improvements of working conditions in China, and worries that "if Nike and Reebok go, this pressure evaporates.". . .

Corporations have not acquired more power through free trade. Indeed, they used to be far more powerful—and still are in dictatorships and controlled economies. Large corporations have chances to corrupt or manipulate when power is distributed by public officials who can be hobnobbed over luncheons to give protection through monopolies, tariffs, or subsides. Free trade, on the other hand, exposes corporations to competition. Above all, it lets consumers ruthlessly pick and choose across national borders, rejecting companies that don't measure up. . . .

Companies in free competition can grow large and increase their sales only by being better than others. Companies that fail to do so quickly go bust or get taken over by someone who can make better use of their capital, buildings, machinery, and employees. Capitalism is very tough—but mainly on firms offering outdated, poor-quality, or expensive goods and services. Fear of established companies growing so large as to become unaccountable has absolutely no foundation in reality. In the U.S., the most capitalist large country in the world, the market share of the 25 biggest corporations has steadily dwindled over recent decades.

Freer markets make it easier for small firms with fresh ideas to compete with big corporations. Between 1980 and 1993, the 500 biggest American corporations saw their share of the country's total employment diminish from 16 to 11 percent. During the same period, the average personnel strength of American firms fell from 17 to 15 people, and the proportion of the population working in companies with more than 250 employees fell from 37 to 29 percent.

Of the 500 biggest enterprises in the United States in 1980, one third had disappeared by 1990. Another 40 percent had evaporated five years later. Whether they failed to grow enough to stay on the list, died, merged, or broke up, the key lesson is that big corporations have much less power over consumers than we sometimes imagine. Even the most potent corporation must constantly re-earn its stripes, or tumble fast. . . .

Many people fear a "McDonaldization" or "Disneyfication" of the world, a creeping global homogeneity that leaves everyone wearing the same clothes, eating the same food, and seeing the same movies. But this portrayal does not accurately describe globalization. Anyone going out in the capitals of Europe today will have no trouble finding hamburgers and Coca-Cola, but he will just as easily find kebabs, sushi, Tex-Mex tacos, Peking duck, Thai lemongrass soup, and cappuccino. . . .

The world is indeed moving toward a common objective, but that objective is not the predominance of a particular culture, rather it is pluralism, the freedom to choose from a host of different paths and destinations. The market for experimental electronic music or film versions of novels by Dostoevsky may be small in any given place, so musicians and filmmakers producing such material could never produce anything without access to the much larger audience provided by globalization.

This internationalization is, ironically, what makes people believe that differences are vanishing. When you travel abroad, things look much the same as in your own country: The people there also have goods and chain stores from different parts of the globe. This phenomenon is not due to uniformity and the elimination of differences, but by the growth of pluralism everywhere. . . .

⌇❦⌇

In the age of globalization, the ideas of freedom and individualism have attained tremendous force. There are few concepts as inspiring as that of self-determination. When people in other countries glimpse a chance to set their own course, it becomes almost irresistible. If there is any elimination of differences throughout the world, it has been the convergence of societies on the practice of allowing people to choose the sort of existence they please.

Global commerce does undermine old economic interests, challenge cultures, and erode some traditional power centers. Advocates of globalization have to show that greater gains and opportunities counterbalance such problems. . . .

Lasse Berg and Stig Karlsson record Chinese villagers' descriptions of the changes they experienced since the 1960s: "The last time you were here, people's thoughts and minds were closed, bound up," stated farmer Yang Zhengming. But as residents acquired power over their own livelihoods they began to think for themselves. Yang explains that "a farmer could then own himself. He did not need to submit. He decided himself what he was going to do, how and when. The proceeds of his work were his own. It was freedom that came to us. We were allowed to own things for ourselves."

Coercion and poverty still cover large areas of our globe. But thanks to globalizing economic freedom, people know that living in a state of oppression is not natural or necessary. People who have acquired a taste of economic liberty and expanded horizons will not consent to be shut in again by walls or fences. They will work to create a better existence for themselves. The aim of our politics should be to give them that freedom.

Martin Hart-Landsberg  **NO**

Neoliberalism: Myths and Reality

Agreements like the North American Free Trade Agreement (NAFTA) and the World Trade Organization (WTO) have enhanced transnational capitalist power and profits at the cost of growing economic instability and deteriorating working and living conditions. Despite this reality, neoliberal claims that liberalization, deregulation, and privatization produce unrivaled benefits have been repeated so often that many working people accept them as unchallengeable truths. Thus, business and political leaders in the United States and other developed capitalist countries routinely defend their efforts to expand the WTO and secure new agreements like the Free Trade Area of the Americas (FTAA) as necessary to ensure a brighter future for the world's people, especially those living in poverty. . . .

Therefore, if we are going to mount an effective challenge to the neoliberal globalization project, we must redouble our efforts to win the "battle of ideas." Winning this battle requires, among other things, demonstrating that neoliberalism functions as an ideological cover for the promotion of capitalist interests, not as a scientific framework for illuminating the economic and social consequences of capitalist dynamics. It also requires showing the processes by which capitalism, as an international system, undermines rather than promotes working class interests in both third world and developed capitalist countries.

The Myth of the Superiority of 'Free Trade': Theoretical Arguments

According to supporters of the WTO and agreements such as the FTAA, these institutions/agreements seek to promote free trade in order to enhance efficiency and maximize economic well being. This focus on trade hides what is in fact a much broader political-economic agenda: the expansion and enhancement of corporate profit making opportunities. In the case of the WTO, this agenda has been pursued through a variety of agreements that are explicitly designed to limit or actually block public regulation of economic activity in contexts that have little to do with trade as normally understood.

For example, the Agreement on Trade-Related Aspects of Intellectual Property Rights (TRIPS) limits the ability of states to deny patents on certain products (including over living organisms) or control the use of products patented in their respective nations (including the use of compulsory licensing to ensure affordability of critical medicines). It also forces states to accept a significant increase in the length of time during which patents remain in force. The Agreement on Trade Related Investment Measures (TRIMS) restricts the ability of states to put performance requirements on foreign direct investment (FDI), encompassing those that would require the use of local inputs (including labor) or technology transfer. A proposed expansion of the General Agreement on Trade in Services (GATS) would force states to open their national service markets (which include everything from health care and education to public utilities and retail trade) to foreign providers as well as limit public regulation of their activity. Similarly, a proposed Government Procurement Agreement would deny states the ability to use non-economic criteria, such as labor and environmental practices, in awarding contracts.

These agreements are rarely discussed in the mainstream media precisely because they directly raise issues of private versus public power and are not easily defended. This is one of the most important reasons why those who support the capitalist globalization project prefer to describe the institutional arrangements that help underpin it as trade agreements and defend them on the basis of the alleged virtues of free trade. This is a defense that unfortunately and undeservedly holds enormous sway among working people, especially in the developed capitalist countries. And, using it as a theoretical foundation, capitalist globalization advocates find it relatively easy to encourage popular acceptance of the broader proposition that market determined outcomes are superior to socially determined ones in all spheres of activity. Therefore, it is critical that we develop an effective and accessible critique of this myth of the superiority of free trade. In fact, this is an easier task than generally assumed.

Arguments promoting free trade generally rest on the theory of comparative advantage. David Ricardo introduced this theory in 1821 in his *Principles of Political Economy and Taxation*. It is commonly misunderstood to assert the obvious, that countries have or can create different comparative advantages or that trade can be helpful. In fact, it supports a very specific policy conclusion: a country's best economic policy is to allow unregulated international market activity to determine its comparative advantage and national patterns of production. . . .

Like all theories, the theory of comparative advantage (and its conclusion) is based on a number of assumptions. Among the most important are:

- There is perfect competition between firms.
- There is full employment of all factors of production.
- Labor and capital are perfectly mobile within a country and do not move across national borders.
- A country's gains from trade are captured by those living in the country and spent locally.
- A country's external trade is always in balance.
- Market prices accurately reflect the real (or social) costs of the products produced.

Even a quick consideration of these assumptions reveals that they are extensive and unrealistic. Moreover, if they are not satisfied, there is no basis for accepting the theory's conclusion that free-market policies will promote international well being. For example, the assumption of full employment of all factors of production, including labor, is obviously false. Equally problematic is the theory's implied restructuring process, which assumes that (but never explains how) workers who lose their jobs as a result of free-trade generated imports will quickly find new employment in the expanding export sector of the economy. In reality, workers (and other factors of production) may not be equally productive in alternative uses. Even if we ignore this problem, if their reallocation is not sufficiently fast, the newly liberalized economy will likely suffer an increase in unemployment, leading to a reduction in aggregate demand and perhaps recession. Thus, even if all factors of production eventually become fully employed, it is quite possible that the cost of adjustment would outweigh the alleged efficiency gains from the trade induced restructuring.

The assumption that prices reflect social costs is also problematic. Many product markets are dominated by monopolies, many firms receive substantial government subsidies that influence their production and pricing decisions, and many production activities generate significant negative externalities (especially environmental ones). Therefore, trade specialization based on existing market prices could easily produce a structure of international economic activity with lower overall efficiency, leading to a reduction in social well being. . . .

Also worthy of challenge is the assumption that capital is not highly mobile across national borders. This assumption helps to underpin others, including the assumptions of full employment and balanced trade. If capital is highly mobile, then free-market/free-trade policies could produce capital flight leading to deindustrialization, unbalanced trade, unemployment, and economic crisis. In short, the free-trade supporting policy recommendations that flow from the theory of comparative advantage rest on a series of very dubious assumptions. . . .

Neoliberalism: The Reality

The post-1980 neoliberal era has been marked by slower growth, greater trade imbalances, and deteriorating social conditions. The United Nations Conference on Trade and Development (UNCTAD) reports that, "for developing countries as a whole (excluding China), the average trade deficit in the 1990s is higher than in the 1970s by almost 3 percentage points of GDP, while the average growth rate is lower by 2 percent per annum." Moreover,

> The pattern is broadly similar in all developing regions. In Latin America the average growth rate is lower by 3 percent per annum in the 1990s than in the 1970s, while trade deficits as a proportion of GDP are much the same. In sub-Saharan Africa growth fell, but deficits rose. The Asian countries managed to grow faster in the 1980s, while reducing their payments

deficits, but in the 1990s they have run greater deficits without achieving faster growth.

A study by Mark Weisbrot, Dean Baker, and David Rosnick on the consequences of neoliberal policies on third world development comes to similar conclusions. The authors note that "contrary to popular belief, the past 25 years (1980–2005) have seen a sharply slower rate of economic growth and reduced progress on social indicators for the vast majority of low- and middle-income countries [compared with the prior two decades].". . . .

In an effort to keep growing trade and current account deficits manageable, third world states, often pressured by the IMF and World Bank, used austerity measures (especially draconian cuts in social programs) to slow economic growth (and imports). They also deregulated capital markets, privatized economic activity, and relaxed foreign investment regulatory regimes in an effort to attract the financing needed to offset the existing deficits. While devastating to working people and national development possibilities, these policies were, as intended, responsive to the interests of transnational capital in general and a small but influential sector of third world capital. This is the reality of neoliberalism.

The Dynamics of Contemporary Capitalism . . .

Mainstream theorists usually consider international trade, finance, and investment as separate processes. In fact, they are interrelated. And, as highlighted above, the capitalist drive for greater profitability has generally worked to pressure third world states into an overarching liberalization and deregulation. This dynamic has had important consequences, especially, but not exclusively, for the third world. In particular, it has encouraged transnational corporations to advance their aims through the establishment and extension of international production networks. This has led to new forms of dominance over third world industrial activity that involve its reshaping and integration across borders in ways that are ever more destructive of the social, economic, and political needs of working people.

During the 1960s and 1970s, most third world countries pursued state directed import-substitution industrialization strategies and financed their trade deficits with bank loans. This pattern ended suddenly in the early 1980s, when economic instabilities in the developed capitalist world, especially in the United States, led to rising interest rates and global recession. Third world borrowing costs soared and export earnings plummeted, triggering the third world "debt crisis." With debt repayment in question, banks greatly reduced their lending, leading to ever deepening third world economic and social problems.

To overcome these problems, third world states sought new ways to boost exports and new sources of international funds. Increasingly, they came to see export-oriented foreign direct investment as the answer. The competition for this investment was fierce. Country after country made changes in their investment regimes, with the great majority designed to create a more liberalized, deregulated, and "business friendly" environment. Transnational corporations responded eagerly to these changes, many of which they and their governments helped promote. And, over the years 1991–98, FDI became the single greatest source of net capital inflow into the third world, accounting for 34 percent of the total.

New technologies had made it possible for transnational corporations to cheapen production costs for many goods by segmenting and geographically dividing their production processes. They therefore used their investments to locate the labor intensive production segments of these goods—in particular the production or assembly of parts and components—in the third world. This was especially true for electronic and electrical goods, clothing and apparel, and certain technologically advanced goods such as optical instruments.

The result was the establishment or expansion of numerous vertically structured international production networks, many of which extended over several different countries. According to UNCTAD, "it has been estimated, on the basis of input-output tables from a number of OECD and emerging-market countries, that trade based on specialization within vertical production networks accounts for up to 30 percent of world exports, and that it has grown by as much as 40 percent in the last 25 years."

Despite the fierce third world competition to attract FDI, transnational corporations tended to concentrate their investments in only a few countries. In general, U.S. capital emphasized North America (NAFTA), while Japanese capital focused on East Asia, and European capital on Central Europe. The countries that "lost out" in the FDI competition were generally forced to manage their trade and finance problems with austerity. Those countries that "won" usually experienced a relatively fast industrial transformation. More specifically, they became major exporters of manufactures, especially of high-technology products such as transistors and semiconductors, computers, parts of computers and office machines, telecommunications equipment and parts, and electrical machinery.

As a consequence of this development, the share of third world exports that were manufactures soared from 20 percent in the 1970s and early 1980s, to 70 percent by the late 1990s. The third world share of world manufacturing exports also jumped from 4.4 percent in 1965 to 30.1 percent in 2003.

Mainstream economists claim that this rise in manufactured exports demonstrates the benefits of liberalization, and thus the importance of WTO-style liberalization agreements for development. However, this argument falsely identifies FDI and exports of manufactures with development, thereby seriously misrepresenting the dynamics of transnational capital accumulation. The reality is that participation in transnational corporate controlled production networks has done little to support rising standards of living, economic stability, or national development prospects.

There are many reasons for this failure. First, those countries that have succeeded in attracting FDI have usually done so in the context of liberalizing and deregulating their economies. This has generally resulted in the destruction of their domestic import-competing industries, causing unemployment, a rapid rise in imports, and industrial hollowing out. Second, the activities located in the third world rarely transfer skills or technology, or encourage domestic industrial linkages. This means that these activities are seldom able to promote a dynamic or nationally integrated process of development. Furthermore the exports produced are highly import dependent, thereby greatly reducing their foreign exchange earning benefits.

Finally, the transnational accumulation process makes third world growth increasingly dependent on external demand. In most cases, the primary final market for these networks is the United States, which means that third world growth comes to depend ever more on the ability of the United States to sustain ever larger trade deficits—an increasingly dubious proposition. . . .

Our Challenge

As we have seen, arguments purporting to demonstrate that free-trade/free-market policies will transform economic activities and relations in ways that universally benefit working people are based on theories and simulations that distort the actual workings of capitalism. The reality is that growing numbers of workers are being captured by an increasingly unified and transnational process of capital accumulation. Wealth is being generated but working people in all the countries involved are being pitted against each other and suffering similar consequences, including unemployment and worsening living and working conditions.

Working people and their communities are engaged in growing, although uneven, resistance to the situation. While increasingly effective, this resistance still remains largely defensive and politically unfocused. One reason is that neoliberal theory continues to provide a powerful ideological cover for capitalist globalization, despite the fact that it is both generated by and designed to advance capitalist class interests. Another is the dynamic nature of contemporary capitalism, which tends to mask its destructive nature. Therefore, as participants in the resistance, we must work to ensure that our many struggles are waged in ways that help working people better understand the nature of the accumulation processes that are reshaping our lives. In this way, we can illuminate the common capitalist roots of the problems we face and the importance of building movements committed to radical social transformation and (international) solidarity.

POSTSCRIPT

Is Globalization Good for Humankind?

Many believe that economic integration will spawn greater political integration and cultural integration to the benefit of mankind. Others believe that it will destroy some of the protections that people need. There is evidence on both sides but little can be determined now. Both sides are predicting the future state of affairs, so until the future declares one view, the winner cannot be disproved.

There has been an explosion of books on globalization recently. A bestseller is Thomas Friedman's *The Lexus and the Olive Tree* (Farrar, Straus, Giroux, 2000), which tells the story of the new global economy and many of its ramifications. Friedman sees the United States as the nation that is best able to capitalize on that global economy, so it has the brightest future. Other works that explore the role of America in globalization include Jim Garrison, *America as Empire: Global Leader or Rogue Power?* (Berret-Koehler Publishers, 2004); Gary J. Hytrek and Kristine M. Zentgraf, *America Transformed: Globalization, Inequality, and Power* (Oxford University Press, 2008); Ulrich Beck et al. *Global America?: The Cultural Consequences of Globalization* (Liverpool University Press, 2003); and Will Hutton, *World We're In: A Declaration of Interdependence: Why America Should Join the World* (W.W. Norton, 2003). Works that applaud globalization include Barry Asmas, *The Best Is Yet to Come* (AmeriPress, 2001); Diane Coyle, *Paradoxes of Prosperity: Why the New Capitalism Benefits All* (Texere, 2001); John Micklethwait and Adrian Wooldridge, *Future Perfect: The Challenge and Hidden Promise of Globalization* (Crown Business, 2000); and Jacques Bandot, ed., *Building a World Community: Globalization and the Common Good* (University of Washington Press, 2001).

Attacks on globalization are prolific and include Ronaldo Munck, *Globalization and Contestation: The New Great Counter-Movement* (Routledge, 2007); Robert Went, *Globalization: Neoliberal Challenge, Radical Responses* (Pluto Press, 2000); William K. Tabb, *The Amoral Elephant: Globalization and the Struggle for Social Justice in the Twenty-First Century* (Monthly Review Press, 2001); Walden Bello, *Future in Balance: Essays on Globalization and Resistance* (Food First Books, 2001); Vic George and Paul Wilding, *Globalization and Human Welfare* (Palgrave, 2002); Gary Teeple, *Globalization and the Decline of Social Reform* (Humanity Books, 2000); Noreena Hertz, *The Silent Takeover: Global Capitalism and the Death of Democracy* (Free Press, 2002); Alan Tomelson, *Race to the Bottom: Why a Worldwide Worker Surplus and Uncontrolled Free Trade Are Sinking American Living Standards* (Westview, 2000); Richard P. Appelbaum and William I. Robinson, eds., *Critical Globalization Studies* (Routledge, 2005);

Joseph E. Stiglitz, *Globalization and Its Discontents* (W.W. Norton 2003); Vincent Navarro, ed., *Neoliberalism, Globalization, and Inequalities* (Baywood, 2007); Peter Isard, *Globalization and the International Financial System: What's Wrong and What Can Be Done* (Cambridge, 2005); Thom Burnett and Alec Games, *Who Really Runs the World?: The War Between Globalization and Democracy* (Disinformation, 2007); and Robert A. Isaak, *The Globalization Gap: How the Rich Get Richer and the Poor Get Left Further Behind* (Prentice-Hall, 2005).

For relatively balanced discussions of globalization, see Nick Bisley, *Rethinking Globalization* (Palgrave Macmillan, 2007); Arthur P. J. Mol, *Globalization and Environmental Reform: The Ecological Modernization of the Global Economy* (MIT Press, 2001), which points to the environmental degradation that results from globalization but also actions that retard degradation and improve environmental quality; Richard Langhome, *The Coming of Globalization: Its Evolution and Contemporary Consequences* (St. Martin's Press, 2001); Kamal Dervis, *Better Globalization: Legitimacy, Governance and Reform* (Brookings, 2005); Barbara Harris-White, ed., *Globalization and Insecurity: Political, Economic, and Physical Challenges* (Palgrave, 2002); *Global Transformations Reader: An Introduction to the Globalization Debate,* edited by David Held et al. (Policy Press, 2003); Tony Schirato and Jennifer Webb, *Understanding Globalization* (Sage, 2003); and *Globalization and Antiglobalization: Dynamics of Change in the New World,* edited by Henry Veltmeyer (Ashgate, 2004). For interesting discussions of the cultural aspects of globalization, see Paul Kennedy and Catherine J. Danks, eds., *Globalization and National Identities: Crisis or Opportunity* (Palgrave, 2001); Tyler Cowen, *Creative Destruction: How Globalization Is Changing the World's Cultures* (Princeton University Press, 2002); Alison Brysk, ed., *Globalization and Human Rights* (University of California Press, 2002); Elisabeth Madimbee-Boyi, ed., *Beyond Dichotomies: Histories, Identities, Cultures, and the Challenge of Globalization* (SUNY, 2002); and George Ritzer, *The Globalization of Nothing* (Pine Forge Press, 2007).

ISSUE 20

Is America Dominated by Big Business?

YES: G. William Domhoff, from *Who Rules America? Power, Politics, and Social Change,* 5th edition (McGraw-Hill, 2006)

NO: Sheldon Kamieniecki, from *Corporate America and Environmental Policy* (Stanford University Press, 2006)

ISSUE SUMMARY

YES: Political sociologist G. William Domhoff argues that the "owners and top-level managers in large income-producing properties are far and away the dominant power figures in the United States" and that they have inordinate influence in the federal government.

NO: Political scientist Sheldon Kamieniecki's research finds that business interests do not participate at a high rate in policy issues that affect them, "and when they do, they have mixed success in influencing policy outcomes." In fact, environmental and other groups often have considerable influence vis-à-vis business interests.

Since the framing of the U.S. Constitution in 1787, there have been periodic charges that America is unduly influenced by wealthy financial interests. Richard Henry Lee, a signer of the Declaration of Independence, spoke for many Anti-Federalists (those who opposed ratification of the Constitution) when he warned that the proposed charter shifted power away from the people and into the hands of the "aristocrats" and "moneyites."

Before the Civil War, Jacksonian Democrats denounced the eastern merchants and bankers who, they charged, were usurping the power of the people. After the Civil War, a number of radical parties and movements revived this theme of anti-elitism. The ferment—which was brought about by the rise of industrial monopolies, government corruption, and economic hardship for western farmers—culminated in the founding of the People's Party at the beginning of the 1890s. The Populists, as they were more commonly called, wanted economic and political reforms aimed at transferring power away from the rich and back to "the plain people."

By the early 1900s, the People's Party had disintegrated, but many writers and activists have continued to echo the Populists' central thesis: that the U.S. democratic political system is in fact dominated by business elites. Yet the thesis has not gone unchallenged. During the 1950s and the early 1960s, many social scientists subscribed to the *pluralist* view of America.

Pluralists argue that because there are many influential elites in America, each group is limited to some extent by the others. There are some groups, like the business elites, that are more powerful than their opponents, but even the more powerful groups are denied their objectives at times. Labor groups are often opposed to business groups; conservative interests challenge liberal interests, and vice versa; and organized civil libertarians sometimes fight with groups that seek government-imposed bans on pornography or groups that demand tougher criminal laws. No single group, the pluralists argue, can dominate the political system.

Pluralists readily acknowledge that American government is not democratic in the full sense of the word; it is not driven by the majority. But neither, they insist, is it run by a conspiratorial "power elite." In the pluralist view, the closest description of the American form of government would be neither majority rule nor minority rule but *minorities* rule. (Note that in this context, "minorities" does not necessarily refer to race or ethnicity but to any organized group of people with something in common—including race, religion, or economic interests—not constituting a majority of the population.) Each organized minority enjoys some degree of power in the making of public policy.

In extreme cases, when a minority feels threatened, its power may take a negative form: the power to derail policy. When the majority—or, more accurately, a coalition of other minorities—attempts to pass a measure that threatens the vital interests of an organized minority, that group may use its power to obstruct their efforts. (Often cited in this connection is the use of the Senate filibuster, which is the practice of using tactics during the legislative process that cause extreme delays or prevent action, thus enabling a group to "talk to death" a bill that threatens its vital interests.) But in the pluralist view, negative power is not the only driving force: when minorities work together and reach consensus on certain issues, they can institute new laws and policy initiatives that enjoy broad public support. Pluralism, though capable of producing temporary gridlock, ultimately leads to compromise, consensus, and moderation.

Critics of pluralism argue that pluralism is an idealized depiction of a political system that is in the grip of powerful elite groups. Critics fault pluralist theory for failing to recognize the extent to which big business dominates the policy-making process. In the selections that follow, G. William Domhoff supports this view, identifies the groups that compose the power elite, and details the way they control or support social, political, and knowledge-producing associations and organizations that advance their interests. Sheldon Kamieniecki, in opposition, argues that, thanks to new consumer, environmental, and other citizen groups, big business has a much more limited influence on Washington policymakers than Domhoff claims.

YES ⟵

G. William Domhoff

Who Rules America?
Power, Politics, and Social Change

Introduction

Using a wide range of systematic empirical findings, this book shows how the owners and top-level managers in large companies work together to maintain themselves as the core of the dominant power group. Their corporations, banks, and agribusinesses form a *corporate community* that shapes the federal government on the policy issues of interest to it, issues that have a major impact on the income, job security, and well-being of most other Americans. At the same time, there is competition within the corporate community for profit opportunities, which can lead to highly visible policy conflicts among rival corporate leaders that are sometimes fought out in Congress. Yet the corporate community is cohesive on the policy issues that affect its general welfare, which is often at stake when political challenges are made by organized workers, liberals, or strong environmentalists. The book therefore deals with another seeming paradox: How can a highly competitive group of corporate leaders cooperate enough to work their common will in the political and policy arenas?

Partly because the owners and high-level managers within the corporate community share great wealth and common economic interests, but also due to political opposition to their interests, they band together to develop their own social institutions—gated neighborhoods, private schools, exclusive social clubs, debutante balls, and secluded summer resorts. These social institutions create social cohesion and a sense of group belonging, a "we" feeling, and thereby mold wealthy people into a *social upper class*. In addition, the owners and managers supplement their small numbers by financing and directing a wide variety of nonprofit organizations—e.g., tax-free foundations, think tanks, and policy-discussion groups—to aid them in developing policy alternatives that serve their interests. The highest-ranking employees in these nonprofit organizations become part of a general leadership group for the corporate community and the upper class, called the *power elite*.

Corporate owners and their top executives enter into the electoral arena as the leaders of a *corporate-conservative coalition*, which they shape through large campaign contributions, the advocacy of policy options developed by their hired experts, and easy access to the mass media. They are aided by a wide variety of middle-class patriotic, antitax, and single-issue organizations that celebrate the status quo and warn against "big government." These opinion-shaping organizations are funded in good part by the corporate community, but they have some degree of independence due to direct-mail appeals and modest donations by a large number of middle-class conservatives. The corporate leaders play a large role in both of the major political parties at the presidential level and succeeded in electing a pro-corporate majority to Congress throughout the twentieth century. Historically, this majority in Congress consisted of Northern Republicans and Southern Democrats, but that arrangement changed gradually after the Voting Rights Act of 1965 made it possible for a coalition of African-Americans and white liberals to push the most conservative Southern Democrats into the Republican Party.

Since the last quarter of the twentieth century, the corporate-conservative coalition has been joined by the Christian Right, which consists of a wide range of middle-class religious groups concerned with a variety of social issues, including abortion, prayer in schools, teenage sexual behavior, homosexuality, gay marriage, and pornography. The alliance is sometimes an uneasy one because the corporate community and the Christian Right do not have quite the same priorities, yet they work together because of their common mistrust of government power.

The corporate community's ability to transform its economic power into policy influence and political access, along with its capacity to enter into a coalition with middle-class social and religious conservatives, makes it the most important influence in the federal government. Its key leaders are appointed to top positions in the executive branch and the policy recommendations of its experts are listened to carefully by its allies in Congress. This combination of economic power, policy expertise, and continuing political success makes the corporate owners and executives a *dominant class,* not in the sense of complete and absolute power, but in the sense that they have the power to shape the economic and political frameworks within which other groups and classes must operate. They therefore win far more often than they lose on the issues of concern to them.

Who Wins?

There are many issues over which the corporate-conservative and liberal-labor coalitions disagree, including taxation, unionization, business regulation, foreign trade, the outsourcing of jobs, and the funding of Social Security. Power can be inferred on the basis of these issue conflicts by determining who successfully initiates, modifies, or vetoes policy alternatives. This indicator, by focusing on relationships between the two rival coalitions, comes closest to approximating the process of power contained in the formal definition. It is the indicator preferred by most social scientists. For many reasons, however, it is also the most difficult to use in an accurate way. Aspects of a decision process may remain hidden, some informants may exaggerate or downplay their roles, and people's memories about who did what often become cloudy shortly after the event. Worse, the key concerns of the corporate community may never arise as issues for public discussion because it has the power to keep them off the agenda through a variety of means that are explained throughout later chapters.

Despite the difficulties in using the *Who wins?* indicator of power, it is possible to provide a theoretical framework for analyzing governmental decision-making that mitigates many of them. This framework encompasses the various means by which the corporate community attempts to influence both the government and the general population in a conscious and planned manner, thereby making it possible to assess its degree of success very directly. More specifically, there are four relatively distinct, but overlapping processes (discovered by means of membership network analysis) through which the corporate community controls the public agenda and then wins on most issues that appear on it. These four power networks, which are discussed in detail in later chapters, are as follows:

1. The *special-interest process* deals with the narrow and short-run policy concerns of wealthy families, specific corporations, and specific business sectors. It operates primarily through lobbyists, company lawyers, and trade associations, with a focus on congressional committees, departments of the executive branch, and regulatory agencies.
2. The *policy-planning process* formulates the general interests of the corporate community. It operates through a policy-planning network of foundations, think tanks, and policy-discussion groups, with a focus on the White House, relevant congressional committees, and the high-status newspapers and opinion magazines published in New York and Washington.
3. The *candidate-selection process* is concerned with the election of candidates who are sympathetic to the agenda put forth in the special-interest and policy-planning processes. It operates through large campaign donations and hired political consultants, with a focus on the presidential campaigns of both major political parties and the congressional campaigns of the Republican Party.
4. The *opinion-shaping process* attempts to influence public opinion and keep some issues off the public agenda. Often drawing on policy positions, rationales, and statements developed within the policy-planning process, it operates through the public relations departments of large corporations, general public relations firms, and many small opinion-shaping organizations, with a focus on middle-class voluntary organizations, educational institutions, and the mass media.

Taken together, the people and organizations that operate in these four networks constitute the political-action arm of the corporate community and upper class.

How the Power Elite Dominate Government

The power elite build on their structural economic power, their storehouse of policy expertise, and their success in the electoral arena to dominate the federal government on the issues about which they care. Lobbyists from corporations, law firms, and trade associations play a key role in shaping government on narrow issues of concern to specific corporations or business sectors, and the policy-planning network supplies new policy directions on major issues, along with top-level governmental appointees to implement those policies.

However, victories within government are far from automatic. As is the case in the competition for public opinion and electoral success, the power elite face opposition from a minority of elected officials and their supporters in labor unions and liberal advocacy groups. These liberal opponents are sometimes successful in blocking the social initiatives put forth by the Christian Right, but the corporate-conservative coalition itself seldom loses when it is united.

Appointees to Government

The first way to see how the power elite shapes the federal government is to look at the social and occupational backgrounds of the people who are appointed to manage the major departments of the executive branch, such as state, treasury, defense, and justice. If the power elite are as important as this book claims, they should come disproportionately from the upper class, the corporate community, and the policy-planning network.

There have been numerous studies of major governmental appointees under both Republican and Democratic administrations, usually focusing on the top appointees in the departments that are represented in the president's cabinet. These studies are unanimous in their conclusion that most top appointees in both Republican and Democratic administrations are corporate executives and corporate lawyers, and hence members of the power elite. Moreover, they are often part of the policy-planning network as well, supporting the claim that the network plays a central role in preparing members of the power elite for government service.

The Special-Interest Process

The special-interest process consists of the many and varied means by which specific corporations and business sectors gain the favors, tax breaks, regulatory rulings, and other governmental assistance they need to realize their narrow and short-run interests. The process is carried out by people with a wide range of experiences: former elected officials, experts who once served on congressional staffs or in regulatory agencies, employees of trade associations, corporate executives whose explicit function is government liaison, and an assortment of lawyers and public-relations specialists. The process is based on a great amount of personal contact, but its most important ingredients are the information and financial support that the lobbyists have to offer. Much of the time this information comes from grassroots pressure generated by the lobbyists to show that voting for a given measure will or will not hurt a particular politician.

Corporations spend far more money on lobbying than their officers give to PACs, by a margin of ten to one. In 2000, for example, the tobacco industry, facing lawsuits and regulatory threats, spent $44 million on lobbyists and $17 million on the Tobacco Institute, an industry public relations arm, but gave only $8.4 million to political campaigns through PACs. More generally, a study of the top 20 defense contractors showed that they spent $400 million on lobbying between 1997 and 2003, but only $46 million on campaign contributions.

The trend toward increasingly large tax breaks continued from 2001 to 2003, with the effective tax rate on corporations declining from 21.7 percent during the last years of the Clinton Administration to 17.2 percent in 2003. Forty-six of 275 major companies studied for 2003 paid no federal income taxes, a considerable increase from a similar study in the late 1990s. A new tax bill in October 2004 added another $137 billion in tax breaks for manufacturing and energy companies, with General Electric, which spent $17 million in lobbying fees in 2003, once again the biggest beneficiary. At the same time, other legal loopholes have allowed multinational corporations to increase the sheltering of profits in foreign tax havens by tens of billions of dollars.

Special interests also work through Congress to try to hamstring regulatory agencies or reverse military purchasing decisions they do not like. When the Federal Communications Commission tried to issue licenses for over 1,000 low-power FM stations for schools and community groups, Congress blocked the initiative at the behest of big broadcasting companies, setting standards that will restrict new licenses to a small number of stations in the least populated parts of the country. When the Food and Drug Administration tried to regulate tobacco, Congress refused authorization in 2000 in deference to the tobacco industry. The FDA is now so lax with pharmaceutical companies that one-third of its scientific employees have less than full confidence that it tests new drugs adequately, and two-thirds expressed a lack of complete confidence in its monitoring of the safety of drugs once they are on the market.

The special-interest process often is used to create loopholes in legislation that is accepted by the corporate community in principle. "I spent the last seven years fighting the Clean Air Act," said a corporate lobbyist in charge of PAC donations, who then went on to explain why he gave money to elected officials even though they voted for the strengthening of the Clean Air Act in 1990:

How a person votes on the final piece of legislation is not representative of what they have done. Somebody will do a lot of things during the process. How many guys voted against the Clean Air Act? But during the process some of them were very sympathetic to some of our concerns.

Translated, this means there are forty pages of exceptions, extensions, and other loopholes in the 1990 version of the act after a thirteen-year standoff between the Business Roundtable's Clean Air Working Group and the liberal-labor coalition's National Clean Air Coalition. For example, the steel industry has thirty years to bring twenty-six large coke ovens into compliance with the new standards. Once the bill passed, lobbyists went to work on the Environmental Protection Agency to win the most lax regulations possible for implementing the legislation. As of 1998, after twenty-eight years of argument and delay, the agency had been able to issue standards for less than ten of the many hazardous chemicals emitted into the air.

The Big Picture

This book began with two seeming paradoxes. How can the owners and managers of highly competitive corporations develop the policy unity to shape government policies? How can large corporations have such great power in a democratic country? The step-by-step argument and evidence presented in previous chapters provide the foundation for a theory that can explain these paradoxes—a *class-domination theory of power* in the United States.

Domination means that the commands of a group or class are carried out with relatively little resistance, which is possible because that group or class has been able to establish the rules and customs through which everyday life is conducted. Domination, in other words, is the institutionalized outcome of great distributive power. The upper class of owners and high-level executives, based in the corporate community, is a dominant class in terms of this definition because the cumulative effect of its various distributive powers leads to a situation where its policies are generally accepted by most Americans. The routinized ways of acting in the United States follow from the rules and regulations needed by the corporate community to continue to grow and make profits.

The overall distributive power of the dominant class is first of all based in its structural economic power, which falls to it by virtue of its members being owners and high-level executives in corporations that sell goods and services for a profit in a market economy. The power to invest or not invest, and to hire and fire employees, leads to a political context where elected officials try to do as much as they can to create a favorable investment climate to avoid being voted out of office in the event of an economic downturn. This structural power is augmented by the ability to create new policies through a complex policy-planning network, which the upper class has been able to institutionalize because common economic interests and social cohesion have given the corporate community enough unity to sustain such an endeavor over many decades.

But even these powers might not have been enough to generate a system of extreme class domination if the bargains and compromises embodied in the Constitution had not led unexpectedly to a two-party system in which one party was controlled by the Northern rich and the other by the Southern rich. This in turn created a personality-oriented candidate-selection process that is heavily dependent on large campaign donations—now and in the past as well. The system of party primaries is the one adaptation to this constrictive two-party system that has provided some openings for insurgent liberals and trade unionists.

Structural economic power and control of the two parties, along with the elaboration of an opinion-shaping network, results in a polity where there is little or no organized public opinion independent of the limits set by debates within the power elite itself. There is no organizational base from which to construct an alternative public opinion, and there have been until recently no openings within the political system that could carry an alternative message to government.

Finally, the fragmented and constrained system of government carefully crafted by the Founding Fathers led to a relatively small federal government that is easily entered and influenced by wealthy and well-organized private citizens, whether through Congress, the separate departments of the executive branch, or a myriad of regulatory agencies. The net result is that the owners and managers of large income-producing properties score very high on all three power indicators: who benefits, who governs, and who wins. They have a greater proportion of wealth and income than their counterparts in any other capitalist democracy, and through the power elite they are vastly overrepresented in key government positions and decision-making groups. They win far more often than they lose on those issues that make it to the government for legislative consideration, although their lack of unity in the face of worker militancy in the 1930s made it possible for organized workers to have far more independence, income, and power than they ever had in the past.

Many Americans feel a sense of empowerment because they have religious freedom, free speech, and a belief that they can strike it rich or rise in the system if they try hard enough. Those with educational credentials and/or secure employment experience a degree of dignity and respect because there is no tradition of public degradation for those of average or low incomes. Liberals and leftists can retain hope because in recent decades they have had success in helping to expand individual rights and freedom—for women, for people of color, and most recently for gays and lesbians. But individual rights and freedoms do not necessarily add up to distributive power. In the same time period, when individual rights and freedoms expanded, corporate power also became greater because unions were decimated and the liberal-labor coalition splintered. This analysis suggests there is class domination in spite of a widening of individual freedoms and an expansion of the right to vote.

Sheldon Kamieniecki

Corporate America and Environmental Policy: How Often Does Business Get Its Way?

The findings reported in this study directly challenge prevailing assumptions both in- and outside the scholarly community about the regularity of business involvement in agenda building and policymaking as well as the ability of business to influence government decisions concerning pollution control and natural resource management. This outcome was unexpected. When I first began working on this book more than three years ago, I anticipated finding that American corporations are regularly involved in environmental agenda building and policymaking and that they exert a great deal of influence over government decision making. Like many, I accepted the conventional wisdom that business frequently opposes proposals that will improve environmental quality in order to protect its profits. After all, reports in the media nearly always place the blame for the defeat of environmental initiatives on the undue influence of business. As an environmentalist myself, I have been quite disappointed in the lack of progress the United States has made, especially recently, in the areas of pollution control and natural resource conservation. Most policy analysts attribute this lack of progress to the ability of corporate America to block or dilute critical federal legislation and to the inability of environmental groups to compete in the policymaking process. . . .

I was determined to . . . conduct a fair and balanced assessment of the role of business interests in environmental and natural resource policymaking.

As the data show, business interests do not participate in environmental policy debates at a high rate, and when they do, they have mixed success in influencing policy outcomes. These results generally hold when one examines agenda building in Congress, agency rulemaking, and, to some extent, the courts. Analyses of salient conflicts involving pollution control and natural resources also tend to bear this out. Business interests, instead, appear to select strategically the controversies in which they become involved and how much money they spend on lobbying activities of various kinds. A major conclusion of my work is that agenda building within the environmental policy domain is a highly complex process and cannot be explained by a single theory. This and other surprising related findings are the subject of this book. . . .

From *Corporate America and Environmental Policy*, by Sheldon Kamieniecki (Stanford Law and Politics, 2006), excerpts from Preface, chapters 1, 2, and Conclusion. Copyright © 2006 by the Board and Trustees of the Leland Stanford, Jr. University. Reprinted by permission.

The central question of the book is, how often does business get its way on environmental issues? Do corporations, given the immense wealth and resources they command, exert an unequal and unfair influence over American government whereby they are able to compel elected representatives and agency officials to reject or compromise substantially appropriate and necessary environmental rules and regulations? A related concern, often ignored in the interest group literature, is the frequency with which firms are able to prevent environmental and natural resource policy proposals from even reaching the government agenda. Although recent research suggests that firms do not possess the amount of influence necessary to shape or block public policymaking on a consistent basis more generally, few studies have critically analyzed their ability to affect agenda setting specifically within the environmental policy sphere. This investigation addresses this issue by empirically assessing the ability of companies to affect legislative, administrative, and judicial decision making and mold the government's environmental and natural resource policy agenda since the beginning of the environmental movement. . . .

In particular, the size and wealth of business lobbying organizations have grown dramatically since World War Two, prompting some observers to argue that they are now too powerful and are undermining democracy and threatening the well-being of society. The weakening of the political parties, the rising costs of media advertising and election campaigns, and the increasing contributions by Political Action Committees (PACs) to candidates and parties have led to calls for reform in the way American elections are financed. Business interests, among others, are key targets of critics who demand the enactment of meaningful campaign finance reform at the federal level. The campaign finance reform legislation enacted in 2002 bans "soft money," among other things, and is a significant attempt to level the playing field. Loopholes in the act exist, however, and it will be necessary to adopt additional regulations in the future in order to correct inequities in the financing of campaigns. Thus, despite Madison's assurances, the question of how we allow business and other interest groups to form and participate but control their influence remains a dilemma in modern times. . . .

Corporate America and Environmental Policy: Opposing Views

The influence of business over environmental policy is often used as an example of the substantial and unfair leverage certain interest groups have over government actions, especially when compared to the level of influence of average citizens. Many believe that the power business wields in American politics threatens democracy and, among other things, undermines the nation's efforts to control pollution and conserve natural resources. Environmentalists assert that "big business" has continuously been an impediment to the formulation and implementation of clean air and water quality standards. Ranchers and land developers, they argue, have successfully fought endangered species protection; oil, coal, and natural gas companies have opposed strict energy-conservation measures and have lobbied against the adoption of renewable sources of energy; mining companies have thwarted the revision of mining laws and regulations; and chemical companies have fought legislation intended to control pesticides, promote the safe disposal of hazardous waste, and abate old, abandoned toxic waste sites. . . .

Many critics maintain that interest groups subvert democracy, in part by pressing Congress to pass too much "special-interest" legislation that benefits the few at the expense of the majority and in part by blocking legislative initiatives they oppose even when those measures are favored by, or would benefit, the broad public. In addition, critics contend that campaign contributions by interest groups undermine democratic government and degrade the American electoral system. In contrast, Berry rejects these arguments, saying that interest groups help to link citizens to government: "They empower people by organizing those citizens with similar interests and expressing those interests to policymakers. In this regard, the growth of citizen groups reflects an expansion of organizing around interests that have too often received too little attention in Washington." Berry carefully avoids saying that business interests are no longer a force in American politics, but he does argue that their influence has significantly declined. . . .

Interestingly, Berry's findings and conclusions are a throwback to some of the positions of the early pluralists, namely that interest group politics is equitable and fair. For this reason, Berry and his contemporaries, such as Baumgartner and Leech who also share this view, are referred to as *neopluralists* in this volume. Specifically, neopluralists argue that the increasing number and size of citizen groups has furthered democracy and the public good by involving a broad range of interests in policymaking and by substantially countering the influence of business in the political system. The neopluralists, like the early pluralists, point to the positive aspects of group pressures on politics and government. Scholars who believe that public opinion also provides a check on the power of business are considered neopluralists as well. The degree to which environmental groups and public opinion mitigate business influence in environmental policymaking is examined in the present study. . . .

The Business Advantage?

Mark Smith's provocative investigation explores the widely held assumption that business dominates the policymaking process when it is unified on specific policy issues, thereby undermining democracy. Using the policy positions of the U.S. Chamber of Commerce as a guide, he identifies 2,364 unifying issues that were considered by Congress between 1953 and 1996. His list of unifying issues encompasses a wide range of policy areas including employment policy, labor-management relations, and clean air regulation. Agenda building in Congress over time is his dependent variable. Among the independent variables he analyzes are "public mood," public attitudes toward corporations, partisan composition of Congress, "presidential leadership opening" (that is, when partisan turnover in Congress runs in the president's favor), corporate PAC funding, and the state of the economy. Mark Smith finds that unity does not increase the direct influence of business and reduce democratic control by the citizenry. Instead, unity coincides with the opposite results. Issues marked by a common business position are precisely those for which government decisions are affected most strongly by election outcomes and the responsiveness of officeholders to their constituents. Policies match the collective desires of business only when citizens, through their policy preferences and voting choices, embrace ideas and candidates supportive of what business wants. To bolster its odds of winning in politics, business needs to seek backing from the broad public.

According to Mark Smith, therefore, only when the public supports the unified positions of business on policy issues does business achieve its legislative goals. When the public opposes the positions of business, however, Congress tends to follow the public will even though business is unified. Since all unifying policy issues are highly ideological, partisan, and salient. Congress nearly always follows the public on these issues. He concludes by stating, "The long-standing debates over unity among pluralists, elite theorists, and ruling class theorists have focused our attention in the wrong place. Widespread scholarly concerns about business unity are misplaced, for unifying issues are marked by the highest, rather than the lowest, degree of democratic control by the citizenry." Smith's interpretation of his findings places him in the neopluralist camp along with Baumgartner and Leech and Berry. . . .

Baumgartner and Jones report significant changes in the environmental interest group sphere and show dramatic growth in the numbers of environmental groups and the resources available to them. Based on their analysis, the number of environmental organizations nearly tripled from 1960 to 1990, and the combined staff reported by those groups increased nearly ten times. This surge in environmental group membership is one of the most important reasons for the enactment of so many major environmental laws during the 1970s and 1980s, often over the protests of powerful business lobbyists. . . .

This book provided a comprehensive investigation of how much corporate America has influenced agenda building and environmental policymaking since 1970. The study began by charting the development of business interests since the founding of the nation and by raising important issues about democratic theory and the role of business in American politics. A review of the literature on interest groups addressed collective-action issues and the emergence of citizen groups in the agenda-setting process. Research by the neopluralists suggests that public opinion and citizen groups have tempered the influence of business interests in social policymaking. Based on their findings, one would expect this to be the case in environmental and natural resource policy. Theories addressing certain political and economic variables, issue definition, framing processes, and agenda building were introduced and applied in the analysis of the role of business in Congress, at the EPA and natural resource agencies, in federal court, and in environmental and natural resource disputes. . . .

Major Findings

This book reports a number of major findings. In sharp contrast to the conventional wisdom that business interests actively oppose environmental and natural resource protection on a continuous basis, the data presented [clearly shows that] corporations do not take a position on proposed legislation in Congress about four-fifths of the time. The widely held belief that business frequently opposes environmental regulation and natural resource conservation is also not true. Regardless of how companies align (that is, unified or particularized), they tend to support environmental legislation more often than not. . . .

The study also reports several important findings concerning the influence of business over federal agencies and the courts. As the data indicate, the number of public comments on proposed environmental and natural resource rules and which segments of the population participate in the rulemaking process varies depending on the saliency and nature of the policy issue involved. As Golden discovers, a large percentage of those who submit comments are located outside Washington DC. The exceptionally large number of comments submitted by citizen groups on the natural resource rules examined in this research supports the position by the neopluralists that the dramatic rise in the number and size of such groups is effectively competing against the lobbying activities of business interests. Comments by corporations were generally hostile toward the EPA's efforts to promulgate new environmental regulations. Overall, public comments on proposed rules by EPA, the Forest Service, and the FWS have no or very little effect on the composition of final rules. Comments that contain new facts and information normally receive the closest attention by agency officials. Thus, as Golden finds, business does not exercise an undue influence over rulemaking involving environmental and natural resource issues. Instead, what kinds of rules are proposed to begin with is most important. This is determined by who occupies the White House and who the president appoints to senior positions in the environmental protection and natural resource agencies. . . .

The findings from the analyses of business influence in government institutions provide compelling reasons for investigating the influence of corporate interests within specific contexts involving disputes over environmental regulation and the use of natural resources. As this study indicated, in the end GE did not get its way in its fight to block the EPA's order that it clean up the PCBs it had dumped in the Hudson River. Likewise, the coal companies and utilities were unable to persuade Congress to exclude controls on sulfur dioxide emissions to reduce acid rain from the clean Air Act Amendments of 1990. In both cases, the scientific evidence concerning the negative impact of PCBs and SO_2 emissions on the environment and public health was overwhelming and undercut opposing political and economic forces in the debate over policy. Public concern was also high, prompting the FPA and Congress, respectively, to take action against the wishes of powerful economic interests.

The battle over controlling GHG emissions and climate change, however, presents a very different story. Extremely influential energy producers and consumers have teamed up to prevent the U.S. government from ratifying the Kyoto agreement and from taking a leadership role at the international level to address the climate change issue. The ratification of the Kyoto treaty by Russia represents a significant step forward to resolving the global climate change problem. Nonetheless, the global effort is considerably weakened without the participation of large CO_2 emitters such as the United States and Australia. It is unlikely that U.S. policy on climate change will reverse course during President Bush's second term.

In addition, the study explored the influence of business in three controversies concerning natural resource issues. Despite calls for reform, mining interests have successfully beaten back attempts to revise the General Mining Law of 1872. Sugarcane growers and development forces were able to thwart efforts to restore the Florida Everglades until scientists and environmentalists banded together and persuaded the federal government, particularly the U.S. Army Corps of Engineers and Congress, to take action. The state government, which has been continuously pressured from all sides, has waffled in its intentions to improve the wetlands ecosystem in South Florida. Environmentalists have been successful in attracting media attention, expanding the scope of conflict beyond the region and the state, and using the courts to protect the northern spotted owl and old-growth forests in the Pacific Northwest. The ESA continues to provide a strong pillar in the debate over logging old-growth trees on public lands. Revision of the ESA by the Republican-controlled White House and Congress in the coming years could place economic interests ahead of habitat protection and eventually spell the demise of the northern spotted owl and other endangered species across the country. . . .

Implications of the Study's Findings

This study's findings have a number of implications for the way analysts view the role of business in environmental and natural resource policymaking. At the aggregate level it is clear that business interests selectively choose which bills to oppose or support in Congress, and they do not, as environmentalists, media commentators, and some scholars assume, continuously and unrelentingly pressure legislators for favorable treatment. They are most likely to become active in critical and salient policy debates. Although their participation in the legislative process is far less than expected, the controversies in which they decide to become involved tend to be ones where there is much at stake for them *and* the environment. In this sense, the lobbying activities of business can have an enormous impact on the nation's effort to protect the environment and natural resources.

When business does choose to lobby Congress on environmental legislation, it more often supports rather than opposes such legislation. This result probably indicates that the views of business interests are often conveyed and considered during the initial writing of bills. The multiple indicators approach used by Mark Smith and employed in this research unfortunately does not include this somewhat hidden but critical facet of the agenda-building process in Congress. Of course, business interests will actively oppose legislation when their views are not reflected in legislative proposals and when there is much at stake. Such legislation is adopted when pressure from environmental groups and public opinion requires congressional representatives to take immediate action to address urgent pollution or natural resource problems. Congress is unable to always act according to the desires of the business community because of the existence of previous, and oftentimes landmark, law. In such cases corporations seldom get their way. . . .

Analysis of the six case studies, however, offers more support for the position of the neopluralists. Generally, when much is at stake, environmental groups tend to mobilize and provide an effective check on the influence of business interests. This is evident in the conflicts involving GE and the dumping of PCBs in the Hudson River, the promulgation of acid rain regulations, the restoration of the Everglades, and protection of the northern spotted owl and old-growth forests. Public opinion was a factor in all these controversies, though to varying degrees. Therefore, when conflicts are salient, environmental groups and public opinion tend to present an important, countervailing force to business interests. Mancur Olson would not have predicted this finding.

Finally, the overall results of the investigation have important implications for the influence of business in environmental and natural resource policymaking in particular, and democratic theory in general. Corporations strategically select which legislative debates to enter, and they take positions on environmental and natural resource legislation only a small percentage of the time. Furthermore, business interests do not exert an undue influence in the rulemaking process. Yet, they tend to win as many cases as they lose in the federal court of appeals. Overall, however, business does not get what it wants from government institutions a majority of the time, as some argue. This study's findings suggest that the influence of business in environmental and natural resource policymaking is modest at best.

The examination of the case studies presents a similar picture. Although business interests experienced early success in conflicts over the contamination of the Hudson River. SO_2 emissions, the pollution of the Everglades, and the logging of old-growth forests, they eventually were forced to bow to the demands of federal officials. This is not the situation, of course, in disputes over hardrock mining and climate change. In these instances, corporations have thus far been able to defeat efforts to reform the General Mining Act of 1872 and reduce GHG emissions. Based on the overall analysis of the environmental regulatory and the natural resource case studies, however, business interests do not often get their way. As this study shows, they tend to have a mixed rate of success in influencing the outcomes of salient policy controversies.

In addition to environmental groups and public opinion, other factors also mitigate the influence of business in agenda building and policymaking. Competing elites in the media and scientific community, for example, can point out differences between what corporations are claiming and the actual evidence. As this study revealed, the media played a central role in the controversy over the northern spotted owl and old-growth forests. What started out as a regional (Pacific Northwest) issue quickly expanded to the national level as a result of extensive media coverage of the plight of the owl and its habitat.

The timber industry was thus forced to reduce logging on public land considerably. Likewise, scientists brought to light the negative impacts of PCB contamination of the Hudson River, SO_2 emissions on aquatic bodies and forests, and agricultural runoff in the Everglades. In each case business groups were forced to moderate significantly their stands. Federal district trial court judges, too, placed controls on pollution of the Everglades and logging in old-growth forests. This was only possible because of the existence of groundbreaking federal laws governing environmental and natural resource protection (for example, the Clean Water Act and the ESA). As James Madison suggested would generally happen in *Federalist Paper Number 10,* the environmental policy arena is characterized by a healthy balance between competing interests and stakeholders. The system of checks and balances between the three branches of government and the protection of individual rights allow business interests to pursue aggressively their aims but at the same time prevent them from completely destroying the environment and severely harming public health.

POSTSCRIPT

Is America Dominated
by Big Business?

The key issue in this debate is the extent of the influence of corporate power over the making and administrating of government policies on issues that concern them. The dominant view is that neither the public nor mobilized noncorporate interests can effectively counterpose corporate interests. Two political scientists who have advocated this view in a lifetime of publications are G. William Domhoff and Thomas R. Dye. Domhoff's article in this debate contains selections from the fifth edition of his book *Who Rules America?* (McGraw-Hill, 2006). In an earlier book, *Changing the Powers That Be: How the Left Can Stop Losing and Win* (Rowman & Littlefield, 2003), he focused on how to fight this corporate power. Three of Dye's recent books are *Politics in America*, seventh edition (Pearson Prentice Hall, 2007); *Who's Running America?: The Bush Restoration* (Prentice Hall, 2003); and *Top Down Policymaking* (Chatham House, 2001). Other works supporting this view are Michael Parenti, *Democracy for the Few* (Thomson-Wadsworth, 2008); Melissa L. Rossi, *What Every American Should Know about Who's Really Running America* (Plume Book, 2007); Lou Dobbs, *War on the Middle Class: How Government, Big Business, and Special Interest Groups Are Waging War on the American Dream and How to Fight Back* (Viking, 2006); Charles Perrow, *Organizing America: Wealth, Power, and the Origins of Corporate America* (Princeton University Press, 2002); Peter Kobrak, *Cozy Politics: Political Parties, Campaign Finance, and Compromised Governance* (Lynne Rienner, 2002); Arianna Stassinopoulos Huffington, *Pigs at the Trough: How Corporate Greed and Political Corruption Are Undermining America* (Crown, 2003); Ted Nace, *Gangs of America: The Rise of Corporate Power and the Disabling of Democracy* (Berrett-Koehler, 2003); Dan Clawson et al., *Dollars and Votes: How Business Campaign Contributions Subvert Democracy* (Temple University Press, 1998); John B. Parrott, *Being Like God: How American Elites Abuse Politics and Power* (University Press of America, 2003); Russell Mokhiber and Robert Weissman, *On the Rampage: Corporate Predators and the Destruction of Democracy* (Common Courage Press, 2005); Paul Kivel, *You Call this Democracy? Who Benefits, Who Pays and Who Really Decides?* (Apex Press, 2004); and Charles Derber, *Hidden Power: What You Need to Know to Save Our Democracy* (Berret-Koehler, 2005).

Several authors advance the thesis that American corporations also to some degree rule the world, including David C. Korten, *When Corporations Rule the World,* second edition (Kumarian Press, 2001); and Peter Alexis Gourevich and James J. Shinn, *Political Power and Corporate Control: The New Global Politics of Corporate Governance* (Princeton University Press, 2005).

For some pluralist arguments, see Stephen E. Frantzich, *Citizen Democracy: Political Activists in a Cynical Age,* third edition (Rowman & Littlefield, 2008);

Feliz Kolb, *Protest and Opportunities: The Political Outcomes of Social Movements* (Campus Verlag, 2007); Michael Rabinder James, *Deliberative Democracy and the Plural Polity* (University Press of Kansas, 2004); Kevin Danaher, *Insurrection: Citizen Challenges to Corporate Power* (Routledge, 2003); David S. Meyers et al., eds., *Routing the Opposition: Social Movements, Public Policy, and Democracy* (University of Minnesota Press, 2005); Jeffrey M. Berry, *The New Liberalism: The Rising Power of Citizen Groups* (Brookings Institution, 1999); and *Battling Big Business: Countering Greenwash, Infiltration, and Other Forms of Corporate Bullying* (Common Courage Press, 2002). Recently, the pluralist view is being reworked into political process theory. See Andrew S. McFarland, *Neopluralism: The Evolution of Political Process Theory* (University Press of Kansas, 2004).

ISSUE 21

Are Barriers to Women's Success as Leaders Due to Societal Obstacles?

YES: Alice H. Eagly and Linda L. Carli, from "Women and the Labyrinth of Leadership," *Harvard Business Review* (September 2007)

NO: Kingsley R. Browne, from *Biology at Work: Rethinking Sexual Equality* (Rutgers University Press, 2002)

ISSUE SUMMARY

YES: Alice Eagly and Linda Carli argue that women seldom reach the highest levels of corporate America because they face obstacles at every stage of their career that decrease the woman/man ratio at each step upward.

NO: Kingsley Browne argues that biological differences between men and women account for many differences in their behaviors and choices that make women and men better suited for different types of jobs and differences in the way that they handle the same jobs.

The position of women in America has changed dramatically in the past half century to the point that women are outperforming men in many spheres where men used to outperform women. For example, women earned 57 percent of college degrees in 2003, but only earned 35 percent in 1960. They also earned 59 percent of M.A.s and 48 percent of Ph.D.s in 2003. So why are they so rare in leadership positions in large corporations? For example, women represented 50.6 percent of the management, professional, and related occupations of the Fortune 500 companies in 2006, but only 15.6 percent of the corporate officers, 9.4 percent of the highest titles, 6.7 percent of top earners, and 2.6 percent of CEOs. What explains this egregious distribution?

A sociologist would immediately suspect the answer probably is that women are discriminated against. They have been greatly discriminated against in the past, and though the law now makes discrimination in employment illegal, the sociologist would suspect that discrimination continues in subtle ways. If this is true, then something should be done to correct the problem, because the system is unjust to women. But there is another possible explanation: men and women are biologically different, and their differences could affect their abilities, choices, and behavior, which in turn could cumulatively affect their employment prospects. If this is true, then nothing should be done about it because the current situation is the result of women's abilities and choices. Of course there is a third possibility. Both discrimination and biology may be contributing to the failure of women to reach in large numbers the top levels of American corporations. If this were true, then it is likely that the debate would go on without resolution, and the action would be postponed.

We have presented the discrimination and the biological arguments simplistically when there are multiple components to each. The discrimination explanation involves prejudice, old boys' club networks, beliefs about leadership qualities, differential socialization, and the influence of cultural values on gender roles. The biological explanation involves differential abilities (e.g., mathematical competence), differential needs and desires (e.g., the need to relate relative to the need to dominate, or cooperation relative to competition), and differential instincts (e.g., mothering relative to providing). A notable example of the biological explanation is Steven Goldberg's book *The Inevitability of Patriarchy* (1973). He argues that patriarchy is universal, and the claimed exceptions are not exceptions when examined closely. He explains this reported sociological law by the greater innate drive of males to compete and dominate. Thus, we should expect most CEOs to be males forever.

What is interesting is that the past decade has witnessed a change in the management literature, which now preaches the transformational leader who exhibits mainly feminine characteristics such as collaborating, teaching, inspiring, empowering subordinates, and focusing on relationships. The more masculine top-down and command-and-control leader is appropriate in fewer and fewer domains. These changes should favor women getting to top positions in the future.

The following readings debate the causes of the overwhelming dominance of males in top positions in corporate America. Eagly and Carli's selection presents the discrimination theory perspective and identifies many of the ways that women are discriminated against in the workplace. In contrast, Browne presents the biological theory, he arguing that by nature women and men have different interests and talents that better suit them for different jobs.

YES

Alice H. Eagly and
Linda L. Carli

Women and the Labyrinth
of Leadership

If one has misdiagnosed a problem, then one is unlikely to prescribe an effective cure. This is the situation regarding the scarcity of women in top leadership. Because people with the best of intentions have misread the symptoms, the solutions that managers are investing in are not making enough of a difference.

That there is a problem is not in doubt. Despite years of progress by women in the workforce (they now occupy more than 40% of all managerial positions in the United States), within the C-suite they remain as rare as hens' teeth. Consider the most highly paid executives of *Fortune 500* companies—those with titles such as chairman, president, chief executive officer, and chief operating officer. Of this group, only 6% are women. Most notably, only 2% of the CEOs are women, and only 15% of the seats on the boards of directors are held by women. The situation is not much different in other industrialized countries. In the 50 largest publicly traded corporations in each nation of the European Union, women make up, on average, 11% of the top executives and 4% of the CEOs and heads of boards. Just seven companies, or 1%, of *Fortune* magazine's Global 500 have female CEOs. What is to blame for the pronounced lack of women in positions of power and authority?

In 1986 the *Wall Street Journal's* Carol Hymowitz and Timothy Schellhardt gave the world an answer: "Even those few women who rose steadily through the ranks eventually crashed into an invisible barrier. The executive suite seemed within their grasp, but they just couldn't break through the glass ceiling." The metaphor, driven home by the article's accompanying illustration, resonated; it captured the frustration of a goal within sight but somehow unattainable. To be sure, there was a time when the barriers were absolute. Even within the career spans of 1980s-era executives, access to top posts had been explicitly denied. . . .

Times have changed, however, and the glass ceiling metaphor is now more wrong than right. For one thing, it describes an absolute barrier at a specific high level in organizations. The fact that there have been female chief executives, university presidents, state governors, and presidents of nations gives the lie to that charge. At the same time, the metaphor implies that women and men have equal access to entry- and mid-level positions. They do not. The image of a transparent obstruction also suggests that women are being misled about their opportunities, because the impediment is not easy for them to see from a distance. But some impediments are not subtle. Worst of all, by depicting a single, unvarying obstacle, the glass ceiling fails to incorporate the complexity and variety of challenges that women can face in their leadership journeys. In truth, women are not turned away only as they reach the penultimate stage of a distinguished career. They disappear in various numbers at many points leading up to that stage.

Metaphors matter because they are part of the storytelling that can compel change. Believing in the existence of a glass ceiling, people emphasize certain kinds of interventions: top-to-top networking, mentoring to increase board memberships, requirements for diverse candidates in high-profile succession horse races, litigation aimed at punishing discrimination in the C-suite. None of these is counterproductive; all have a role to play. The danger arises when they draw attention and resources away from other kinds of interventions that might attack the problem more potently. If we want to make better progress, it's time to rename the challenge.

Walls All Around

A better metaphor for what confronts women in their professional endeavors is the labyrinth. It's an image with a long and varied history in ancient Greece, India, Nepal, native North and South America, medieval Europe, and elsewhere. As a contemporary symbol, it conveys the idea of a complex journey toward a goal worth striving for. Passage through a labyrinth is not simple or direct, but requires persistence, awareness of one's progress, and a careful analysis of the puzzles that lie ahead. It is this meaning that we intend to convey. For women who aspire to top leadership, routes exist but are full of twists and turns, both unexpected and expected. Because all labyrinths have a viable route to the center, it is understood that goals are attainable. The metaphor acknowledges obstacles but is not ultimately discouraging.

If we can understand the various barriers that make up this labyrinth, and how some women find their way around them, we can work more effectively to improve the situation. What are the obstructions that women run up against? Let's explore them in turn.

Vestiges of prejudice.   It is a well-established fact that men as a group still have the benefit of higher wages and faster promotions. In the United States in 2005, for example, women employed full-time earned 81 cents for every dollar that men earned. . . .

One of the most comprehensive of these studies was conducted by the U.S. Government Accountability Office. The study was based on survey data from 1983 through 2000 from a representative sample of Americans. Because the same people responded to the survey repeatedly over the years, the study provided accurate estimates of past work experience, which is important for explaining later wages.

The GAO researchers tested whether individuals' total wages could be predicted by sex and other characteristics. They included part-time and full-time employees in the surveys and took into account all the factors that they could estimate and that might affect earnings, such as education and work experience. Without controls for these variables, the data showed that women earned about 44% less than men, averaged over the entire period from 1983 to 2000. With these controls in place, the gap was only about half as large, but still substantial. The control factors that reduced the wage gap most were the different employment patterns of men and women: Men undertook more hours of paid labor per year than women and had more years of job experience.

Although most variables affected the wages of men and women similarly, there were exceptions. Marriage and parenthood, for instance, were associated with higher wages for men but not for women. In contrast, other characteristics, especially years of education, had a more positive effect on women's wages than on men's. Even after adjusting wages for all of the ways men and women differ, the GAO study, like similar studies, showed that women's wages remained lower than men's. The unexplained gender gap is consistent with the presence of wage discrimination.

Similar methods have been applied to the question of whether discrimination affects promotions. Evidently it does. Promotions come more slowly for women than for men with equivalent qualifications. . . . Even in culturally feminine settings such as nursing, librarianship, elementary education, and social work, men ascend to supervisory and administrative positions more quickly than women.

The findings of correlational studies are supported by experimental research, in which subjects are asked to evaluate hypothetical individuals as managers or job candidates, and all characteristics of these individuals are held constant except for their sex. Such efforts continue the tradition of the Goldberg paradigm, named for a 1968 experiment by Philip Goldberg. His simple, elegant study had student participants evaluate written essays that were identical except for the attached male or female name. The students were unaware that other students had received identical material ascribed to a writer of the other sex. This initial experiment demonstrated an overall gender bias: Women received lower evaluations unless the essay was on a feminine topic. Some 40 years later, unfortunately, experiments continue to reveal the same kind of bias in work settings. Men are advantaged over equivalent women as candidates for jobs traditionally held by men as well as for more gender-integrated jobs. Similarly, male leaders receive somewhat more favorable evaluations than equivalent female leaders, especially in roles usually occupied by men.

. . . [A] general bias against women appears to operate with approximately equal strength at all levels. The scarcity of female corporate officers is the sum of discrimination that has operated at all ranks, not evidence of a particular obstacle to advancement as women approach the top. The problem, in other words, is not a glass ceiling.

Resistance to women's leadership.   What's behind the discrimination we've been describing? Essentially, a set of widely shared conscious and unconscious mental associations about women, men, and leaders. Study after study has affirmed that people associate women and men with different traits and link men with more of the traits that connote leadership. . . .

In the language of psychologists, the clash is between two sets of associations: communal and agentic. Women are associated with communal qualities, which convey a concern for the compassionate treatment of others. They include being especially affectionate, helpful, friendly, kind, and sympathetic, as well as interpersonally sensitive, gentle, and soft-spoken. In contrast, men are associated with agentic qualities, which convey assertion and control. They include being especially aggressive, ambitious, dominant, self-confident, and forceful, as well as self-reliant and individualistic. The agentic traits are also associated in most people's minds with effective leadership—perhaps because a long history of male domination of leadership roles has made it difficult to separate the leader associations from the male associations.

As a result, women leaders find themselves in a double bind. If they are highly communal, they may be criticized for not being agentic enough. But if they are highly agentic, they may be criticized for lacking communion. Either way, they may leave the impression that they don't have "the right stuff" for powerful jobs.

Given this double bind, it is hardly surprising that people are more resistant to women's influence than to men's. . . .

Studies have gauged reactions to men and women engaging in various types of dominant behavior. The findings are quite consistent. Nonverbal dominance, such as staring at others while speaking to them or pointing at people, is a more damaging behavior for women than for men. Verbally intimidating others can undermine a woman's influence, and assertive behavior can reduce her chances of getting a job or advancing in her career. Simply disagreeing can sometimes get women into trouble. Men who disagree or otherwise act dominant get away with it more often than women do.

Self-promotion is similarly risky for women. Although it can convey status and competence, it is not at all communal. So while men can use bluster to get themselves noticed, modesty is expected even of highly accomplished women. . . .

Another way the double bind penalizes women is by denying them the full benefits of being warm and considerate. Because people expect it of women, nice behavior that seems noteworthy in men seems unimpressive in women. For example, in one study, helpful men reaped a lot of approval, but helpful women did not. Likewise, men got away with being unhelpful, but women did not. . . .

While one might suppose that men would have a double bind of their own, they in fact have more freedom. Several experiments and organizational studies have assessed reactions to behavior that is warm and friendly versus dominant and assertive. The findings show that men can communicate in a warm or a dominant manner, with no penalty either way. People like men equally well and are equally influenced by them regardless of their warmth.

It all amounts to a clash of assumptions when the average person confronts a woman in management. . . . In the absence of any evidence to the contrary, people suspect that such highly effective women must not be very likable or nice.

Issues of leadership style.   In response to the challenges presented by the double bind, female leaders often struggle to cultivate an appropriate and effective leadership style—one that reconciles the communal qualities people prefer in women with the agentic qualities people think leaders need to succeed. . . .

It's difficult to pull off such a transformation while maintaining a sense of authenticity as a leader. Sometimes the whole effort can backfire. In the words of another female leader, "I think that there is a real penalty for a woman who behaves like a man. The men don't like her and the women don't either." Women leaders worry a lot about these things, complicating the labyrinth that they negotiate. For example, Catalyst's study of *Fortune* 1000 female executives found that 96% of them rated as critical or fairly important that they develop "a style with which male managers are comfortable."

Does a distinct "female" leadership style exist? There seems to be a popular consensus that it does. . . .

More scientifically, a recent meta-analysis integrated the results of 45 studies addressing the question [comparing three leadership styles]. . . . Transformational leaders establish themselves as role models by gaining followers' trust and confidence. They state future goals, develop plans to achieve those goals, and innovate, even when their organizations are generally successful. Such leaders mentor and empower followers, encouraging them to develop their full potential and thus to contribute more effectively to their organizations. By contrast, transactional leaders establish give-and-take relationships that appeal to subordinates' self-interest. Such leaders manage in the conventional manner of clarifying subordinates' responsibilities, rewarding them for meeting objectives, and correcting them for failing to meet objectives. Although transformational and transactional leadership styles are different, most leaders adopt at least some behaviors of both types. The researchers also allowed for a third category, called the laissez-faire style—a sort of non-leadership that concerns itself with none of the above, despite rank authority.

The meta-analysis found that, in general, female leaders were somewhat more transformational than male leaders, especially when it came to giving support and encouragement to subordinates. They also engaged in more of the rewarding behaviors that are one aspect of transactional leadership. Meanwhile, men exceeded women on the aspects of transactional leadership involving corrective and disciplinary actions that are either active (timely) or passive (belated). Men were also more likely than women to be laissez-faire leaders, who take little responsibility for managing. These findings add up to a startling conclusion, given that most leadership research has found the transformational style (along with the rewards and positive incentives associated with the transactional style) to be more suited to leading the modern organization. The research tells us not only that men and women do have somewhat different leadership styles, but also that women's approaches are the more generally effective—while men's often are only somewhat effective or actually hinder effectiveness.

Another part of this picture, based on a separate meta-analysis, is that women adopt a more participative and collaborative style than men typically favor. The reason for this difference is unlikely to be genetic. Rather, it may be that collaboration can get results without seeming particularly masculine. As women navigate their way through the double bind, they seek ways to project authority without relying on the autocratic behaviors that people find so jarring in women. A viable path is to bring others into decision making and to lead as an encouraging teacher and positive role model. . . .

Demands of family life.   For many women, the most fateful turns in the labyrinth are the ones taken under pressure of family responsibilities. Women continue to be the ones who interrupt their careers, take more days off, and work part-time. As a result, they have fewer years of job experience and fewer hours of employment per year, which slows their career progress and reduces their earnings. . . .

There is no question that, while men increasingly share housework and child rearing, the bulk of domestic work still falls on women's shoulders. We know this from time-diary studies, in which people record what they are doing during each hour of a 24-hour day. So, for example, in the United States married women devoted 19 hours per week on average to housework in 2005, while married men contributed 11 hours. That's a huge improvement over 1965 numbers, when women spent a whopping 34 hours per week to men's five, but it is still a major inequity. And the situation looks worse when child care hours are added.

Although it is common knowledge that mothers provide more child care than fathers, few people realize that mothers provide more than they did in earlier generations—despite the fact that fathers are putting in a lot more time than in the past. . . . Thus, though husbands have taken on more domestic work, the work/family conflict has not eased for women; the gain has been offset by escalating pressures for intensive parenting and the increasing time demands of most high-level careers.

Even women who have found a way to relieve pressures from the home front by sharing child care with husbands, other family members, or paid workers may not enjoy the full workplace benefit of having done so. Decision makers often assume that mothers have domestic responsibilities that make it inappropriate to promote them to demanding positions. . . .

Underinvestment in social capital.   Perhaps the most destructive result of the work/family balancing act so many women must perform is that it leaves very little time for socializing with colleagues and building professional networks. The social capital that accrues from such "nonessential" parts of work turns out to be quite essential indeed. One study yielded the following description of managers who advanced rapidly in hierarchies: Fast-track managers "spent relatively more time and effort socializing, politicking, and interacting with outsiders than did their less successful counterparts . . . [and] did not give much time or attention to the traditional management activities of planning, decision making, and controlling or to the human resource management activities of motivating/reinforcing, staffing, training/develping, and managing conflict." . . .

Even given sufficient time, women can find it difficult to engage in and benefit from informal networking if they are a small minority. In such settings, the influential networks are composed entirely or almost entirely of men. Breaking into those male networks can be hard, especially when men center their networks on masculine activities. The recent gender discrimination lawsuit against Wal-Mart provides examples of this. For instance, an executive retreat took the form of a quail-hunting expedition at Sam Walton's ranch in Texas. Middle managers' meetings included visits to strip clubs and Hooters restaurants, and a sales conference attended by thousands of store managers featured a football theme. One executive received feedback that she probably would not advance in the company because she didn't hunt or fish.

Management Interventions That Work

Taking the measure of the labyrinth that confronts women leaders, we see that it begins with prejudices that benefit men and penalize women, continues with particular resistance to women's leadership, includes questions of leadership style and authenticity, and—most dramatically for many women—features the challenge of balancing work and family responsibilities. It becomes clear that a woman's situation as she reaches her peak career years is the result of many turns at many challenging junctures. Only a few individual women have made the right combination of moves to land at the center of power—but as for the rest, there is usually no single turning point where their progress was diverted and the prize was lost.

What's to be done in the face of such a multifaceted problem? A solution that is often proposed is for governments to implement and enforce antidiscrimination legislation and thereby require organizations to eliminate inequitable practices. However, analysis of discrimination cases that have gone to court has shown that legal remedies can be elusive when gender inequality results from norms embedded in organizational structure and culture. The more effective approach is for organizations to appreciate the subtlety and complexity of the problem and to attack its many roots simultaneously. More specifically, if a company wants to see more women arrive in its executive suite, it should do the following:

> **Increase people's awareness of the psychological drivers of prejudice toward female leaders, and work to dispel those perceptions.** . . .
>
> **Change the long-hours norm.** . . . To the extent an organization can shift the focus to objective measures of productivity, women with family demands on their time but highly productive work habits will receive the rewards and encouragement they deserve.
>
> **Reduce the subjectivity of performance evaluation.** . . . To ensure fairness, criteria should be explicit and evaluation processes designed to limit the influence of decision makers' conscious and unconscious biases.

Use open-recruitment tools, such as advertising and employment agencies, rather than relying on informal social networks and referrals to fill positions. . . . Research has shown that such personnel practices increase the numbers of women in managerial roles.

Ensure a critical mass of women in executive positions—not just one or two women—to head off the problems that come with tokenism. Token women tend to be pegged into narrow stereotypical roles such as "seductress," "mother," "pet," or "iron maiden." . . . When women are not a small minority, their identities as women become less salient, and colleagues are more likely to react to them in terms of their individual competencies.

Avoid having a sole female member of any team. Top management tends to divide its small population of women managers among many projects in the interests of introducing diversity to them all. But several studies have found that, so outnumbered, the women tend to be ignored by the men. . . . This is part of the reason that the glass ceiling metaphor resonates with so many. But in fact, the problem can be present at any level.

Help shore up social capital. As we've discussed, the call of family responsibilities is mainly to blame for women's underinvestment in networking. When time is scarce, this social activity is the first thing to go by the wayside. . . . When a well-placed individual who possesses greater legitimacy (often a man) takes an interest in a woman's career, her efforts to build social capital can proceed far more efficiently.

Prepare women for line management with appropriately demanding assignments. Women, like men, must have the benefit of developmental job experiences if they are to qualify for promotions. . . .

Establish family-friendly human resources practices. These may include flextime, job sharing, telecommuting, elder care provisions, adoption benefits, dependent child care options, and employee-sponsored on-site child care. Such support can allow women to stay in their jobs during the most demanding years of child rearing, build social capital, keep up to date in their fields, and eventually compete for higher positions. . . .

Allow employees who have significant parental responsibility more time to prove themselves worthy of promotion. This recommendation is particularly directed to organizations, many of them professional services firms, that have established "up or out" career progressions. People not ready for promotion at the same time as the top performers in their cohort aren't simply left in place—they're asked to leave. But many parents (most often mothers), while fully capable of reaching that level of achievement, need extra time—perhaps a year or two—to get there. . . .

Welcome women back. It makes sense to give high-performing women who step away from the workforce an opportunity to return to responsible positions when their circumstances change. . . .

Encourage male participation in family-friendly benefits. Dangers lurk in family-friendly benefits that are used only by women. Exercising options such as generous parental leave and part-time work slows down women's careers. More profoundly, having many more women than men take such benefits can harm the careers of women in general because of the expectation that they may well exercise those options. Any effort toward greater family friendliness should actively recruit male participation to avoid inadvertently making it harder for women to gain access to essential managerial roles.

Managers can be forgiven if they find the foregoing list a tall order. It's a wide-ranging set of interventions and still far from exhaustive. The point, however, is just that: Organizations will succeed in filling half their top management slots with women—and women who are the true performance equals of their male counterparts—only by attacking all the reasons they are absent today. Glass ceiling-inspired programs and projects can do just so much if the leakage of talented women is happening on every lower floor of the building. Individually, each of these interventions has been shown to make a difference. Collectively, we believe, they can make all the difference.

The View from Above

Imagine visiting a formal garden and finding within it a high hedgerow. At a point along its vertical face, you spot a rectangle—a neatly pruned and inviting doorway. Are you aware as you step through that you are entering a labyrinth? And, three doorways later, as the reality of the puzzle settles in, do you have any idea how to proceed? This is the situation in which many women find themselves in their career endeavors. Ground-level perplexity and frustration make every move uncertain.

Labyrinths become infinitely more tractable when seen from above. When the eye can take in the whole of the puzzle—the starting position, the goal, and the maze of walls—solutions begin to suggest themselves. This has been the goal of our research. Our hope is that women, equipped with a map of the barriers they will confront on their path to professional achievement, will make more informed choices. We hope that managers, too, will understand where their efforts can facilitate the progress of women. If women are to achieve equality, women and men will have to share leadership equally. With a greater understanding of what stands in the way of gender-balanced leadership, we draw nearer to attaining it in our time.

Kingsley R. Browne

Biology at Work: Rethinking Sexual Equality

Modern evolutionary biology and psychology pose an even more direct challenge to the [Standard Social Sciences Model] (SSSM) with their insight that human behavioral predispositions are ultimately attributable to the same cause as the behavioral predispositions of other animals—evolution through natural selection. The centrality of mating and reproduction to evolutionary success, coupled with the differential investment of mammalian males and females in offspring, makes behavioral and temperamental identity of the sexes highly improbable. Just as no farmer expects to see identical patterns of behavior from the mare as from the stallion, from the cow as from the bull, or from the hen as from the rooster, no social scientist should expect to see identical patterns of behavior from men and women.

Claims for the existence of a recognizable "human nature" or for predictable behavioral differences between the sexes should be inherently suspect only to those who believe that the forces that created humans were importantly different from those that created the rest of the animal kingdom. If males and females are at their core psychologically identical, they are unique among mammals. This is not to deny the importance of social influences or the fact that societies have certain emergent characteristics that no amount of atomistic study of individuals could ever predict. But it is critical to understand that some social practices are more likely to arise than others precisely because human *minds* are more likely to settle on some social practices than others and that males and females tend to have different psychologies independent of the influence of cultures that expect them to be different.

The Division of Labor by Sex

A proper understanding of psychological sex differences would go far toward an understanding of the modern workplace, the study of which has heretofore been heavily biased toward the SSSM orientation. One human universal that is apparently a product of human nature is the division of labor by sex. All societies label some work "men's work" and other work "women's work." Although the content of the categories is by no means fixed—what some cultures

From *Biology at Work: Rethinking Sexual Equality*, 2002, pp. 4–6, 33–34, 215–217. Copyright © 2002 by Rutgers University Press. Reprinted by permission.

label "men's work" is "women's work" in others—there are, nonetheless, some consistent patterns. Big-game hunting and metalworking are almost always "men's work" and cooking and grinding grain are almost always "women's work." While some divisions are obviously related to physical capacity, this is not always the case. For example, carrying water is almost always "women's work," and manufacture of musical instruments is almost always "men's work."

Modern Western societies are breaking down these age-old divisions, so that workers increasingly find themselves in what anthropologists call an "evolutionarily novel environment"—an environment that differs from that in which our hominid ancestors evolved—in this case a workplace environment in which men and women work side by side and compete for position in the same status hierarchies. Today, almost all positions in the labor market are formally open to women, the primary exception being certain combat positions in the military. Nonetheless, a high degree of de facto occupational segregation continues to exist, so that in practice there are many occupations that remain "men's work" and "women's work." Thus, most men work mostly with other men, and most women work mostly with other women. Moreover, even in largely integrated occupations, men are more likely than women to achieve the highest organizational positions.

The architects of sexual equality appear to have assumed that lifting formal barriers to women in the workplace would result in parity with men because men and women inherently have identical desires and capacities. When prohibitions on formal discrimination have not resulted in sexual parity, hidden discrimination is often assumed responsible. If hidden discrimination can be disproved, then informal barriers, such as sexist attitudes of parents or teachers are identified as the culprit. If direct external forces must finally (and reluctantly) be abandoned because the paths that women's lives have taken must be attributed to their own choices, then their choice becomes a "choice" that is attributed to their internalization of "patriarchal" notions about the proper role of the sexes and to their life constraints. While the causal attribution may shift over time, what does not change is the persistent invocation of causes other than women's inherent predispositions. Given the human propensity for self-deception, it may not be possible to answer the question whether these shifting arguments reflect actual beliefs or are merely opportunistic arguments to advance a political agenda.

The social-role view of sex differences is that "men and women have inherited essentially the same evolved psychological dispositions" and that behavioral sex differences are simply results of "two organizing principles of human societies: the division of labor according to sex and gender hierarchy." How is it that a sexually monomorphic mind came up with the division of labor by sex and gender hierarchy? Certainly the social explanation is not the most parsimonious explanation for sex differences in behavior. Humans evolved from other creatures surely having sexually dimorphic minds. The notion that humans evolved away from the primate pattern of behavioral sex differences—presumably because it was advantageous to do so—but simultaneously replaced the preexisting biological pattern with cultural patterns having the same effect is difficult to credit. Moreover, the direction of causation in this explanation is implausibly unidirectional. Even if behavioral sex differences originated from a sexually monomorphic mind, one would expect that they would be reinforced through selection over the hundreds of thousands or millions of years that these social phenomena existed.

Stasis and Change

Trends in women's work-force participation are not easily explained in terms of broad themes such as "patriarchy," "subjugation of women," or even the waning power of a monolithic male hierarchy. The progress of women has not been uniformly slow or uniformly fast, as might be expected if it were solely a consequence of such wide-ranging forces; instead, the pattern has been much more complex, and it is that pattern that any theory of workplace sex differences must attempt to explain.

In some respects, the role of women in the work force has been massively transformed in just a few decades. In 1960, women constituted just one-third of the American work force compared to over 46 percent today. During that same period, the percentage of married women who work doubled to 61 percent. Only 4 percent of lawyers in 1970 were women, while today the figure for law school graduates exceeds 42 percent. The percentage of female physicians increased from 10 to 24 percent between 1970 and 1995, and the percentage of female medical students now exceeds 40 percent. In business, the change has been no less impressive. In 1972, women held only 18 percent of managerial and administrative positions, compared to 43 percent of such positions in 1995. These changes represent a genuine revolution in the American workplace.

Despite these striking advances, however, women are far from achieving parity in a number of areas. They constitute only 5 to 7 percent of senior executives in the largest corporations, and the average full-time female employee makes less than 75 cents for every dollar earned by the average full-time male, if factors that influence wages such as hours worked and nature of the occupation are not considered. Many occupations remain highly sex segregated. Among the occupations in the United States that remain 90 percent or more female are bank teller, receptionist, registered nurse, and preschool and kindergarten teacher. Among the occupations that are less than 10 percent female are engineer, firefighter, mechanic, and pest exterminator. Large numbers of women pursue education in some scientific fields—such as biology and medicine—yet far fewer are found in other scientific fields—such as mathematics, physics, and engineering. Despite frequent assertions that women are victims of widespread discrimination, for the past two decades unemployment rates of the two sexes have not diverged by as much as a percentage point. Thus, women's progress has not been uniformly stifled nor has it uniformly advanced; instead it has been quite patchy.

The question is why. Part of the answer lies in the sexually dimorphic human mind. . . . The means by which any animal "makes a living" is intimately related to the animal's physical and psychological makeup. If the physical and psychological makeup of a species varies substantially by sex, we would expect that males and females may make their livings in a somewhat different manner. The culturally universal division of labor by sex appears to be a manifestation of that principle.

Even in today's relatively egalitarian Western societies, men and women tend to seek different jobs, favor different occupational attributes, and sometimes even perform the same jobs in a somewhat different manner. Because workplace choices often influence both tangible and intangible rewards, systematically different preferences tend to result in systematically different rewards. A social environment in which individuals of both sexes are free to pursue their own priorities cannot therefore be expected, a priori, to produce identical rewards to members of the two sexes.

Sex differences in temperament and cognitive abilities, as well as occupational preferences, are at least partially responsible for a number of workplace phenomena that are sometimes labeled "problems"—the "glass ceiling," the "gender gap" in compensation, and occupational segregation. Although sex discrimination can also play a role, complete understanding of workplace patterns requires us to look honestly at other factors. Some individuals, for example, are more likely to seek, and make the requisite sacrifices and investments to achieve, the highest positions in business, government, and academia. Those who achieve positions of high status tend to be those for whom status is a high priority. Those who have high earnings tend to be those for whom high earnings are a sufficiently high priority that the sacrifices and tradeoffs necessary to achieve them are worthwhile. Because men and women vary systematically along these and other dimensions, occupational outcomes for men and women are not identical. Whether this is a problem or merely a fact is to some extent a value judgment. However, one's beliefs about the causes of the outcomes—for example, discrimination by employers or personal choice of the affected individuals—may influence the extent to which the outcomes are deemed acceptable. . . .

Conclusion

The evidence and arguments put forward in this book will be troubling to many. Some may believe that invocation of biology is implicitly (or perhaps even explicitly) a defense of the status quo—a paean to the virtue of existing arrangements or at least a testament to their inevitability. The defense, however, is more limited. It is that many of the workplace patterns that are laid at the foot of nefarious causes such as discrimination by employers or sexist socialization have causes that are less invidious and less attributable to an anti-female ideology than is commonly recognized.

A consensus about the causes of workplace patterns does not foreordain consensus about policy responses. One's values are important, and values are not directly derivable from scientific fact. Proponents of laissez-faire policies will likely draw free-market implications, while those more inclined toward governmental intervention may settle on more activist approaches. Everyone interested in workplace policy, however, whatever his political or social outlook, should desire an accurate understanding of the underlying causes of current patterns.

It would be a mistake to interpret average temperamental or cognitive sex differences as limitations on the potential of individual girls and women. Nothing contained in this book implies that women cannot or should not be corporate presidents or theoretical physicists, only that equal representation of women in these positions is unlikely to occur unless selection processes are modified with the specific purpose of guaranteeing proportional representation.

Sufficient overlap exists on most traits that there are few occupations that should be expected to remain the exclusive domain of one sex, but many occupations will remain overwhelmingly male or overwhelmingly female if people continue to select occupations on the basis of their preferences and abilities. Expansion of the choices available to women (and to men) increases the influence of individual preferences on workplace outcomes. To the extent that individuals' preferences differ, we should expect them to seek different workplace rewards. Because the average endowment of men and women differs—in temperament, cognitive ability, values, and interests—it would be astonishing if their occupational preferences and behaviors were identical.

Modern attitudes about preferences are somewhat conflicted. The value that Western liberals place upon individual liberty rests heavily on the assumption that the preferences of individuals differ. Each individual should be free, within broad limits, to pursue his own ends. There is, therefore, something vaguely illiberal about both the assumption that all individuals *should* have the same preferences and attempts to ensure the outcomes that would result if they did.

Some people believe that even if sex differences exist, there is harm in publicizing them because they can become self-fulfilling prophecies. Even if the "correct" ratio of professional mathematicians is, say, 5 males to 1 female, it is harmful to make that fact widely known, because then mathematics will be labeled a "male field," and girls will assume that it is *only* for males. Although that is a rational concern, it is not well supported empirically. Clark McCauley found, for example, that when asked to estimate the proportion of males or females in a number of sex-stereotyped occupations, subjects showed no evidence of stereotypic exaggeration. The correlation between estimates and actual percentages was high, indicating that people rank-ordered them accurately, but where the subjects erred, it was almost always in the direction of underestimating the difference between men and women in the occupation. Similarly, Mary Ann Cejka and Alice Eagly found that participants systematically underestimated the extent to which male-dominated and female-dominated occupations were segregated.

It may seem odd that this book implies the near-inevitability of disproportionate male representation at the highest levels in corporate and other hierarchies, at least under current incentives, at the same time that other writers are predicting seemingly contrary trends. In 1999, two books appeared on the market, coincidentally both by Rutgers University anthropologists: *The First Sex* by Helen Fisher and *The Decline of Males* by Lionel Tiger. Both chronicled changes in the workplace, in education, and in broader social forces such as increasing female control over reproduction. Fisher's book emphasized the positive—the ascendancy of females—but gave little attention to the social effects of the "displaced males" that ascendancy of females implies. Tiger analyzed many of the same trends, but his view was more pessimistic, as the specter of large numbers of marginalized males does not bode well for any society. Neither Fisher's nor Tiger's analysis is inconsistent with that provided here, however. [T]he gender gap in compensation shrinks with changes in work that favor women. Nonetheless, men will continue to dominate the scarce positions at the top of hierarchies as long as it is necessary to devote decades of intense labor-market activity to obtain them, even if women come to predominate in middle-management positions and even if men also disproportionately occupy the bottom of hierarchies. Men will similarly continue to dominate math-intensive fields, as well as fields that expose workers to substantial physical risks.

The extent of one's willingness to live with the sex differences in outcomes described here depends to some extent on one's definitions of equality. If current workplace outcomes are a cumulative consequence of millions of individual choices made by men and women guided by their sexually dimorphic psyches, are the outcomes of those choices rendered suspect because those sexually dimorphic minds incline men and women to make their choices in systematically different ways? This question resembles, if not entails, the familiar question of whether the equality that ought to be of importance to policy makers is "equality of opportunity" or "equality of result." Those who place primary importance on equality of opportunity may say that as long as both men and women are given the opportunity to pursue the opportunities that the workplace provides, the outcomes are unimportant. Those who look to group outcomes, on the other hand, may say that the critical question is what the different groups end up with. However, we cannot say that the "outcome" for women is deficient without specifying with precision what that outcome is. We cannot, that is, simply look at women's income and occupational attainment without also considering what they get in return for the occupational tradeoffs that they make.

The question of agency is at the core. Are women, like men, active agents in their own lives, making rational decisions based upon their own preferences? Or are they pawns of both men and society—making suboptimal "choices" that are forced on them by others? All indications are that the former is closer to the mark. Women, though somewhat constrained by life circumstances, as are men, make rational and responsible choices that are most compatible with their temperaments, abilities, and desires.

POSTSCRIPT

Are Barriers to Women's Success as Leaders Due to Societal Obstacles?

Alice H. Eagly and Linda L. Carli present convincing evidence that women face discrimination in employment and prejudice against their capacity as leaders. Kingsley R. Browne makes a good case that men and women are biologically different in ways that would affect work choices and performances. Neither destroys the argument of the other, so both could be true. If so, women will never be equally represented in the leadership positions in large corporations unless women are better suited for transformational leadership, and large businesses need this type of leadership for today's challenges. But it is also clear that women should be better represented at the highest levels of businesses than they are now. The research indicates that the promotion of more women would be in the interest of the businesses as well as in the interest of justice.

Further reading on this issue should start with Alice H. Eagly and Linda L. Carli's book length treatment of the topic in *Through the Labyrinth: The Truth about How Women Became Leaders* (Harvard Business School Press, 2007). Two works that support their line of thinking are Alicia E. Kaufmann, *Women in Management and the Life Cycle: Aspects That Limit or Promote Getting to the Top* (Palgrave Macmillan, 2008) and Barbara Kellerman and Deborah L. Rhode, eds., *Women and Leadership: The State of Play and Strategies for Change* (Jossey-Bass, 2007). Works on women and leadership include Jean Lau Chin et al., eds., *Women and Leadership: Transforming Visions and Diverse Voices* (Blackwell, 2007); Linda Coughlin, Ellen Wingard, and Keith Hollihan, eds., *Enlightened Power: How Women Are Transforming the Practice of Leadership* (Jossey-Bass, 2005); Sue Hayward, *Women Leading* (Palgrave Macmillan, 2005); and John E. Butler, ed., *New Perspectives on Women Entrepreneurs* (Information Age Publishers, 2003). Books that focus on women as political leaders include Lori Cox Han and Caroline Heldman, eds., *Rethinking Madam President: Are We Ready for a Woman in the White House* (Lynne Reinner, 2007); Vicki Donlan, *Her Turn: Why It's Time for Women to Lead America* (Praeger, 2007); Gunhild Hoogensen and Bruce O. Solhein, *Women in Power: World Leaders since 1960* (Praeger, 2006); Marie C. Wilson, *Closing the Leadership Gap: Why Women Can and Must Help Run the World,* revised edition (Penguin Books, 2007); and Barbara Palmer and Dennis Simon, *Breaking the Political Glass Ceiling: Women and Congressional Elections* (Routledge, 2008). More basic works on gender include Mary Holmes, *What Is Gender?: Sociological Approaches* (Sage, 2007); Harriet Bradley, *Gender* (Polity Press, 2007); Julia T. Wood, *Gendered Lives: Communication, Gender and Culture* (Wadsworth/Thompson Learning, 2005); and Michael W. Kimmel, *The Gendered Society,* 2nd edition (Oxford University Press, 2004).

One aspect of the professional attainment of women that should receive more attention is the gender differences in socialization. Boys and girls are not treated the same nor socialized the same, and differences in socialization continue throughout the life course. Gender socialization is thoroughly treated in textbooks about gender such as Margaret L. Andersen, *Thinking about Women: Sociological Perspectives on Sex and Gender*, 8th edition (Allyn & Bacon, 2008).

ISSUE 22

Is the World a Victim of American Cultural Imperialism?

YES: Julia Galeota, from "Cultural Imperialism: An American Tradition," *The Humanist* (2004)

NO: Philippe Legrain, from "In Defense of Globalization," *The International Economy* (Summer 2003)

ISSUE SUMMARY

YES: Julia Galeota interprets the flooding of the rest of the world with American products and images as cultural imperialism. She argues that multinational corporations' strategy is to impose American values and ideals on the world community and to advance American culture at the expense of other cultures.

NO: Philippe Legrain examines the idea of American cultural imperialism and concludes that it is a myth. Furthermore, the advance of globalization and whatever cultural attachments that go with it are positive, not negative, developments.

Years ago a very popular picture that hung in many houses including my own was the picture of the Earth from the moon. Many of us liked this picture because it says better than a thousand words that the world is one. Humans may be separated into groups, tribes, and nations, but we are all one. Or is that only a dream? It was only a pipe dream while the United States and the Soviet Union had thousands of nuclear missiles pointed at each other, but when the Berlin wall came down in 1989 and the Soviet Union ceased to exist two years later, the dream revived and billions expected a long period of relative peace. One dissenter was Samuel Huntington, who in 1996 wrote *The Clash of Civilizations*, which predicted that the axis of world conflict would shift away from the clash of political ideologies and toward the clash of religious and cultural ideologies. At the same time, other writers were identifying the evolution of a one world culture that reflected the culture of America more than other countries. More recently some writers, including Julia Galeota, are interpreting this trend as an outcome of American cultural imperialism.

Another important trend is economic globalization. Some see this as a positive trend which spreads economic growth and wealth around the world. After all, jobs lost in America mean many good-paying jobs (compared other available jobs) in developing countries without causing high unemployment in America. It also lowers the prices of the goods that we buy so everyone wins. These ideas are hotly debated in another issue in this book, but the issue of economic globalization comes up here because it may be a major cause of the diffusion of American values throughout the world. It is certainly associated with the values of capitalism, free markets, freedom, rational self-interest, and materialism. It is also associated, though less tightly, with the values of democracy, science, anti-traditionalism, and secularism. It does erode traditional cultures, which raises the question of whether this is good or bad. Americans, of course, believe that their values are the best in the world so their spread benefits the world. Many members of the impacted cultures do not agree. Hence the debate. One of the questions in this debate is whether American culture is embodied in the products sold by many multinational corporations. Is buying American goods or watching American movies a step toward being Americanized?

Julia Galeota gives voice to the victims of American global cultural imperialism. She argues that the dissemination of American values through consumerism is eroding other cultures and threatening peoples' traditional identities. Philippe Legrain counters that the cultural imperialism thesis is a myth. It is absurd to think that culture and identity are destroyed by purchases. External images may influence us but not at the level of our basic identity and culture.

YES ↩

Julia Galeota

Cultural Imperialism:
An American Tradition

Travel almost anywhere in the world today and, whether you suffer from habitual Big Mac cravings or cringe at the thought of missing the newest episode of MTV's *The Real World,* your American tastes can be satisfied practically everywhere. This proliferation of American products across the globe is more than mere accident. As a byproduct of globalization, it is part of a larger trend in the conscious dissemination of American attitudes and values that is often referred to as *cultural imperialism.* In his 1976 work *Communication and Cultural Domination,* Herbert Schiller defines cultural imperialism as:

> The sum of the processes by which a society is brought into the modern world system, and how its dominating stratum is attracted, pressured, forced, and sometimes bribed into shaping social institutions to correspond to, or even to promote, the values and structures of the dominant center of the system.

Thus, cultural imperialism involves much more than simple consumer goods; it involves the dissemination of ostensibly American principles, such as freedom and democracy. Though this process might sound appealing on the surface, it masks a frightening truth: many cultures around the world are gradually disappearing due to the overwhelming influence of corporate and cultural America.

The motivations behind American cultural imperialism parallel the justifications for U.S. imperialism throughout history: the desire for access to foreign markets and the belief in the superiority of American culture. Though the United States does boast the world's largest, most powerful economy, no business is completely satisfied with controlling only the American market; American corporations want to control the other 95 percent of the world's consumers as well. Many industries are incredibly successful in that venture. According to the *Guardian,* American films accounted for approximately 80 percent of global box office revenue in January 2003. And who can forget good old Micky D's? With over 30,000 restaurants in over one hundred countries, the ubiquitous golden arches of McDonald's are now, according to Eric Schlosser's *Fast Food Nation,* "more widely recognized than the Christian cross." Such American domination inevitably hurts local markets, as the

From *The Humanist,* vol. 64, no. 3, May/June 2004, pp. 22–24, 46. Copyright © 2004 by Julia Galeota. Reprinted by permission of American Humanist Association and Julia Galeota.

majority of foreign industries are unable to compete with the economic strength of U.S. industry. Because it serves American economic interests, corporations conveniently ignore the detrimental impact of American control of foreign markets.

Corporations don't harbor qualms about the detrimental effects of "Americanization" of foreign cultures, as most corporations have ostensibly convinced themselves that American culture is superior and therefore its influence is beneficial to other, "lesser" cultures. Unfortunately, this American belief in the superiority of U.S. culture is anything but new; it is as old as the culture itself. This attitude was manifest in the actions of settlers when they first arrived on this continent and massacred or assimilated essentially the entire "savage" Native American population. This attitude also reflects that of the late nineteenth-century age of imperialism, during which the jingoists attempted to fulfill what they believed to be the divinely ordained "manifest destiny" of American expansion. Jingoists strongly believe in the concept of social Darwinism: the stronger, "superior" cultures will overtake the weaker, "inferior" cultures in a "survival of the fittest." It is this arrogant belief in the incomparability of American culture that characterizes many of our economic and political strategies today.

It is easy enough to convince Americans of the superiority of their culture, but how does one convince the rest of the world of the superiority of American culture? The answer is simple: marketing. Whether attempting to sell an item, a brand, or an entire culture, marketers have always been able to successfully associate American products with modernity in the minds of consumers worldwide. While corporations seem to simply sell Nike shoes or Gap jeans (both, ironically, manufactured *outside* of the United States), they are also selling the image of America as the land of "cool." This indissoluble association causes consumers all over the globe to clamor ceaselessly for the same American products.

Twenty years ago, in his essay "The Globalization of Markets," Harvard business professor Theodore Levitt declared, "The world's needs and desires have been irrevocably homogenized." Levitt held that corporations that were willing to bend to local tastes and habits were inevitably doomed to failure. He drew a distinction between weak multinational corporations that operate differently in each country and strong global corporations that handle an entire world of business with the same agenda.

In recent years, American corporations have developed an even more successful global strategy: instead of advertising American conformity with blonde-haired, blue-eyed, stereotypical Americans, they pitch diversity. These campaigns—such as McDonald's new international "I'm lovin' it" campaign—work by drawing on the United States' history as an ethnically integrated nation composed of essentially every culture in the world. An early example of this global marketing tactic was found in a Coca-Cola commercial from 1971 featuring children from many different countries innocently singing, "I'd like to teach the world to sing in perfect harmony/I'd like to buy the world a Coke to keep it company." This commercial illustrates an attempt to portray a U.S. goods as a product capable of transcending political, ethnic, religious, social, and economic differences to unite the world (according to the Coca-Cola Company, we can achieve world peace through consumerism).

More recently, Viacom's MTV has successfully adapted this strategy by integrating many different Americanized cultures into one unbelievably influential American network (with over 280 million subscribers worldwide). According to a 1996 "New World Teen Study" conducted by DMB&B's Brain-Waves division, of the 26,700 middle-class teens in forty-five countries surveyed, 85 percent watch MTV every day. These teens absorb what MTV intends to show as a diverse mix of cultural influences but is really nothing more than manufactured stars singing in English to appeal to American popular taste.

If the strength of these diverse "American" images is not powerful enough to move products, American corporations also appropriate local cultures into their advertising abroad. Unlike Levitt's weak multinationals, these corporations don't bend to local tastes; they merely insert indigenous celebrities or trends to present the facade of a customized advertisement. MTV has spawned over twenty networks specific to certain geographical areas such as Brazil and Japan. These specialized networks further spread the association between American and modernity under the pretense of catering to local taste. Similarly, commercials in India in 2000 featured Bollywood stars Hrithik Roshan promoting Coke and Shahrukh Khan promoting Pepsi (Sanjeev Srivastava, "Cola Row in India," BBC News Online). By using popular local icons in their advertisements, U.S. corporations successfully associate what is fashionable in local cultures with what is fashionable in America. America essentially samples the world's cultures, repackages them with the American trademark of materialism, and resells them to the world.

Critics of the theory of American cultural imperialism argue that foreign consumers don't passively absorb the images America bombards upon them. In fact, foreign consumers do play an active role in the reciprocal relationship between buyer and seller. For example, according to Naomi Klein's *No Logo,* American cultural imperialism has inspired a "slow food movement" in Italy and a demonstration involving the burning of chickens outside of the first Kentucky Fried Chicken outlet in India. Though there have been countless other conspicuous and inconspicuous acts of resistance, the intense, unrelenting barrage of American cultural influence continues ceaselessly.

Compounding the influence of commercial images are the media and information industries, which present both explicit and implicit messages about the very real military and economic hegemony of the United States. Ironically, the industry that claims to be the source for "fair and balanced" information plays a large role in the propagation of American influence around the world. The concentration of media ownership during the 1990s enabled both American and British media organizations to gain control of the majority of the world's news services. Satellites allow over 150 million households in approximately 212 countries and territories worldwide to subscribe to CNN, a member of Time Warner, the world's largest media conglomerate. In the words of British sociologist Jeremy Tunstall, "When a government allows news importation, it is in effect importing a piece of another country's politics—which is true of no other import." In addition to politics and commercials, networks like CNN also present foreign countries with unabashed accounts of the military and economic superiority of the United States.

The Internet acts as another vehicle for the worldwide propagation of American influence. Interestingly, some commentators cite the new "information economy" as proof that American cultural imperialism is in decline. They argue that the global accessibility of this decentralized medium has decreased the relevance of the "core and periphery" theory of global influence. This theory describes an inherent imbalance in the primarily outward flow of information and influence from the stronger, more powerful "core" nations such as the United States. Additionally, such critics argue, unlike consumers of other types of media, Internet users must actively seek out information; users can consciously choose to avoid all messages of American culture. While these arguments are valid, they ignore their converse: if one so desires, anyone can access a wealth of information about American culture possibly unavailable through previous channels. Thus, the Internet can dramatically increase exposure to American culture for those who desire it.

Fear of the cultural upheaval that could result from this exposure to new information has driven governments in communist China and Cuba to strictly monitor and regulate their citizens' access to websites (these protectionist policies aren't totally effective, however, because they are difficult to implement and maintain). Paradoxically, limiting access to the Internet nearly ensures that countries will remain largely the recipients, rather than the contributors, of information on the Internet.

Not all social critics see the Americanization of the world as a negative phenomenon. Proponents of cultural imperialism, such as David Rothkopf, a former senior official in Clinton's Department of Commerce, argue that American cultural imperialism is in the interest not only of the United States but also of the world at large. Rothkopf cites Samuel Huntington's theory from *The Clash of Civilizations and the Beginning of the World Order* that, the greater the cultural disparities in the world, the more likely it is that conflict will occur. Rothkopf argues that the removal of cultural barriers through U.S. cultural imperialism will promote a more stable world, one in which American culture reigns supreme as "the most just, the most tolerant, the most willing to constantly reassess and improve itself, and the best model for the future." Rothkopf is correct in one sense: Americans are on the way to establishing a global society with minimal cultural barriers. However, one must question whether this projected society is truly beneficial for all involved. Is it worth sacrificing countless indigenous cultures for the unlikely promise of a world without conflict?

Around the world, the answer is an overwhelming "No!" Disregarding the fact that a world of homogenized culture would not necessarily guarantee a world without conflict, the complex fabric of diverse cultures around the world is a fundamental and indispensable basis of humanity. Throughout the course of human existence, millions have died to preserve their indigenous culture. It is a fundamental right of humanity to be allowed to preserve the mental, physical, intellectual, and creative aspects of one's society. A single "global culture" would be nothing more than a shallow, artificial "culture" of materialism reliant on technology. Thankfully, it would be nearly impossible to create one bland culture in a world of over six billion people. And nor should we want to. Contrary to Rothkopf's (and George W. Bush's) belief that, "Good and evil, better and worse coexist in this world," there are no such absolutes in this world. The United States should not be able to relentlessly force other nations to accept its definition of what is "good" and "just" or even "modern."

Fortunately, many victims of American cultural imperialism aren't blind to the subversion of their cultures. Unfortunately, these nations are often too weak to fight the strength of the United States and subsequently to preserve their native cultures. Some countries—such as France, China, Cuba, Canada, and Iran—have attempted to quell America's cultural influence by limiting or prohibiting access to American cultural programming through satellites and the Internet. However, according to the UN Universal Declaration of Human Rights, it is a basic right of all people to "seek, receive, and impart information and ideas through any media and regardless of frontiers." Governments shouldn't have to restrict their citizens' access to information in order to preserve their native cultures. We as a world must find ways to defend local cultures in a manner that does not compromise the rights of indigenous people.

The prevalent proposed solutions to the problem of American cultural imperialism are a mix of defense and compromise measures on behalf of the endangered cultures. In *The Lexus and the Olive Tree,* Thomas Friedman advocates the use of protective legislation such as zoning laws and protected area laws, as well as the appointment of politicians with cultural integrity, such as those in agricultural, culturally pure Southern France. However, many other nations have no voice in the nomination of their leadership, so those countries need a middle-class and elite committed to social activism. If it is utterly impossible to maintain the cultural purity of a country through legislation, Friedman suggests the country attempt to "glocalize," that is:

> to absorb influences that naturally fit into and can enrich [a] culture, to resist those things that are truly alien and to compartmentalize those things that, while different, can nevertheless be enjoyed and celebrated as different.

These types of protective filters should help to maintain the integrity of a culture in the face of cultural imperialism. In *Jihad vs. McWorld,* Benjamin Barber calls for the resuscitation of nongovernmental, noncapitalist spaces—to the "civic spaces"—such as village greens, places of religious worship, or community schools. It is also equally important to focus on the education of youth in their native values and traditions. Teens especially need a counterbalance to images of American consumerism they absorb from the media. Even if individuals or countries consciously choose to become "Americanized" or "modernized," their choice should be made freely and independently of the coercion and influence of American cultural imperialism.

The responsibility for preserving cultures shouldn't fall entirely on those at risk. The United States must also recognize that what is good for its economy isn't necessarily good for the world at large. We must learn to put people before profits. The corporate and political leaders of the United States would be well advised to heed these words of Gandhi:

> I do not want my house to be walled in on all sides and my windows to be stuffed. I want the culture of all lands to be blown about my house as freely as possible. But I refuse to be blown off my feet by any.

The United States must acknowledge that no one culture can or should reign supreme, for the death of diverse cultures can only further harm future generations.

Philippe Legrain  **NO**

In Defense of Globalization

Fears that globalization is imposing a deadening cultural uniformity are as ubiquitous as Coca-Cola, McDonald's, and Mickey Mouse. Many people dread that local cultures and national identities are dissolving into a crass all-American consumerism. That cultural imperialism is said to impose American values as well as products, promote the commercial at the expense of the authentic, and substitute shallow gratification for deeper satisfaction.

Thomas Friedman, columnist for the *New York Times* and author of *The Lexus and the Olive Tree,* believes that globalization is "globalizing American culture and American cultural icons." Naomi Klein, a Canadian journalist and author of *No Logo,* argues that "Despite the embrace of polyethnic imagery, market-driven globalization doesn't want diversity; quite the opposite. Its enemies are national habits, local brands, and distinctive regional tastes."

But it is a myth that globalization involves the imposition of Americanized uniformity, rather than an explosion of cultural exchange. And although—as with any change—it can have downsides, this cross-fertilization is overwhelmingly a force for good.

The beauty of globalization is that it can free people from the tyranny of geography. Just because someone was born in France does not mean they can only aspire to speak French, eat French food, read French books, and so on. That we are increasingly free to choose our cultural experiences enriches our lives immeasurably. We could not always enjoy the best the world has to offer.

Globalization not only increases individual freedom, but also revitalizes cultures and cultural artifacts through foreign influences, technologies, and markets. Many of the best things come from cultures mixing: Paul Gauguin painting in Polynesia, the African rhythms in rock 'n' roll, the great British curry. Admire the many-colored faces of France's World Cup-winning soccer team, the ferment of ideas that came from Eastern Europe's Jewish diaspora, and the cosmopolitan cities of London and New York.

Fears about an Americanized uniformity are overblown. For a start, many "American" products are not as all-American as they seem; MTV in Asia promotes Thai pop stars and plays rock music sung in Mandarin. Nor are American products all-conquering. Coke accounts for less than two of the 64 fluid ounces that the typical person drinks a day. France imported a mere $620 million in food from the United States in 2000, while exporting to

From *The International Economy* by Philippe Legrain, vol. 17, no. 3, Summer 2003, pp. 62–65.

America three times that. Worldwide, pizzas are more popular than burgers and Chinese restaurants sprout up everywhere.

In fashion, the ne plus ultra is Italian or French. Nike shoes are given a run for their money by Germany's Adidas, Britain's Reebok, and Italy's Fila. American pop stars do not have the stage to themselves. According to the IFPI, the record-industry bible, local acts accounted for 68 percent of music sales in 2000, up from 58 percent in 1991. And although nearly three-quarters of television drama exported worldwide comes from the United States, most countries' favorite shows are homegrown.

Nor are Americans the only players in the global media industry. Of the seven market leaders, one is German, one French, and one Japanese. What they distribute comes from all quarters: Germany's Bertelsmann publishes books by American writers; America's News Corporation broadcasts Asian news; Japan's Sony sells Brazilian music.

In some ways, America is an outlier, not a global leader. Baseball and American football have not traveled well; most prefer soccer. Most of the world has adopted the (French) metric system; America persists with antiquated British Imperial measurements. Most developed countries have become intensely secular, but many Americans burn with fundamentalist fervor—like Muslims in the Middle East.

Admittedly, Hollywood dominates the global movie market and swamps local products in most countries. American fare accounts for more than half the market in Japan and nearly two-thirds in Europe. Yet Hollywood is less American than it seems. Top actors and directors are often from outside America. Some studios are foreign-owned. To some extent, Hollywood is a global industry that just happens to be in America. Rather than exporting Americana, it serves up pap to appeal to a global audience.

Hollywood's dominance is in part due to economics: Movies cost a lot to make and so need a big audience to be profitable; Hollywood has used America's huge and relatively uniform domestic market as a platform to expand overseas. So there could be a case for stuffing subsidies into a rival European film industry, just as Airbus was created to challenge Boeing's near-monopoly. But France's subsidies have created a vicious circle whereby European film producers fail in global markets because they serve domestic demand and the wishes of politicians and cinematic bureaucrats.

Another American export is also conquering the globe: English. By 2050, it is reckoned, half the world will be more or less proficient in it. A common global language would certainly be a big plus—for businessmen, scientists, and tourists—but a single one seems far less desirable. Language is often at the heart of national culture, yet English may usurp other languages not because it is what people prefer to speak, but because, like Microsoft software, there are compelling advantages to using it if everyone else does.

But although many languages are becoming extinct, English is rarely to blame. People are learning English as well as—not instead of—their native tongue, and often many more languages besides. Where local languages are dying, it is typically national rivals that are stamping them out. So although, within the United States, English is displacing American Indian tongues, it is not doing away with Swahili or Norwegian.

Even though American consumer culture is widespread, its significance is often exaggerated. You can choose to drink Coke and eat at McDonald's without becoming American in any meaningful sense. One newspaper photo of Taliban fighters in Afghanistan showed them toting Kalashnikovs—as well as a sports bag with Nike's trademark swoosh. People's culture—in the sense of their shared ideas, beliefs, knowledge, inherited traditions, and art—may scarcely be eroded by mere commercial artifacts that, despite all the furious branding, embody at best flimsy values.

The really profound cultural changes have little to do with Coca-Cola. Western ideas about liberalism and science are taking root almost everywhere, while Europe and North America are becoming multicultural societies through immigration, mainly from developing countries. Technology is reshaping culture: Just think of the Internet. Individual choice is fragmenting the imposed uniformity of national cultures. New hybrid cultures are emerging, and regional ones re-emerging. National identity is not disappearing, but the bonds of nationality are loosening.

Cross-border cultural exchange increases diversity within societies—but at the expense of making them more alike. People everywhere have more choice, but they often choose similar things. That worries cultural pessimists, even though the right to choose to be the same is an essential part of freedom.

Cross-cultural exchange can spread greater diversity as well as greater similarity: more gourmet restaurants as well as more McDonald's outlets. And just as a big city can support a wider spread of restaurants than a small town, so a global market for cultural products allows a wider range of artists to thrive. If all the new customers are ignorant, a wider market may drive down the quality of cultural products: Think of tourist souvenirs. But as long as some customers are well informed (or have "good taste"), a general "dumbing down" is unlikely. Hobbyists, fans, artistic pride, and professional critics also help maintain (and raise) standards.

A bigger worry is that greater individual freedom may undermine national identity. The French fret that by individually choosing to watch Hollywood films they might unwittingly lose their collective Frenchness. Yet such fears are overdone. Natural cultures are much stronger than people seem to think. They can embrace some foreign influences and resist others. Foreign influences can rapidly become domesticated, changing national culture, but not destroying it. Clearly, though, there is a limit to how many foreign influences a culture can absorb before being swamped. Traditional cultures in the developing world that have until now evolved (or failed to evolve) in isolation may be particularly vulnerable.

In *The Silent Takeover,* Noreena Hertz describes the supposed spiritual Eden that was the isolated kingdom of Bhutan in the Himalayas as being defiled by such awful imports as basketball and Spice Girls T-shirts. But is that such a bad thing? It is odd, to put it mildly, that many on the left support multiculturalism in the West but advocate cultural purity in the developing world—an attitude they would tar as fascist if proposed for the United States. Hertz appears to want people outside the industrialized West preserved in unchanging but supposedly pure poverty. Yet the Westerners who want this supposed paradise preserved in aspic rarely feel like settling there. Nor do most people in developing countries want to lead an "authentic" unspoiled life of isolated poverty.

In truth, cultural pessimists are typically not attached to diversity per se but to designated manifestations of diversity, determined by their preferences. Cultural pessimists want to freeze things as they were. But if diversity at any point in time is desirable, why isn't diversity across time? Certainly, it is often a shame if ancient cultural traditions are lost. We should do our best to preserve them and keep them alive where possible. Foreigners can often help, by providing the new customers and technologies that have enabled reggae music, Haitian art, and Persian carpet making, for instance, to thrive and reach new markets. But people cannot be made to live in a museum. We in the West are forever casting off old customs when we feel they are no longer relevant. Nobody argues that Americans should ban nightclubs to force people back to line dancing. People in poor countries have a right to change, too.

Moreover, some losses of diversity are a good thing. Who laments that the world is now almost universally rid of slavery? More generally, Western ideas are reshaping the way people everywhere view themselves and the world. Like nationalism and socialism before it, liberalism is a European philosophy that has swept the world. Even people who resist liberal ideas, in the name of religion (Islamic and Christian fundamentalists), group identity (communitarians), authoritarianism (advocates of "Asian values") or tradition (cultural conservatives), now define themselves partly by their opposition to them.

Faith in science and technology is even more widespread. Even those who hate the West make use of its technologies. Osama bin Laden plots terrorism on a cellphone and crashes planes into skyscrapers. Antiglobalization protesters organize by e-mail and over the Internet. China no longer turns its nose up at Western technology: It tries to beat the West at its own game.

Yet globalization is not a one-way street. Although Europe's former colonial powers have left their stamp on much of the world, the recent flow of migration has been in the opposite direction. There are Algerian suburbs in Paris, but not French ones in Algiers. Whereas Muslims are a growing minority in Europe, Christians are a disappearing one in the Middle East.

Foreigners are changing America even as they adopt its ways. A million or so immigrants arrive each year, most of them Latino or Asian. Since 1990, the number of foreign-born American residents has risen by 6 million to just over 25 million, the biggest immigration wave since the turn of the 20th century. English may be all-conquering outside America, but in some parts of the United States, it is now second to Spanish.

The upshot is that national cultures are fragmenting into a kaleidoscope of different ones. New hybrid cultures are emerging. In "Amexica" people speak Spanglish. Regional cultures are reviving. The Scots and Welsh break with British monoculture. Estonia is reborn from the Soviet Union. Voices that were silent dare to speak again.

Individuals are forming new communities, linked by shared interests and passions, that cut across national borders. Friendships with foreigners met on holiday. Scientists sharing ideas over the Internet. Environmentalists campaigning together using e-mail. Greater individualism does not spell the end of community. The new communities are simply chosen rather than coerced, unlike the older ones that communitarians hark back to.

So is national identity dead? Hardly. People who speak the same language, were born and live near each other, face similar problems, have a common experience, and vote in the same elections still have plenty in common. For all our awareness of the world as a single place, we are not citizens of the world but citizens of a state. But if people now wear the bonds of nationality more loosely, is that such a bad thing? People may lament the passing of old ways. Indeed, many of the worries about globalization echo age-old fears about decline, a lost golden age, and so on. But by and large, people choose the new ways because they are more relevant to their current needs and offer new opportunities.

The truth is that we increasingly define ourselves rather than let others define us. Being British or American does not define who you are: It is part of who you are. You can like foreign things and still have strong bonds to your fellow citizens. As Mario Vargas Llosa, the Peruvian author, has written: "Seeking to impose a cultural identity on a people is equivalent to locking them in a prison and denying them the most precious of liberties—that of choosing what, how, and who they want to be."

POSTSCRIPT

Is the World a Victim of American Cultural Imperialism?

One of the strengths of sociology is its readiness to see the connections between society's different sectors. A sociologist would not be surprised to find that technologically and economically driven globalization would have profound cultural impacts. In fact both authors argue this point. They differ, however, in the type of cultural change that takes place. Galeota focuses on the Americanization of other cultures and Legrain focuses on a global culture that is multicultural. Galeota points to McDonald's 30,000 restaurants in over 100 countries, the ubiquity of Coca-Cola, and the worldwide audience of MTV as examples of American dominance. Legrain points out that much of best of American culture involves cultural mixing such as "Paul Gauguin painting in Polynesia, the African rhythms in rock 'n' roll, the great British curry." They also differ on the imperialism label for the cultural impact of globalization. Galeota argues that multinational corporations are attempting to impose American culture on other cultures to increase their sales. Then she condemns this practice and supports preservation of indigenous cultures. In contrast Legrain argues that cultural imperialism is a myth and even argues that some adjustment of traditional cultures to modernity would be beneficial.

Many references on globalization are provided in the Postscript to Issue 19. Below we provide recent references on globalization and culture. General discussions of globalization and culture include J. Macgregor Wise, *Cultural Globalization: A User's Guide* (Blackwell, 2008); Paul Hopper, *Understanding Cultural Globalization* (Polity, 2007); Tyler Cowen, *Creative Destruction: How Globalization Is Changing the World's Cultures* (Princeton University Press, 2002); and Sarah A. Radcliffe, ed., *Culture and Development in a Globalizing World* (Routledge, 2006). Works that focus on the globalization of American culture include Lane Crothers, *Globalization and American Popular Culture* (Rowman & Littlefield Publishers, 2007); Ulrich Beck et al., *Global America?: The Cultural Consequences of Globalization* (Liverpool Univeristy Press, 2003); Richard Crockatt, *After 9/11: Cultural Dimensions of American Global Power* (Routledge, 2007); and Ashley Dawson and Malini Johar Schueller, eds., *Exceptional State: Contemporary U.S. Culture and the New Imperialism* (Duke University Press, 2007). Works that focus on identities include Chan Kwok-bun, Jan W. Walls, and David Hayward, eds., *East-West Identities: Globalization, Localization, and Hybridization* (Brill, 2007); Pam Nilan and Carles Feixa, eds., *Global Youth? Hybrid Identities, Plural Worlds* (Routledge, 2006); Paul Kennedy and Catherine J. Danks, eds., *Globalization and National Identities: Crisis or Opportunity* (Palgrave, 2001); and Elisabeth Madimbee-Boyi, ed., *Beyond Dichotomies: Histories, Identities, Cultures, and the Challenge of Globalization* (Pine Forge Press, 2007).

Finally, we list works that focus on the resistance to cultural imperialism including Jerry Mander and Victoria Tauli-Corpuz, eds., *Paradigm Wars: Indigenous Peoples' Resistance to Globalization* (Sierra Club Books, 2006); Catarina Kinnvall, *Globalization and Religious Nationalism in India* (Routledge, 2006); Marisol de la Cadena and Orin Starn, eds., *Indigenous Experience Today* (Berg, 2007); and Makere Stewart-Harawira, *The New Imperial Order: Indigenous Responses to Globalization* (Hula Publishers, 2005).

Contributors to This Volume

EDITOR

KURT FINSTERBUSCH is a professor of sociology at the University of Maryland at College Park. He received a B.A. in history from Princeton University in 1957, a B.D. from Grace Theological Seminary in 1960, and a Ph.D. in sociology from Columbia University in 1969. He is the author of *Understanding Social Impacts* (Sage Publications, 1980), and he is the coauthor, with Annabelle Bender Motz, of *Social Research for Policy Decisions* (Wadsworth, 1980) and, with Jerald Hage, of *Organizational Change as a Development Strategy* (Lynne Rienner, 1987). He is the editor of *Annual Editions: Sociology* (McGraw-Hill/Contemporary Learning Series); *Annual Editions: Social Problems* (McGraw-Hill/Contemporary Learning Series); and *Sources: Notable Selections in Sociology*, 3rd edition (McGraw-Hill/Dushkin, 1999).

AUTHORS

CONSTANCE AHRONS is co-chair of the Council on Contemporary Families. She is a therapist and author of three books: *The Good Divorce, Divorced Families,* and *We're Still Family.* She is Professor Emerita from the Department of Sociology and former director of the Marriage and Family Therapy Doctoral Training Program at the University of Southern California in Los Angeles.

DAVID A. ANDERSON is a Blazer Associate Professor of Economics. He teaches many courses including law and economics, as well as the economics of crime. He is the author of *Environmental Economics* (Southwestern, 2004).

RONALD BAILEY is the science editor for *Reason* magazine and frequently publishes in papers and magazines. He has written several books on the environment.

FRED BARNES was the executive editor of *The Weekly Standard* from 1985 to 1995. He has a news TV talk show.

GARY S. BECKER is a university professor in the Department of Economics and Sociology and professor in the Graduate School of Business. He is a senior fellow at the Hoover Institute and past president of the American Economic Association.

LAWRENCE D. BOBO is the Martin Luther King Jr. Centennial Professor at Stanford University, where he is also director of the Center for Comparative Study in Race and Ethnicity and director of the Program in African and African American Studies. He is a founding co-editor of the *Du Bois Review: Social Science Research on Race* published by Cambridge University Press. He is coauthor of the award-winning book *Racial Attitudes in America: Trends and Interpretations* (Harvard University Press, 1997). His latest book is *Prejudice in Politics: Public Opinion, Group Position, and the Wisconsin Treaty Rights Dispute,* (Harvard University Press, 2006).

CLINT BOLICK is vice president of the Institute for Justice, and has litigated many crucial school choice decisions. His book *Voucher Wars: Waging the Legal Battle Over School Choice* has just been published by the Cato Institute.

ROBERT H. BORK is a senior fellow at the American Enterprise Institute. He has been a partner at a major law firm, taught constitutional law as the Alexander M. Bickel Professor of Public Law at the Yale Law School, and served as Solicitor General and Attorney General of the United States. He is the author of the bestselling *Slouching Toward Gomorrah: Modern Liberalism and American Decline* (HarperCollins Publishers).

LESTER R. BROWN was the founder and president of the Worldwatch Institute, a non-profit organization dedicated to the analysis of the global environment. He served as advisor to Secretary of Agriculture Orville Freeman and served as administrator of the International Agricultural Service in that department. In 1969, he helped James Grant establish the Overseas Development Council. He is the author and coauthor of numerous books.

KINGSLEY R. BROWNE is a professor at Wayne State University Law School. He specialized in labor and employment law when he was previously a partner in the San Francisco-based law firm of Morrison & Foerster. He has written *Co-ed Combat: The New Evidence That Women Shouldn't Fight the Nation's Wars* (Sentinel, 2007). His work deals primarily with employment discrimination law and the legal implications of evolved differences between the sexes.

PATRICK BUCHANAN was a presidential candidate in 2000. Currently, he is a political analyst, television commentator, and the author of *The Death of the West* (Thomas Dunne Books, 2000), which focuses on the issue of immigration.

LINDA L. CARLI, Ph.D., is an associate professor in the Psychology Department at Wellesley College, where she has been since 1991. Her current research focuses on women's leadership, particularly the obstacles that women leaders face and ways to overcome those obstacles. She teaches a variety of courses, including organizational psychology, the psychology of law, and research in applied psychology.

ANDREW G. CELLI, JR. is a lawyer practicing in New York City, and has served as chief of the Attorney General's Civil Rights Bureau from 1999 to 2003. He has recently published in the *New Republic*, "A Democratic Vision for the New Economy" (March 16, 2004).

LINDA CHAVEZ is chairman of the Center for Equal Opportunity and a high-ranking official in several Republican administrations. She is a prominent Hispanic-American conservative author and TV commentator.

DAVID COATES is the Worrel Professor of Anglo-American Studies in the Political Science Department at Wake Forest University. He just published *The Liberal Toolkit: Progressive Answers to Conservative Arguments* from which the reprinted articles were taken.

MICHELLE CONLIN is a journalist and the editor of the Working Life department of *BUSINESS WEEK* magazine, where she covers workplace culture and careers.

LARRY COX is the executive director of Amnesty International USA.

CURTIS CRAWFORD is the editor and coauthor of the Web site www. DebatingRacialPreference.org.

G. WILLIAM DOMHOFF has been teaching psychology and sociology at the University of California, Santa Cruz, since 1965. His books on political sociology include *Who Rules America?* (Prentice-Hall, 1967); *The Power Elite and the State: How Policy Is Made in America* (Aldine de Gruyter, 1990); and *Diversity in the Power Elite* (Yale University Press, 1998*)*.

ALICE EAGLY, a social psychologist, is the James Padilla Chair of Arts and Sciences, professor of psychology, faculty fellow of Institute for Policy Research, and department chair of psychology, all at Northwestern University. She has received numerous awards including the 2007 Interamerican Psychologist Award from the Interamerican Society of Psychology for contributions to psychology as a science and profession in the Americas, as well as the 2005 Carolyn Wood Sherif Award from Society for the Psychology of Women for contributions to the field of the psychology of women as a scholar, teacher, mentor, and leader.

BARBARA EPSTEIN was a writer and founding co-editor of *The New York Review of Books.*

JULIA GALEOTA is a 20-year-old student whose essay as a 17-year-old won the 2004 Humanist Essay Contest.

NEIL GILBERT is the Chernin Professor of Social Welfare at the University of California at Berkeley, co-director of the Center for Child and Youth Policy, and director of the Center for Comparative Family Welfare and Poverty Research. He was also the founding director of the Family Welfare Research Group.

MARTIN HART-LANDSBERG is professor of economics and director of the Political Economy Program at Lewis and Clark College.

HUMAN RIGHTS CAMPAIGN is the largest national gay, lesbian, bisexual, and transgender political organization with members throughout the country.

KAY S. HYMOWITZ is a senior fellow at the Manhattan Institute and a contributing editor of *City Journal*. She writes extensively on education. Her latest book is *Liberation's Children: Parents and Kids in a Postmodern Age* (Ivan R. Dee, 2003).

SHELDON KAMIENIECKI is Dean of the Division of Social Sciences at the University of California, Santa Cruz. He was a member of the Department of Political Science at the University of Southern California (USC) between 1981 and 2006. He was chair of the Political Science Department and the founding director of the Environmental Studies Program at USC. He received the Raubenheimer Award for Outstanding Senior Faculty in the College of Letters, Arts and Sciences at USC in 1999.

ROBERT F. KENNEDY, JR. is an environmental and political activist. He is an environmental lawyer and co-host of *Ring of Fire* on the Air America Radio Network and also serves as a senior attorney for the Natural Resources Defense Council.

JAMES KURTH is a Claude Smith Professor of Political Science at Swarthmore College, where he teaches defense policy, foreign policy, and international politics. He is also editor of *Orbis*.

PHILLIPE LEGRAIN is chief economist of Britain in Europe, the Campaign for Britain to Join the Euro. He is the author of *Open World: The Truth about Globalization* (Abacus, 2002).

BJORN LOMBORG is a statistician at the University of Aarhus and the author of the controversial book *The Skeptical Environmentalist: Measuring the Real State of the World* (Cambridge University Press, 2001).

ELIZABETH MARQUARDT is the director of the Center for Marriage and Families and authored *Between Two Worlds: The Inner Lives of Children of Divorce* (Crown, 2005).

KEVIN M. MURPHY is the George J. Stigler Distinguished Service Professor of Economics at the University of Chicago Graduate School of Business and a Senior Fellow at the Hoover Institution.

ETHAN A. NADELMANN is director of the Lindesmith Center of the Drug Policy Foundation, a New York drug policy research institute, and professor of politics and public affairs in the Woodrow Wilson School of Public and International Affairs at Princeton University. He is the author of *Cops Across Borders: The Internationalization of U.S. Criminal Law Enforcement* (Pennsylvania State University Press, 1993).

JOHAN NORBERG is a senior fellow at the Washington D.C.-based Cato Institute. From 1999 to 2005, he was in charge of the ideas policy at the Swedish think-tank Timbro where he was also the editor of smedjan.com. His most recent book is *In Defense of Global Capitalism* (Cato Institute, 2003).

KATE O'BEIRNE is the editor of *National Review* and a frequent panelist on TV news shows.

JEFFREY REIMAN is the William Fraser McDowell Professor of Philosophy at American University in Washington, DC. He is the author of *Justice and Modern Moral Philosophy* (Yale University Press, 1992) and *The Rich Get Richer and the Poor Get Prison: Ideology, Class, and Criminal Justice*, 6th edition (Allyn & Bacon, 2001). He is also editor, with Paul Leighton, of *Criminal Justice Ethics* (Prentice Hall, 2001).

MICHAEL J. SANDEL is the Anne T. and Robert M. Bass Professor in the Political Science Department at Harvard. His recent book is *Public Philosophy: Essay on Morality in Politics* (Harvard University Press, 2005).

ELIOT SPITZER has served New York as State Attorney General and as Governor. He has advanced initiatives in environmental protection, public safety, civil rights, and consumer affairs. He often presses cases against the major Wall Street firms.

PETER SPRIGG serves as Vice President for Policy at the Family Research Council and oversees FRC research, publications, and policy formulation. He is also the author of the book *Outrage: How Gay Activists and Liberal Judges Are Trashing Democracy to Redefine Marriage* (Regnery, 2004), and the co-editor of the book *Getting It Straight: What the Research Shows about Homosexuality.*

JOHN STOSSEL works for the ABC news magazine *20/20*, has received 19 Emmy Awards, and has been honored five times for excellence in consumer reporting by the National Press Club.

CLAUDIA WALLIS is editor-at-large at *TIME*. She has been both a writer and editor specializing in stories about health and science, women's and children's issues, education, and lifestyle. She was the founding editor of *TIME for Kids*.

JOHN P. WALTERS is the director of the Office of National Drug Control Policy and as such is the official "Drug Czar" who coordinates all aspects of federal drug programs and spending.

JOEL WENDLAND is managing editor of *Political Affairs*, a monthly magazine of ideology, politics, and culture, and a member of UAW Local 1981 (national writers union) who has written for numerous publications. He also writes and maintains *ClassWarNotes*.

RON WOLK is a former vice president of Brown University and is chairman of the board of Editorial Projects in Education. He founded *Education Week* and *Teacher Magazine*. He edited with Blake Hume Rodman *Classroom Crusaders: Twelve Teachers Who Are Trying to Change the System* (Jossey-Bass Publishers, 1994).